MUBARAK'S EGYPT

MUBARAK'S EGYPT

Fragmentation
of
the Political Order

Robert Springborg

Westview Press
BOULDER & LONDON

Copyright © 1989 by Westview Press, Inc.

Published in 1989 in the United States of America by Westview Press, Inc., 5500 Central Avenue, Boulder, Colorado 80301, and in the United Kingdom by Westview Press, Inc., 13 Brunswick Centre, London WC1N 1AF, England

Library of Congress Cataloging-in-Publication Data
Springborg, Robert.
  Mubarak's Egypt: fragmentation of the political order/Robert Springborg.
    p.   cm.
  Includes index.
  ISBN 0-8133-7643-2
  1. Egypt—Economic policy. 2. Egypt—Politics and
government—1981–   I. Title.
HC830.S68   1989
338.962—dc19   88-11096
                                                                              CIP

Printed and bound in the United States of America

 The paper used in this publication meets the requirements of the American National
Standard for Permanence of Paper for Printed Library Materials Z39.48-1984.

10   9   8   7   6   5   4   3   2

CONTENTS

ACKNOWLEDGMENTS

The bulk of the field research on which this book is based was conducted in Egypt in 1986. It was made possible by a grant from the National Endowment for the Humanities administered by the American Research Center in Egypt, and by further assistance from Macquarie University. I would particularly like to thank Paul Walker, Richard Verdery, and Robert Betts of ARCE for facilitating the smooth transition from a southern to a northern hemisphere academic year and for assisting me and my family while we were in Cairo.

Having first become enamored of Egypt while working as a front desk clerk in an international hotel in Cairo in 1965, I have over the years accumulated an enormous debt of gratitude to innumerable Egyptians. Ahmad Fawzi and Ali Darwish, close friends of mine for more than twenty years, have made me feel as much at home in their country as in mine by sharing their knowledge of Egyptian society and politics with me. Others with whom I have been in contact over the years and who facilitated this and other projects include Adil Hussain, Tahsin Bashir, Hilmi Murad, and Sayed, Omar, Nasr, and Hassan Marei. Sayid Yassin and Salama Ahmad Salama, both of *al-Ahram*, generously shared with me their insights into contemporary events. Various members of the Ministry of Foreign Affairs, including Muhammad Assim, Badair Ghamrawi, and the recently deceased Salah Hindawi, assisted and encouraged this project at various stages. Sayid al-Kholi, also of that ministry, has not only taught me a great deal about the Egyptian political economy but has also provided documentation and other assistance that was vital to this endeavor. He was also the first to read an early draft of the manuscript, correcting numerous errors and encouraging me to push on. I have also benefited from interacting with various Egyptian academics. Ali Dessouki, Assim Dessouki, and Ibrahim Soliman have been particularly helpful. To all of these warmhearted, hospitable men I would like to express my deepest appreciation.

Various individuals employed in western institutions in Egypt were also of great help to me. Sylvia Mitchell, director of the Development Information Center of USAID, guided me professionally through the labyrinth of the Center's extremely useful collection. William Janssen,

Ken Weigand, and Robert Mitchell, also of USAID, spent many hours describing to me the nuances of USAID–Egyptian government relations. Nicholas Hopkins, Enid Hill, and Walid Kazziha of the American University in Cairo provided useful insights into several policy issues. Hamilton McMillan of the British Embassy and Peter Rogers of the Australian Embassy instructed me on numerous occasions on contemporary events. Lee Travers of the Ford Foundation was both a stimulating and informed professional colleague and an ideal landlord. Ron and Anne Wolfe of Professional Business Services introduced me to a great many of the prominent personages with whom they have established close rapport and shared with me their unequalled knowledge of the inner workings of the Egyptian professional and business worlds. More than anyone else they ensured that a year in Cairo was for all members of my family a rewarding and unforgettable experience.

Bent Hansen, Clement Henry, George Lenczowski, and John Waterbury stimulated my thinking about numerous aspects of Egypt's contemporary political economy and read part or all of the manuscript. I would also like to thank Jim Bill, Ira Lapidus, and Yahya Sadowski for having read and commented on the manuscript. General Fakhr, a member of Field Marshal Abu Ghazala's staff, provided useful verbal and written comments on a draft of Chapter 4.

Helma Neuman of Macquarie University and Kate Herman, Nadine Zelinski, and Micky Skronski of the University of California at Berkeley overcame the obstacles of interpreting my rough drafts and integrating three highly idiosyncratic computer systems while processing the manuscript in a timely and professional manner. The Institute of International Studies and the Department of Political Science of UC, Berkeley, generously provided computer time and staff assistance, for which I would particularly like to thank Bent Hansen and Ken Messerer.

An abbreviated version of Chapter 4 appeared as "The President and the Field Marshal: Civil-Military Relations in Egypt Today," in *MERIP Middle East Report* 17, 4 (July-August 1987), pp. 4–17. I would like to thank the publishers of that journal for their permission to republish some of that material here.

Lastly, my wife, Patricia, who turned to good purpose a year in Cairo by researching and writing a book on the Pharaonic origins of kingship, was as always my greatest supporter and most perceptive critic. Our sons Ziyad and George bore up admirably under the strain of having two obsessed parents. To their credit both managed to carve out their own spheres of competence and to develop respect and appreciation for the country and its people. To Patricia, Ziyad, and George this book is dedicated.

Robert Springborg

A NOTE ON TRANSLITERATION

The method of transliteration is geared primarily to the interests of readers not proficient in Arabic. No diacritical marks have been used and the Arabic letter *ayn* has not been represented by a single quotation mark as is commonly the case, except in the term *gama'at*, which is its typical spelling in the Western press. The vowels "e" and "o" appear only in those place names relatively familiar to Western readers (e.g., Beni Suef); in proper names of authors published in the West or of prominent persons (e.g., Heikal, Marei, Nasser); and in place of the dipthong "aw" in the case of the Cairo newspaper, *Akhbar al-Yom*. The doubled *ya* appears as a single "y" (e.g., Minufiya, not Minufiyya; Sayid, not Sayyid). Plurals are formed by adding "-s" to the italicized singular (e.g., *imam*-s). The *jim*, which is pronounced as a hard "g," is represented by "g" except in the word *jihad*, which is its most common spelling in the West. Uthman is rendered as the more common Osman, Umar as Omar, Quran as Koran, and Muslim as Moslem.

1

EGYPT CONFRONTS
THE NEW ORTHODOXY
OF DEVELOPMENT

As one of the world's great riverine civilizations, Egypt has like a magnet attracted powerful states endeavoring further to expand their influence. The great powers and their successors, including since the Napoleonic invasion of 1798 the French, British, Russians, and now the Americans, have sought to remake the Egyptian political economy according to a distorted, dependent, mirror image of their own. The French *mission civilisation*, undertaken by Napoleon and his countrymen who followed, was too abbreviated to restructure the economic foundations of the state, although Egyptian elites continued to imitate French culture long after France's paramountcy had waned. The French language and accompanying behavioral style afforded some defense, however symbolic and psychological, against the reality of British hegemony. For their part the British succeeded in establishing an export-oriented agricultural economy presided over by a semifeudal notability and aristocracy, arrangements that satisfied British economic demands and accorded with English perceptions of the politically right and proper. Three-quarters of a century later the Soviets exported a pale image of their "scientific socialism," which was reerected along the Nile in the form of Gamal Abdel Nasser's Arab Socialism. The Nasserite political system, with its emphasis on the single party, was made in the 1960s to conform stylistically, if not substantively, with the Leninist model. U.S. efforts since 1974 have contributed to the emergence of an economy with some recognizable neoclassical elements, while a version of political democracy has sent down a few tentative roots.

None of this is unique in the history of the modern world. Most Third World states have had to stage cultural, economic, and political retreats, either as a result of an immediate colonial presence or because cliental relations with superpowers are fatally attractive, in part because they hold the promise of potential economic and other advantages, at

1

least to some portion of the population. But Egypt is unusual in that it has had so many such relationships in the nineteenth and twentieth centuries and because of the degree of enthusiasm and commitment that outsiders have devoted to their Egyptian entanglement. Within the space of a decade Egypt has been the largest recipient of Soviet aid and, after Israel, the leading beneficiary of U.S. aid. The desire to garner influence in Cairo seems to be impelled by more than sheer strategic concerns. Because it is so old, so apparently immutable, and so intriguing, Egyptian civilization offers an irresistible lure to those who are intent on proving the worth of their cultures and economic and political systems on a global scale. If Egypt can be remade in the image of the conqueror or patron, the rest of Africa and Asia has been put on notice.

U.S. attempts to influence the path of development in Egypt since World War II are illustrative. In the late 1940s and early 1950s, when U.S. influence in Egypt was less than it is now, Western ideas on development were nevertheless incorporated readily into the plans of those who were to rule in the name of Nasserism. Those notions, heavily influenced by Keynesian theories and by the involvement of European economists in the League of Nation's efforts to rebuild Eastern Europe in the wake of World War I, began to appear in U.S. writings on development after World War II. Influenced by their European colleagues, impressed by their successes in mobilizing the governmental war effort, and in some cases encouraged by their previous efforts in using the federal government and its New Deal to combat the Great Depression, these apostles of development, newly entrenched in academic institutions and in the United Nations, the International Monetary Fund (IMF), and other development agencies, called for the state to play the leading role in Third World economies. Mobilization of sufficient capital, integration of national efforts through planning, pursuit of a consistent policy of import substitution, and management of the country's agricultural resources required, in this view, direct governmental intervention. Less concerned with the political structure in which these choices were to be made than with the commitment to governmental dynamism, these theorists believed that the newly emerging nationalist middle classes would in any case be politically more sophisticated than, and preferable to, the entrenched, neofeudalist elites that the European powers had nurtured.[1] Consistent with these political and economic preferences was the prescription of land reform, which, it was believed, would strike a blow against retrograde elites while simultaneously enhancing governmental capability to manage this critical sector.

Such advice fell on fertile ground in Egypt. At the broadest level it seemed compatible with the basic trends of Egyptian economic history. The quintessential hydraulic society of antiquity, Egypt had long experience with governmental intervention into the economy during the pharaonic and mamluk eras, even with direct management of the always vital agricultural sector.[2] The experiment with neofeudal, *latifundia*-style agriculture, which was initiated by Muhammad Ali and brought to fruition under the British, was, according to this reading of economic history, a retrograde step and one alien to Egyptian economic traditions. Since colonialism had imposed the emphasis on agriculture and its neofeudal organization, proper decolonization and one consistent with this version of Egypt's historiography required a land reform regulated by the state, coupled with industrialization.

But it was not just reaction to colonialism and consonance with prevailing Egyptian interpretations of the nation's history that underlay the attraction to Egypt's new masters of the writings of Doreen Warriner, Arthur Lewis, Gunnar Myrdal, and the other apostles of the Big Push by the state.[3] After July 1952, the revolutionary elite sought to uproot and displace vestiges of the *ancien regime*, for which there seemed no better tool than centralized control of the economy and polity. The prescriptions of the West's leading theorists of development fortuitously dovetailed with this preference. This, in retrospect, was unfortunate, for it raised U.S. expectations. Egypt was elevated to the status of a test case for the viability of U.S. endorsed and supported modernization programs led by nationalist-inclined middle classes armed with progressive theories of reform. That these hopes were not realized and that Egypt turned away from the U.S. approach and embraced a mixture of the Yugoslav and Soviet models contributed substantially to the stormy U.S.-Egyptian relationship of the next two decades and more.

Neither side, however, appears to be guided by the maxim of "once burned, twice shy." Since the October 1973 Arab-Israeli War, U.S. Egyptian relations have grown steadily closer. Accompanying this rapprochement has been increasing U.S. pressure for Egypt to adopt the new orthodoxy of development subscribed to by political and academic elites in the United States and, to a lesser extent, other Western nations. This orthodoxy, which like the previous one just outlined is concerned mainly with Third World economies rather than polities, is founded on the assumption that real economic growth can be had through broad-based, systematic efforts to integrate national economies into the world capitalist order. Inward-looking import substitution strategies are condemned as counterproductive. Protectionism is seen as leading to distortions of the economy that will become either albatrosses around the necks of the nation's taxpayers or targets for long-overdue "rationalizations." Overvalued currencies, excessive tariffs, and other barriers to trade are described as bugbears of export-led growth. Recommendations for domestic economic reform concentrate on reducing governmental controls and increasing incentives, particularly through the neoclassical pricing mechanism. Governmental efficiency is to be improved by contracting the scope of the public sector while the private sector is encouraged to move into the vacuum. Foreign aid is, at least in part, to be redirected toward the private sector, aid to government being increasingly restricted to programs designed to develop administrative capacity based on adaptive management principles. The relatively successful export-oriented economies of the Pacific Rim are offered by adherents of the new orthodoxy as proof of the pudding, with occasional references to Turkey as a Middle Eastern example of what policies of currency devaluation coupled with economic liberalization can achieve.[4]

As the recommended package of policies has become more standardized under the Reagan Administration, so too has the approach to facilitating its adoption. Out of the belief that the doctor knows best, ailing Third World economies have been forced to swallow stiff doses of appropriate fiscal remedies. These bitter pills have been sweetened by aid and loan programs, which increasingly are withheld from those who refuse to take their medicine. Members of the U.S. academic community have been recruited to facilitate the application of leverage. According to Anne Krueger, a staunch advocate of economic liberalization for the Third World, "difficulties of the transition" (from closed to open economies) should provide foci for research agendas.[5] Similarly, "policy space research" has been proposed as a method whereby social scientists should investigate specific Third World decision-making environments for the purpose of assisting those in aid programs to design packages that are most likely to achieve maximum leverage to bring about reforms.[6] Antecedents for the role of academics as midwives to reform are to be found in a previous era of U.S. enthusiasm for exporting its development orthodoxy, which was the early 1960s. The most noteworthy and durable contribution of that period was Albert O. Hirschman's *Journeys Toward Progress*, which provides a handbook for savvy elites seeking to build reform coalitions.[7] For Hirschman and for his successors, reform—in reality a synonym for adopting policies currently in vogue in Washington—is virtually always possible. It is just a question of pulling the right political levers.

EGYPT'S RELUCTANCE
TO ADOPT THE NEW ORTHODOXY

Egypt, currently the Third World's leading beneficiary of Western aid and among the most carefully studied of non-Western societies, has been painfully slow in adopting the new orthodoxy of development. Disappointment with Egypt's pace of change among officials within the United States Agency for International Development (USAID) and among others committed to liberalization is growing and is compounded by three factors. First, it is remembered that Egypt in the post-World War II period was a leader among the less developed countries in adopting U.S.-endorsed reform programs. Why then and not now, it is asked? Was it just because those reforms endorsed an expanded role for the state? Second, in most senses Egypt remains the leading Arab state. Its role as bellwether and even cause of change in the Arab World is reduced but still potent. If Egypt remains recalcitrant in the face of U.S. pressure, it suggests there is little hope for spreading the new orthodoxy elsewhere in the region. Finally, hopes for liberalization of the Egyptian economy and polity were raised by Anwar al-Sadat's *infitah* (opening), a reform program that survived its author's assassination but in modified form. The excesses of the *infitah* served to discredit economic liberalization among broad sectors of the population. Reforms in the directions of export-led growth and privatization now confront more political obstacles than they did under Sadat, when large numbers of Egyptians saw in such changes a panacea for their economic problems. The bungled reform has, in short, made the task of the Muhammad Husni Mubarak generation of reformers more difficult.

Students of Egypt's political economy differ in their assessments of the possibility for structural changes. There are those who emphasize patterns of continuity in Egypt's bureaucratic political culture and in the composition of its elite, thereby suggesting that a transformation of the way in which the Egyptian political economy operates is improbable.[8] Another view is that while Egypt's political economy is in its basic form immutable, it will oscillate between "heavily statist structures and considerably more liberal ones."[9] Cooper sees this dynamic as the consequence of class relations in state capitalism, whereas Bianchi, for whom Egypt is an example of "state corporatism," sees the pendulum being driven by groups assuming relatively pluralist or corporatist forms.[10]

A third academic view concurs in the basic assessment of Egypt as being an authoritarian state prone to semiliberal digressions from the norm, but admits of the possibility that real structural changes could occur. Moore, for example, argues that privatization is primarily "a political tactic for sustaining authoritarian regimes rather than a set of reforms for stimulating free enterprise or markets." But, continues Moore, privatization may set in motion a process whereby group interests, particularly those of "private entrepreneurs and their financial backers," become sufficiently cohesive to "transform the clientelist bases of [authoritarian] politics."[11] Richards concurs in much of this, arguing that the process of liberalization in Egypt over the past decade has greatly enhanced the power of the bourgeoisie. The breakthrough suggested as possible by Moore has not come about simply because the incumbent elite has been spared making fundamental choices by virtue of "rents," by which Richards means income from oil, worker remittances, Suez Canal revenues, and tourism. Accordingly, now that income from the "big four" has seriously deteriorated, Richards predicts that the Egyptian political economy could undergo real structural change.[12]

Waterbury, like Richards, sees the key variable determining the shape of the political economy as being sources of income arising outside the productive sectors of the Egyptian economy, although for Waterbury those sources are entirely external: In the earlier era of import-substitution industrialization, he includes cheap energy, Food for Peace aid, expanding international trade, and significant aid generated by the Soviet-U.S.

competition for influence. "Easy money" has for Egypt made possible a "softhearted" authoritarianism. "Neither leader (Nasser or Sadat) felt that it was necessary or desirable to sweat significant segments of the citizenry for the sustained savings that might have made relatively autonomous growth possible." But with the change of the external environment Egypt has been forced to abandon import-substitution industrialization, and in 1979, according to Waterbury, it moved into an export-led growth phase of accumulation in which the state is "acting as catalyst to and partner in alliances with foreign private capital and technology, and, on occasion, with the Egyptian private sector." As far as political changes are concerned, Waterbury sees a "surface liberalism" as having accompanied the shift from import substitution to export-led growth. He suggests that the political system is too weak to impose the "policing of labor and general belt tightening" necessary to make Egyptian goods internationally competitive, although he admits of the possibility that in the coming years this could change in the direction of the corporatist Latin American states as foreign capital in alliance with Egyptian affiliates in banking and manufacturing could impose a much more austere political regimen.[13]

Most writers concur then in the observation that Egypt since Nasser has had a weak authoritarian state that is now having to preside over an economic liberalization as a result principally of externally imposed financial stringencies. There is disagreement as to whether this in turn will lead to only a transitory "surface liberalism," to a more institutionalized pluralism, or to a Latin American-style corporate state in which the military, allied with the captains of private industry and finance, rules.

Those in charge of attempting to induce Egypt to adopt the various elements of the new orthodoxy of development, a category that includes officials not only from USAID but also those of the World Bank, IMF, and other bilateral and multilateral aid agencies, have not given as much thought, at least in print, to the connection between economics and politics. Their operating assumption, to the degree that it can be identified, appears to be that a more liberal economic system is likely to facilitate the emergence of a more liberal polity.[14] The academic theoreticians and the bureaucratic practitioners are therefore of like mind in the belief that inducing economic change will cause reverberations through the political system. They also agree that Egypt has reached a crossroads. Revenues arising from sources outside the economy's productive sectors are now seen as insufficient to meet the obligations of maintaining the soft authoritarian state that doles out subsidies to the poor and unconscionable profits to the rich and powerful. The social contract negotiated by the weak state between contending classes is under severe threat, and most Western opinion concurs that it will have to be revised.

What continues to amaze and irritate those charged with the task of forcing Egypt to see the irrefutable logic of choosing the new orthodoxy of development as the way out of the current impasse is that Egyptian decision makers remain surprisingly unwilling or unable to take the requisite steps to put the program in place. One such individual, an official in the economic section of the U.S. Embassy in Cairo, had become so frustrated by the end of his posting that he resorted to racialist interpretations. He bemoaned to the author that the inability of Egyptians to grasp the seriousness of their plight and to comprehend that liberalization offered the only real hope for salvation was due to a deterioration of their racial stock as a result of generations of endogamous marriages and immigration of the more talented.

Needless to say, the Egyptians see matters differently. The excesses of Sadat's *infitah* discredited the general idea of integration into the world capitalist system and, among many, the benefits of privatization. Under a political leader more committed to careful supervision of the economic reform program, Egypt may indeed have played a pioneering role in the Middle East and even in the Third World in adopting successfully and at an early stage the main features of the new development orthodoxy. But Sadat was anything but a fastidious manager of the economy, and a chance for a quick breakthrough in uniquely favorable circumstances of rising revenues and enhanced political legitimacy was lost. Subsequently the forces negatively disposed to or just wary of economic liberalization have had ample time to ponder its suitability, to express their views, and to mobilize opposition. Egypt, therefore, remains hesitant in the face of pressure to convert the economy into one more export-oriented and led by the private sector. Although the Mubarak government has taken several steps in the direction of liberalizing trade and fostering private sector activities, it has also imposed numerous restrictive measures. At the level of public pronouncements Mubarak has identified self-sufficiency as the principal goal of his government, a slogan that sounds very much like a call for a strategy of import substitution predicated on protectionism. While not necessarily contradictory, the mixed rhetoric of the regime and its vacillating economic policies do not trace a clear path in the direction of adopting an export-led mode of economic growth, nor do they lead sharply away from that alternative. Indecisiveness on the key issues of currency controls and values, tariffs and other forms of protectionism, and allocations of investments to the public or private sectors suggest continued unresolved conflicts within the decision-making elite.

ALTERNATIVE SCENARIOS

In these unsettled circumstances one can concoct widely varying scenarios of Egypt's even short-term future, to say nothing of what lies in store in the 1990s. Those foreign experts charged with plotting such changes and, not incidentally, attempting to guide them in directions indicated by the new orthodoxy tend to adopt highly optimistic or deeply pessimistic outlooks. Many optimists are of the opinion that Egypt is finally on the road to reform, some even contending that the regime is working on a flexible timetable and that the obvious digressions are planned tactical maneuvers. Other optimists doubt this, but remain convinced that Egypt, given the bleakness of its economic situation and prospects, just has to adopt a thoroughgoing reform program. The worse the economic crisis, in this view, the better the prospects for real change.

Those convinced of this reasoning can take cheer from Egyptian economic indicators in the mid-1980s. In 1984 Egypt's official hard-currency remittances from expatriates, which then as now constitute a fraction of the total—for considerably more leak in unofficially—totaled $4 billion. In 1985 these remittances fell to $3.7 billion and in 1986 they dropped to $2.7 billion. Foreign-currency earnings from tourism traced a parallel trajectory, falling from $1 billion in 1985 to $500 million in 1986. Oil revenues fell in the same period by $1.1 billion. In total, hard-currency earnings declined from $9.7 billion in 1985 to $6.9 billion in 1986.[15] While they recovered somewhat in 1987, the current account deficit continued to widen through 1987 and the foreign debt grew from some $38 billion in 1986 to well over $40 billion in early 1988. If bad news is good news, then Egypt ought to be on the road to reform. To ensure that will be the case USAID, IMF, the World Bank, and others have coordinated efforts to tighten conditions on grants and loans so that Egypt cannot squirm off the hook at this critical juncture.

Pessimists, however, doubt that the leverage provided by a deteriorating economy, even when combined with efforts to drive the point home by aid agencies and international financial institutions, will in the end bring about the desired result. They scoff at the proposition that the regime has a blueprint for reform and contend alternatively that it is paralyzed by indecision. They point to seemingly contradictory measures as reflecting temporary ups and downs of contending forces within the elite or exigencies of domestic politics at any given moment. They appraise as worthless promises by ministers to those who hand out aid and loans to reform this or that program, citing an endless chain of broken pledges to bring anomalies into line with recommendations agreed upon in the "policy dialogue." What strategic and tactical planning they see under-taken by the political elite is principally to confront pressure applied by aid agencies and foreign governments, with the preferred tactics being temporary conciliation, stonewalling, and/or subterfuge. To pessimists the regime behaves as the dancer with seven veils, beguiling her audience while removing the first six and then slipping away before the last, critical, veil is shed. The historical precedent for duplicity is to these pessimists provided by the Khedive Ismail's trail of broken promises to his many creditors.[16]

With disagreements of this magnitude over the regime's intentions, it follows that specific policy decisions are interpreted in widely varying fashions. What an optimist sees as indicative of real change a pessimist sees as a clever ploy to disarm foreign critics and gain access to the funds of yet another *tranche* (installment). There is, however, general agreement on one matter. Mubarak's regime is thought to be much more fragmented than those of either Nasser or Sadat. Indications of this fragmentation are a lack of organizational and ideological cohesiveness within the elite, increasing lassitude within state structures, emergence of counterelites and ideologies within the increasingly active legal and underground political oppositions, and the growing independence of associational groups and even governmental bodies, such as the judiciary. But while observers concur that the highly centralized system erected by Nasser and maintained, albeit not religiously, by Sadat is now fissured much more deeply, they disagree over the consequences of this fragmentation. One view is that this is a favorable development. Fragmentation of the Nasserite authoritarian political system is interpreted as a prerequisite for political and economic reform and an indication that such reforms are making headway. The facts are that the elite is now less homogeneous in social origins and ideological commitment than it was during the Nasser and Sadat eras, that voluntary associations and institutions of the state are striving to establish autonomy from the executive branch, and that multiple points of view are represented in organized form within the political opposition. All these suggest that a more pluralistic political system is emerging out of the ashes of its authoritarian predecessor. It, in turn, can be expected to preside over a further liberalization of the economy.

An alternative perspective is that the regime is simply decaying. Buffeted by contending domestic, regional, and international forces, lacking coherence and a clear sense of direction, and led by an uninspiring president challenged by the military, the regime is sinking into chaos. For reforms to be meaningful and lasting they have to be carried out by self-conscious reformers, capable of projecting positive images of their vision of the future and ever-alert to the possibilities of widening their coalition. Real reforms do not just emerge out of the breakdown of political order, they are engineered. Disorder in political and economic systems is as much an enemy of reform as it is of the status quo. Its consequences are a volatility and unpredictability that can easily lead to a regression to strict control or to a progression into revolution. Sensible reforms, in which some sacrifices are exchanged for general improvements, require at least a quasi-rational political environment in which arguments can be made with effect and deals struck to an observable purpose.[17] In Mubarak's Egypt, however, the government, according to these skeptics, is too weak to articulate and implement significant reforms but too strong for alternative elites to take up that challenge. In the meantime the public has lapsed into a cynicism that automatically rejects any plan for reform as inadequate or perceives it as self-serving and demands instead root and branch change—a reversion to the strongman or progression into the revolutionary unknown.

Whichever view of contemporary Egyptian politics is correct, there is little doubt that Egypt is at a crossroads. The internally and externally generated "rents," which prolonged the life of the soft state, may well now be insufficient to service the requirements of the social contract on which that weak state has rested. The choices thus appear to be four:

1. To attempt to continue to muddle through and hope that the political system does not collapse before rental receipts miraculously increase;
2. To squeeze the middle and upper classes and revert to a more egalitarian, populist politics, in accordance with a secular or Islamic ideology;
3. To opt for a Latin American solution with order imposed partly or wholly by the military, economic profits generated by indulging the preferences of the captains of industry and commerce, and legitimacy provided by a veneer of Islamism;
4. To devise a political economy according to the guidelines of the new orthodoxy.

Supporters of the last option, whether Egyptian or otherwise, contend that since the first alternative is likely to fail, it will be either of the unpalatable options two or three, both of which would be associated with significant repression or could even stimulate revolutionary chaos, that will develop unless somehow the reforms required to bring the new orthodoxy into existence can be engineered. Those reforms will require a significant reduction of governmental involvement in the economy, greater reliance on markets and price mechanisms generally, devaluation and unrestricted flotation of the Egyptian pound, enhanced productivity through increasing investment in the private sector, a general tightening of labor discipline, and a significant reduction in governmental and public sector employment. This is a tall order. It immediately raises the question of whether such reforms could conceivably emerge from the political system as currently structured.

The official line of the supporters of the new orthodoxy is that the present regime can adopt the basic tenets of the faith without having to undergo a political transformation. The government is strong enough, commands enough of the country's resources, and would enjoy sufficient backing from the beneficiaries of such reforms, to say nothing of the international aid community, to bring about the required changes. Unofficially there are doubts about the regime's capabilities and fears that a mishandling of reforms could be fatal. Behind closed doors in embassy and aid offices there is much talk of an Iranian-style disaster, something that no official wants to be associated with for at least personal career reasons, if not out of general political predispositions. Many of these quasi-participants in the Egyptian decision-making process believe that the dilemma of the reform package requires more pressure than the semiliberal system can apply and will eventually have to be resolved by stiffening the latter with the necessary measure of authoritarianism. For some this process sounds very much like a preference for the Latin American option of an alliance between the military and the bourgeoisie presiding over a corporate, authoritarian state. For others involved in pushing the new orthodoxy the political changes required fall considerably short of this and are in any case intended to be temporary, just allowing sufficient time for the benefits of reform to appear and thereby lend support to a more open polity. While there is no official U.S. policy on this matter, tightening of pressure on Egypt to adopt economic reforms, the close bilateral military relations and strong U.S. support for the head of the military, and the lack of any effort to force the pace of political liberalization suggest that Washington is perfectly willing to tolerate a fair measure of "stiffening" of the political order, if that is necessary to stabilize the economy and safeguard the bilateral military relationship.

Egyptian bourgeois liberals, whose chief organizational vehicle is the New Wafd Party, scoff at the contention that a truly privatized, export-oriented economic system can be brought into being by the contemporary regime or one yet more authoritarian. Their reasoning is that the authoritarian political system inherited by Mubarak from Sadat and Nasser rests on control of the economy and will, therefore, never abdicate voluntarily to the private sector. Consequently, economic reform, if it is to be accomplished, will have to be preceded rather than followed by political liberalization, which Wafdists, not incidentally, anticipate as paving the way for their return to power. In that event, or so the party faithful promises, the shackles binding private initiative would be removed, the public sector would be slimmed down, and markets would be awarded the task of determining prices. The result: The new orthodoxy would be enshrined as that prevailing in Egypt. The self-serving nature of the argument aside, there is much to recommend the basic proposition that an openly competitive capitalist economy requires real capitalists, rather than soldiers and managers lurking in the interstices of the network that links the public to the private sector. After all, if Arab Socialism foundered because there were no real socialists, what would be the fate of Arab Capitalism without real capitalists? But this logic has made no discernible impact on U.S. policy toward Egypt, which is committed to twisting the arms of those in power to force them to adopt the new orthodoxy, rather than working behind the scenes to facilitate the emergence of a reform coalition that would necessarily include elements from what is now the opposition.[18]

A cursory glance at comparative attempts to adopt policies of private sector-based strategies of export-led growth suggests that in the initial stages they may be compatible with almost any type of regime, but that after a certain point further progress may be impeded by the structure of political authority. Within the Middle East and North Africa, for example, the single-party regimes of Iraq and Algeria have embarked on reform programs, as have the monarchial regimes of the Persian Gulf, but none has yet managed a real breakthrough. The impression these experiences convey is that political elites are behaving as Moore hypothesized—they are seeking to maintain authoritarian rule by privatizing the resource requirements of patronage. While over the long haul that may so erode the base upon which authoritarian rule rests it will collapse, that is by no means a certainty and there is as yet no historical example to suggest it is even possible. On the other hand, the two Middle Eastern states with the most highly institutionalized patterns of political participation, Turkey and Israel, have pursued most successfully the strategy of reform dictated by the new orthodoxy of development.

It is, however, premature to assert a necessary relationship between regime type and willingness and ability to pursue strategies of privatization and export-led growth. In this region of the world the process is insufficiently advanced. For this reason the Egyptian case, in which conflict over the adoption of the new orthodoxy of development is most open and has the longest history, contains the potential to be very instructive. If the Egyptians cannot engineer economic reforms because their political system is insufficiently flexible, then there is little hope for the yet more authoritarian systems of the Fertile Crescent, the Gulf, or North Africa. Conversely, if meaningful reforms can be achieved within the present political framework, then the possibility that the new economic orthodoxy will spread through the region are commensurately greater.

ORGANIZATION OF FOLLOWING CHAPTERS

The starting point for the investigation of the relationship between political authority and economic change in Egypt will be the presidency and the highest level of the political elite. The political persona of Husni Mubarak remains shrouded in considerable ambiguity. Since presidential preferences and style are so important in this executive-centered system, it is essential that an attempt be made to specify the ways in which Mubarak has defined his role and his impact on the political elite and policy making. As will be suggested in Chapter 2, fragmentation of authority is due in part to the way in which Mubarak has structured the inner core of the elite, which in turn results from changes in Egypt's political economy in the past decade and from the President's personal political style. Unlike his predecessor, Mubarak has not gathered around himself a coterie of high-profile advisers with extensive connections into the *infitah* bourgeoisie, a personnel resource which Sadat seized upon as a means with which to monitor and control private sector economic activities.

Mubarak's freedom of action is constrained by two social forces that have flourished in the partial vacuum of power. The first, the weaker of the two, is the *infitah* bourgeoisie, which emerged as a result of Sadat's opening and to whom both Sadat and Mubarak turned to provide the resources to maintain patronage networks upon which presidential power rests. The trade-off has been that this bourgeoisie has accumulated at the very least veto power in some areas of decision making,[19] and, according to some accounts, virtually across-the-board influence.[20] In Chapter 3 the composition and political influence of the bourgeoisie will be investigated, with particular attention given to divisions within the class. The existence of contending factions of the bourgeoisie accounts in part for the reticence of the state to adopt the new economic orthodoxy. It is by no means the case that all sections of this class favor a liberal, export-oriented economy of the sort USAID and IMF officials describe in glowing terms. Indeed, the wing of the bourgeoisie that is politically most influential, which includes those who operate in the interstices between the public and the private sectors, is reluctant to support an economic opening that would lead to a truly competitive, free enterprise economy.

Of related interest is the means by which the bourgeoisie articulates its interests. To some observers key elements of this class constitute cliques that operate behind the scenes and manipulate policy to serve individual rather than broad, impersonal class purposes, whereas to others the key feature of interest is that the bourgeoisie is increasingly incorporated in pluralist groups. While the former mode suggests a continuation of the authority of presidential-centered patrimonialism, the latter points to the possibility of system transformation in the direction of pluralism or Latin American-style corporatism. This issue will be taken up in both Chapters 3 and 6.

The second social force that has encroached upon presidential power and that contributes to the fragmentation of political authority more generally is the military. At this stage there has been no appreciable increase in the presence of military officers in political and administrative institutions, the principal indicator that has frequently been used to argue the decline in importance of the military from the Nasser to the Sadat eras. But what has indisputably occurred is that the military has acquired substantial economic resources, both independently and in alliance with the civilian bourgeoisie. These resources not only enhance the organizational distinctiveness and power of the armed forces, but they provide the basis upon which their leader, Field Marshal Abd al-Halim Abu Ghazala, has constructed a clientage network that rivals that of the President himself. As a consequence the possibility of a creeping or a dramatic intervention by the military into the political system, a process intimated by the high-level duel between Mubarak and Abu Ghazala, now looms over civilian politicians. This new role for the military and the reaction of politicians to it are the subject of Chapter 4.

Sadat's *infitah*, which directed resources away from the state and into private hands, Mubarak's unwillingness or inability to construct a powerful and far-flung presidential clientage network, and the emergence of an articulate if still somewhat disorganized opposition have all contributed to the fragmentation of the state's control system, which Nasser carefully erected and upon which Sadat relied but did not expend many resources in maintaining. This fragmentation is manifested both within particular institutions and among them. So, for example, discontent within the key security agencies under the minister of interior, an unthinkable development under Nasser or Sadat, is now clearly evident.[21] Unseemly squabbles among undersecretaries in other ministries charged with controlling particular domains likewise have become the daily fare of Egypt's avid readers of the opposition press. The most dramatic example of conflict between control institutions was the pitched battle that broke out between the Ministry of Interior's Central Security Force on the one hand and the army and air force on the other in February 1986. Similarly, the regime's political party, the National Democrats, which inherited from the old Arab Socialist Union via Sadat's Socialist Party of Egypt the duties to contain the opposition and recruit loyal political leadership, is riven with strife. It now requires unconstitutional electoral laws, combined with embarrassingly heavy-handed vote rigging, to retain its electoral majority at local, provincial, and national levels. The party, formerly a principal vehicle for controlling syndicates and student politics, now has its hands full just holding itself together and ensuring that the opposition in parliament does not embarrass it. The fragmentation of the control system and its consequences will be discussed in Chapter 5.

If one side of the coin is the decay of the state's system of control, the other is the proliferation of various manifestations of pluralism, from private voluntary associations to opposition political parties. Of such groups there has been a veritable explosion under Mubarak, with all manner of Egyptians rushing to form organizations or participate in those already existing. Provincial and city politics, long-dominated by the government in Cairo through the bureaucracy and the party, are now more independent of central control. Upper Egypt has been consumed by the issue of Islamic fundamentalism, Port Said's politics turn on the issue of import controls, and politicians in the frontier provinces of North and South Sinai and Matruh, along the northwest Mediterranean coast, are concerned chiefly with issues relating to tourism and drug smuggling. Student politics are similarly diverse and much more independent than they were under Sadat or Nasser. Despite persistent efforts by the Ministry of Interior and the National Democratic Party to break the hold of Islamic activists on student unions, campuses continue to be dominated by this trend. Professional syndicates likewise have become battlegrounds for the various political tendencies, with the regime unable to contain them as it did even as recently as 1980, when syndicates that dared to flaunt Sadat's desires were systematically purged.

While there is no doubt that political participation has flourished as the state's control system has fragmented, what is less clear is whether interests articulated by such groups are in turn aggregated by the various opposition parties. Put differently, have the parties been able to capitalize on the spread of political participation by gaining recruits from these newly formed and active organizations, so that the linkage is made between what might be termed a citizen-level politics and national decision making? The degree of integration between these various interest groups and political parties is a measure of the density and effectiveness of political participation and may provide a guide to whether the system is likely to consolidate a new pluralism as a result of politicization or is simply going to collapse under the load of unorganized and unprocessed demands. Indicators of these critical dimensions will be sought in Chapter 6.

Waterbury has speculated on the effectiveness of a tripartite reform coalition consisting of the state, private entrepreneurs, and foreign actors.[22] Chapter 7 addresses this issue, paying special attention to the role of USAID. Because of the terms of the bilateral agreement under which USAID operates and its organizational shortcomings and because of Egyptian resistance, the hypothetical reform coalition has yet to come into existence. "Policy dialogue," which is a USAID euphemism for attempts to induce recipient parties to adopt recommended reforms, has in Egypt been conducted in a political vacuum. USAID is without sufficiently powerful allies from the state apparatus or the bourgeoisie to tilt the balance in the chosen direction. The new orthodoxy of development remains conspicuously the guiding philosophy of USAID rather than the agenda of broad sectors of the Egyptian articulate public. Politically and ideologically isolated after more than a decade of high-profile existence in Egypt, USAID exemplifies problems encountered by external agents of reform.

The puzzle of Egypt's future will be taken up in the concluding chapter. As in many other states of the Third World, political fragmentation induced by development failures, economic pressures, and social mobilization has brought the country to a crossroads. Whether the signals it has already given of an impending economic and political liberalization indicate that a real turning is at hand, or whether they are just temporary phenomena indicating that a pendular swing of the weak authoritarian state is reaching its outer limit, remains to be seen. The primary purpose of this book is to provide a basis upon which a more informed estimate of the likely outcome can be made.

NOTES

1. I am indebted to Bent Hansen for information about the pioneering role played by European economists in the "old orthodoxy of development." For a recent review of the works of the early U.S. development economists, see Gerald M. Meier, *Emerging from Poverty: The Economics That Really Matters* (New York: Oxford University Press, 1984), esp. pp. 130–158. The most compelling statement of support for the emerging middle classes in the Middle East is Manfred

Halpern, *The Politics of Social Change in the Middle East and North Africa* (Princeton: Princeton University Press, 1963).

2. On the organization of pharaonic agriculture see A.H.M. Jones, "Egypt and Rome," in S.R.K. Glanville, ed., *The Legacy of Egypt* (Oxford: Oxford University Press, 1942), pp. 283–295.

3. Doreen Warriner, *Land Reform and Development in the Middle East* (New York: Oxford University Press, 1962). On Warriner's impact on Egyptian decision makers, see Robert Springborg, *Family, Power, and Politics in Egypt: Sayed Bey Marei—His Clan, Clients, and Cohorts* (Philadelphia: University of Pennsylvania Press, 1982), p. 135. For a discussion of the impact of Lewis, Myrdal, and other early development economists on the Third World more generally, see Meier, *Emerging from Poverty*, pp. 130–158.

4. See for example Anne O. Krueger, *Foreign Trade Regimes and Economic Development: Liberalization Attempts and Consequences* (Cambridge: Ballinger Publishing Company, 1978). See also the other volumes in this series, and Vittorio Corbo, Anne O. Krueger, and Fernando Ossa, *Export-Oriented Development Strategies* (Boulder: Westview Press, 1985); Sherry M. Stephenson of the Directorate of Trade of the OECD in an interview with an Egyptian journalist claimed that Egypt could successfully imitate Taiwan's, Korea's, and Hong Kong's strategies of export-led growth and, because of its relatively favorable resource endowment, even outperform them. Cited in *al-Ahram al-Iqtisadi* (4 May 1987).

5. Anne O. Krueger, "Loans to Assist the Transition to Outward-looking Policies," *The World Economy*, 4, 3 (September 1981), 271–281.

6. John M. Cohen, Merilee S. Grindle, and S. Tjip Walker, "Foreign Aid and Conditions Precedent: Political and Bureaucratic Dimensions," *World Development*, 13, 12 (December 1985), pp. 1211–1230.

7. Albert O. Hirschman, *Journeys Toward Progress: Studies of Economic Policy-Making in Latin America* (New York: The Twentieth Century Fund, 1963), pp. 227–298.

8. See for example Nazih N. M. Ayubi, *Bureaucracy and Politics in Contemporary Egypt* (London: Ithaca Press, 1980); and Leonard Binder, *In a Moment of Enthusiasm: Political Power and the Second Stratum in Egypt* (Chicago: University of Chicago Press, 1978).

9. Mark N. Cooper, "State Capitalism, Class Structure, and Social Transformation in the Third World: The Case of Egypt," *International Journal of Middle East Studies*, 15, 4 (November 1983), pp. 451–469.

10. Robert Bianchi, "The Corporatization of the Egyptian Labor Movement," *The Middle East Journal*, 40, 3 (Summer 1986), pp. 429–444.

11. Clement Henry Moore, "Money and Power: The Dilemma of the Egyptian *Infitah*," *The Middle East Journal*, 40, 4 (Autumn 1986), pp. 634–650.

12. Alan Richards, "Ten Years of *Infitah*: Class, Rent, and Policy Stasis in Egypt," *Journal of Development Studies*, 20, 4 (July 1984), pp. 323–338. While oil and canal revenues are clearly "rents" in that they accrue directly to the state, remittances and tourist-generated income are only partially so for they depend on labor and for the most part are earned and held privately. On this distinction see Lisa Anderson, "The State in the Middle East and North Africa," *Comparative Politics*, 20, 1 (October 1987), pp. 1–11.

13. John Waterbury, *The Egypt of Nasser and Sadat: The Political Economy of Two Regimes* (Princeton: Princeton University Press, 1983), pp. 7–12. Also see by the same author "The 'Soft State' and the Open Door: Egypt's Experience with Economic Liberalization, 1974–1984," *Comparative Politics*, 18, 1 (October

1985), pp. 65–83. Waterbury's contention that Egypt shifted into an export-led growth phase in 1979 is not supported by data on export performance. From this time until the mid-1980s, exports in constant pounds actually decreased.

14. This conclusion is based on conversations with officials of these agencies and on selective reviews of *Finance and Development*, the quarterly publication of the IMF and the World Bank, and of various USAID publications.

15. *al-Akhbar* (4 December 1986).

16. The classic study of the relationship between Ismail and his creditors is David Landes, *Bankers and Pashas: International Finance and Economic Imperialism in Egypt* (Cambridge: Harvard University Press, 1958).

17. See Hirschman, *Journeys Toward Progress*, pp. 227–298.

18. In the late 1970s U.S. Ambassador Hermann Eilts was quite active in maintaining contacts with prominent Wafdists and others in the semilegal opposition. Since that time there have been surprisingly few contacts and most leading Wafdists have become suspicious of U.S. intentions, while for their part the staff of the U.S. Embassy generally consider the Wafd a spent force and not worth an investment of their time or interest. In late 1986, however, there were indications that the new Ambassador, Frank Wisner, might seek to reopen contacts with Wafdists.

19. Richards, "Ten Years of *Infitah*."

20. See for example "Egypt's Infitah Bourgeoisie," *MERIP Reports*, 142 (September-October 1986), pp. 40–41.

21. The opposition press has made much of the factionalization of security agencies. In mid-April 1986, for example, it reported that security officers unhappy with the appointment of Zaki Badr as Minister of Interior had formed a secret organization and were circulating pamphlets against their boss. See *al-Ahali* (16 April 1986). In the previous month Ibrahim Saada, editor of *Akhbar al-Yom* in his weekly column of 14 March revealed a conflict between Badr and the head of State Security, which was resolved by the former sacking the latter.

22. Waterbury, *The Egypt of Nasser and Sadat*, pp. 423–434.

2

MUBARAK, THE POLITICAL ELITE, AND THE CHANGING POLITICAL ECONOMY

After six years in office Muhammad Husni Mubarak remains an enigma. To some he is a skillful manager, methodically channeling the major streams of political thought and action so they flow together in reasonable tranquility. That the potentially contradictory liberal, Nasserist, and Moslem activist tendencies have been forced by Mubarak into a state of competitive but more or less peaceful coexistence attests to his sagacity and skill. He is by nature a balancer, who seeks to find fulcrums between the many polar extremes toward which Egyptian foreign and domestic policies could slide. His management of the economy requires that compromise be sought between the rich and poor; between the demands of the IMF for "restructuring" and the anger of those threatened by economic contraction; between the public and the private sectors; and between national self-sufficiency and its alternative, which is further integration into the world economic order through pursuit of a policy of export-led growth. The political choices are equally polarized, pitting secularism against theocracy, authoritarian control against liberalization, and those who venerate the memories of Sadat, Nasser, Saad Zaghlul, and Hassan al-Banna against one another. As if the potentially centrifugal forces of domestic policies were not threatening enough, Mubarak has also to avoid destructive imbalances in Egypt's foreign policy. At the regional level he somehow has to reconcile normalization of relations with Israel with reintegration into the Arab fold, while his dealings with the superpowers require that he retain the U.S. commitment to Egypt's well-being while enticing the Soviets to forgive and forget outstanding loans and previous violations of trust so that fruitful bilateral relations can be reestablished. Given these complexities and the utter probability that a very high price would be paid by Egypt and its leader for a serious misstep, it is not surprising that Mubarak treads warily. According to this interpretation of Mubarak the measure of his success to date is

19

that he has so far not fallen into any of the pitfalls that might have claimed a less cautious president.

Other pundits are not so charitable. To them Mubarak is not a masterful political tactician but a slow-witted ex-officer who lacks the native ability successfully to make the transition from bomber pilot to president. Political voluntarism is spreading not because Mubarak is expertly implementing a strategy of reform through reconciliation, but because his indecisiveness has given rise to political chaos. Having failed to indicate the direction in which Egypt ought to be moving in order to escape the economic quagmire, put behind it the scornful political cynicism that now prevails, and to somehow impart an effective identity to Egypt before the Arabs, the superpowers, and the world, Mubarak will go down in Egyptian history as a leader with no vision and no followers. There are, for example, Nasserists, Sadatists, Wafdists, Moslem Brothers, and so on, but there are no Mubarakists. Indeed, there cannot be, for no one knows what policy line such a label would imply. Egyptian political jokes, always an indicator of the public's attitude, played off of Nasser's dogmatism and authoritarianism, Sadat's capriciousness and cunning. Now they find Mubarak's alleged stupidity a convenient butt. After completing his first term in office in October 1987 he remains the "laughing cow," this uncomplimentary caricature being based on his alleged resemblance to the cow that appears on the label of a French cheese popular in Egypt. As this is hardly a compelling image for potential loyalists, Egyptian political activists, especially of the younger generation, are drifting into other channels in which they may express their hopes and desires. For Islamic activists, Wafdists, and others, Mubarak is the logical conclusion of the mindless and destructive "1952 Revolution" that aborted the real course of Egyptian history, which to the Wafdists was bourgeois liberal nationalism and to the Islamic activists was theocratic rule under the Moslem Brotherhood. To many supporters of that revolution, Mubarak is not a legitimate son of it.

Paradoxically, the "street" of Egyptian politics is populated by many who firmly believe that Mubarak is neither a clever manager of contending political forces nor a fool, but instead is a closet Nasserist awaiting the opportunity to leap out with a large red N on his chest. The proof offered in support of this interpretation consists principally not of what Mubarak has done, but of whom he has placed in positions of power. Gradually staffing a Nasserist apparatus behind the scenes, Mubarak will be ready to move when the phalanxes are in place and the opposition is weakened. Presidential adviser Usama al-Baz, who formerly was head of the office of archconspirator Sami Sharaf when Sharaf was *Chef d'Cabinet* for Nasser, is the *bête noire* of the Mubarak-is-Nasser school. He is seen as the point man organizing the infiltration and guiding policy in Nasserist directions. Other prima facie cases of Nasserists in power are Mubarak's information managers Safwat al-Sharif and Mustafa al-Faqi, the former of whom, after serving in military intelligence, became an apparatchik in Nasser's agitprop organizations, while the latter is a younger, Nasserist intellectual; Rifat al-Mahgub, Speaker of the parliament now and previously head of the Arab Socialist Union; a bevy of newspaper and magazine editors including Mahfuz al-Ansari at *al-Gumhuriya*, Makram Muhammad Ahmad at *al-Musawwur* and Ibrahim Nafa at *al-Ahram*; and scores of reporters, among whom, for example, is Assam Kursh, who covers the presidency for *al-Ahram*. The return in 1986 of Muhammad Hassanein Heikal to the world of Cairo journalism is proof of the pudding to those who cannot abide Nasser's former mouthpiece. That, coupled with the regime's willingness to permit publication of the Nasserist weekly newspaper, *Sawt al-Arab*, from August 1986,[1] and to allow a conference on Nasserism to be held in May 1986, at one of Cairo's swankiest hotels,[2] indicates just where Mubarak's real sympathies lie.

With regard to Nasserist influence on policy, the signs of this are the continued defense of and investment in the public sector, despite its (alleged) appalling record of mismanagement, corruption, and waste; the regime's reliance on the National Democratic Party (NDP), which inherited the human, physical, and to some extent the ideological resources of the old Arab Socialist Union after they had previously passed through the hands of Sadat's Egyptian Socialist Party; the selection of Nasserists for almost one-half of NDP candidates in the 1984 parliamentary elections,[3] the increasingly virulent attacks on U.S. policy toward Egypt and the Middle East more generally that regularly appear in the opposition press and occasionally creep into the progovernment media, especially since 1986; and the progressively more insistent overtures to the Soviet Union, including cabinet-level exchanges of visits and posting of top-ranking ambassadors to both capitals. In sum, Mubarak, who after all was one of the countless beneficiaries of Nasser's expansion of the military and who trained at the Frunze Military Academy in the Soviet Union, is carefully laying the groundwork for a return to the 1960s.[4]

Other observers scoff at this interpretation, for to them Mubarak is a Sadatist in all but name. By that they mean he is undermining the public sector and encouraging private investment, the evidence of that being the increase from less than 30 percent to about 40 percent of the private sector's share of investments scheduled in the five-year plan for 1987–92 as compared to its predecessor; the introduction of market determined prices into public-sector transactions; pledges to sell various public-sector enterprises to private buyers; and so on. Military and economic ties to the United States are, according to this view, being strengthened rather than weakened, as indicated by the increasing dollarization of the Egyptian economy; by the role of U.S. aid in setting Egyptian development priorities; by the purchase of ever-larger amounts of advanced U.S. military equipment; and by increasing coordination of military activities, including joint exercises, granting U.S. forces access to Egyptian "facilities," and coordination of counterterrorist measures.

Normalization of relations with Israel, including importation of Israeli goods and services, is a further indication of the Sadatist trend.

The domestic political scene, far from being infiltrated by Nasserists, is characterized by the continued preeminence of those who rose to power during the Sadat period or who are influenced by liberal ideology. Mubarak's Prime Ministers, for example, either emerged into the political limelight under his predecessor (i.e., Fuad Muhyi al-Din and Kamal Hassan Ali) or are economists of the neoclassical school (i.e., Ali Lutfi and Atif Sidqi), who support policies of privatization, rationalization of subsidies, and emphasis on price mechanisms generally. The National Democratic Party, which Sadat bequeathed to Mubarak just as Nasser had previously left to his political heir the Arab Socialist Union, has not been completely purged of its Sadatist core by Egypt's new president. Increasingly it represents the privileged rather than the workers and peasants who had previously benefited from Nasserism. From this perspective Mubarak is a conservative, a supporter of the West and economic and political liberalism more generally. That he has not moved more rapidly and energetically in pursuing policies consistent with this orientation reflects the presence of opposition rather than the absence of good intentions.

Others interpret Mubarak as victim of powerful antagonistic forces. Evidence proffered in support of this interpretation is his failure to move against controversial public figures and increasingly independent political institutions that allegedly constrain his power. Those who subscribe to either class-based theories of political behavior, or to cabalistic ones, are of the opinion that Mubarak is rendered powerless by *munfatihun*, (openers), or the beneficiaries of the open door policy that Sadat instituted. These are the importers, the middlemen between foreign firms and the government, and the money changers and the fixers who emerged from the ranks of government officials, private entrepreneurs, or the *ancien regime* bourgeoisie that had been sitting it out under Nasser, or even in a few cases the urban lower class.[5] Whether this parasitic element constitutes a full-blown comprador bourgeoisie, or simply a mafia, as many, including journalist David Hirst, describe them,[6] the consequence is the same—namely, they are more powerful than the president himself.

A related interpretation downgrades the importance of cabalistic behavior, of the idea that a mafia is operating behind the scenes to derail Mubarak's reforms. The argument instead is that his power is limited as a result of the transformation of the corporatist interest groups, which Nasser created and then contained, into truly pluralist ones, whose semiautonomous existence both testifies to and results in the president's inability to force Egyptians to toe his political line. While the groups that have most frequently been identified as having successfully encroached on executive decision making are those that represent *munfatihun* and the larger category of businessmen from which they are drawn, it is occasionally argued that associations representing more humble interests have also made their presence felt.[7] Although the conspiratorial and the corporatist/pluralist views present alternative explanations of how the president's will is thwarted, they concur in the view that Mubarak's instincts tend to be the right ones—that he wants to clean up the Augean stables left by Sadat, but that he has been unable to do so.[8]

The disagreement even among the cognoscenti of Egyptian politics over Mubarak's intentions and capabilities is not a novel phenomenon. Mystery surrounded both Nasser and Sadat in the early days of their rule. Nasser was seen by the Egyptian left and by the Soviets as a U.S. agent in the wake of his coup, a view that was dispelled eventually by the dramatic events of 1955–1956. Sadat gave little indication of his subsequent behavior before he established legitimacy and unquestioned political supremacy as a result of the semisuccessful October war. If history is a guide, there remains the possibility that Mubarak could, with relatively short notice, lead Egypt decisively in a new direction. But there is no gainsaying the fact that he has fallen so far behind the pace set by Nasser and Sadat in establishing their power and authority that there is doubt he will ever do so. Were he suddenly to embark down some new path, the nation might not follow. His personality and political style, the structure of the political elite, and the nature of the political economy that he inherited from Sadat have worked together to frustrate his efforts to consolidate presidential rule.

MUBARAK'S POLITICAL STYLE

On succeeding to the presidency after Sadat's assassination, Mubarak immediately adopted a low-key, conciliatory tone. He released political prisoners who had been rounded up by Sadat in the month preceding his death, and he reinvigorated the process of political liberalization that had been launched in 1976 but that had been aborted by Sadat in 1978–1979. In so doing he won considerable goodwill from an Egyptian population that had grown tired of his two predecessors' grand gestures and the costs, personal and national, they frequently carried. But after a certain point what had first appeared as caution and reconciliation began to seem more as indecision and indifference to alternative viewpoints. By the parliamentary elections of 1984, the Egyptian public appeared to be missing the more flamboyant style of Sadat and the forcefulness of Nasser, almost as if they were in need of a fix of the political adrenalin that had surged on those occasions when Nasser had challenged the superpowers and Sadat had outsmarted them. Mubarak appeared to have lost the initiative to his opponents, foreign and domestic, a failing that Sadat's most trenchant critics could never accuse him of and a fact that they now began to remember.[9] As the domestic economic crisis intensified after 1985 and the Arab World continued to drift rudderless and virtually without regard to Egypt's presence, Egyptians have grown increasingly desperate for signs that Mubarak is going to lead them out of their difficulties.

But Mubarak is not a charismatic figure, nor even one who appears comfortable in a political environment. He is principally a military officer accustomed to routine imposed by bureaucracy and chain of command. More than ten years younger than Sadat and Nasser, he graduated from the military academy in 1949 and from the air force academy some four months before the July 1952 coup d'etat that brought Nasser and the Free Officers to power. But Mubarak was not in those or his subsequent military days a political activist. He was half a generation younger than the bulk of the Free Officers. Given the importance of loyalties based on age cohorts and graduating classes in civilian and military tertiary institutions in Egypt,[10] that gap was enough to separate Mubarak and most of his contemporaries from the political activism of their predecessors. The son of a provincial civil servant from Shabin al-Kum in the Delta province of Minufiya, Mubarak diligently pursued a military career in the air force, staying away from the eccentric and ambitious officers who formed the clientele of Field Marshal Abd al-Hakim Amer and his protege, Shams Badran, all of whom were purged in the wake of the 1967 war.[11]

Mubarak's lack of political involvement in the 1950s and 1960s may have stemmed not only from a sense of military professionalism but also from his lack of sociability. Egyptian politics are intensely personal, constructed on the foundations of countless social relations given shape in small groups known as *shilla*-s.[12] Mubarak, however, is not given to small talk, to idling away long hours with *shilla* partners, or to seeking out new social contacts. When asked by Egyptian television what his favorite pasttime is, he replied that he had none.[13] When interviewed by *Oktober* magazine on his daily habits, he provided a timetable of his day, which other than a break for squash is spent almost entirely behind a desk, with breaks coming in the form of presidential visits to various installations.[14] By comparison, Sadat indulged his passion for socializing late into the night, while Nasser could sit for hours listening to the tales of *ancien regime* politics and personalities as related by raconteurs such as Ahmad Abdu Sharabasi, whose proficiency in this area earned him a cabinet portfolio.[15] Mubarak, by contrast, prefers his own company. When visiting his wife's relatives in Great Britain, he has been known to spend long hours alone in his hotel room, not seeking the companionship of Egyptian diplomats, other members of the large Arab community in London, or that of English politicians, academics, or reporters, to all of whom he would have ready access.[16] He is a private person who prefers the structured environment of the workplace to less formal social settings.

Mubarak's lack of social skills, including a visible awkwardness in repartee, has unfortunate consequences for his political persona. He is stiff not only in physical appearance, with his arm moving up and down rigidly as he seeks to emphasize a point, but in his manner of dealing with subordinates. He has, while on tours of inspection, literally pushed cabinet ministers and abused them in intemperate language when apparently irritated by their lack of haste or other inadequacies. His aides cringed when, in the summer of 1986 on a visit to a factory, he attempted to make small talk with a female process worker. After she responded to his first question about the amount of her salary (£E60 per month, or about $30), he proceeded to ask her if she managed to spend all of it. This suggested either a sadistic streak or remarkable naivete, for inflation in prices for basic commodities was the issue in the country and £E60 a laughably inadequate sum.[17] His lack of ease before television cameras and inability to come up with the right answers were apparent from the first interview he gave to a U.S. network in the wake of the Sadat assassination. On that occasion he was asked what he most feared. He replied, "Nothing." While to a Western audience this bisyllabic answer was acceptable if uninformative, to a Moslem audience a man not fearing God, especially when his predecessor had just been gunned down by Islamic extremists, was either a fool or a nonbeliever.

His set piece performances are not appreciably better. Potentially his most important speech of 1986, indeed, of his entire presidential career, was the one he delivered at the People's Assembly (parliament) in the wake of the 25–26 February riots by Central Security Force conscripts. It was widely anticipated that having not only survived this near disaster, but having won considerable admiration for his handling of it, Mubarak would seize the opportunity to ride the crest of the wave of popularity by announcing a set of policy initiatives. Instead the speech was a dull rehash of the violent events and a recitation of the regime's vague remedies for Egypt's pressing problems, with the real punch line of the speech being a prohibition on the Assembly's discussion of the riots until after judicial proceedings had been completed. In other words the riots were to be defined as a criminal rather than political affair. The opportunity to consolidate a significant measure of presidential popularity was squandered for a marginal tactical gain in the petty political game with the parliamentary opposition. A man who seems not to value intimate social contacts, Mubarak gives the impression of being cut off from popular sentiments. He does not read public opinion well and has difficulty in articulating and encapsulating popular desires in appropriate words and actions. His sense of timing is, correspondingly, inadequate.[18]

While Mubarak is widely viewed as indecisive, his self-image seems to be the opposite, or at least his mannerisms suggest he is very much trying to project such an image. The brusque public style is coupled with the presentation of him by his advisers as a man who solicits different viewpoints and then immediately reaches a decision.[19] As a result of this preoccupation with decisiveness, which probably results from an interaction of personality factors and the military environment in which he was conditioned, Mubarak does not relate well to individuals or audiences he needs to win over. A senior official in the U.S. Embassy in Cairo who often dealt directly with Mubarak found his compulsion to appear decisive as somewhat comical.[20] Others find it downright offensive. In spring 1985, while on a trip to Washington, Mubarak met with a group of foreign correspondents. Several of them expressed their apprehensions about the future of President Gaafar Numairi of the Sudan. Mubarak upbraided them in no uncertain terms, asserting dogmatically and without qualification that Numairi was there to stay and that his information on the subject was infinitely better than theirs. One of the reporters present described Mubarak's style as "assertive, belligerent, and it did not impress those listening. It was as if he wanted to appear very decisive, very much in control."[21] Within weeks of this off-the-record session Numairi was overthrown.

Mubarak has an accentuated concern for privacy. It is manifested in part by his reticence to discuss aspects of his youth or upbringing. This stands in contrast to Sadat's fondness for glorifying his village life in Mit Abul Kom and to Nasser's recollections of his feelings as a young officer with revolutionary ideas.[22] Mubarak, on the other hand, has given no clues as to the personally significant events of his early life, his emotional or political maturation, or even to his current feelings. His wife passed almost anonymously through the American University in Cairo, where she went by the name of Susan Sabet.[23] The presidential household is neither the very ostentatious palace along the Nile that Sadat preferred nor the much-photographed suburban dwelling that Nasser inhabited. Instead it is a villa adjacent to the army base in the suburb of Heliopolis. For literally blocks around the streets are closed off. Egyptians have no idea of what the presidential home looks like, whereas Nasser's house and Sadat's palace were familiar public landmarks.

While the privacy that surrounds Mubarak and his family is no doubt in part a calculated reaction to his predecessor's grand public style, which grated on the Egyptian public as it became ludicrously excessive, it also seems to reflect strong personal preferences. Mubarak's attitude about the public's interest in his life is "It's none of their business." The glossy weekly photo magazine specials on him, which began to appear in the autumn of 1986 as his need for reelection in 1987 dictated a public relations campaign, were a far cry from equivalent treatments of Sadat, both in terms of what they revealed about the man and in their professionalism. The accompanying interviews with Mubarak gave the impression he begrudged the time spent with the reporter.[24]

The persisting inability to shed the aura of remoteness that surrounds him, or to turn it to his advantage by appearing to be a demigod, as Nasser did, may reflect Mubarak's limited breadth of perspective, hence lack of ease in dealing with a variety of situations. While next to nothing in detail is known about his early youth in Minufiya, from the time he was a teenager he has lived in the womb of the military. He attended its college in Heliopolis, virtually a stone's throw from where he now lives. For much of his career he has been stationed at the main Cairo air base, which is located just down the road. The social environment of the military subsociety of Heliopolis and Nasr City, the adjacent suburb, is quintessentially secular middle class, replete with medium-sized villas, medium-sized Fiats, and medium-sized families supervised by mothers who have college degrees and speak reasonable French or English and who, until recently, have shunned Islamic dress, although as that attire has been glamorized it has become increasingly popular with even this set. Husbands' closest social contacts are typically with members of the same graduating class, sometimes reinforced by shared origins in a particular province.[25] Mubarak, in short, has lived a comfortable, middle-class, military existence for almost forty years, with one academic year when he was already a family man spent in the Soviet Union, where he also had a shorter training mission. He did travel in official capacities after becoming Vice President in 1975, but this was a far cry from the sort of formative experiences that Nasser and Sadat had. They moved about Egypt extensively in their earlier years, and both prowled through the underground of revolutionary nationalist politics in the heady days of anticolonialism. Sadat even tried his hand at acting, while Nasser plotted from sunrise to sunset. By comparison Mubarak's life has been staid, predictable, and unlikely to produce a deep and complex personality fired by a sense of historical destiny.

While the President's strong desire for privacy is unobtrusive, if nevertheless noticeable and remarked upon, his accompanying passion for security is obtrusive, possibly obsessive, and further contributes to his isolation from the public. The sprawling security net that spreads out from his Heliopolis villa far exceeds any previous efforts to protect presidents. His phalanx of bodyguards is truly formidable and as constraining as the Secret Service cocoon around the U.S. president. The conveniences and liberties of normal citizens are, in comparison to presidential security precautions, of no concern. Whole city quarters are blocked off in advance of presidential movements, whereas Sadat and Nasser used to make do with presidential cavalcades. Helicopters sometimes oversee presidential forays into urban districts, lending a menacing air to presidential visits.

The lack of concern with the negative public impact of security precautions was manifested in particularly stark fashion at the celebration of the Feast of the Sacrifice in the summer of 1986. Mubarak chose on that occasion to demonstrate his religious piety by praying at the Imam Hussain mosque, which is adjacent to the al-Azhar complex and smack in the middle of Cairo's oldest quarters. It draws an intriguing mixture of urban poor, faculty and students of al-Azhar, mystics and members of Sufi orders, innumerable political activists hoping to spread their message and expand their networks of supporters, journalists seeking to tap into these sources, and police spies leavening the mixture. About seven in the evening prior to the dawn prayer of the morning of the

Feast of the Sacrifice, Mubarak's security men swooped down on the Khan al-Khalili quarter in which the Imam Hussain mosque is located. They forced shopkeepers to close up and go home, chased habitues out of the coffee houses and sent them on their way, and issued orders that the streets were to be kept clear until after the President's visit was concluded. The following morning with television cameras grinding the President conducted his prayers in the mosque before an overflow crowd, virtually the entirety of which was composed of security officers brought in for the occasion. This performance provided grist for the already overworked rumor mills of this politically sensitive quarter of Cairo for days. While reconciling the demands of presidential security with image creation is difficult, the mix that Mubarak has settled upon suggests he places insufficient emphasis on the latter.

The combination of Mubarak's desire for privacy and security and his wish to appear decisive does not mesh well with the gears that drive politics. One indicator of this is that the office of the presidency is not well managed. Announcements are frequently made that subsequently have to be retracted. In the fall of 1986, for example, it was announced that Mubarak would be visiting Washington before the end of the year. When the necessary spadework in the form of economic reforms demanded by Washington clearly could not be completed by that date, the visit was pushed back until January. Rescheduled again for 25 February, Mubarak then canceled the trip in protest against the Iran arms deal and the U.S. response to Egyptian proposals for reducing interest on the military debt. In November of the same year Mubarak abruptly sacked Prime Minister Ali Lutfi and replaced him with Atif Sidqi, but the task of putting the cabinet together did not go smoothly. On 11 November al-Akhbar announced that there would be eight new faces in the cabinet, but on the following day ten new names were included in the list of portfolios. Cairo was buzzing with rumors about Minister of Supply Nagi Shatla's refusal to stay on in the post and how Fuad Sultan, Minister for Tourism in the Ali Lutfi government, was dropped from the new cabinet and then brought back in with the portfolio of Civil Aviation added at the last minute. Again Mubarak's decisiveness seemed not to be translated into effective political management.

A second indication of the inappropriateness of the Mubarak style within the context of elite politics is his failure to recruit into policy positions top-caliber technical and administrative expertise, with which Egypt is particularly well endowed. This shortcoming may be a consequence of Mubarak's inability to come to terms with the porous nature of Egyptian politics, a world in which secrets are very hard to keep. For a man who values privacy as much as Mubarak does, leakages from decision-making elites to the articulate public and beyond are irksome. He is willing to incur considerable costs, including those of recruiting less-qualified personnel, to avoid such embarrassments.

The willingness to sacrifice quality in personnel selection in order to maintain secrecy is reflected most clearly in the process of cabinet formation. The abrupt reshuffle in November 1986 was very similar to that of September 1985, which in turn was a reaction to the delay and uncertainty surrounding the formation in 1984 of the Kamal Hassan Ali government. When Prime Minister Fuad Muhyi al-Din died in the wake of the 1984 parliamentary elections, it took from 5 June until 16 July for a new cabinet to be cobbled together, during which time it became abundantly clear that Mubarak was having great difficulty in finding suitable candidates for various important portfolios. This upset Mubarak, who surprised everyone, including the principals, the following year when he abruptly dismissed Kamal Hassan Ali and appointed the little-known Ali Lutfi as his replacement. An honest, competent economist who had served as Minister of the Economy in 1978–1979 and as Chairman of the National Democratic Party's Economic Committee in the critical January-April 1985 period during which that committee challenged the program of the incumbent Minister of the Economy, Mustafa al-Said, Lutfi appealed to Mubarak precisely because of his relative obscurity. His selection surprised virtually all observers of and participants in Egyptian elite politics, a response in which Mubarak took delight.[26]

But for that presidential triumph Ali Lutfi and the country had to pay a price. A more powerful and prominent candidate than Lutfi could have expected to nominate short lists for a minimum of seven or eight of the nonsensitive cabinet positions. In that way a new prime minister normally takes a small team of loyalists with him into the cabinet who support him against the President's direct selections, which invariably include those in the key portfolios of defense, interior, and foreign affairs, as well as others. But in this instance Mubarak permitted his prime minister designee only two such nominations, principally because he did not want Lutfi to engage in protracted negotiations that would tip off the country that a cabinet change was imminent.[27] The upshot of Mubarak's desire for secrecy and his wish to appear decisive in dictating his choice of prime minister was that Ali Lutfi, a technocrat elevated far above any political base he might have had in a more circumscribed domain and lacking a sufficiently large nucleus of allies in the cabinet, was, along with his government, completely immobilized. His public agony dragged on for a year before he was mercifully replaced. The public generally sympathized with this good and honest fellow who was the wrong man for the job.

Although human talents are not easily measured or compared, there exists little doubt among close observers that the caliber of cabinet ministers, party officials, and parliamentarians loyal to the government's cause has deteriorated under Mubarak. The list of ministers who served under Nasser and who established themselves within Egypt and even internationally as competent experts in their particular fields includes such individuals as Sayed Marei, Aziz Sidqi, Abd al-Munain Qaissuni, Muhammad Hassanein Heikal, Mustafa Khalil, and others. Sadat's choices were not as impressive, but his cabinets included some of the above luminaries as well as a few new figures of note, including Abd al-Aziz Hijazi, Ismail Sabri Abdulla, Ibrahim Shukri, and possibly others. The relative dearth of really talented ministers in Mubarak's cabinets and elsewhere in his governmental apparatus reflects on his leadership. His personal style—the need to emphasize decisiveness, the emotional austerity, remoteness from ordinary social intercourse—does not facilitate contacts with potential political recruits. Nor does it encourage loyalty or frank advice. Mubarak prizes organizational men who exemplify the principles of rational-legal rather than charismatic authority and who are not conspicuous by virtue of talent or other characteristics. The political elite that has emerged since 1981 is, therefore, markedly different, at least at its highest level, from the one that surrounded Nasser and Sadat.

MUBARAK AND THE POLITICAL ELITE

The inner core of the political elite includes the President and his closest advisers. Under both Nasser and Sadat this group was relatively visible. Its members were known to the articulate public and they generally occupied formal posts in government other than just offices in the presidency. But this is not to say that the clientele group was stable over time. During his eighteen years as leader, Nasser shuffled through, first, the original members of the Revolutionary Command Council and then, in the 1960s, pulled up into the inner elite second-ranking members of the Free Officers, as well as a few civilian technocrats. Virtually all of these clients of the President at one time or another occupied ministerial or other high-ranking posts. Under Sadat those who were gathered around the President included a very few former officers, most notable of whom was Hassan Tuhami; prominent civilian figures with long careers in the public limelight, including Osman Ahmad Osman, Sayed Marei, Mustafa Khalil; and other, younger men who were pulled into the elite from comparative obscurity, such as Mansur Hassan. Most of these figures held cabinet portfolios at one time or another. Moreover, they and their predecessors under Nasser sought to enhance their own powers by building up personal patronage networks in the various state apparatuses, while for their parts the presidents took precautions to ensure that these clienteles would not grow too large and threatening.

The Mubarak presidency has witnessed a departure from this pattern. The men he has chosen as his closest advisers were not previously prominent, they are not now high-profile public figures, and they have not been given important positions outside the presidency. The majority are military officers with whom Mubarak came into contact during his air force career or while he was Vice President, a position which gave him access to the sprawling presidential bureaucracy and to the officers who constitute its nucleus. The two civilians who are known to have unimpeded access to Mubarak owe their positions at least in part to those very same officers. These civilians' vocational backgrounds, career trajectories, and modus operandi also mirror the managerial style of their boss.

The more senior of these two presidential confidants is Usama al-Baz, who joined the Foreign Ministry as a third secretary in 1956 after he had completed a law degree and worked briefly as a niyaba, or court investigator. He was sent by the government in the early 1960s to undertake graduate work at Harvard University, where he was suspected by fellow Egyptian students of being employed by the security service that Nasser had established to monitor activities of Egyptian students overseas.[28] He returned to Egypt without having obtained a degree and went to work immediately as the director of the office of Sami Sharaf, a former Free Officer who at that time was in charge of Nasser's personal intelligence network. In that post al-Baz had day-to-day contact with the scores of officers who staff the presidency. It was due to support he accumulated in this quarter that his career was not terminated prematurely when Sharaf was purged by Sadat in May 1971. When Mubarak was elevated to the vice presidency in 1975, it was through the assistance of these same officers that al-Baz was assigned the job of briefing the new man on foreign affairs.

Al-Baz worked assiduously to cement his fortuitous connection, so by the time of Sadat's assassination he had become Mubarak's closest civilian adviser and the head of his office. From that position he has played a key role in advancing or blocking the careers of several members or potential members of the upper ranks of the political elite.[29] He is therefore feared, hated, and occasionally admired. His public persona is that of presidential confidant, an image reinforced by frequent interviews in which he is asked to convey and interpret Mubarak's thoughts on this or that subject.[30] His political views have not been articulated in writing at any length, although it is widely believed that he is a Nasserist, an interpretation consistent with his public utterances. Similarly, there is little ambiguity regarding his character, which is almost universally thought of as ambitious and conspiratorial, an interpretation for which there is considerable evidence.[31]

The second prominent civilian who is reputedly very close to the President is Mustafa al-Faqi, who previously was a client of al-Baz. Al-Faqi was a Nasserist student activist who was then sent off to London, where he completed a doctorate on the role of Makram Ubaid and the Copts in Egyptian politics. On his return to Cairo, where he was employed by the Ministry of Foreign Affairs, he came to the attention of al-Baz, who prides himself on the high level of talent he disposes of in his retinue. But al-Baz lost a client and gained a competitor when al-Faqi, managing his boss's office when in 1985 he had to leave Egypt for medical treatment, came to the attention of the President. Impressed by al-Faqi, Mubarak promoted him to the post of Secretary to the President for Information, where he has subsequently operated as a counterbalance to al-Baz.

Superficially the equivalents to the presidential clients who formerly attended upon Nasser and Sadat, al-Baz, al-Faqi, and the nameless and faceless officers who cluster around Mubarak are in fact performing quite different roles. They are managers, advisers, and assistants, devoid of independent power bases in government or in private activities and without significant national reputations that could facilitate a semiautonomous exercise of power. Such presidential clients can intervene intermittently into ministries and other agencies to affect high-level personnel and policy matters, but not having day-to-day management responsibility for organizations outside the presidency, they cannot establish the impressive networks of clients that their predecessors amassed. Mubarak's inner elite is not the equivalent of the "centers of power" that encroached upon Nasser's authority while expanding their own within the state apparatus, nor are they the multimillionaire capitalists of the sort that surrounded Sadat and who built vast empires in the *infitah* economy.

This departure from established practice is not only an indication of Mubarak's managerial orientation and his repugnance of cronyism, but it is also a consequence and further cause of the decline of presidential power. Nasser and Sadat organized their clusters of clients as management teams of which they were the boss. Clients were assigned specific responsibilities. Under Nasser this resulted in a handful of former officers taking charge of various organizations in the state apparatus in order to direct the society, economy, and polity in the direction mandated by the President's inclinations. Under Sadat the restoration of political and economic power to the bourgeoisie was effected in part by expanding the cluster of presidential clients and extracting through them patronage from the private sector. Both leaders were committed to change and neither believed it could be achieved solely by working through the bureaucracy. They used their underlings to punish and reward and in so doing push policy in preferred directions.

Mubarak's approach differs in that his commitment to change is less compelling and his preferred management style requires only the standard bureaucratic chain of command supplemented by a few back-room advisers who occasionally intervene in subordinate domains but who lack sufficient delegated authority to really terrify officials into action. By relying on an ideal-typical organizational model rather than on the more fluid executive patronage system favored by his predecessors, Mubarak has attempted to operate without a powerful and homogeneous inner elite. Nasser and Sadat appreciated that bureaucratic and economic elites were heterogeneous in composition and outlook, hence requiring direction and control by a smaller, more homogeneous group in close contact with the chief executive. Both leaders delegated sufficient power to enable their clients to manage presidentially backed initiatives. Coordination of policy formulation and implementation was achieved at least in part through the extensive social interaction that characterized both inner elites. Under Nasser such socializing derived from the bonds that brought together the members of the Free Officers conspiracy, while under Sadat ties of friendship and kinship that linked the President and the inner core of the elite manifested themselves in frequent social gatherings in some of the country's most attractive locations. The inner elite of the Mubarak presidency, different from its predecessors in that presidential clients are comparatively weaker, is also less intimate. Its members are drawn together principally by overlapping career paths and by sheer chance, not by shared political commitments, kinship, or strong bonds of friendship. Policy formation and execution, difficult with even a united group around an active chief executive, are challenges that the loosely integrated and weak inner elite around Mubarak have yet to master.

THE POLITICAL ELITE AND
THE CHANGING POLITICAL ECONOMY

Mubarak's failure to structure a client group through which he could more forcefully direct Egypt's affairs is due, as suggested above, in some measure to his personal style and preferences. Another contributing factor is that the political economy that surrounds him differs substantially from that within which Nasser operated and even from the *infitah* political economy of Sadat. Nasser's Arab Socialism obliterated domestic alternatives to patronage that were not ultimately under the control of the President himself. Externally the Soviets provided some backing for those it believed to be sympathetic to Soviet concerns and interests. At least one of the recipients, Ali Sabri, managed to convert such support into a useful political resource. But these Soviet interventions were of insufficient duration, breadth, or depth to create a large group, to say nothing of a class, that would have been bound together by shared dependence on externally generated resources and thus independent of the President.

Under Sadat the means of production were increasingly privatized and externalized, hence possibilities for generating and distributing patronage outside the ambit of presidential authority were multiplied. The tremendous upsurge in foreign investment and aid provided innumerable opportunities for comprador activities, some of which could only be undertaken in conjunction with President Sadat and/or his clients or wife, but others of which were up for grabs. The real political impact of the *infitah*, which paid lip service to political liberties, was in fact to generate the capital base upon which independent political initiatives (usually by wealthy managers, entrepreneurs, and professionals but also by the more humble) could be contemplated and carried through. By the end of the Sadat period the old command structure, which had ensured that Nasser could open and close the valves through which virtually all scarce resources passed, was in ruins.

Sadat, however, was not a passive bystander in the face of this potentially devastating erosion of presidential power. He attempted to benefit from the injection of capital into the system and from its privatization by forcing it into partnerships over which he had direct or indirect control. Such authority was exercised either directly by the President and his family, by his cronies, or by the governmental apparatus over which he presided. The first pattern amounted to a return to tradition in the presidency. A personalistic network of patronage and control was erected alongside the state bureaucracy, much in the way Khedive Ismail, the most profligate of Egypt's nineteenth-century rulers, had done. The distinction between the public treasury and the ruler's private purse became increasingly blurred as Sadat and his immediate family became principal beneficiaries of the *infitah*. Sadat was not a carbon copy of the Shah of Iran or of Ferdinand Marcos for he did not openly pursue business interests or acquire assets in his own name; but his wife, siblings, and others, not the least of whom was the heavy-handed Minister of the Interior, Nabawi Ismail, ensured that the President's family secured a substantial piece of the action. The political consequence of this neo-Khedival system of almost direct presidential involvement in business was to reinforce Sadat's power while undermining his legitimate authority, for domestic competitors and outsiders looking for opportunities in Egypt had to take account of the Sadats, but the public was repelled by this wheeling and dealing. But Sadat died as a president with no real challengers, a testament in some measure to the contribution to his power base of his personal financial relationship to the changing economy.

A related method by which Sadat permitted the proliferation of private economic activities but maintained political control was to channel those activities through the members of his inner elite. Osman Ahmad Osman, Sayed Marei, Mansur Hassan, Ashraf Marwan, and others at one remove from the inner circle were encouraged to undertake profitable ventures. Closely associated with the regime, it was unimaginable that they would attempt to use their resources to resist presidential will. Indeed, Sadat could rest assured that the combined weight of these substantial members of the elite would be a significant resource upon which he could draw if necessary.

But the preservation of presidential power in the face of rapidly proliferating and decentralizing sources of wealth, hence patronage, was achieved primarily through Sadat's continued control over the governmental apparatus itself. Deals were struck between the public sector and/or government as one partner and domestic or foreign private capital as the other. The latter was granted access to resources controlled directly or indirectly by the state, including markets, while the government and those who controlled it were compensated with new and much expanded resources for patronage. Since the state's resource base was shrinking and the President was committed to the continuation of the *infitah*, he had no choice but to pursue this strategy. As Clement Henry Moore points out, "Supporting client groups then becomes less expensive because some of the costs are farmed out." Those private interests with whom such deals were struck included state oligopolists like Osman Ahmad Osman, whose private resources could "service patron-client networks cutting across Egypt's vast, compartmentalized government bureaucracies."[32] Other useful partners were multinational corporations, whose entry into the Egyptian market was in many cases made conditional on their forming joint ventures with public-sector firms, the managers of which invariably benefited from the new arrangement by converting their control over state resources into personal wealth. This was accomplished by legal means, such as by appointment to boards of directors in newly formed entities, or through an endless variety of partially or completely illegal strategems, the end result of which was to "privatize the profits and socialize the risks and losses."[33] Joint-venture banks became a favored vehicle for farming out the costs of patronage, with loyal, long-serving ministers frequently being assigned a position on the board or in the management structure of such a bank following their retirement from the cabinet.[34]

But these strategems for the retention of presidential power in the face of progressive penetration of the old command economy by private interests were both difficult to bequeath to a successor, especially one of Mubarak's temperament, and of declining effectiveness. The absence of a client cluster around Mubarak, whose members could play a role similar to that of Sayed Marei, Osman Ahmad Osman, or others under Sadat, has restricted the sources of patronage upon which the President can draw. Mubarak is also not the type to pursue a neo-Khedival strategy of blurring the distinction between his personal and the public purse. But of greatest potential significance is the peril inherent in the process of farming out patronage to the private sector, a process that could continue to gain momentum and eventually result in the liberation of private interests from governmental, hence presidential, control. As Moore states, "The trouble with this cozy relationship and the theory behind it is that public sector officials had little incentive to keep control over their private benefactors."[35] While there were signs that the privatization of patronage was beginning to undermine presidential control prior to Sadat's death, his other personalistic mechanisms of control were still in place, and his arbitrary, despotic proclivities served as a warning to those who sought to colonize patronage networks for their own benefit.

Mubarak inherited the dilemma of requiring a network of supporters yet lacking resources in the government and public sector to ensure loyalties. Unwilling or unable to engineer the fundamental change of the political economy that would restore a sufficiently high proportion of the nation's resources to the state for patronage to be centered there, he has had to continue the strategy of trading the state's capital and regulatory prerogatives to the private sector in return for access to resources. This may not be a satisfactory resolution of the dilemma from Mubarak's standpoint: It could lead to further deterioration of presidential power, and it does appear to contradict a central feature of his claim to legitimacy, which is that of honesty in government coupled with careful management of the economy. But so far Mubarak has not come up with any alternatives and so the consolidation of presidential power continues to elude him.

What Mubarak has done to prevent his position from being further eroded by the *infitah* bourgeoisie and those allied with it is to grant increased freedoms to the formal, legal opposition. Through their newspapers, parliamentary presence, and general impact on the articulate public, the opposition parties, almost regardless of their class bases and political programs, provide Mubarak a counterbalance to the *munfatihun*. The opposition's members are whistle blowers, using their extensive networks of connections within the private and public sectors to collect information on the wheelings and dealings of prominent members of the *infitah* class and their allies in the state. The never-ending stream of scandals generated from such sources provide Mubarak with ammunition he uses to move against selected targets.

But for the political opposition to be sufficiently powerful and in its majority predisposed to constrain the *infitah* bourgeoisie as a class rather than using it just to provide individual targets for scandalmongering, the base of political participation would have to be significantly widened. This, however, is a step Mubarak, out of the fear of its implications for his own role, has been unwilling to countenance. Prevented from cementing linkages to interest groups, subject to various restrictions and controls on their activities, and manipulated ceaselessly from above so that internal divisions rapidly widen into permanent factions, the opposition parties remain little more than gadfly critics of those abusing power, a role that perfectly suits Mubarak's short-term interests.

Mubarak has also fostered a more pluralistic climate for Egypt's voluntary associations. But they, too, are still tethered to the regime, although they are now on longer ropes. Moreover, despite the fact that they represent more specific interests and frequently enjoy more committed support from their membership than do the opposition parties, their coverage of the population is extremely uneven. Indeed, with the exception of the *infitah* bourgeoisie, which is comparatively well organized and generally too powerful for the regime to attack directly, other sectors are more or less entirely unorganized. The groups with any cohesion, such as some elements of labor and the Islamic activists, arouse the repressive instincts of the state immediately on coming to its notice.

It is not the case, however, that Mubarak's weak authoritarian state can afford entirely to ignore the interests of unorganized constituencies. In fact, the very isolation of the decision-making elite from the society at large imposes serious constraints on the consideration of policy alternatives. It is recognized that there is an amorphous, inchoate, but nevertheless real, increase in political awareness and sensitivity throughout society, which results from the combined forces of social mobilization that have buffeted Egyptian society for a very long time. Ominously this largely unchanneled politicization has increased at the very time that elite-mass linkages have deteriorated. Nasser's mobilizational structures have withered or been infiltrated by opportunistic elements; Sadat's pie-in-the-sky substitute for mobilization activity has proved to be an empty promise; and Mubarak's tentative pluralism has yet to establish that it can achieve a reasonably fair balance of interests. This pluralism has not sent roots downward into the great unincorporated constituencies of the Egyptian political system, and as a result accurate appraisal of the limits of public tolerance is increasingly difficult. Security agents now substitute for party cadres in reading public reaction to trial balloons.[36] The regime is far more frightened of the possible anomic response of the alienated than it is of the schemes of the organized, for the latter are susceptible to surveillance, manipulation, and control, whereas the former may simply explode. The regime's poorly informed perception of the outer limits of mass acceptance thus defines the policy space within which alternatives are considered.

MUBARAK: THE ENIGMA REVEALED?

Mubarak has encouraged a limited form of political pluralism in order to reinforce presidential power in the face of challenges from the *infitah* bourgeoisie and forces allied to it and also because his managerial talents are best displayed while balancing off and reconciling the major political tendencies. The paradox posed by the continued presence of Nasserists in a regime that in its social base and political program is a far cry from the original article arises out of the same basic considerations. Mubarak's managerial orientation toward politics predisposes him to select those with similar skills, and none are better suited than Nasserist apparatchiks, regardless of ideological differences between them and the President. The other attraction of Nasserists to Mubarak is that they provide a direct counterbalance to the bourgeoisie that emerged as a powerful force under Sadat and to the rising tide of Islamic activism.

But for the same reason that Mubarak sets limits on the mobilizational activities of all opposition parties and most interest groups, he places obstacles in the path of a broad-based Nasserist upsurge. He wants from Nasserism a tame force that he can manipulate for his own purposes, not an independent political movement coordinated by a cabal situated outside or within the command structures of the state. So

Mubarak has recruited into his service lower-ranking Nasserists such as Rifat al-Mahgub and Safwat al-Sharif, but he has shunned the really big names, such as Ali Sabri, Abd al-Muhsin Abu al-Nur, Aziz Sidqi, and others. Moreover, he permitted in early 1987 the unofficial re-emergence of a Nasserist party, but its leadership had to be drawn not from among Nasserist luminaries but from the second string, such as Farid Abd al-Karim, the new party's secretary-general. Muhammad Hassanein Heikal began in autumn 1986 to write weekly columns in *Akhbar al-Yom,* but they dealt with such politically innocuous subjects as "Leaders I Have Known." While Nasserists were able to convene a large conference in spring 1986, they were still complaining in early 1987 of on-again, off-again harassment of their attempts to organize seminars.[37] All of this suggests that Nasser's legacy is to Mubarak a two-edged sword. It is a useful tool to use against those who constrain his exercise of power, chief among whom are the bourgeoisie who flourished once Nasserism faded. But it is also a potential threat that he must guard against. Mubarak is not a closet Nasserist, but he does appreciate the organizational skills of its standard bearers and is happy to utilize its political weight as a much-needed counterbalance.

Equally, Mubarak is not a Sadatist. Most of the powerful, visible members of the Sadat inner core have, as Egyptians put it, been "put on the shelf." Sayed Marei, despite his vigor, political acumen, and the fact that in the last two to three years of the Sadat era he was increasingly distant from the President, has not been called out of retirement to play any political role. His youngest son, Hassan, who is anxious to inherit his father's political mantle, has been prevented by Mubarak from offering his candidacy for a parliamentary seat in the home constituency of Minya al-Qamh in Sharqiya Province. Nabawi Ismail has been struggling since Mubarak removed him from the Ministry of Interior to avoid prosecution for his involvement in the torture of political prisoners and for various financial irregularities. Mustafa Khalil remains as head of the NDP's Foreign Affairs Committee, but he represents Egypt's bridge to Israel and as such is a symbol whose removal would be awkward. He is also protected by Osman Ahmad Osman, but he exercises little influence over policy and is now concerned primarily with his activities as chairman of the Arab International Bank. Abd al-Munaim Qaissuni, the informal dean of Egypt's Keynesian economists and the former Minister of the Economy who presided over the 1977 food riots, is provided with occasional newspaper space but little else.

Only Osman Ahmad Osman of the high-profile Sadatists retains a powerful political role. That is because he, as the principal oligopolist to whom Sadat had farmed out patronage, was too powerful for Mubarak to displace. There are indications that Mubarak had to learn that lesson firsthand. On succeeding to the presidency Mubarak is reputed to have ordered that government contracts be directed away from Osman's company, Arab Contractors. He is known to have demanded that various of the privileges to which Osman had become accustomed as Sadat's friend and ally be suspended. Cairenes noted that Arab Contractors' earth-moving equipment and concrete mixing plants, which for years had occupied sites on government-owned land in Cairo, were hastily removed. Several government projects on which Arab Contractors had been working in dilatory fashion, in some cases for years, were finished with haste after Mubarak came to power. The vast Salhiya reclamation project in Osman's fiefdom of Ismailiya, which had been handed over to Osman's Arab Contractors by Sadat as a pledge of his friendship and their political alliance and which had received lavish funding from the state until Sadat's death, was placed by Mubarak on a much more restricted budget.

The evidence suggests that Mubarak was testing Osman and that the latter responded by indicating his loyalty to the new President and his eagerness to comply with Mubarak's wishes. Osman, the preeminent inside operator in the Egyptian political economy since the early 1960s, was far too clever to attempt a head-on confrontation with state authority. His skillful manner of handling Mubarak, in combination with his massive economic support base and sprawling network of political clients, led within two years of Sadat's death to a reasonable relationship between him and the new President. But the relationship is not nearly as intimate as that which Osman enjoyed with Sadat. Consequently, the profits of the Osman empire are still respectable, but they are not what they were when Osman, as Minister for Reconstruction, wrote the tenders and as chairman of Arab Contractors drew up the bids.[38]

Other aspects of Mubarak's personnel management confirm his desire to escape the Sadat legacy. In addition to the Nasserists he has brought into the state apparatus, he has replaced many middle to higher ranking activists of the 1970s with those who were either junior to them or were not previously involved in politics. Yusuf Wali, a career bureaucrat in the Ministry of Agriculture, who also dabbled in politics under both Nasser and Sadat, has, for example, emerged as one of Mubarak's chief political fixers. Appointed Minister of Agriculture in 1982, following Prime Minister Fuad Muhyi al-Din's death in 1984 he also became Secretary General of the NDP. From this post he has supervised the gradual replacement of second level politicians who made their careers in the party and parliament under Sadat with a new crop of NDP activists and parliamentarians whose fates are now tied to Mubarak's. Almost 50 percent of the candidates endorsed by the NDP for the April 1987 parliamentary elections, for example, had not served in the Peoples' Assembly under Sadat. Wali, the most prominent and powerful of Mubarak's political managers, is by no means the only new face of this sort. His deputy at the NDP, Kamal Shazli, is a similar figure, as in some respects is Zaki Badr, the career detective and security specialist who has become a highly contentious Minister of Interior as a result of his obtrusive interventions into the political arena. Other bureaucrat-politicians Mubarak has brought into positions of power include Subhi Abd al-Hakim, the President of Cairo University who was made Speaker of the *Maglis al-Shura* (Consultative Assembly), and Amal Osman, who has served as Minister of Social Affairs in all of Mubarak's cabinets and who plays a critical role in supervising voluntary associations and interest groups of all sorts. These and others whose careers have blossomed under Mubarak are primarily apparatchiks unassociated with any specific political ideology. They are not required to identify political goals, articulate a persuasive or coherent ideology or mobilize mass support. Even the President himself rarely attempts these challenges.

Identifying what Mubarak is not and does not do is in fact easier than specifying who he is and what he is attempting to accomplish. The process of elimination suggests that he is neither a Nasserist or a Sadatist nor an ideologue of any particular coloring. His exhortations and slogans, such as his call in 1985 for a "Great Awakening," in 1986 for "Self-Sufficiency," or the 1987 election program of "Development, Stability and Democracy," are devoid of ideological content. He does not appear to make connections between various issues and problems, but treats each as if it were a discrete phenomenon requiring a specific solution. He obviously does not use the new orthodoxy of development as an overall framework in which to conceptualize Egypt's economy and from which to deduce solutions to problems. But on the other hand he does not reject all the elements of the new orthodoxy either. He has a pragmatic rather than programmatic approach, so will adopt specific measures rather than overall designs.

In the particular case of the new orthodoxy, however, Mubarak has a further disincentive for its adoption. His foreign policy is predicated on the desire to reintegrate Egypt into the Arab World and bring the Soviet Union back into the Middle Eastern equation. For this he must establish some distance between Cairo and Washington. Moreover, his domestic political balancing act prohibits too close an embrace of the United States, for such an act would reinforce the power of the *infitah* bourgeoisie and its allies. It would probably terminate his tactic of using Nasserists as political managers and derail his basic approach to establishing political legitimacy, which is to create an image of a firm, fair, and decisive moderator between the various political tendencies. Thus Mubarak can accept elements of the economic strategy called for by the new orthodoxy, but not the package as a whole with a label on it and tag saying "Made in the United States."

Mubarak's basic goal is the limited but nevertheless challenging one of retaining Egypt's social peace and political cohesion in the face of economic and other difficulties. To achieve this end he appears to believe that he needs some democracy (but not uncontrolled political participation), a continuation of the dualistic economy composed of the public and private sectors, and the assistance of political activists of previous eras in managing the political system (but not in providing ideologically derived objectives for it). His greatest difficulty has been an inability to establish the presidency as an institution perceived as being above and impartial toward the various parties to the social contract. Indeed, the most widespread perception is that the presidential will is constrained by more powerful forces. Just how accurate those perceptions are will now be investigated with regard to those social forces most commonly nominated as standing between Mubarak and the implementation of his ideas and the consolidation of an insurmountable position of authority. In Chapter 3 the role of the *infitah* bourgeoisie and in Chapter 4 that of the military will be investigated.

NOTES

1. The editor in chief of *Sawt al-Arab* is Abd al-Azim Munaf, who after spending several years in the Gulf established in Cairo *Mawqif al-Arabi*, a publishing house that turns out Nasserist tracts. This press and the newspaper are widely suspected of receiving payments from Libya. The level of their operations and the fees that they pay journalists, including a reported £E500 per article to prominent columnist Fathi Radwan, certainly suggest some outside support.

2. This conference was attended by most prominent Nasserites, including Muhammad Hassanein Heikal, Aziz Sidqi, Labib Shuqair, Muhammad Faiq, Tharwat Ukasha, and many others associated with Nasser's regime or its intellectual legacy. It was given extensive coverage in the press. See, for example, Yusuf al-Qaid and Nigwan Abd al-Latif, "The Nasserists Reconsider the July Experiment," *al-Musawwar* (16 May 1986).

3. According to Muhammad Farid Zakariya, the exact number of Nasserist NDP candidates in 1984 was 174. See his "Secrets of Mubarak's Political Kitchen," *al-Ahrar* (25 August 1986).

4. That Mubarak is fostering a return of Nasserism is a theme most frequently enunciated by the conservative opposition. *Al-Ahrar*, the weekly newspaper of the conservative Liberal Party, for example, alleged in June 1986 that Nasser's old secret vanguard organization was being reconstituted, and it announced in August of that year that a diplomatic report from "a large western embassy," (i.e., the U.S. Embassy) affirmed the return of that Nasserist secret organization. See Kamal Khalid, "The Mafia of the Vanguard Organization . . . Men for all Regimes," *al-Ahrar* (16 June 1986); and "Western Diplomatic Reports Confirm the Return of the Secret Organization to Dominate Government," *al-Ahrar* (25 August 1986).

5. On the *munfatihun* see John Waterbury, *The Egypt of Nasser and Sadat* (Princeton: Princeton University Press, 1983), pp. 172–180.

6. See his series of three articles in *The Guardian* (7, 8, and 9 April 1986).

7. Robert Bianchi, "Businessmen's Associations in Egypt and Turkey," *Annals*, 482 (November 1985), pp. 147–159; and by the same author, "The Corporatization of the Egyptian Labor Movement," *The Middle East Journal*, 40, 3 (Summer 1986), pp. 429–444. Most Egyptians who write on this topic stress the fact that business interests are better organized than any others. See for example *The Arab Strategic Report 1985* (Cairo: al-Ahram Publishing, 1986), pp. 339–344 (in Arabic); Ihab Salam, "The Political Opposition and Pressure Groups,"

al-Ahram al-Iqtisadi (21 April 1986); Imani Qandil, "Political Pluralism and an Examination of the Bases of Decision Making," *Qadiya Fikriya* (August-October 1986), pp. 215–225, and by the same author, "Decree 119 and Interests Making Economic Policy," *al-Ahram al-Iqtisadi* (14 April 1986); Mustafa Kamel al-Sayed, "A Study of Interest Groups in Egypt: Some Theoretical Issues," paper delivered to the Seminar on the Egyptian Political System, 2-3 April 1986, Syndicate of Merchants, Cairo (in Arabic); and Nahed Dajani, "Corporatism Within the Egyptian Context: A Profile of Business and Professional Politics in Egypt," unpublished M.A. thesis, Department of Economics, Mass Communication, and Political Science, American University in Cairo, 1982.

8. For one of the many assessments of Mubarak as being too weak to confront the powerful forces around him, see Robert Bianchi, "Egypt: Drift at Home, Passivity Abroad," *Current History* (January 1986), pp. 71–74, 82–83.

9. This point was made to the author by a prominent critic of Sadat, Adil Hussain, the editor of *al-Shaab*. Interview, Cairo (19 February 1986).

10. See Robert Springborg, "Patterns of Association in the Egyptian Political Elite," in George Lenczowski, ed., *Political Elites in the Middle East* (Washington: American Enterprise Institute, 1975), pp. 83–108.

11. Mubarak differed temperamentally from most of the clients of Amer and Badran, who were generally sociable, sometimes hard drinking, and frequently enamored of their clandestine political-military activities in Yemen during the war there and in the Gaza Strip, where many were involved in organizing and containing the Palestine national movement. Many of these officers were in the same graduating class as Mubarak, and although he was not close to them, many had a high opinion of his professional abilities, as they expressed to the author.

12. See Robert Springborg, *Family, Power, and Politics in Egypt: Sayed Bey Marei—His Clan, Clients and Cohorts* (Philadelphia: University of Pennsylvania Press, 1982), pp. 100–109.

13. The author is indebted to al-Sayed al-Kholi, Counselor, Egyptian Ministry of Foreign Affairs, for this information.

14. *Oktober* (12 October 1986).

15. The author is indebted to Clement H. Moore for this information.

16. The author is indebted to P. J. Vatikiotis for this information.

17. Comments on this incident circulated widely among Egyptian journalists in summer 1986. The author is indebted to Ali Darwish, Press Counselor, U.S. Embassy, Cairo, for bringing this matter to his attention.

18. Mubarak does not have a shrewd sense of public relations. He nearly missed the opportunity to associate himself with the referendum held in early 1987 on the issue of dissolving the parliament and holding new elections. Only when his advisers pointed out that he should personally announce the referendum and thereby associate himself with "democracy" did he appreciate its public relations value. I am indebted to Ali al-Din Hillal Dessouki for this information.

19. To commemorate the fifth anniversary of Mubarak's succession to the presidency, the issues of *Oktober* on 12 and 19 October 1986 included lift-out supplements on democracy and decision-making, respectively, under Mubarak. The emphasis upon Mubarak's commitment to gathering information from various sources and then reaching a quick decision characterizes both issues, although in its starkest form it is to be found in an interview with Usama al-Baz, the Director of the Office of the Presidency for Political Affairs, in the second supplement.

20. I would like to thank various officials in that Embassy for generously providing much useful information.

21. David Ottaway, interview, Cairo (28 July 1986).

22. See Anwar al-Sadat, *In Search of Identity* (London: Collins, 1977); and Gamal Abdel Nasser, *The Philosophy of the Revolution* (Buffalo: Economics Books, 1959).

23. Earl L. Sullivan, *Women in Egyptian Public Life* (Syracuse: Syracuse University Press, 1986), pp. 93–99.

24. See in particular the October 1986 issues of *Oktober* and *al-Musawwar.*

25. Mubarak's closest friend, for example, is a fellow officer from Minufiya with whom he plays squash on a regular basis.

26. On the suddenness of the decision and the element of surprise, see Osama Saraya, "Egypt's New Premier to Put Fresh Focus on Economy," *The Middle East Times* (15–21 September 1985). For the interpretation of Mubarak's reaction I am indebted to a political officer in the U.S. Embassy who was also caught unaware by the cabinet change and who subsequently investigated the decision in some detail.

27. Muhammad Abdilla, Chairman of the Foreign Relations Committee of the People's Assembly, interview, Cairo (18 February 1986).

28. This information was provided by the son of one of al-Baz's student colleagues in the Boston, Massachusetts area.

29. Mubarak's ambassador to the Soviet Union, for example, was prior to that assignment in 1985 expecting to be sent to London. His name, in fact, had already been submitted to and approved by the British government as Egypt's ambassador-designate. But at the last moment and unbeknown to the very talented Salah Basyuni, Usama al-Baz ordered that he be sent not to London, where he would come into repeated contact with Mubarak, but to Moscow, where he was unlikely to have much sustained access to the President.

30. In the wake of Vice President George Bush's visit to Egypt in August 1986, for example, Usama al-Baz gave an extended interview to *al-Musawwar* in which he played down the importance of the visit, saying there was "nothing new in it related to efforts for peace." This was interpreted by the U.S. Embassy as a slight on the Vice President and an indication that Mubarak was taking a tougher line with Washington. See "We and America: Conversation of the Week with Usama al-Baz," *al-Musawwar* (22 August 1986).

31. Upon Mubarak's succession to the presidency, for example, al-Baz immediately cut his ties to individuals with whom he had worked closely during the Sadat period and to whom he feared that Mubarak might not be favorably disposed.

32. Clement Henry Moore, "Money and Power: The Dilemma of the Egyptian infitah," *The Middle East Journal*, 40, 4 (Autumn 1986), p. 636.

33. *Ibid.*, p. 640.

34. By the mid-1980s this practice had become so common that even the progovernment press was moved occasionally to comment on it in unfavorable terms. Badawi Mahmud, for example, writing in *al-Gumhuriya* in January 1987, observed that the appointment to private banks of former prime ministers and occupants of governmental posts crucial to the regulation of the economy was a means by which those banks influenced economic policy. He provided the following list of recent appointments: Ali Nigm, former governor of the Central Bank, to the vice presidency of the board of directors of the Egyptian International Bank, of which the president is former Prime Minister Mustafa Khalil, who also

is president of the board of directors of the Egypt-Iran Company for Hotels, which controls the Gezira Sheraton Hotel; former Prime Minister Kamal Hassan Ali to the presidency of the Egyptian Gulf Bank; Abd al-Aziz Hijazi, who served as Prime Minister under Sadat and who was appointed president of the Merchants Bank as well as several large companies, including the prominent joint venture Chloride-Egyptian Battery Company; and various other former cabinet members and key political figures, including Hassan Abbas Zaki, Saad Mamun, Sayid Fahmi, Fuad Abu Zahlah, Ahmad Abu Ismail, Suliman Nur al-Din, Nassif Tahun, Salim Muhamidin, Fuad Hussain, and Hilmi Abd al-Akhar. The writer, Badawi Mahmud, observed that gadfly NDP Member of Parliament Tawfiq Zaghlul was of the opinion that such appointments contravened the law. This article is reprinted in *al-Shaab* (13 January 1987).

35. Moore, "Money and Power," p. 648.

36. The presidency has a large network of such agents upon whom it relies for information on public reactions to policy changes both before and after the event.

37. In an editoral entitled "No to the Police State" on 28 January 1987, *al-Ahali* complained of the prohibition by the government of a meeting scheduled for 22 February by the soon-to-be formed Arab Socialist Nasserite Party. In the following issue on 4 February, Amina Naqash chronicled the problems faced by Nasserites in dealing with governmental harassment. In November 1987, the Political Parties Committee that screens applications for the formation of new parties recommended against granting a license to the Nasserists on the grounds that their goals were the same as those of the NDP. See Hassan Amer, "Panel Says Nasserite Party Offers Nothing That Is Both New and Legal," *Middle East Times* (15–21 November 1987).

38. In fact the relatively low ratio of profits to invested capital in Arab Contractors in the mid-1980s has caused the opposition to allege that Osman is milking that public-sector concern in order to provide profits to the private companies with which it has business dealings and which are controlled directly by Osman and his family. Sana al-Sayid, commenting that Arab Contractors' net profits for the financial year 1984–85 were said to be only £E900,000, asked Osman in the middle of a lengthy interview in the 10 November 1986 issue of the progovernment weekly *Mayo*, why that was the case. He responded by saying that total assets were £E1.16 billion, that £E650 million worth of work had been completed in that year, and that the low rate of profitability was due to the government policy on interest charges and loan repayments imposed on the public sector. He denied ever having heard of the company Asmetal, which members of the opposition had accused him of controlling and using as a vessel into which he siphoned funds from the public-sector Arab Contractors.

3

THE BOURGEOISIE
AND THE STATE

Triggered by the oil boom and policies of *infitah*, of which Sadat's is the most well known but by no means only example, dramatic change over the past fifteen years has affected the political economies of most Arab countries. With regard to the impact on class structures, it has been widely observed that an *infitah* bourgeoisie has emerged as the most powerful social force in domestic economies and political systems. What remains in question is how cohesive that class is and whether it has succeeded in rendering the state subservient to it. The general weight of expert opinion on Egypt is that the *infitah* bourgeoisie has emerged from the coalescence of segments of the bourgeoisie that previously were isolated or antagonistic and through the mobilization of altogether new elements. These fragments that together constitute the *infitah* bourgeoisie include leftovers from the *ancien regime*, those who had been "sitting out" Nasserism in the West or the Gulf, members of Nasser's "new class" of managers and technocrats who established linkages to the private sector, upwardly mobile financial wizards who successfully rode the roller coaster propelled by the fast money of the *infitah*, and various other smaller components. Not surprisingly, as the *infitah* has lost its steam due to disenchantment with its excesses, falling oil prices, and global recession, factionalization of this class has become evident, suggesting that the fragments of which it was said to be composed may never have merged as thoroughly as was previously thought. The diversity of the larger category of the bourgeoisie will be illustrated in this chapter, and an attempt will be made to demonstrate that the true *infitah* bourgeoisie, which is more accurately termed parasitic, is not currently nor was it previously homogeneous.

The related issue of the power of this class vis-à-vis the state has likewise stirred controversy. Waterbury contends that the state continues to enjoy relative autonomy from this and other social forces.[1] Richards objects to this interpretation, claiming that at the very least the *infitah* bourgeoisie enjoy veto power over critical decisions.[2] A host of observers are of the opinion that the state has in fact been captured lock, stock, and barrel by it.[3] Much of this disagreement turns on the issue of what constitutes evidence. The pattern of spending of state revenues, which undoubtedly has favored the *infitah* bourgeoisie, is offered by some as proof of the autonomous power of that class fragment and of the subordination of the state to it.[4] But as Batatu argues in his review of a similar thesis about the Iraqi political economy, favorable expenditures are insufficient grounds on which to argue for the ascendance of this class over the state. To Batatu the issue must be decided on empirical grounds through an investigation of the leverage of these capitalists over the state structure. Only then can the question of whether "we are witnessing the growth of an autonomous or of an essentially parasitic type of capitalism" be determined.[5]

While there has been no in-depth study of the role of the *infitah* bourgeoisie in national or local level decision making in Egypt, commonly offered in the place of such evidence is a case that is said to illustrate the power of the bourgeoisie. That incident involved the failed attempt by former Minister of Economy Mustafa al-Said during the period from January to April 1985 to extend governmental control over foreign-currency transactions and imports. It is widely cited as confirmation of the power of the illegal money changers, of the bourgeoisie more generally, and/or of the businessmen's organizations that are said to represent them.[6]

But the Mustafa al-Said case cannot serve as a litmus test of the power of the *infitah* bourgeoisie simply because his reforms affected not only this class but virtually all Egyptians dependent directly or indirectly on imported goods. Said's draconian restrictions on the so-called parallel market (i.e., the legal black market) dried up virtually overnight foreign currency for import financing. Caught unaware by Said's initiatives, the banks had insufficient funds to meet demand. The interruption of imports affected public and private sector enterprises alike. Small independent proprietors joined with Egypt's infamous oligopolists in demanding Said's scalp. Moreover, his policies were from the outset opposed by other members of the government's economic team and were not supported even by Said's boss, the Prime Minister. Unless the concept of the *infitah* bourgeoisie is stretched to include all the disparate elements that objected to Said's ways and means, the incident cannot be offered as proof of its power.[7]

But there is a more recent episode in which the government targeted a specific sector of the bourgeoisie for closer regulation, and it, more or less single-handedly, successfully resisted the pressure. This incident was the attack in the fall of 1986 by the governor of the Central Bank and other officials on Islamic investment companies. This campaign, like Said's, backfired, resulting in the removal of that governor. It also contributed to the fall of the Ali Lutfi government. Because it highlights the fragmented nature of the state and indicates the relative power and autonomy of this class segment, it is worth recounting in some detail.

ISLAMIC INVESTMENT COMPANIES
VERSUS THE STATE

Approximately one million Egyptians have since 1974 invested in the Islamic investment companies that came into being as a result of the investment law of that year, which was the legal cornerstone of the *infitah*. The majority of those who have deposited their funds with such companies are of the middle strata, whose savings, typically acquired while working abroad, are insufficient to purchase an attractive flat for rental and for which there are few other outlets. Having as much as several tens of thousands of dollars or pounds to invest, these Egyptians have been attracted to such companies because they claim to operate on the basis of Islamic principles; they pay dividends typically four or more times the interest paid on deposits by the secular banks; they operate internationally and in various currencies; and/or because they offer services tailored to the needs of these investors, particularly those who have acquired their capital outside Egypt.[8] These firms, of which 18 were operating by 1986 as individual proprietorships and as many as 150 (although not all claiming to be Islamic) as limited-liability joint stock companies, are owned and managed by Egyptians from various class backgrounds. The less successful of the companies, which maybe not coincidentally are those not generally identified as Islamic, appear to be controlled by that segment of the *infitah* bourgeoisie that emerged in the 1970s from the state, including former ministers, heads of government agencies, former police and army officers, and the relatives of such members of the "new class."[9] Paradoxically, the major operators and those who have been most studious in identifying their operations as Islamic are typically from more humble origins. Muhammad Ashraf Saad, for example, head of the Saad group of companies and son of a low-ranking official in a provincial office of the Ministry of Housing, was raised in a medium-sized town in Daqahliya Province. His tertiary education was obtained at the less than illustrious Institute for Cooperative and Commercial Studies, while what may have been more valuable experience was gained during a sojourn in France spent washing dishes and picking grapes. Converted to a much more devout and activist Islam on his return to Egypt, by the end of 1986, while still less than 32 years of age and after less than two years of operations, he had amassed £E60 million, according to his own account. He claims to have accomplished this by shrewdly investing funds provided him first by friends and acquaintances and, as his reputation grew, by the general public.[10]

Virtually the same story is told by Fathi Tawfiq Abd al-Fattah, head of the sprawling al-Rayan conglomerate, which boasts of 20 companies, over 300,000 investors, and assets that have been estimated as high as a staggering £E6.5 billion.[11] Abd al-Fattah, apparently lacking tertiary credentials, spent fourteen years working in various Arab countries before returning to Egypt in 1982. With his savings and those of his brothers and friends he claims to have "begun working in cheese and eggs."[12] True or not, within four years his was the largest investment company in Egypt. In 1986 he set Cairo tongues wagging when for £E14 million he purchased the newly completed residence for the U.S. Ambassador, a structure the U.S. government had, because of various construction defects, declared unfit for habitation.

The company widely thought to be second in size to al-Rayan is that known as al-Sharif, whose founder is a Moslem Brother who was imprisoned by Nasser in 1965. Together with other members of that organization who were released by Sadat in the early 1970s, he founded a company which engaged in the manufacturing of plastics and the construction of apartments, particularly in Alexandria. Similarly, the largest such company in Asyut, Talia al-Iman (Vanguard of the Faith), was founded by the son of a Moslem Brother who was executed by Nasser in 1954.

These biographical sketches point to the possibility that an Islamic sector has emerged within the larger category of *infitah* bourgeoisie. Alternatively, the known political affiliations of these proprietors suggest the hypothesis that organized, activist Islam, receiving support from abroad, is utilizing Islamic investment companies to finance its social and political revival. In other words, the owners and managers of these companies may owe their wealth and status to their connections and possible total dependence on a broadly based, internationally supported, religiously oriented political movement. If true, they would better be conceptualized as political apparatchiks rather than as Moslem capitalist entrepreneurs. Crucially important then is whether the Islamic bourgeoisie, of which those in the Islamic investment companies are a vital component, is composed of independent entrepreneurs seeking profits like any other members of this class, but doing so within what is at least a nominally Islamic context, or whether these money managers are the agents of organized, activist Islam.

The likely answer is that both types exist. The Moslem Brotherhood and some activist organizations associated with it have not only been the breeding grounds from which principals of Islamic investment companies have emerged, but those companies exist primarily if not exclusively further to spread the message of those organizations. This is especially so in Asyut, the epicenter of Islamic activism in Egypt. There the Talia al-Iman group of companies requires that its customers be "good Moslems" and be recommended by someone with "Islamic connections."[13] By contrast, Fathi Tawfiq Abd al-Fattah boasts that among al-Rayan's clients are innumerable Christians and two Jews.[14] Male clerical and manual staff of Talia al-Iman must not shave their beards and the veil is required of women. Donations are provided to the students' union at Asyut University, which, like all others in the country, is controlled by those of the Islamic tendency. These funds are used to purchase Islamic dress for female students, to pay for lodgings, to distribute

Islamic books and political tracts, and in general to build up an ever-larger network of Islamic activists within the ranks of students. Given that the majority shareholder of Talia al-Iman is a committed Moslem Brother and persistent rumors that disbursement of funds is so excessive that they must be coming from outside sources, it is conceivable that this particular investment company, and probably many like it, are intended principally as vehicles of political mobilization by dedicated Islamic activists bent on establishing theocratic rule in Egypt.[15]

This is also the conclusion reached by many secular political activists, especially those on the left. *al-Ahali*, the organ of Tagamu (the National Progressive Unionist Party), has in recent years repeatedly leveled the charge that at least some of these companies are fronts for political subversion by Islamic extremists. Specifically, it has been alleged that such companies have planned to purchase arms for the Moslem Brotherhood;[16] that the Brotherhood puts pressure on Egyptians working in Saudi Arabia and the Gulf to deposit their money in companies controlled by the organization;[17] that similar institutions financed Gaafar Numairi in the Sudan;[18] that the security authorities warned the Minister of Redevelopment and Land Reclamation against assigning 7,000 *feddan*-s (1 *feddan* = 1.038 acres) of desert land for reclamation to al-Sharif Company since it would subsequently be used as a training camp by the Brotherhood;[19] that in the April 1987 parliamentary elections some of the companies financed Islamic activist candidates in many of the 48 seats reserved for those not on party lists;[20] and so on. Some of these allegations may be dismissed as hyperbole intended to discredit both the Islamic investment companies and the Islamic political tendency, neither of which appeal to those in Tagamu. Nevertheless, that such charges have been made repeatedly over a considerable period, that they have not been denied by government agencies identified in some instances as the sources of the information, that they are believed by a wide cross section of the Egyptian public, and that they are supported by a sizable body of circumstantial evidence are all facts that suggest the veracity of the claim that the Islamic investment companies are in some cases nothing more or less than the financial arms of the Islamicist movement.

But even the staunchest critics of these companies do not claim that they are all cut from the same Islamicist cloth. While some are, others are simply financial ventures that are self-identified as Islamic because the use of that term makes good business and political sense. Those that are independent of organized Islam are not any more palatable to most critics, however. As far as their putative Islamic credentials and practices are concerned, it is maintained by many commentators that they are a sham, for to these critics Islamic law prohibits speculation in precious metals and currencies. The companies' claims to be patriotic are also scoffed at, for it is alleged that the bulk of their funds are held outside the country and therefore deprive the Egyptian economy of much needed investment capital. Various calculations have been offered in support of these claims. The Nasserist newspaper *Sawt al-Arab*, for example, claims that al-Rayan's projects in Egypt are worth no more than £E300 million, whereas that company's net worth is some £E6.5 billion. *Sawt al-Arab* further claims that speculation on the London and New York stock and bullion exchanges accounts for the vast bulk of al-Rayan's "investments."[21]

That a number of such enterprises are pyramid schemes whose perpetrators intend to flee the country before their financial houses of cards come tumbling down is another of the standard charges and one supported by precedent, although the actual number of such cases of fraud and flight in comparison to the generalized allegation seems small. Ali Nigm, the governor of the Central Bank who made it his mission to destroy these companies, was asked to provide examples of such swindles; he could remember the name of but one such case, that being the al-Rida Company, whose owner was a Palestinian.[22] The only other specific example provided in the government and opposition press of the principal of a company fleeing with depositors' funds was that of Samir Fawzi, who *al-Ahali* claims fled to Australia.[23] There is no denying the fact, however, that there is little protection of depositors' interests, for the assets of those companies are held in the name of their principals. While Abd al-Fattah, the owner of al-Rayan, and others like him argue that a relationship of personal trust between depositors and owners is sufficient and "Islamic,"[24] most critics believe that since these companies are operating for all intents and purposes as banks, they should be subject to the same controls as their secular counterparts.

STRATEGIES TO FORESTALL GOVERNMENT CONTROL

The investment companies themselves have not been idle in the face of allegations made against them and the general threat to restrict or close down their activities altogether. In the first instance they have sought to enlist the support of the *ulama*. The Islamic establishment as represented by the *Mufti* (chief Islamic jurist), the shaikhs of al-Azhar, and others, are caught between a government that pays their salaries and wants to control the Islamic investment companies and the kudos these companies enjoy among the devout, who consider them as genuine manifestations of the Islamic economy. Confronted with this dilemma the *ulama* lean as far toward the investment companies and their supporters as their indebtedness to the government permits.[25] Many of them, including six of the twelve members of al-Azhar's Supreme Fatwa Committee, head "*sharia* committees" for Islamic banks and investment companies. These committees are charged with passing on the Islamic legality of the institution's financial activities. For these services the shaikhs are paid quite handsomely, an arrangement that has led critics to allege that the Islamic establishment has been suborned by the banks and investment companies.[26]

The principals of the major Islamic investment companies have engaged in sophisticated and expensive advertising campaigns, purchasing more space in government and opposition publications than any other financial institutions, public or private. Indeed, they probably spend more on newspaper and magazine advertising than any other concerns in the country. The Saad group of companies alone, for example, spent more than £E100,000 in less than a fortnight in May 1986, placing advertisements in *al-Ahram* and *al-Akhbar* to counter various allegations made against this and other Islamic investment firms in the opposition press.[27] al-Rayan spent in excess of £E150,000 in November of that year defending itself from attack from another quarter.[28]

The content of the advertisements is suggestive of the purposes they are intended to serve. The commercial motive of attracting custom is manifested through the manipulation of Islamic symbols and imagery as well as through secular means of assuring potential investors of the trustworthiness and high rates of return provided by the companies. The diversity, sheer size, and standing of these firms in the national and even international financial community is emphasized. This approach also serves the important purpose of creating a broadly based constituency of supporters to forestall negative action by government. For this purpose the investment companies also claim to devote substantial portions of their assets to "food security" and other projects to which the government has accorded priority through its five year plan or by virtue of presidential or ministerial decrees and pronouncements. When the government, for example, prohibited the further manufacture of bricks from agricultural soil, at least two of the investment companies claimed to have financed ventures in the production of cement bricks, advertising this as a symbol of their commitment to the preservation of a scarce national resource and of their willingness to allocate funds in accordance with governmental desires. Most illustrative material accompanying advertisements emphasizes the companies' involvement in food production and distribution, whether in the form of dairy farms, poultry installations, bakeries—especially those producing "popular" loaves, "Islamic" restaurants, or large scale reclamation schemes; or they target the companies' efforts to "resolve the housing crisis." Even their projects with dubious claims to contributing to national production are cast in a way that emphasizes that they are providing a public service. Fathi Tawfiq Abd al-Fattah was pictured in *al-Ahram* cutting the ceremonial opening ribbon of a new jewelery store in Heliopolis, the purpose of which was identified as "serving the people and the citizens."[29]

Additional tactics in the strategies of Islamic investment companies to defend themselves from governmental control and regulation are to garner the support of local government officials and to render the government at least partially dependent upon them for local projects.

Such tactics have been implemented with particular thoroughness by Muhammad Ashraf Saad in his home province of Daqahliya. There he has cultivated the support of the governor and much of the provincial administrative hierarchy by agreeing to participate in schemes backed by the governorate, including housing complexes and bakeries, and by pledging to supplement Daqahliya's transportation system by providing a fleet of microbuses and ferries. These and similar activities elsewhere caused the minister of local government and subsequently the prime minister to endorse cooperation between such companies and governorate administrative bodies.[30] The Talia al-Iman group in Asyut has secured its connection to local officialdom through another channel. Two-thirds of the venture is owned by the son of Abd al-Qadir Awda, a Moslem Brother hanged by Nasser, while the remaining one-third is owned by Muhammad al-Bakri, friend and business partner of the former governor of the province.[31]

A related tactic has been for the Islamic investment companies to form joint ventures with the Popular Development Companies that first came into existence under the guidance of Osman Ahmad Osman when he was serving as Minister for Popular Development under Sadat. Such companies, intended as integral components of the *infitah*, were to encourage the private sector, in partnership with the government, to invest in production and service projects. Overall coordination and control was to be exercised by Osman's ministry and, when that was abolished, by the President's political party. While the Popular Development Companies have not fulfilled the role some envisioned for them, they continue to operate and they remain under Osman's supervision, for legally they are attached to the NDP's Popular Development Committee, of which he remains chairman. While there may be financial advantage in Islamic investment companies acquiring some portion of the ownership of Popular Development enterprises, such as gaining access to capital equipment that was imported when the Egyptian pound was of higher value and tariffs were lower or nonexistent, the chief incentive is political. Participation in these ventures not only provides general goodwill, but it links the investment companies to influential members of the bourgeoisie, who in turn are well connected with the NDP and, in many cases, to Osman himself.

A final and even more direct manner of gaining political access and leverage has been for the Islamic investment companies to hire prominent politicians as "consultants," much in the way that the secular banks have made room on their boards of directors for retired cabinet ministers. The most notable example of this practice is the retention by al-Rayan Company of the services of former Minister of Interior Nabawi Ismail, a connection that became the subject of innuendo when the principal of that company narrowly escaped prosecution, an episode shortly to be recounted.

THE FIRST MOMENT OF TRUTH

By 1986 the Islamic investment companies clearly constituted a growing challenge to the secular banking system and possibly to secularism more generally. They had succeeded in penetrating various of the regime's control systems, including provincial government bodies and the party. They had politicians on the payrolls and they enjoyed tremendous support among the devout and considerable admiration with the public more generally. More than a million Egyptians had demonstrated their confidence by placing their funds with them, and the companies' total assets had reached as much as £E16 billion.[32] The largest of them disposed of assets in excess of those held by the public-sector banks, and as a group they had access to more foreign currency than the Central Bank itself could lay claim to. This was a situation that the latter, in particular, found intolerable.

The principal opponents of the Islamic investment companies were the secular leftist opposition and those in government responsible for economic management. Unlike several other targets on which the opposition directed its fire and scored some hits, such as the Arab-African International Bank, the governor of Alexandria, and the brother of the speaker of parliament, these companies proved to be far more elusive. This was due in part to the fact that the opposition itself was divided on the issue, as suggested by its press coverage. *Al-Ahali*, which had come back into print at the time of the 1984 elections, was critical of the companies, but the remainder of the opposition press, with the exception of the limited circulation *Sawt al-Arab*, was silent on the issue. The political alliances of the parties for which the papers spoke dictated their respective approaches. The Wafd Party had linked up with the Moslem Brotherhood prior to the 1984 election and could not, therefore, launch an attack on ostensibly Islamic financial activities, whatever their real nature. It was not until after that alliance was on its last legs in late 1986 that the Wafd was willing to mount an attack. It convened a seminar of its leading economic spokesmen, who proceeded to roundly condemn the Islamic investment companies, as was recorded verbatim in *al-Wafd*.[33] The Socialist Labor Party, which from the time of the 1984 elections began a drift in the direction of a more avowedly Islamic doctrine, a shift that culminated in an electoral alliance with the Moslem Brotherhood in 1987, forswore criticism of Islamic financial practices of any sort in its paper, *al-Shaab*. The Liberal Party, which joined the Socialist Labor–Moslem Brotherhood coalition in 1987 and which after 1984 also relied increasingly on Islamicist appeals, similarly avoided negative comments in its mouthpiece, *al-Ahrar*. So for most of 1986 it was only *al-Ahali* that wielded the cudgels against al-Rayan, Saad, Sharif, the Egyptian Guidance Company, and so on.

The focal point of opposition to Islamic investment companies within government was the Central Bank and, in particular, its Governor, Ali

Nigm. Promoted to that post in March 1985 after a long career in the institution, Nigm immediately identified the need for regulation of these companies as one of his top priorities.[34] He reiterated this demand on numerous occasions, and a year after becoming governor he was able to induce Ali Lutfi's cabinet to place appropriate legislation on its parliamentary calendar.[35] But that government's enthusiasm for tackling al-Rayan and the other companies, in the middle of an ongoing economic crisis that was consuming most of its energies and dividing its members, was noticeably weaker than Nigm's ardor. The upshot was that the government, not wanting to stir up a hornet's nest, slipped the legislation through without debate on 16 June 1986, the last sitting day of parliament. The government clearly hoped that the summer holidays would overtake criticism of this and other controversial legislation it spirited through in this manner. It took the further precaution with this particular legislation of inserting a clause that rendered the various mechanisms of supervision and control assigned to the Capital Market Authority applicable only to companies established after that date. The stable door had been bolted only after the horses had fled. Eighteen such companies were already in existence and for over two years no sizable newcomer had entered the field. Law 89 was obviously an ineffective device designed as a sop to Ali Nigm and others who had been calling for action.

But those involved in this stratagem apparently misjudged the resolve of the Central Bank's governor and his supporters. Toward the end of the period of parliamentary recess Ali Nigm orchestrated an attack on the Islamic investment companies, apparently with the purpose of forcing parliament to revise the legislation to make the eighteen companies subject to the provisions of Law 89 for 1986. On 22 September a lengthy article appeared in the government weekly *Mayo*. It stated that the police had apprehended the principals of several investment companies as they were trying to escape. The author, Siham Abd al-Al, claimed that many of the projects such companies identified as highly profitable were in fact illusory. A similar article appeared in *al-Musawwar* on 31 October. Its author, a Coptic leftist, Magid Atiyah, compared the behavior of Islamic investment companies to that of the Kuwaiti speculators who precipitated the Suq al-Manakh crash and drew the further comparison to the Lebanese Intra Bank debacle of 1966.[36] He claimed that in a typical Islamic investment company only 4 percent of its funds were in Egypt and that in general they were a threat to the stability of the Egyptian economy. Moreover, according to Atiyah, they did not adhere to Koranic principles, for they speculated on currency and precious metals in Western markets. Writing in the following week's issue, Atiyah alleged that Popular Development Companies in Port Said, Alexandria, Asyut, and Ismailiya had been taken over by Islamic investment companies for the purpose of asset stripping.[37]

In the meantime Nigm had been working behind the scenes to engineer the downfall of the largest of the companies, al-Rayan. A report in the magazine *Middle East Money* that al-Rayan had lost $100 million at Morgan Guarantee Bank while speculating in gold, which al-Rayan's principal, Fathi Tawfiq Abd al-Fattah, later claimed was planted by Nigm, was photocopied and, according to Fattah, distributed to every bank and prominent businessman in Egypt.[38] Abd al-Fattah also claimed this was done on Nigm's instructions, an allegation not denied by the Central Bank's governor and a tactic consistent with those employed by the Central Bank in 1984 when it brought down Sami Ali Hassan, the "king of the money changers," and the Jammal Trust Bank.[39] Then on 9 November a small article appeared in *al-Akhbar* reporting that eight owners of four Islamic investment companies had been prohibited from leaving Egypt. This decision had been taken, according to *al-Akhbar,* because of the "instability in the situation of these companies in the recent period" and because one of the companies had lost millions in speculating on European exchanges.

Within hours of the newspaper hitting the streets a crowd of some 2,000 depositors gathered in front of al-Rayan's headquarters on Pyramids Street in Giza. Demands for withdrawal of funds were met by checks drawn on al-Rayan's accounts in the major public-sector banks.[40] This continued for several days as depositors refused to be mollified by advertisements placed by al-Rayan in all major government and opposition publications. The ads placed on 10 November included copies of telexes from various international banks confirming al-Rayan's status as a valued, solvent customer. On 12 November in an ad entitled "The Truth . . . Before All," al-Rayan quoted in Arabic a Reuter dispatch that stated that al-Rayan "had in the past few days faced a fierce campaign of misleading rumours and lies, the aim of which is to strike fear in the hearts of investors and depositors. . . . " In the accompanying English language copy of the dispatch it was clear that Reuter was simply quoting al-Rayan's press release. The desperate tone of the ads, however, did not presage disaster for the company. On the very day this one appeared the government signaled that it was the first to blink in its confrontation with Fathi Tawfiq Abd al-Fattah. In the back pages of *al Ahram* it included a photograph of him in obvious good humor opening a new shop in Heliopolis. Shortly thereafter the crowds began to dissipate and on 16 November the government weekly *Oktober* ran the al-Rayan incident as its cover story, most space being given over to a long and sympathetic interview with Abd al-Fattah.

During that turbulent week Abd al-Fattah had the satisfaction not only of persevering in the face of the challenge, but also of seeing the demise of his adversaries. On 9 November it was announced that Prime Minister Ali Lutfi had resigned. Shortly thereafter it was further announced that Mubarak had accepted Ali Nigm's resignation. The latter, who was quickly appointed to the board of directors of former Prime Minister Mustafa Khalil's Egyptian-Arab International Bank, had paid the ultimate political price for his failed campaign against al-Rayan. Lutfi, according to most sources, also lost his post at least in part because of his complicity in the campaign. Playing a major if not crucial role in toppling the government and forcing the replacement of the governor of the Central Bank is no small accomplishment for anyone, let alone an individual who had been targeted for a major governmental reform drive. How he succeeded has been the subject of much speculation.

Abd al-Fattah himself explained the causes and the outcome of the crisis on both economic and political levels.[41] He alleged that the crisis had been precipitated by Ali Nigm, who wanted to frighten investors into withdrawing their funds from al-Rayan and other companies and depositing them in public-sector banks. Nigm miscalculated on two counts, however. The first was that al-Rayan itself had large deposits in the public-sector banks and it drew on these to pay those demanding their funds. Those banks, chronically short of liquid capital, were forced to issue postdated checks and to request that the checks be converted into deposits. Their inability to cover even this relatively small but sudden rash of withdrawals stemmed from the fact that the Central Bank, acting as fiscal agent of the government, requires Egyptian banks to surrender to it one-quarter of their deposits, which the Central Bank in turn supplies as an interest-free loan to the government. In order to maintain a reasonable level of profitability the banks have to obtain maximum returns from their remaining capital, which dictates that they operate at very low levels of liquidity. This fact Abd al-Fattah fully appreciated and capitalized on.

The second economic factor that Abd al-Fattah saw as operating to al-Rayan's benefit was that while some doubt its financial integrity and stability, Egyptians distrust the large public-sector banks even more because they are perceived as tools of government. This impression has been reinforced by increasing governmental restrictions on foreign currency deposits and by a move in January 1986 to freeze them, a move that was hastily abandoned after its destructive consequences for future investment and general financial stability were made apparent. Abd al-Fattah's assessment was that in the battle for investors' confidence the government was bound to lose. Those depositing funds are attracted not only by high rates of return, but are driven by a desire to protect their savings from the fiscal depredations of the government. The government, on the other hand, could not allay these fears without undertaking major changes of its general fiscal and monetary policies. Among other changes it would have to increase interest rates, which it wants desperately to avoid not only because such a step would raise costs to government, but because it would inflame those of the Islamicist tendency who are already critical of the un-Islamic practices of government banks.[42]

But Abd al-Fattah did not permit his future and that of al-Rayan to be decided by impersonal economic mechanisms alone. As he explained, after the campaign was launched against his company, he went to Deputy

Prime Minister and Secretary General of the NDP, Yusuf Wali, and "gave him the complete file on all the operations." The choice of Wali was not accidental. An ambitious apparatchik, he was responsible to Mubarak for overseeing the impact of policies on the regime's popularity, a responsibility that, among others, he was using to erode the power of his competitors, including the Prime Minister and the governor of the Central Bank. Abd al-Fattah demanded of Wali that the government "make the matter clear so that the stability of al-Rayan and the whole economy not be undermined." Presumably Wali obliged. It would not have been difficult to convince Mubarak, who was simultaneously being besieged by anxious bankers, that it was courting economic disaster to persist in the campaign against the Islamic investment companies. That it would also drive away from the President the increasingly important constituency of those who wanted the application of the *sharia* must also have been uppermost in Wali's briefing of Mubarak.

Various other commentators provided additional insights into the episode. *Al-Wafd's* reporters confided that the government launched the campaign because al-Rayan refused to loan it $50 million at the exchange rate of US$1=£E1.35, al-Rayan holding out for the then free market rate of US$1=£E1.85. They also pointed out that various unsavory elements had joined in the campaign. These included some of the oligopolists who controlled the trade in steel, cement, timber, and corn. *Al-Wafd* also contended that the campaign had been joined by some elements in the media opposed to an Islamic economy, by which it meant principally *al-Musawwar*, whose Nasserist editor, Makram Muhammad Ahmad, is known to harbor and protect journalists of his own predisposition. For good measure *al-Wafd* added to the list of al-Rayan's enemies "zionist elements which monopolize the European gold market."[43] *Al-Shaab* claimed *al-Musawwar* had been anxious to join in the campaign not because of the Nasserist tendencies of its editor, but because al-Rayan had refused to renew its £E250,000 annual advertising account with the magazine.[44]

What appeared to be the epilogue to the story of the aborted assault on the Islamic investment companies was provided during the election campaign in the early spring of 1987. Never before having allowed his person or the presidency to be associated in any way with the Islamic investment companies, Mubarak suddenly permitted himself to be made the centerpiece of advertising campaigns by several of them. Photographs of the smiling President surrounded by the principals of various of the companies appeared in ads placed in the government and opposition press.[45] The unmistakable message was that the government, despite continued appeals in *al-Ahali* and *Sawt al-Arab*, had at least temporarily called off its campaign against the investment companies and was now trying to woo them. The implied trade-off was that the political appeal these companies possessed would be placed at the disposal of the President and his ruling party. Since the latter was in the midst of a bitter electoral campaign against the Moslem Brotherhood and various other Islamicist elements and had chosen to identify itself in some districts in the Delta as "the party of God" and in general was seeking to wrap itself in a cloak of Islamic legitimacy,[46] it would have been highly impolitic for the government to persist in attacking Islamic investment companies.

THE GOVERNMENT TRIES AGAIN

The government renewed its campaign against Islamic investment companies in May 1987. Its timing was dictated by the completion of elections and by the need to reach agreement with the IMF on reforms required for a standby loan. Those measures were announced on 11 May and included a substantial devaluation and partial flotation of the pound. These steps were accompanied by the arrest of some 150 black market currency dealers, most of whom worked for or with Islamic investment companies. Preceded by a renewal of criticism in government media of those companies and by press reports that the government was preparing to subordinate the companies to the appropriate laws and to the supervision of *al-Raqaba al-Idariya* (Administrative Supervision),[47] the 11 May economic reform package was targeted principally at the foreign currency operations of the Islamic investment companies.

Despite the wave of arrests, which by the end of July had netted almost 400 dealers, including Sami Ali Hassan, the former "king of the moneychangers," the move against Islamic investment companies was tempered by conciliatory gestures designed to induce them to cooperate with government policy. Announcement of the reform package had been delayed for twenty-four hours so that a meeting could be held between high-level government officials, including Minister of Economy Yusri Mustafa, Minister of Interior Zaki Badr, Minister of Agriculture Yusuf Wali, and Minister of State for Cabinet Affairs Atif Ubaid, on the one hand, and eleven representatives of leading investment companies on the other. While that meeting was highly confrontational and both sides refused to comment to the press in its wake, it appears that a deal was struck whereby the companies, in return for not actively seeking to undermine the new measures by speculating against the pound, were to be allowed to diversify their activities and acquire other enterprises.[48] Another conciliatory gesture was offered by Mubarak in July when he implicitly criticized Minister of Interior Badr's mass arrests of Islamic activists and currency dealers under the provisions of the emergency laws and instructed the Minister to process the cases as quickly as possible. The President's statement was widely interpreted as an attempt to distance himself from the crackdown and as an indication that the government, anxious not to repeat the debacle of Mustafa al-Said's reforms—which had led to a catastrophic drying up of sources of foreign exchange—wanted to leave open a small window for black market activities so that the needs of private importers could be adequately serviced.[49]

The government did, however, maintain pressure on the companies. It stepped up the press campaign against them, with some attacks being particularly virulent.[50] It also sought to compete directly with the Islamic investment companies at the principal source of their profits, which is in the Gulf where remittances are generated. The government placed advertisements in Gulf newspapers informing expatriate Egyptians that they could maintain legal dollar accounts in Egyptian banks and that they would be ensured "realistic" rates of exchange when they converted those dollars into Egyptian currency.[51] The government also dispatched prominent spokesmen to the Gulf bearing the same message.[52] Additional leaks to the press in the summer of 1987 intimated the government's intent to introduce further legislation to impose much stricter controls on the companies.[53] Prime Minister Sidqi confirmed this intention in his governmental policy statement to parliament on 16 November.[54] The fact that such legislation still had not been introduced by the end of 1987, some seven months after the May reforms, and that during that period pressure on black market currency dealers had been gradually relaxed, suggested that the government still hoped to placate Islamic investment companies and induce them to modify their practices by offering carrots rather than by applying the stick.

For their part the Islamic investment companies chose not to confront the government directly. They sought instead to vitiate the impact of the reforms and to utilize the opportunity further to expand their economic and political influence. Following their eleventh-hour meeting with government representatives just prior to the announcement of the 11 May reforms, the principals of the leading investment companies signaled that they would heed the warning not to speculate heavily against the pound by posting notices in their Cairo headquarters that they were no longer dealing in foreign currencies. Simultaneously, however, they continued to appeal to Egyptians in the Gulf to deposit foreign currencies with them, offering rates slightly higher than the £E2.16 to the dollar that the government had set on 11 May. The Islamic investment companies were, in other words, forced to forfeit their near-monopoly over currency exchanges with tourists to the government banks, for street-corner money changers were vulnerable to harassment and arrest. But the companies fought to maintain their overwhelming market share of currency transactions with expatriate Egyptians, and in this they were more or less successful. Their position was strengthened by virtue of the fact that the government-imposed credit squeeze and strict allocation of foreign currency left private-sector importers with no option but to turn to investment companies for dollars. The gap between the official and the black market rate, which had all but disappeared in the immediate aftermath of the 11 May reforms, had by July opened up to almost 20 piasters on the dollar, or around 7 percent. By the end of the year the government had been forced to allow the pound to slip down by a further six piasters on the dollar, but the black market rate by then offered about a 10 percent premium.[55]

While the struggle between the government and the investment companies to attract foreign currencies was being played out behind the scenes in Egypt and the Gulf, the companies set about reinforcing their political defenses. They placed more advertisements that emphasized their Islamic credentials, refuted claims that their gains were ill-gotten, and stressed their involvement in productive projects.[56] Al-Rayan began publication of new, leather-bound editions of Islamic classics, which it offered for sale at nominal prices. Al-Rayan also led the way in seeking to legitimate itself through association with prominent public figures. It hired as a consultant the former Minister of Planning and International Cooperation, Abd al-Razzaq Abd al-Magid, through whom it made a request to the Central Bank to purchase Bank of America's 40 percent share of the Misr American International Bank.[57]

Simultaneously the companies began rapidly to diversify their operations, a move impelled by economic calculations and by the desire to bolster their image as patriotic enterprises and to forestall governmental efforts to subject them to various controls. As the credit squeeze tightened in the wake of the reforms and partly as a result of IMF pressure, the shortage of foreign currency began to place many private firms at risk. Some sought their way out of difficulties by offering part or all of their equity for sale. Potential purchasers with greatest liquidity were the Islamic investment companies, which quickly snapped up a wide range of firms. Saad Investment Company bought Zanussi, a leading producer of refrigerators and other appliances. It also entered into negotiations to purchase Schweppes, which has a large market share of the soft drink business, from the nephew of Osman Ahmad Osman. Simultaneously Saad added to its network of automobile distributorships and repair shops. Sharif commenced construction of an industrial complex at the 10 Ramadan new city site and signed agreements with Japanese firms to produce appliances under license. It acquired a foothold in the banking sector with the purchase of a 30 percent stake in the Islamic International Bank, on the board of which it placed four members. Al-Rayan expanded its livestock fattening and meat packing operations, began producing detergents, purchased several more supermarkets, and in August announced that it was setting up al-Rayan Finance Company, a joint stock venture that would be subject to supervision by banking authorities.[58] Even the Moslem Brotherhood established a direct presence in the financial sector. It formed a Bahamas-registered investment bank with headquarters in Geneva, capitalized at $30 million and named appropriately Bank al-Taqwa (Devoutness Bank).[59]

In summary, both the Islamic investment companies and the government made some marginal gains in this round. Banks under governmental control seized the near-monopoly previously held by the companies over street corner transactions with tourists and some of those with expatriate Egyptians. The margin between the official and black market rates for the pound was significantly reduced, although by the end of the year it appeared as if that margin might be on the verge of widening once again. While the government declared in November that it intended to introduce legislation to control the companies, that had not been done by the end of 1987 and was in any case rendered almost completely irrelevant by the transformation of these companies into sprawling conglomerates. Legislation designed to combat fraud, were it to be enacted, would probably have no greater impact on the Islamic investment companies than any other firms. It is also doubtful that Egyptian legislation could effectively or even legally restrict the activities of Islamic investment companies in the Gulf. While the government may claim success in inducing investment companies to commit their capital to productive agricultural and industrial enterprises and to the formal, legal financial sector, the companies were able to acquire many of these operations on extremely favorable terms and are likely in the future to expand significantly their market shares, for they have access to foreign currency while much of their competition does not. If the government's intent had been to garner control over tourist receipts and channel some additional funds into domestic production, it had won this round. If, on the other hand, it had sought to reduce the political and economic clout of the companies, it had clearly been frustrated.

"RENT" COLLECTORS
AND FRAGMENTED GOVERNMENT

Attempts to regulate Islamic investment companies suggest, as did the aborted reforms of Minister of Economy Mustafa al-Said, that the government is weak and fragmented. At moments of truth in confrontations with social forces, it is very likely to retreat. Whether those social forces are the bourgeoisie, as was the case in these instances, or the urban masses, as was the case when the government hastily rescinded the price rises that stimulated the January 1977 food riots, the government is predisposed to cut and run when faced with serious opposition. This reflects the fact that the government is not united either organizationally or ideologically. In 1985 the government economic team included Minister of Economy Mustafa al-Said, who firmly believed that economic progress could only be made if the government assumed control over foreign-currency transactions. Another member of that team, Ali Lutfi, who was then Chairman of the NDP Economic Committee, expressed grave reservations about the wisdom of steps to achieve that goal. When Said's reforms ran into trouble, they and their author were disowned by the Prime Minister and his government, and the entire episode was kept at arm's length from the presidency. Similarly, Ali Nigm, although not alone in his desire to force the Islamic investment companies to submit to governmental supervision, was certainly the most dedicated to that cause among high-ranking officials and politicians. Most others kept a discreet silence. When the political and economic costs of Nigm's campaign were raised to levels that Mubarak found unacceptable, he jettisoned the Central Bank's governor.

The President, heading a highly fragmented political elite, protects himself by not becoming personally identified with controversial policy initiatives, allowing and probably encouraging them to be pressed not even by the Prime Minister, to whom he is too close, but by cabinet ministers, from whom he is insulated. The government as a whole is not committed to such reforms because Mubarak prefers it that way, because its individual members would not agree on specific proposals, and because such commitment would carry for all too many personal political risks. The process of government thus is one in which trial balloons are launched by individual ministers, who may or may not receive the backing of the government, depending on how their proposals are received.

All social forces, however, do not dispose of equivalent political resources in this system of policy making by anticipated reaction, trial balloons, and remote presidential control. While the urban masses must rely principally on violence and the threat of its use, the bourgeoisie have more subtle and easily mobilized economic and political resources at their disposal. The former consist principally of control of capital and, to a lesser extent, domination of the means of production (as distinct from the sheer manipulation of money). In the Egyptian economy, which is heavily dependent on "rents," those who collect them have power. While the state gathers virtually all rents generated by the Suez Canal and most of those earned in the oil industry, even after the May 1987 reforms it still collects only a portion of worker remittances. It is this latter source in particular that has provided the financial power of the money changers who, alone or in concert, blocked Mustafa al-Said's reforms; it is also that source that has underlaid the success of the Islamic investment companies. The spreading dollarization of the Egyptian economy also siphons an increasing amount of internally generated savings into the hands of the private money managers, whether secular or Islamic, for Egyptians now convert their extra pounds into dollars as quickly as they can and as far from the government's purview as possible.

The government is thus caught in a dilemma in its relations with this element of the private financial sector. If it attempts to regulate private investment companies more closely or to destroy them altogether, it risks a massive flight of capital compounded by a future reluctance on the part of those Egyptians still outside the country to remit their earnings back home in any form. On the other hand, if it permits this sector to operate more or less as it has been, Islamic investment companies and other private money managers will control an increasing share of the country's liquid wealth, which has implications for the banking system, fiscal and monetary policies, and investment priorities. Additionally, it has potentially serious political ramifications. As capital accumulates in private hands, it provides its owners with a political resource for those who care to use it appropriately. While the secular money changers who opposed Mustafa al-Said seemed to have little inclination to convert economic into political resources on a permanent basis, this is not the case with regard to the companies that Ali Nigm challenged. Some are clearly instruments of a political movement, while others seek to manipulate Islamicist constituencies in order to protect and enlarge their personal financial holdings. Both, however, contribute to an increasing Islamicization of political life in the country and therefore to its predictable backlash. The *infitah*, in sum, let the genie out of the bottle, and the Mubarak government is still too weak to put it back in. Too many resources are in private hands for them to be harnessed directly by the government without the use of draconian measures that could destabilize the economy and the political system.

SEGMENTS OF THE BOURGEOISIE

Specific segments of the bourgeoisie have demonstrated an ability to block some governmental initiatives, as has just been described. That these elements together constitute a unified class in and for itself, one whose power has reduced the state to the role of a "committee for managing the common affairs of the bourgeoisie," as Karl Marx put it in the *Communist Manifesto*, is an altogether different and more questionable proposition. It is abundantly clear that this social class is fragmented into various categories according to religion, place of residence, type of economic activity, the period in which economic success was achieved, and so on. The degree to which these fragments, however disparate, perceive and act upon common economic interest is a much more ambiguous matter. At the very least it can be asserted that there are relatively few visible intraclass connections, be they intermarriages between families drawn from the different sectors or the formation of formal or semiformal organizations of a political nature. Before examining the issue of such linkages, however, it is first necessary to illustrate the relative diversity of the bourgeoisie.

The Modern Islamic Bourgeoisie:
Haute and Petite

The existence of an Islamic bourgeoisie as distinct from a secular one has been suggested. Obvious candidates for inclusion in such a category include the owners and managers of Islamic banks and investment companies. That they are separate from the secular bourgeoisie is suggested not just by the "Islamic" character of their financial activities, but by their general absence from the formal organizations favored by the latter, such as the Chamber of Commerce, Council of Businessmen, American-Egyptian Chamber of Commerce, Rotary Club, and so on. To the extent that they are involved in organizations, it is Islamic ones, and especially the Moslem Brotherhood, that they favor. The milieu of Islamic banks and investment companies is Arab-Islamic, whereas that of the secular banks is distinctly Western in flavor. This is marked by differences in dress, life-style preferences, the use of Arabic as opposed to Western languages, and so on. Bankers all, members of these two groups are competitors for economic and political hegemony in Egypt and in "the struggle for Egypt's soul," as Ajami put it, by which he meant the conflict to decide whether Egypt's culture is primarily Mediterranean or Arab-Islamic.[60]

There are differences, moreover, in the loan and investment portfolios of the Islamic investment companies and Islamic banks, on the one hand, and the secular financial institutions, on the other. While the former do engage directly in importation and in the financing thereof, foreign banks operating in Egypt, of which there are twenty, do virtually nothing other than that. Financing imports also accounts for the bulk of joint-venture banks' activities. Islamic financial institutions, however, have under Mubarak moved noticeably to broaden their range of investments in the production and service sectors. This has occurred because some of these investments have been profitable, but also because the Islamic institutions have needed to defend themselves against charges that they are parasitic. The Feysal Islamic Bank, for example, much the largest of such institutions, was caught up in the 1984 scandal that involved Sami Ali Hassan, the Jammal Trust Bank, and the al-Ahram Bank.[61] In a weakened position the Feysal Islamic Bank gave ground in the face of Mustafa al-Said's charges that it was engaged principally in speculation rather than investment. It dropped its managing director, Fuad Sarraf, and embarked on a series of highly visible investment projects in Egypt, including the construction of several thousand housing units.

The joint ventures of the secular and Islamic financial institutions are also of a different character, with the latter typically involved with Arab or other non-Western partners. The Saad group of companies, for example, formed in December 1986 a £E60 million joint venture for the manufacture of clothing and carpets with a state-owned Chinese firm.[62] Thus while Egypt's secular bankers are involved largely in dealings with their Western counterparts and with members of the Egyptian bourgeoisie, those in the Islamic sector have a much wider range of activities and contacts, both externally and internally.

The Islamic bourgeoisie, however, is not all cut from the same cloth. Those associated with Islamic banks are much more likely to have upper class origins than those who are connected to the Islamic investment companies. The Feysal Islamic Bank provides an insight into the backgrounds of those involved in Islamic banking. On its establishment in

Egypt in the mid-1970s it recruited its management from among Egypt's most prominent families. One of the most active founding members of the board of directors was Omar Marei, half brother of the politically durable Sayed Marei. Omar, a successful businessman and, since 1980, chairman of the Foreign Affairs Committee of the *Maglis al-Shura* (Consultative Council, a sort of legislative upper house), had been jailed by Nasser for conspiring, along with other members of the Moslem Brotherhood, to overthrow the regime.[63] He recruited into the bank's management individuals with similar backgrounds and commitments. Drawn from elite families of the *ancien regime*, such men look down upon those in the Islamic investment companies, whom they consider in some cases as shady operators and in general as nouveau riche.

Despite the very considerable wealth of many of the investment company entrepreneurs, the principals and managers of the Islamic banks seek to retain social and even political distance from them. The latter consideration may result from the competition Islamic banks are facing from the investment companies, which have been successful in attracting clients away from the banks. So self-interest rather than just snobbery may explain why the banks did not aid the investment companies in their time of trouble with Ali Nigm. As far as political connections are concerned, those in the Islamic banks are typically associated with the Moslem Brotherhood, especially its more conservative elements, and with the NDP. Their counterparts in the Islamic investment companies are less likely to enjoy extensive contacts in the NDP, and their main ties are to younger, more radical elements of the Islamicist movement. In sum, the labels *haute* and *petite* bourgeoisie are suggestive of the differences between those clustered around the Islamic banks as opposed to those who have utilized Islamic investment companies as their vehicles of upward mobility.

Traditional Islamic Bourgeoisie

A fragment of the bourgeoisie that is Islamic by virtue of origins, outlook, and practices, but whose members would never think of labeling themselves as such, is that group of businessmen who dominate various sectors of the traditional economy, most notably the manufacture of petty commodities, such as shoes, leather goods more generally, bazaar articles, kitchen utensils, furniture, and so on. In Egypt's large cities and provincial capitals a significant component of this type of manu-facturing, which still comprises a surprisingly large percentage of total industrial output, is organized on a putting-out basis.[64] Those who supply the inputs and collect the finished goods comprise the traditional bourgeoisie that is Islamic by background and orientation but typically not by virtue of personal "rebirth" and/or mobilization by activist organizations.

While members of the traditional bourgeoisie in provincial centers are necessarily small-time operators, those in the large cities can accumulate real wealth. A handful of them, for example, control traditional shoe manufacturing in Cairo and Alexandria, which accounts for upward of 90 percent of leather shoe output in those two major markets.[65] That modern manufacturers have not displaced the putting-out system is due in part to the power of this segment of the bourgeoisie. Shoe manufacturers, using their connections to suppliers of inputs and to government officials in charge of import licensing, and by employing various competitive commercial practices, set about defending their market share well more than twenty years ago. At that stage the government, in a joint venture with the Bally Corporation, sought to modernize the production of shoes. But neither Bally nor any other firm, public or private, has succeeded in establishing a significant niche in the leather shoe market, nor has the government ever permitted the importation of shoes.

The traditional bourgeoisie are Islamic in religious belief and in economic practice. They do not charge interest in a direct, visible form to the craftsmen to whom they supply inputs and capital. Instead, the extraction of surplus value is achieved through setting appropriate prices for inputs and finished articles. According to a study of small-scale manufacturing in Damietta, the "interest" obtained in this way averaged 25 percent at an annual rate. It is interesting to note that as part of this study the craftsmen were asked if they would be willing to accept subsidized low-interest loans from the government in order to free themselves from their current arrangements. The majority said they would not because it violated Islamic principles.[66]

The relationship between these members of the bourgeoisie and their client craftsmen is the key to the former's success. Big-time operators keep large "stables" of producers, control over whom may be contested by alternative patrons. The rewards for those who are able to sustain dependency relations with large numbers of producer-clients are apparently worth the effort expended. The central business districts of Cairo and Alexandria, for example, have a higher percentage of shoe shops than most comparable locations elsewhere in the world. This is not because these shops come cheaply. In the spring of 1987 one of 500 square feet in central Cairo went at auction for £E1.4 million in "key money" (payment required to obtain contract), while one twice that size obtained £E3.5 million.[67] The clustering of shoe shops in the high-rent districts occurs because of the favorable profit margins in the sale of this commodity, for which there is no effective government price control.

The shoe kings of Cairo, of which there are a handful, are extremely wealthy, generally uneducated, and invariably tough. These men, and countless others like them in other locations and working with other commodities, are not associated with Islamic investment companies or banks. They have their own sources of capital and investment outlets. Although generally independent of the state, some value political connections and work to establish themselves within the regime's organizations, especially the party.

A similar situation exists with regard to labor contracting, both in rural areas and in the urban-centered construction industry. Labor contractors tend to be of rural middle- to lower-class origins. Unlike the bourgeoisie who control putting-out industries, they depend on strategic contacts rather than capital as their primary resource. The control of craftsmen rests primarily on an ability to supply large quantities of inputs on credit. Labor gangs, on the other hand, are built and maintained by the ability to provide employment. In the construction industry this depends principally on relationships with large firms, such as Arab Contractors, while in the rural sector it rests on connections to government officials, such as those in the cooperatives and the Ministries of Irrigation and Agriculture. Ahmad Yunis, for example, who served in various capacities in the administration of agricultural cooperatives, including a stint as Director of the Federation of Cooperatives, amassed a sizable fortune from labor contracting, a portion of which he presumably doled out to others in the cooperative "movement" who had authority to award labor contracts. Yunis was an active member of the Arab Socialist Union and of parliament in both the Nasser and Sadat eras. In the mid-1970s, however, he erred in imagining he could move away from the regime when it declared legal the formation of political parties other than the ASU. When he let it be known that he was intending to join the Wafd Party in 1977, he was informed that he would be indicted for violations of labor laws. He returned to the government fold and the case was never prosecuted.[68]

The extent to which a traditionally based, arriviste provincial bourgeoisie has emerged as a result at least in part of their labor contracting activities is suggested by the significant percentage of so-called peasant members of parliament and local government bodies who have engaged in this business at some stage in their careers. The most common form of labor contracting is providing gangs of workers to the Ministry of Irrigation, or to the public-sector companies under its control, for the purpose of canal clearing, a task that is increasingly mechanized but that still requires large numbers of unskilled and semiskilled laborers. A study of the backgrounds of members elected to parliament from Sharqiya in the "peasant" category and to local government bodies in that province reveals that politically and economically upwardly mobile provincial activists have frequently been successful labor contractors.[69] In the 1964 elections, for example, of the five peasant members elected from Sharqiya, two had begun their careers in the agrarian reform organization and then moved into labor contracting for canal cleaning. Subsequently, one also engaged in mercantile activities while remaining active in provincial politics. The other, who had begun his career as a *qabaani* (person who weighs crops) at the cooperative, another crucial post for those seeking to obtain funds and influence, went from this job to labor contracting, an activity in which he retains an interest. Currently he is head of the NDP Peasant Committee, president of the National General Society for Agrarian Reform Cooperatives, and he was reelected to parliament in April 1987. He owns several stores and an automobile showroom.

The career trajectory of another typical "peasant" political activist from Sharqiya likewise points to the interconnection between labor contracting and strategic connections to the state apparatus. This individual owned a small plot of land in addition to working as a *qabaani* in the cooperative. In 1963 he joined the ASU and became a member of the board of the agricultural cooperative society. According to the study in which this biographical sketch appears, this individual then "utilized his presence in the ASU and the cooperative" to facilitate his work as a supplier of labor for canal clearing, which vastly increased his assets. In 1968 he became a member of the ASU Central Committee and a member of the city council of Zagazig, the provincial capital. Political upward mobility further facilitated his contracting activities, which expanded from canal maintenance to road building. Capital from these endeavors was invested in land, and by the early 1980s he owned in excess of 20 acres.

Such individuals are typical of the bourgeoisie that has emerged as a consequence of the rural policies of the Nasser, Sadat, and Mubarak governments. Although similar in class origins and degree of upward mobility to the bourgeoisie that has flourished in the traditional manufacturing sector, the two class fractions have fundamentally different relations to the state. The upwardly mobile rural bourgeoisie has, because of the dominance of the state over the rural economy, had to rely on strategic connections to it in order to extract surplus value from the abundant supplies of unskilled labor. The bourgeoisie in the traditional manufacturing sector, however, has operated in an area more or less free from governmental control and has, therefore, relied principally on the mobilization of capital as its chief resource for the further extraction of surplus value. Furthermore, because of their independence, wealth, and potential political influence, the state apparatus and particularly the party have sought to recruit the traditional bourgeoisie, whereas the rural bourgeoise "recruited" the state for their purposes. It would not be surprising, therefore, if these two fractions of the traditional bourgeoisie had different attitudes about the proper relationship between state and economy, with the rural bourgeoisie not at all adverse to a continuation of a significant governmental role in at least the rural sector. On the other hand, the state and modern capitalists, which might seek singly or jointly to compete with traditional manufacturing enterprises, are the chief potential threats to those involved in the putting-out industries.

These two class fragments, in short, have little common ground on which to pursue joint interests. The differences stemming from their separate relations to the means of production are further exacerbated by the geographical and cultural gap between rural and urban Egypt. Although members of both these fragments are Moslem in that they emerged from the religious milieu that characterizes these strata of Egyptian society, that is not an identification they have chosen out of political or economic motives, nor is it one that has been crucial in shaping their career strategies. They do not, therefore, constitute an integral part of the self-conscious Islamicist tendency.

The Secular Bourgeoisie

Fragmentation. Just as the Islamic bourgeoisie is divided into two subfactions, (i.e. *haute* versus *petite,* urban industrial versus rural), so too is the modern secular bourgeoisie less than homogeneous. The principal divisions are temporally determined, a consequence of the abrupt and thoroughgoing changes that have affected the Egyptian political economy during this century. While even the semicolonial state was not static during the first half of the twentieth century, after that time the Egyptian political economy was ratcheted with breathtaking speed through its experiments with Nasser's Arab Socialism, Sadat's *infitah,* and now Mubarak's "productive *infitah.*" As a result, according to Robert Bianchi,

> the Egyptian business world has experienced abrupt shifts and frequent reversals in its sources of recruitment, concentration of ownership, sectoral distribution of investments, relative importance vis-à-vis state enterprise, and degree and direction of integration into foreign markets. The result has been a highly fragmented bourgeoisie, divided not only by such conventional cleavages as sector, region, size, and international competitiveness, but by equally important differences in age, education, ethics, family background, and, of course, political loyalty.[70]

It has been contended, nevertheless, that these various fragments, the most crucial of which are composed of the families prominent during the *ancien regime,* those of the Nasserist new class, and the *munfatihun* who rose from other origins to amass fortunes under Sadat, have since the demise of Nasserism coalesced into a reasonably coherent social force, an *infitah* bourgeoisie.

There is some evidence for the proposition of increasing class coherence. It is possible to discern, for example, the emergence of business coalitions drawn from two or more elements that are said to constitute the *infitah* bourgeoisie. Such alliances are to be found in joint-venture banks, whose boards of directors typically include a mixture of foreigners, Egyptians of prominent *ancien regime* families, and political luminaries from the Nasser and Sadat eras. The Egyptian-Gulf Bank, for example, was the product of the labors of Ahmad Abaza, the patriarch of that wealthy and powerful family that has been a force in Sharqiya and in national politics since the time of Muhammad Ali. Capital for the bank was provided by the Abazas and other prominent Egyptian families and by Gulf Arabs, principally Kuwaitis. But capital and a good name proved to be insufficient, for the bank's profitability began to decline, along with that of most other foreign and joint-venture banks, as the Egyptian economy deteriorated during the Mubarak era. In 1985 Abaza and his fellow board members seized on the opportunity to appoint the recently dismissed Prime Minister, Kamal Hassan Ali, as their chairman.[71] He provided not only general governmental connections, but the much more valuable asset of ties to the military, in which he had served as head of intelligence, Chief of Staff, and finally, as Minister of Defence. Previously engaged principally in the financing of civilian imports, after Ali's appointment the Egyptian-Gulf Bank became involved in military procurement transactions and in its "food security" projects. The Egyptian-Gulf Bank had thus tied itself much more closely to the regime, or at least to the military component of it, while for his part Kamal Hassan Ali signaled a willingness to identify himself more closely with the *infitah* bourgeoisie. He joined various businessmen's organizations and voiced increasingly conservative opinions about the need to reduce subsidies, free the private sector, and so on.[72] This example of linkage of *ancien regime* notables with a representative of the post-1952 military-technocratic elite indicates the possible existence of a broader pattern of integration of these two fragments of the bourgeoisie.

The proliferation of organizational activity by businessmen might likewise be interpreted as evidence for an increasingly coherent bourgeoisie. Invigoration of the Chamber of Commerce and the Federation of Industry, creation of the Businessmen's Association and of the American-Egyptian Chamber of Commerce, and other manifestations of organizational pluralism have involved many thousands of businessmen in sustained interpersonal contact and semipolitical activities. Equally, the transformation of professional syndicates into virtual corporate business enterprises, for which Osman Ahmad Osman's Engineers' Syndicate paved the way, has greatly increased the density and multiplexity of connections between professionals and businessmen and presumably, therefore, of the various fragments of the bourgeoisie.

But increased organizational dynamism may signal instead, as Bianchi argues, the separate incorporation of the various segments of the bourgeoisie rather than their coalescence.[73] This interpretation rests on an assessment of demands from below, which are said to remain particularistic, and on the alleged desire of the weak authoritarian state to encourage duplication and competition in order to weaken this social force. This view appears to fit the facts more closely. Rather than a gradual harmonizing of relations within and among these organizations, as one would predict if they were emerging from and further contributing to a cohesive bourgeoisie, relations are increasingly acrimonious and noncooperative.

The Chamber of Commerce, for example, fought against the establishment of the Businessmen's Association and has continued to oppose it as well as its offshoot, the Businessmen's Council, which was formed in early 1986 as a result of consultations between the Association and the government of Ali Lutfi.[74] Underlying the conflict are personal and organizational jealousies and the fact that the Association is composed principally of a Mubarak generation of businessmen, or, more precisely, those who currently enjoy good access to the elite. The Chamber of Commerce, on the other hand, tends to combine generations of the bourgeoisie that matured in previous eras; hence it includes those with no significant political connections and those who emerged through the public sector, as well as the more traditional, smaller operators. The Chamber of Commerce and its organizational kin, the Federation of Industries, are therefore in many instances closely associated with the state apparatus at lower levels, while the Businessmen's Association and Businessmen's Council are well connected to the political elite. The Chamber of Commerce, representing many who believe their interests are ignored by the political elite, has been willing to coordinate some activities with the political opposition, whereas the Businessmen's Association remains tied to the government's line. The Port Said and Alexandria branches of the Chamber of Commerce, for example, are comprised largely of importers and other prototypical *munfatihun*. In attempting to combat governmental restrictions on imports they have turned to the Wafd Party, which in the case of Port Said has had a decisive impact on political relations. There the Wafd, in the 1987 elections, won two of the five seats, its best showing in the entire country. The Businessmen's Association, acting in line with the government's instructions and maybe on its own interests, had steadfastly opposed the Port Said branch of the Chamber, charging its members with undercutting the price of Egyptian products with their imported merchandise. The Federation of Industries, which nominally represents Egyptian manufacturers, has supported the Port Said branch of the Chamber of Commerce in this battle, suggesting the possibility of economic linkages between the importers and public-sector managers as well as hostility harbored by members of the Federation toward those businessmen who have made it under Mubarak.

Relations within these organizations are also not free from friction nor suggestive of the emergence of a cohesive *infitah* bourgeoisie. The various branches of the Chamber of Commerce, particularly those in Port Said and Alexandria, tend to go their own way and resist intrusion into their affairs by the national body. The American-Egyptian Chamber of Commerce (AMCHAM), established in 1982 with behind-the-scenes assistance from the commercial section of the U.S. Embassy, was intended to be a vehicle to bring together Egypt's most prominent businessmen and representatives of U.S. corporations. It rapidly acquired over 200 members, of which some 60 percent were Egyptian. But instead of AMCHAM serving as a body in which Egyptian and American businessmen could effectively "network," which its executive director identified as its chief function,[75] the souring of relations between some of the prominent Egyptian members and a general feeling by U.S. members that the organization had been taken over by a particular Egyptian faction rendered that objective difficult of attainment. Underlying the organization's deterioration was a protracted power play by the second most powerful figure in the Osman dynasty, Ismail Osman, a son of Osman Ahmad Osman's older brother who, after his father's death, was raised in his very rich uncle's household. Utilizing the enormous resources of the Osman empire, Ismail won over a majority of the Egyptian members to his cause. When the 1986 elections for AMCHAM's board of directors were declared open, he stood and announced that he had seventy proxies, more than enough to guarantee his election and that of his slate of candidates.[76] The Osman empire had succeeded in adding another fiefdom to its domains, suggesting in the process that the *infitah* bourgeoisie, even at the exalted heights represented by AMCHAM, was not so much an independent social force as a constituency that the state's leading oligopolists could manipulate for their own purposes.

That business organizations are unable to achieve a modicum of unity and dedication of purpose is indicative of the underlying diversity of their membership. Despite the fact that various businesses, including the joint-venture bank discussed above, have succeeded in uniting two or more fragments of the bourgeoisie, its components remain for the most part caught up in the particularistic identities and attitudes typical of their class fragment. Marriage patterns, a key indicator of inter- and intra-class relations, remain structured by family status. Arriviste elements of the bourgeoisie, despite their wealth, are still not thought of as appropriate marriage partners for the offspring of Egypt's prominent families. The managerial-technocratic element is likewise a closed universe as far as social interaction and marriage patterns are concerned. Just as the Egyptian political system resembles a museum, with exhibits from various stages of Egypt's twentieth-century history on display, so too is the class structure segmented by historically determined outlooks and commitments. Attitudes formed in previous eras persist in diluted form among younger generations, and they remain as significant barriers to the sort of broad, middle-class social interaction that characterizes political organizations in Western industrial societies. Status remains a critical factor of social evaluation in Egypt. It, as well as perceived differences in interest, stands in the path of the development of political organizations based on common membership in broad, horizontal social categories.

Political Power of the Secular Bourgeoisie. The ability of Islamic investment companies to thwart efforts to subject them to governmental control was due to their relationship, whether real or just generally perceived, to a broader, at least partially organized political movement, and to the fact that they have devised schemes whereby they have direct access to one of the principal sources of rent that sustains the Egyptian economy. Neither of these conditions obtains for the much larger category of the secular bourgeoisie. Although politically articulate, they cannot claim to speak for any society-wide movement. Their loyalties are divided between the government and the opposition. Although they constitute the most powerful social force within the ruling NDP, that party is an integral element of the state's system of control and is therefore subject to manipulation from above. Profits of this segment of the bourgeoisie are not derived from a direct tap into one of the principal sources of rent. Their activities are generally less remunerative, not as secure, and more susceptible to governmental regulation. This is true whether the bourgeoisie in question are engaged in secular banking, importation, manufacturing, construction, domestic trade, exportation, or virtually any other legal economic activity. In all of these areas governmental regulatory mechanisms exist in the form of legislation and agencies of control. Profits can be generated in spite of or in cooperation with the state, but its presence cannot be ignored. For the secular bourgeoisie, then, escape from the state is not an option as it has been for Islamic investment companies and for the traditional Islamic bourgeoisie. The choice before the modern secular bourgeoisie is whether to seek to penetrate and subvert the state or to stay as far from its purview as possible. The class is divided according to which of these strategies its members pursue.

That the state is not the captive of this class is suggested by its ability under Mubarak to deal effectively not only with many of the most successful *munfatihun* of the Sadat era, but also by its gradual tightening of controls over one of the most powerful segments of the *infitah* bourgeoisie, the importers. Prominent Sadatist *munfatihun* whom Mubarak singled out for the attention of the state's judicial system included President Sadat's brother Ismat, as well as Rashid Osman, who rose spectacularly above his humble origins in Alexandria by combining drug smuggling and other illegal activities with political activism in the regime's party. A variety of smaller operators were also cut loose from the state apparatus and/or had their particular rackets closed down. Sadat's favorite governor of Alexandria, for example, Naim Abu Talib, came perilously close to a stint behind bars. A former professor of economics and a bon vivant, Abu Talib had delighted in redecorating the governor's mansion, throwing tea parties, and in general trying to create the impression that the days of *The Alexandrian Quartet* had returned. When investigated by the *niyaba* in the wake of Sadat's assassination, it turned out that he was also receiving a retainer of £E3,000 monthly from a joint-venture bank. Instead of being sentenced he was allowed to sink into political obscurity.[77]

Against the most prominent survivor of the Sadat era Mubarak had to move much more cautiously. Jihan Sadat had not only created a bureaucratic institution that paralleled her husband's, so that the presidency had his and hers branches, the latter of which Mubarak had by 1983 expertly pruned back, but she had engaged in business ventures with influential Egyptians, including Osman Ahmad Osman, Nabawi

Ismail, Mustafa Khalil, and Mansur Hassan, and with foreigners.[78] Moreover, she remains associated with the Rockefeller-Kissinger set that had also protected the Shah and which, under the Reagan Administration, continues to enjoy access at the very highest levels of the U.S. government. In 1986 her son Gamal was hired by David Rockefeller to work at the New York headquarters of Chase Manhattan Bank. Jihan, therefore, still possesses leverage that can be brought to bear on Mubarak. He has, consequently, moved carefully but continuously against the legacy of her influence in Egypt. One tactic has been to undermine her credibility and integrity. The presidency, for example, did nothing to dampen and most probably encouraged the widespread media reporting in 1986 of the former First Lady's association with the University of South Carolina. Picking up U.S. reports, the Cairo press described her appointment as having been arranged by her powerful U.S. backers, identified her salary as US$80,000 and her duties as consisting of giving occasional lectures, for which she was delivered to campus by helicopter.[79] While this media campaign was brewing Mubarak moved against one of her principal remaining sources of power in the country, her remote control of the charity she had founded, Wafa wal Amal (Faith and Hope). This organization has been widely suspected of providing Jihan with a patronage network and of serving as the organizational vehicle by which she controls certain assets in Egypt.[80] Mubarak ordered Minister of Social Affairs Amal Osman, a former close friend of Sadat's widow, to engineer the defeat of Jihan's candidate for president of Wafa wal Amal. Because all charities come under supervision of this ministry, supervision which includes overseeing elections, the outcome was a foregone conclusion. Possibly as an indication of her contempt for the successor regime, Jihan left town only after throwing one of the season's most talked-about parties.[81]

The political and economic muscle of importers similarly dictated that Mubarak could move against them only incrementally. But he has made significant progress in bringing this critical element of the *infitah* bourgeoisie under control. Accomplishment of this task was facilitated by macroeconomic trends, most notably the continual depreciation of the Egyptian pound, especially since 1985. This has made importation a less profitable and much more risky business. But in the absence of specific policy changes importers might have been able to devise ways and means, such as selling goods in hard currency, to protect their profits. The government, however, took advantage of circumstances and fashioned mechanisms to restrict the sheer quantity of imports and to alter their composition.

Although Mubarak had moved against prominent individual importers as part of his purge of the most notorious Sadatist *munfatihun*, the first step against importers as an economic category was taken by the controversial Minister of Economy, Mustafa al-Said. Part of the reform package he announced in January 1985 was the creation of an import rationalization committee. Its purpose was to review, in secret, applications for permission to import merchandise and commodities. That it was arbitrary and the cause of delay was agreed by all. But the rationalization committee was the only one of Said's reforms not rescinded when he was chased from the cabinet in April 1985. The new Minister of Economy, Sultan Abu Ali, announced on coming into office that the committee would be abolished within six months and replaced by a list system, whereby goods would be grouped in four categories, ranging from those whose further importation would be banned to those that would attract negligible duty.

In the event, the replacement of the rationalization committee by a list system was not achieved until August 1986, over a year behind schedule. This delay was due to discord within decision-making circles and to resistance by importers, who disliked the secret rationalization committee but who feared that a more effective, across-the-board ban might replace it. Additionally, in August 1985 importers in Port Said staged a series of demonstrations against government attempts to impose customs duties on four of their main import lines—fabrics, ready-made clothes, apples, and plastic products. Prime Minister Kamal Hassan Ali, burned in effigy by the protesters, rescinded the decision by his finance minister to impose these duties. It appeared as if the government would abandon its attempt to more carefully regulate imports, an impression that was reinforced the following spring when on 25 March, Minister of Supply Nagi Shatla announced Ministerial Decree 121, which granted permission to the private sector to import some twenty food commodities that under the previous regime of Ministerial Decree 119, which dated back some ten years, had been reserved for importation by the public sector. Moreover, Decree 121 raised the officially permissible profits for importers from 6 percent of the total cost of goods, inclusive of expenses, to 10 percent, with similar increases granted to wholesalers and retailers. Decree 121 was greeted enthusiastically by the thirty or so large operators who dominate food importation.[82]

But this enthusiasm had turned to howls of protest by the summer when it became clear that Decree 121, far from opening up profitable new lines for importation, was in fact leading to the closing down of those that had previously been most remunerative. This was due to several factors. First, the public sector was continuing to import the food commodities listed in Decree 121 and to sell them at subsidized prices. As a consequence some importers who had rushed to land consignments had incurred substantial losses. A second deterrent was the procedure by which permission was granted for customs clearance. Importers had to submit accredited documentation of prices for the goods and associated expenditures on each consignment and were prohibited from selling the goods before permission had been granted and wholesale and retail prices assigned. The Ministry of Supply and the customs service adopted the practice of ignoring the "accredited documentation," claiming that importers as a matter of course forged such documents or had suppliers provide false papers. Instead the ministry and customs "estimated" costs, which importers claimed were consistently less than actual ones. A third problem was the exchange rate upon which calculations of costs were based. Although Decree 121 had raised the rate from a maximum of £E1.50=US$1 to £E1.80=US$1, the real market rate was substantially higher, at that time occasionally reaching two pounds to the dollar. By September, importers had frozen many of their activities so sugar, rice, tea, cooking oil, soap, and other basic commodities were increasingly in short supply.[83]

In the meantime the government had finally enacted the reforms promised in 1985 by the Minister of Economy, Sultan Abu Ali. They, too, had the effect of restricting the profits and range of activities of importers. All customs exemptions were canceled, which had amounted to 40 percent of the total value of imports, and 210 items, from pork sausages to office furniture, were banned. Duty on luxury items, such as videos, cars, and wine, were raised dramatically. The exchange rate on which duty is calculated was lifted from £E.70=US$1 to £E1.35=US$1. Mustafa al-Said's import rationalization committee was also abolished. These measures were calculated to yield an additional £E500 million in customs receipts in the first twelve months. The reforms announced on 22 August simultaneously granted importers permission to deal in various commodities previously reserved for the public sector, including certain foodstuffs.

These changes in import regulations and customs duties were designed to stem the flood of nonessential commodities, to derive additional revenues from customs receipts, which are the government's major source of taxation, and to encourage importers to provide commodities, especially basic foodstuffs, for which the government's foreign currency reserves were increasingly inadequate. But this window the government opened for the private sector was not attractive to importers. Profit margins in foodstuff importation were low and closely regulated, while the threat of competition from the public sector remained. Importers were well aware that the government, fearful of a popular backlash, could not allow food prices to escalate at the rate required to keep pace with the diminution of subsidies and devaluation of the pound. The government attempt to induce importers to absorb some of this burden therefore was unsuccessful. It had demonstrated its power to force importers out of business, but it could not induce them to operate at a loss.

While this may not be the last chapter in the story of the rise and fall of the importers who profited so handsomely during the *infitah*, it must be very close to the end of the saga. The combined forces of economic recession and governmental policy changes have rendered this business relatively unattractive. Importers have fled in droves into other avenues of investment, some of which are productive and encouraged by government, others of which are parasitical, speculative, or of marginal contribution to the economy and society and hence not consciously encouraged by the policy changes described above. In any case the hemorrhage of currency from the national economy to pay for imports has been slowed and the era of the real *munfatihun* brought to a close.

Importers have not been the only segment of the bourgeoisie who profited during the Sadat and early Mubarak eras and who subsequently have suffered from declining returns and increasing regulation. Shopkeepers for example, have had to confront economic recession and, under the Lutfi and Sidqi governments, relatively vigorous price surveillance. Throughout 1986 the Minister of Supply waged a highly publicized campaign to enforce price ceilings on retailers, an activity in which he was occasionally joined by the Minister of Interior. Early morning visits were paid by both, for example, to Cairo's main fruit and vegetable market at Rod al-Farrag. The ranks of retailers were thinned out appreciably after 1985 by a high level of bankruptcies. The rate of declared insolvency would have been much higher had the banks not been reluctant to call in their loans out of fear of general collapse.[84]

Bankers have also been unable to induce the government systematically to adopt favorable policies. The twenty foreign banks operating in Egypt have suffered serious declines in profitability. They have laid off hundreds of staff as a result not only of the general profit squeeze on banks, but because they are prohibited from dealing in local currency. With a rapidly devaluing pound this is a critical restriction, for they dare not lend in dollars when earnings to repay such loans have to be generated in pounds. A way around this problem, which was for debtors simultaneously to borrow the equivalent of their dollar loan in pounds and immediately convert those funds to dollars, thereby covering themselves against changes in the exchange rate, was stopped by Ali Lutfi in the spring of 1986. He alleged that its widespread practice had further depressed the pound's value. Despite repeated approaches to Mubarak by foreign bankers, the government has persisted in its defense of their local competitors by refusing to allow branches of international banks to compete directly with Egyptian ones.

But the local joint-venture and public-sector banks have had their own grievances. Until the spring of 1987 there had been various restrictions on their dealings in hard currencies. These restrictions were lifted not as a result of lobbying by these banks, but because they were demanded by the IMF as part of the package to float the pound, which was itself one of the economic reforms required by the IMF for the rescheduling of Egypt's debts.[85] Another long-standing grievance of public-sector banks has been the requirement that they deposit some 25 percent of their funds with the Central Bank, which in reality is a massive interest-free loan to government. This requirement the authorities have steadfastly refused to modify.

Importers, retailers, and bankers comprise a significant percentage of the bourgeoisie who flourished under Sadat. That they have not done nearly as well under Mubarak is the result of national and global economic trends and of the regime's generally unsympathetic approach to their problems. This suggests that the secular bourgeoisie as a whole is now less powerful than previously and than as alleged by leftist critics of Mubarak. There is, moreover, no evidence to suggest that in their decline importers or other segments of the bourgeoisie have sought to broaden their political base to resist governmental encroachments. When they have contested decisions it has been through channels closely associated with their particular line of business.

The government, intent since 1985 on implementing monetarist policies, has been willing and able to engineer a forced reduction of consumption that has affected both the subsidies for the lower and middle classes and the profits of the wealthy, although it has done little if anything to reduce the gap between rich and poor and it has not enjoyed much success in shifting investment from consumption to production. This in turn suggests that it has been able to contain the bourgeoisie, but not direct it as it would like.

ENTREPRENEURIAL CAPITALISTS
AND THE STRATEGY OF AVOIDANCE

It previously was stated that the secular bourgeoisie could relate to the state either by attempting to subvert it or by seeking to avoid it. The latter alternative, which is to engage in entrepreneurial, capitalist ventures, is generally the least profitable and the most fraught with peril, thereby attesting to the fact that the distribution of power between the bourgeoisie and the state continues to favor the latter despite a clear decline in the cohesion and authority of the state since the Nasser period. A two-way struggle may not, however, be the proper way to conceptualize the contest for dominance over the political economy. It might be better thought of as a three-way contest in which the bourgeoisie on the one hand and the president and inner elite on the other contest for control over a state apparatus that is itself also an actor in the game and that may cast its lot with either suitor. This point will be taken up below.

Entrepreneurial capitalists are those who perceive a market for goods and services and attempt more or less without assistance from the state to fill that market. The category includes the traditional (Islamic) bourgeoisie previously described, as well as a modern component, which in turn is comprised of *ancien regime* elements, those from the Nasserist managerial-technocratic "new class," small-scale operators who have accumulated considerable capital, and some resident aliens. They may be involved in importation, exportation, service industries, agriculture or industry. What they share in common is that their business venture does not rest on a strategic relationship with the bureaucracy, civilian or military, or the political elite. They are unprotected from the depredations of the state because they lack personal access to it and because there is no organized group that could defend collective interests. They are capitalist in their political orientation. They want a minimum of state control, encouragement of the private and reduction of the public sector, low taxes, removal of hindrances to exports, and so on. In short, they are supporters of the basic tenets of the new orthodoxy of development. But of the bourgeoisie they are furthest from exercising political power, hence unable to provide political support for the proponents of that package of reforms.

Kamal Abd al-Nur is an example of an entrepreneur in the agricultural sector. Until 1985 he was the largest grower and exporter of roses in Egypt. A Christian from a large landowning family in Girga in Upper Egypt that had provided Wafdist members of parliament, Kamal Abd al-Nur sold in 1959 his share of the family estates. With two of his brothers he purchased the Minufiya property of the Takhla family, Syrian Christians whose ancestors had founded *al-Ahram* and who, having had their newspaper nationalized, fled to France. On his one-third share of the land Abd al-Nur planted horticultural crops and roses, the latter of which he marketed in Egypt as well as in Europe and North America. In 1985 he was presented a bill for £E1.5 million by the Ministry of Finance for tax arrears, a very sizable figure indeed considering that in 1985 total government revenues derived from personal income taxes levied on those in the private sector amounted to only £E140 million. He appealed to the *Maglis al-Dawla* (Council of State), which is composed of prominent jurists upon whose advisory opinions the courts normally rely. The legal issue at hand was whether by packing his roses in boxes for export he was adding value, in which case he was liable for 40 percent tax on net profits. The *Maglis al-Dawla* determined that this was not a case of added value, hence that he was not liable for tax. The Ministry of Finance did not relent, however, so Abd al-Nur, neither desiring nor able to pay the tax, nor having been informed of the basis upon which the assessment was calculated, pulled what capital he had out of the bank, stuffed it in his mattress, and ripped up 80 percent of his rose gardens, leaving the remainder to service the local market. Egypt's other flower exporters, aware of the Abd al-Nur case and fearing similar treatment, terminated export contracts. As of late 1986 the Ministry of Finance was still demanding its due, and Abd al-Nur and other rose growers were dumping their production on the local market, where wholesale prices were driven down to £E.05 and less per rose (about US$.03), a level at which profitability, despite the extensive employment of child labor at £E1 per day, could not be maintained. Regardless of the prominence of his family, his personal wealth, numerous political connections, particularly among *ancien regime* elements, and the fact that he was not alone in his plight, Abd al-Nur could not obtain redress of his grievance.[86]

Another entrepreneur engaged in modern, intensive agricultural production who has encountered problems with the bureaucracy is Egypt's largest producer of mushrooms, Bairam Murad. His story, however, has a happy ending. Not of a prominent *ancien regime* family, he had acquired capital while working as an undersecretary in the Ministry of Petroleum and for a multinational oil company. A chemist by training, he decided that the relative scarcity of mushrooms on the local market and their commensurate high price provided an opportunity for a modern, large-scale producer. He approached Minister of Agriculture Yusuf Wali through his brother Ali Wali, a former official in the Ministry of Petroleum and close friend of Murad's. Murad was informed by Yusuf Wali that he himself had tried to grow mushrooms, but had failed. This was not for technical reasons, but because Wali, despite holding the portfolio of Agriculture, could not secure the necessary authorizations to produce on his estates in Fayum what in Egypt is a novel crop. Wali nevertheless promised his assistance and within a week had issued a ministerial decree giving Murad permission to grow mushrooms on the few *feddans* he owns outside of Tanta. Murad retired from the Ministry of Petroleum and set about obtaining the other authorizations required. That effort took three years, an additional forty-two signatures, and eleven further ministerial decrees. It involved departments and agencies at the national and provincial levels and such matters as whether the ministry concerned intended to build a road, canal, or power pylon on or through his farm, as well as issues related specifically to mushrooms and any potentially harmful consequences they might have.[87] Finally, after having obtained the required signatures he invested £E500,000 in sheds and equipment and commenced production. After a protracted teething period he is now successfully producing and marketing his crop. Prices remain high because the labyrinthine procedure of obtaining permission from the state to grow mushrooms has deterred other potential growers.[88]

Enterprises that aim to operate autonomously from the government include both highly capitalized ventures as well as much more humble ones. Their common fate is that they are subject to arbitrary and frequently destructive interventions by the bureaucracy. This harassment results from a desire to regulate and control according to law, but an absence of adequate and effective machinery to do so; a prevailing hostile attitude among state employees toward private sector activities; and it occurs because such interventions, or the threat thereof, are used to extort side payments from individuals or firms. Legitimate business premises attract an endless stream of petty officials from various agencies at the municipal, provincial, and national levels, including those in the areas of health, labor, utilities, and taxation, who are routinely offered *bakshish* as the alternative to a vindictive application of whatever regulation it is they are charged with enforcing. The overheads of doing business are commensurately high, hence profitability in these entrepreneurial ventures is much more at risk than it is in situations where profits are more or less guaranteed as a result of a strategic relationship with the state apparatus.

PARASITIC BOURGEOISIE
AND THE STRATEGY OF SUBVERSION

Activities in which profits are generated principally through the subversion of the state and the conversion of its resources into private wealth range literally from street vending to the largest oligopolistic enterprises, and from those that are technically legal to those that are criminal beyond question. The distribution and utilization of subsidized commodities illustrate the vast range of parasitical activities. At the bottom end are those who individually or in small gangs obtain subsidized commodities from the state's retail outlets, either by bribing or intimidating clerks or by manipulating the system of rationing. The most humble and conspicuous of these operators are the *dalalla*-s, the older women robed in their traditional black garments who camp in front of the consumer cooperatives. They utilize ration cards, frequently issued in the names of deceased relatives, to purchase subsidized goods that in turn they sell to their clients who lack ration cards or, being of the middle class, are too busy or too embarrassed to stand in queues in front of these invariably shabby shops. The next step up are the *bultagi*-s, the male toughs who gain access to the goods on sale at these shops by intimidating clerks, scaring away other customers, or by working a profit-sharing system with the state employees responsible for the distribution of subsidized goods. These generally small-time racketeers have minimal protection from the various enforcement agencies under the Ministries of Supply and Interior, as the staggering number of arrests of them indicates. In 1986, for example, there were 102,000 arrests for "supply violations," the vast majority of which were for relatively petty infringements.[89]

At a much more sophisticated level are operations involving large consumers of commodities, such as bakeries or macaroni factories, and their partners in crime, who are officials in the distribution network. Whereas the relatively low total of 34,000 metric tons of stolen subsidized goods was seized in 1986, a report by the *Mabahith al-Tamwin* (Supply Investigator) claimed that 800,000 kilos of flour per day were being diverted to the black market, principally to unnamed large macaroni producers.[90] Of such firms al-Muhandis Company of Ismailiya, part of the Osman empire, is most prominent. Shortly before this report was leaked *al-Shaab* had alleged that the governor of Ismailiya, Abd al-Munaim Amara, a close associate of Osman Ahmad Osman, was engaged in a massive diversion of subsidized flour into the black market.[91] Similar operations have been reported elsewhere. In Gharbiya, for example, it was revealed that the inspectors of the Ministry of Supply were intimidated and physically assaulted by bakery owners to whom the members of the board of the local consumer cooperative, the majority of whom were also elected members of the provincial or district popular councils, were diverting flour.[92]

The Ministry of Supply, responsible both for distributing subsidized goods and for investigating the theft of them, appears to be penetrated at the highest levels by what the opposition press refers to as "the supply mafia." On 5 March 1986, the Disciplinary Court for Higher Administration of the Council of State issued indictments for cooperating with black marketeers against the president of the Central Directorate for Supervision and Price Control, who held the rank of undersecretary; the director of the General Directorate for Price Control; the principal investigator of the Directorate of Investigations; and various lower ranking officials also responsible for defending the supply system against crime. The opposition press alleged that the Minister of Supply, Nagi Shatla, attempted to protect his high ranking administrators, but that he had been unable to dissuade the court from issuing the indictment.[93] Almost a year later, however, the indictments had yet to result in trials, and massive leakage from the supply system continued.

Profiteering from access to subsidized commodities is by no means always an illicit, undercover activity. Indeed, in virtually all sectors of the economy various forms of it assume an institutionalized, open character. Feed mill operators who receive subsidized yellow corn, manufacturers who are provided electricity at a fraction of its real cost, furniture makers who obtain subsidized cotton, and countless others strive to increase the magnitude of subsized inputs and to reduce government restrictions on the marketing of their finished goods. One such restriction is that goods or services produced with subsidized inputs are not to be exported, but this requirement is circumvented by those with influence. The ZAS airline company, for example, has made a considerable profit through dodging this regulation. It is Egypt's only private air freight carrier. Funded in 1982 by several prominent individuals from Sharqiya Province, including a leading member of the NDP and a prominent conservative journalist, it was granted the right to purchase subsidized jet fuel. This was a virtual guarantee of success and by 1987 ZAS had expanded from its original fleet of one Boeing 707 to six. While Egyptian importers and exporters may have benefited marginally from more competitive freight rates, the principal beneficiaries are the owners of ZAS. The larger percentage of their business is in fact not carrying goods to and from Egypt at all. Rather, they transport cargo between various destinations in Europe, filling their tanks in Egypt and making two or more European stops before returning to refuel.[94]

Decisions such as that to award the privilege to ZAS to purchase unlimited quantities of subsidized aviation fuel are made at the very highest levels and require influence, exchange of favors, and/or bribes. Businessmen who have gained access to the resources of the state in this way and those in the state apparatus and/or political elite who have made such access possible have no interest in changing this system. For them, the milking of the state's resources, combined with monopolistic and oligopolistic control of markets, guarantees substantial rewards.[95]

Similar arrangements exist in the provision of goods and services by private entrepreneurs to the state, especially when the capital for their acquisition is provided by external sources, such as bilateral or multilateral aid donors. Whereas the state monitors its direct expenditures with comparative competence and thoroughness, when the cash is coming from others parasitic capitalists frequently succeed in inserting themselves between that source and the state. Shafiq Gabr, for example, made a handsome profit out of brokering deals between Egypt's municipalities and U.S. manufacturers of fire and garbage trucks, purchases of which were 100 percent financed by USAID. Gabr, the 34-year-old son of Egypt's former Ambassador to Greece and grandson of a Wadist parliamentarian, is a close confidant of Ismail Osman. Possibly through that connection he established a working relationship with the third ranking official in the Cairo USAID office. When Gabr opened a branch of his Columbia Company in Washington, D.C., in 1986, his contact in USAID resigned from his position to take up the directorship of that office.

A more lucrative scam and one that was the subject of a sustained attack by the opposition has been run by an emigre former Vice President of North Yemen, Abd al-Rahman al-Baidani. Not trained as an engineer, Baidani nevertheless established Egycon, an engineering consulting firm that obtained the contract to provide, in conjunction with a British-American firm, overall design and technical management for the world's largest public health engineering project, the $3 billion overhaul of Cairo's sewer system. Relying on his many contacts with Egyptian military intelligence that dated to the Yemenese civil war and on his tactic of indulging expatriate suppliers and consultants, Baidani reportedly made millions from the project.[96] Through much of 1986 al-Wafd regaled its readers with stories of kickbacks, overcharging, bribes to the Minister of Housing, and so on. Baidani retaliated by offering the editor of that paper a £E100,000 bribe to terminate the campaign. As the money was changing hands the police, tipped off by Baidani, seized the editor and charged him with blackmail.

Despite the prevalence of illegal, parasitic activities, it probably is the case that more capital is converted from public to private control through perfectly legal strategems, the most well known of which are joint ventures linking the state with the private sector, Egyptian and foreign. It is this device that the most powerful oligopolists, such as Osman, and prominent political figures, such as former Prime Minister Abd al-Aziz Higazi, have utilized so effectively. Of the joint ventures created until 1983 under the provisions of Law 43 of 1974, 65 percent of all invested capital was provided from Egyptian sources and just less than one-quarter of total capital was provided by the state. In the area of industry the government provided 35 percent.[97]

The manner in which that capital has been progressively privatized is illustrated by the Suez Canal Bank, 63 percent of the equity of which was contributed by four public-sector banks and a public-sector insurance company. The balance of the capital was subscribed by the employees' fund of Arab Contractors, the Suez Canal Authority, and by individuals. Once established, this joint venture, like all others, is considered under law a private entity. Its chairman, a close associate of Osman, is Zakariya Tawfiq Abd al-Fatah, one of Sadat's ministers of Trade and Supply. By 1982 the Suez Canal Bank had invested capital in 41 other banks and companies in the private sector. One such investment was in al-Muhandis Bank, of which the Suez Canal Bank subscribed 60 percent of the capital and the Engineers' Syndicate the remainder. Al-Muhandis, the chairman of the board of which is Ahmad Ali Kamal, a former Minister of Irrigation who in 1975 issued the ministerial decree governing the Engineers' Syndicate, in turn formed several joint ventures with Arab Contractors.[98] In 1986 the Suez Canal Bank became one of the principal shareholders in the joint venture involving General Motors and the Egyptian public-sector firm Nasr Automotive Company (NASCO) for the purpose of assembling GM cars in Egypt. Even the most dedicated of the state's accountants would, as a result of this complex pattern of ownership, have extreme difficulty in tracing the ultimate destination of the government's original investment. That a very significant share of such funds have ultimately been siphoned off by private interests at the other end of the labyrinth of companies is suggested not only by innumerable specific allegations, but by the fact that the state has, according to reliable accounts, lost millions in its joint ventures.[99]

Not even the Central Bank is immune from the process of privatizing profits and socializing losses. It has a 42 percent share in the joint-venture Arab-African International Bank, the capital of which was hastily increased from £E200 million to £E500 million in 1986. As a result of a muckraking campaign in the summer of that year by al-Akhbar's independent columnist Gallal al-Hammamsi and al-Shaab's Nimat Fuad, it became clear that the bank had been perilously close to collapse prior to the injection of capital. It had been brought to the brink by its chairman, the Kuwaiti Ibrahim al-Ibrahimi, who had doled out the bank's capital to his friends and relatives while buying the complicity of prominent state officials. The incorruptible Directorate of Supervision had issued a series of reports on his illegal activities dating back to 1979, but in each case they were buried as a result of Ibrahimi's timely interventions. In 1979 he forced the Egyptian representative on the board of directors to resign after that honest banker had confirmed the report of the Directorate of Supervision. The contents of the secret report and the Egyptian representative's endorsement of it were leaked to Ibrahimi by the Minister of Economy, who on leaving the cabinet was made president of the bank. During a similar episode five years later the Prime Minister, Kamal Hassan Ali, countermanded a demand by his Minister of Economy, Mustafa al-Said, that the Kuwaiti government relieve Ibrahimi of his post. Ali was subsequently appointed chairman of the board of the Egyptian-Gulf Bank, of which the majority share holding is Kuwaiti.

In the meantime Hammamsi and Fuad had done their sums and found that the total cost to the Egyptian government of the "mismanagement" of the bank was in the neighborhood of £E1 billion. The cynical interpretation was that Ibrahimi was finally forced out not because his behavior was fundamentally different from that of other custodians of governmental assets in joint ventures, but because of his rude and arrogant nature, the fact that he was a foreigner, and because he converted such a massive amount of public assets to private wealth without taking the usual precautionary measures. Virtually all of Cairo's journalists were aware, for example, that Ibrahimi had provided the prominent pro-government editor, Ibrahim Saada, with a new Mercedes.[100]

CONCLUSION

From the humble *dalalla*-s squatting in front of the consumer cooperatives to the expensively dressed bankers in their boardrooms, the modus operandi of subverting the state is the same. The profits are shared out between those in the private sector and the state employees or members of the political elite who make those profits possible. These arrangements enervate the state and sap its will to regulate such interests. It cannot, for example, organize the effective distribution of subsidized goods, for they are siphoned off at various levels, whether by millionaire feed mill operators or by gangs of tough young *bultagi*-s. Attempts to stimulate business investment and the expansion of entrepreneurial activities are frustrated by the fact that entrepreneurial elements who do invest their resources fall prey to the state apparatus, which seeks individually and collectively to enhance its wealth, status, and power at the expense of the unprotected. Finally, and most importantly, a significant element of the bourgeoisie has tapped into the state's coffers through innumerable legal and semilegal activities, most profitable of which are joint ventures.

In his relations with parasitic capitalists the President cannot even count on his Prime Minister to defend the abstract interests of the state, hence presidential authority. This was made clear to Mubarak when on coming to power he attempted to reduce the influence of Osman. While Mubarak slowed the rate at which Osman converts public resources into private wealth, he could do little to disconnect the tangled web of personal ties to strategic elites that provide Osman with his power and influence. Mubarak had to rely on numerous ministers and party officials, including even the Secretary General of the NDP and Minister of Agriculture Yusuf Wali, who were known to be closely associated with Osman. By the mid-1980s Mubarak had settled on a policy of peaceful coexistence with Egypt's wealthiest man, a policy that he extended to others of the parasitic bourgeoisie. While he makes occasional object lessons of the most voracious of those feeding off the state, his purposes thus far have been to set the limits and to reassure the public, rather than to launch a systematic campaign to destroy the linkages between the state and the parasitic bourgeoisie that lives off it. Presumably he adjudges that nexus as still too powerful to permit a successful attack on it.

The undoubted potency of the parasitic element should not disguise, however, the fact that as a class the bourgeoisie is neither cohesive nor able to dictate policies uniformly supportive of its interests. It is divided between Islamic and secular wings, between importers and manufacturers, between traditional bosses and foreign-educated technocrats, between Wafdists and NDP regulars, and so on. Each of these segments is a self-contained constituency. Some of these groups, such as the bourgeoisie represented by the Islamic investment companies, have benefited from a confluence of economic and political factors that have raised the cost to the President of bringing them under control, although he has clearly signaled his desire to do so. Others, such as the traditional bourgeoisie involved in small-scale manufacturing, carry out their activities more or less beyond the purview of the political elite and the state. Still others, including many modern entrepreneurial bourgeoisie, attempt to replicate that strategy of avoidance in the modern sector, but with only mixed results. They are considerably less united and powerful than even the importers, who eventually lost their protracted struggle against the government.

It is in fact only the core of the *infitah* bourgeoisie, its parasitic element—which consists of those who gained access to the state's resources through joint ventures with it, through appropriation of subsidized commodities, or through other means—that so far has remained too powerful for Mubarak to confront directly. This is not because it is a cohesive class fragment. Instead it is better conceptualized as a collection of mafia-style operations by independent "gangs." By far the most powerful one is that headed by Osman, but there is no evidence to suggest that he provides an umbrella for those not of his "family," or for the parasitic bourgeoisie as a whole. The power of the oligopolists of the parasitic bourgeoisie stems from the fact that Sadat farmed out presidential patronage to them. They were created by virtue of an innovative strategy of patrimonial rule whereby it could be perpetuated through a partial privatization. Mubarak, for the reasons discussed in Chapter 2, has not been able to bring that patronage back under his control. But there is little evidence to suggest that this parasitic bourgeoisie is further expanding or that its intraclass alliances are solidifying. Mubarak, unable to overpower Osman and similar forces, has brought the system more or less into equilibrium or, more accurately, immobility. Osman is not growing dramatically richer, and Mubarak is not becoming significantly more powerful. It remains conceivable that in the future the President could launch a successful attack against the parasitic bourgeoisie, but so far he has contented himself with the occasional skirmish. The question remains open then as to whether the farming out of patronage has created a class segment with such power that it is forever immune to regulation and control or whether it is presidential caution or incompetence that just causes it to appear as such.

As far as the new orthodoxy of development is concerned, the current distribution of power within the bourgeoisie is not supportive of its eventually serving as a guide for the reorganization of Egypt's political economy. The most powerful segment of the bourgeoisie derives its wealth and influence from parasitic relations with the state, not through entrepreneurial activities. Osman sang the praises of capitalism in his memoirs not because he is an entrepreneur but because its anti-Nasser overtones were what Sadat wanted to hear.[101] Osman, after all, started to accumulate his fortune when Nasser assigned state projects to him and went on to multiply it many times over as a result of the governmental largesse bestowed on him by Sadat. The Osman empire has been built in the shadow of the state and would wither were it placed in the direct sunlight of open economic competition, as would its smaller counterparts. So Osman and others of the powerful parasitic bourgeoisie are not at all in favor of the tenets of the new orthodoxy of development as preached by U.S. academics and USAID officials. Those Egyptian bourgeoisie who are, such as the struggling rose and mushroom growers, lack the power to bring such a program into being. Whether a reform coalition including these elements and bypassing the parasitic bourgeoisie could be patched together will be taken up in Chapter 7. Previous to that, however, it is necessary to investigate what is an even more potent constraint on Mubarak's exercise of power, the military, and its connections to the parasitic bourgeoisie.

NOTES

1. John Waterbury, *The Egypt of Nasser and Sadat: The Political Economy of Two Regimes* (Princeton: Princeton University Press, 1983).

2. Alan Richards, "Ten Years of Infitah: Class, Rents, and Policy Stasis in Egypt," *Journal of Development Studies* 20, 4 (July 1984), pp. 323–328.

3. That this interpretation has become commonplace is suggested by its appearance, albeit in somewhat diluted forms, even in non-Marxist interpretations of Egyptian politics. See for example Paul Jabber, "Egypt's Crisis, America's Dilemma," *Foreign Affairs* (Summer 1986), pp. 960–980.

4. See for example Marie-Christine Aulas, "Sadat's Egypt: A Balance Sheet," *Merip Reports* 12, 6 (July-August 1982), pp. 6–19.

5. Hanna Batatu, "State and Capitalism in Iraq: A Comment," *Merip Middle East Report*, 142 (September-October 1986), pp. 10–12.

6. Bianchi, for example, writing shortly after the event, emphasized the behind-the-scenes role of the money changers, while a year later he attributed Mustafa al-Said's demise to pressure exerted by businessmen's organizations. See Robert Bianchi, "Businessmen's Associations in Egypt and Turkey," *Annals* 482 (November 1985), pp. 147–154; and "Egypt: Drift at Home, Passivity Abroad," *Current History* (January 1986), pp. 71–74, 82–83. See also "Egypt's Infitah Bourgeoisie," *Merip Middle East Report*, 142 (September-October 1986), p. 39.

7. This point is made clear by Clement Henry Moore, "Money and Power: The Dilemma of the Egyptian *Infitah*," *The Middle East Journal*, 40, 4 (Autumn 1986), pp. 634–650. That a major portion of the government's economic officials opposed the reforms from the outset was made clear by Said's successor, Sultan Abu Ali, in an interview in *Oktober* (1 March 1987).

8. These observations are based on conversations with individuals who have entrusted their funds to these companies and on various public statements by their owners and by others involved in similar activities. See for example Muhsin Hassanain, "Former King of the Money Changers Speaks," *Oktober* (15 February 1987).

9. Mahmud al-Hadari, "Islamic Investment Companies," *al Ahali* (28 May 1986).

10. Tahir Salah, "Conversation with a President of an Islamic Investment Company," *al-Ahram* (11 February 1987).

11. Ismail Muntasir, "Tornado on Pyramids Road," *Oktober* (16 November 1986); and Mahmud al-Maraghi, "al-Rayan and the Prime Minister 'Super,'" *Sawt al Arab* (16 November 1986).

12. Muntasir, "Tornado on Pyramids Road."

13. Alexandre Buccianti, "Egypt Faced with Rising Tide of Fundamentalist Violence," *The Guardian* (25 May 1986).

14. Muntasir, "Tornado on Pyramids Road."

15. This is the conclusion suggested by Buccianti, "Egypt Faced with Rising Tide of Fundamentalist Violence."

16. Hadari, "Islamic Investment Companies."

17. *Ibid.*

18. Abd al-Azim Anis, "Meaning of Words," *al-Ahali* (21 May 1986).

19. "Secrets of the Week," *al-Ahali* (11 June 1986).

20. Amir Ahmad Amir, "The Conflict Between the Government and the Investment Companies over the Independent Seats," *al-Ahali* (11 February 1987).

21. Maraghi, "al-Rayan and the Prime Minister 'Super.'"

22. "Conversation of the Week," *al-Musawwar* (26 September 1986).

23. Hadari, "Islamic Investment Companies."

24. Muntasir, "Tornado on Pyramids Road," and Salah, "Conversation with a President of an Islamic Investment Company."

25. An example of this sometimes awkward stance was provided in the government weekly *Mayo*, which in its 22 September 1986 issue carried a lengthy indictment of Islamic investment companies. Seeking to enlist the support of someone who could be said to speak on behalf of al-Azhar, the author, following his recitation of the standard charges of chicanery and violation of Islamic principles, interviewed the dean of al-Azhar University's faculty of commerce. This "shaikh" carefully avoided blanket condemnation of such companies and instead provided a discourse on their different characteristics according to Islamic law. He then proceeded to argue that the reason such companies were so successful was that the Islamic banks had not expanded sufficiently and that the government was slower still in making available to Egyptians, especially those working in foreign countries, suitably attractive investment opportunities. He was noticeably reluctant to echo the reporter's call for restrictions to be imposed on the investment companies. Siham Abd al-Al, "Investment Companies After the New Law," *Mayo* (22 September 1986).

26. Hassan Amer, "Islamic Banks Under Fire for Bending *Sharia* for Profit," *Middle East Times* (8–14 March 1987).

27. "Secrets of the Week," *al-Ahali* (4 June 1986).

28. Maraghi, "al-Rayan and Prime Minister 'Super.'"

29. *al-Ahram* (12 November 1986).

30. Ibrahim Abu Zaid and Nagwa Mahmud, "Investigation Presented to the Prime Minister," *Ruz al-Yusuf* (30 June 1986). The al-Sharif company has similarly established an economic and political presence in the Delta. Attending the ceremonial laying of the foundation stone for one of al-Sharif's new industrial establishments at Inshas in Sharqiya in April 1987 were Dr. Muhyi al-Din Gharib, Vice President of the Investment Organization, Amin Mitkis, Governor of Sharqiya, and various of the province's officials and notables. See *al-Shaab* (28 April 1987).

31. Buccianti, "Egypt Faced with Rising Tide of Fundamentalist Violence."

32. For differing estimates of their assets see al-Al, "Investment Companies After the New Law" and Maraghi, "al-Rayan and the Prime Minister 'Super.'"

33. Ali Khamis, "The Legal and Economic Frameworks of the Investment Companies," *al-Wafd* (25 December 1986).

34. See Nigm's comments in Osama Soraya, "New Central Bank Head Key Figure in Rationalizing Monetary Policies," *Middle East Times* (29 June–6 July 1985).

35. Muhsin Hassanain, "Governor Number Six of the Central Bank," *Oktober* (22 March 1986).

36. "So That the Deposits of Egyptians are Not Lost in the Investment Companies," *al-Musawwar* (31 October 1986).

37. "Secrets and News," *al-Musawwar* (7 November 1986).

38. Muntasir, "Tornado on Pyramids Road." See also "al-Rayan's Gold Rumble," *Middle East Money* (November 1986).

39. Moore recounts that episode in "Money and Power."

40. "The Banks Suffer Liquidity Deficit," *al-Wafd* (13 November 1986).

41. See his lengthy explanation in Muntasir, "Tornado on Pyramids Road."

42. Egyptian negotiators have on numerous occasions informed IMF and World Bank officials of their inability to raise interest rates in the face of the Islamicist challenge. For this information I am indebted to Olaf Gondley of the IMF.

43. "The Banks Suffer Liquidity Deficit."

44. "What Is Behind the Campaign Against Al-Rayan?" *al-Shaab* (11 November 1986).

45. See for example the ad by al-Rayan on 28 February in *al-Akhbar* and that by al-Sharif in *al-Ahram* on 22 March. These same ads also appeared in various of the opposition papers.

46. Imam Ahmed, "Islamic Fever Infects Egypt's General Elections," *Middle East Times* (5–11 April 1987).

47. A statement to this effect was attributed to Adli Abd al-Shahid, Minister for Emigrants' Affairs, by *al-Wafd* (20 March 1987).

48. On this meeting see "Investment Companies Delay the Declaration of the Economic Decrees," *al-Ahram al-Iqtisadi* (18 May 1987). Among the 11 representatives of investment companies was a Coptic financier whose investment company, modeled on the Islamic counterparts but servicing the needs of Coptic investors, had by 1987 become one of the largest in Egypt. See Mohsen Hassanein, "Conflict Intensifies Between Egypt and Islamic Companies," *Middle East Times* (21–27 June 1987).

49. This interpretation appeared credible in light of the fact that the large public-sector firms had absorbed much of the foreign currency captured by the official banking system, leaving the private sector with insufficient funds to cover its import requirements and causing businessmen to complain bitterly of their plight. See *Middle East Economic Digest* (*MEED*) (25 July 1987) and *Egypt: Country Report*, Economist Intelligence Unit, 3 (1987), p. 6.

50. A caricature of whisky-swilling businessmen "pilgrims," referred to as Hagg-a-go-go, featured repeatedly in this campaign. See for example *al-Ahram al-Iqtisadi* (28 September 1987), p. 5. See also David Butter, "Mubarak Leads Egypt into the 1990s," *MEED* (10 October 1987).

51. Mohsen Hassanein, "Egypts Banks Poised in Scramble for Savings of Returning Workers," *Middle East Times* (5–11 July 1987).

52. For the reflections of one such spokesman after returning from the Gulf, see Muhsin Muhammad's column in *al-Gumhuriya* (16 August 1987).

53. Imam Ahmed, "Egypt Readies Moves to Rein in Islamic Investment Companies," *Middle East Times* (2–8 August 1987); and Imam Ahmed, "Egypt's New Government Moves Confidently to Resolve Old Problems," *Middle East Times* (25–31 August 1987).

54. He stated that the government was preparing a bill to regulate the operations of investment companies "in such a way as to safeguard national interests and ensure the rights of investors." *al-Ahram* (17 November 1987).

55. MEED (11 and 17 July 1987). See also "Mubarak Tries to Awaken Egypt," *Middle East Times* (20–26 December 1987).

56. See for example the advertisement by al-Rayan in *al-Ahram* (28 May 1987).

57. "Islamic Capital Firms Buy Bank Shares," *Middle East Times* (7–13 June 1987).

58. MEED (22 August 1987). See also Osama Gheith, "Egypt's Islamic Companies Try to Clean up Their Image," *Middle East Times* (6–12 September 1987).

59. "Ikhwan Form Islamic Investment Co.," *Middle East Times* (4–10 October 1987).

60. Fuad Ajami, "The Struggle for Egypt's Soul," *Foreign Policy* (Summer 1979), pp. 3–30.

61. Moore, "Money and Power," p. 644.

62. Salah, "Conversation with a President of an Islamic Investment Company."

63. On Omar Marei's activities see Robert Springborg, *Family, Power, and Politics in Egypt: Sayed Bey Marei—His Clan, Clients, And Cohorts* (Philadelphia: University of Pennsylvania Press, 1982).

64. Several observers have commented on the surprising persistence of traditional, small-scale industries. A World Bank team, for example, stated the following: "Despite the uninviting climate, small-scale industries have managed to hold their own and even grow, accounting for about one-third of total value added generated in industry." Khalid Ikram, *Egypt: Economic Management in a Period of Transition* (Baltimore: Johns Hopkins University Press, 1980), p. 246. According to Waterbury, the private petty manufacturing sector, despite innumerable handicaps in the Nasser and Sadat eras, "managed to hold its own in total industrial output." *The Egypt of Nasser and Sadat*, p. 187.

65. I am indebted to Dr. Ibrahim Soliman of the Department of Economics, Zagazig University, for information about the Egyptian shoe industry.

66. This study was conducted during 1986 as part of a pilot project supported by the Ford Foundation. I am indebted to Mustafa Murad, a summer intern at the Ford Foundation, for this information.

67. "Prices of Shop and Office Space Escalates," *Middle East Times* (12–18 April 1987).

68. On this incident see Springborg, *Family, Power, And Politics in Egypt*, p. 238.

69. Muhamed Salah al-Din Mansi, *The Political Participation of Peasants* (Cairo: Nafa Publishing, 1984) (in Arabic).

70. Bianchi, "Businessmen's Associations in Egypt and Turkey," p. 153.

71. The Kuwaiti connection was instrumental in Ali's appointment.

72. See, for example, the interview with him in *Middle East Times* (16–22 February 1986). See also his recently published autobiography, Kamal Hassan Ali, *Warriors and Negotiators* (Cairo: Al-Ahram Publishing, 1986) (in Arabic). His increasingly conservative views were conveyed to the author in interviews on 20 July and 14 September 1986, during which he stated that food subsidies should be withdrawn, that the agrarian reform laws should be relaxed, and that the private sector should be given responsibility for all land reclamation.

73. Bianchi, "Businessmen's Associations in Egypt and Turkey."

74. For an overview of the conflict between these organizations, see Hassan Amer, "Businesses Quarrel over Government's Role in Trade," *Middle East Times* (2–8 February 1986).

75. "Egypt's Amcham: Business Social Workers," *Middle East Times* (28 April– 5 May, 1984).

76. I am indebted to Anne Wolfe, former Executive Director of AMCHAM, for information about that organization.

77. I am indebted to Mustafa Murad for information about Naim Abu Talib.

78. Jihan Sadat, Mansur Hassan, and various members of the office of the presidency, for example, were partners in an agribusiness reclamation project in Sinai operated by Osman Ahmad Osman. See Talat Kamih, "Ali Baba and the 29," *al-Shaab* (17 March 1987).

79. These details were reported in various articles that appeared in *al-Shaab* and *al-Ahali* in August and September 1986.

80. Nimat Ahmad Fuad claimed, for example, that Wafa wal Amal received far more donations from various Western governments than it expended on charitable projects. She demanded that Wafa wal Amal be subjected to governmental accounting procedures. See Nimat Ahmad Fuad, *The Industry of Ignorance: A Book About Politics* (Cairo: Dar al-Mustaqbal al-Arabi, 1984), pp. 321–327 (in Arabic).

81. Subsequently Jihan Sadat gave several interviews to Western publications in which she criticized various aspects of the Mubarak regime, including what she claimed was its refusal to grant her an adequate pension. The President responded through Ibrahim Saada, editor of *Akhbar al-Yom*, whose column of 23 May 1987, entitled "Letter to Jihan al-Sadat," accused her of disloyalty, personal aggrandizement, and misrepresentation of the facts about her personal finances. Her farewell party is described in *al-Wafd* (7 August 1986). Mubarak's involvement in the removal of Jihan's influence over *Wafa wal Amal* was described to the author by Salama Ahmad Salama, managing editor of *al-Ahram*, interview (21 September 1986).

82. Osama Gheis, "New Decree Increasing Private Sector Powers Comes into Effect," *Middle East Times* (30 March–5 April 1986).

83. Ahmed El Mahdi, "Importers Try to Force Change in New Marketing Policy," *Middle East Times* (31 August–6 September 1986).

84. The conservative editorialist Muhammad al-Hayawan made a plea in his column in *al-Gumhuriya* of 16 September 1986 for the government to come to the assistance of the banks and companies. He claimed that as many as 300 companies of significant size were threatened with bankruptcy unless action was taken and that the banking sector itself would therefore be shaken. Businessmen had themselves previously approached government for support, but had been unsuccessful in obtaining a formal commitment that their debts would be rescheduled. See Osama Gheis, "Businessmen Call on Banks to Reschedule Debts," *Middle East Times* (11–17 May 1986).

85. Abd al-Rahman Aql, "A New System to Attract Deposits of Foreign Currency," *al-Ahram* (28 April 1987); and Imam Ahmed, "Egypt Anticipates IMF Deal by Easing Hard Currency Law," *Middle East Times* (26 April–9 May, 1987.

86. I am indebted to Kamal Abd al-Nur and his son Hani Abd al-Nur for providing this information.

87. The Ministry of Health's director for Gharbiya Province, for example, at first refused permission on the grounds that mushrooms are poisonous. Murad brought that official a chart of over 1,000 mushrooms, which indicated those that are poisonous and those that are not. The provincial office of the Ministry of Supply also refused permission initially. This was because a secretary, when copying the executive summary of Murad's proposal, wrote in Arabic *mushrub* instead of *mushrum*, which translates as drink, implying that it is an alcoholic beverage. It took weeks for the consequences of his error to be rectified.

88. I am indebted to Bairam Murad for providing this information.

89. Izzat al-Saadani, "A Record of Investigations by the Minister of Interior," *al-Ahram* (31 January 1987).

90. This report appeared in *al-Ahrar* (16 June 1986).

91. Ahmad Mahmud Hassan, "Investigation of the Governor of Ismailiya for Manipulation of the Flour Market," *al-Shaab* (20 May 1986); and "The Governor of Ismailiya: No Basis to the Incident of Playing with Flour," *al-Shaab* (27 May 1986).

92. Mustaf al-Said, "The Disappearance of Flour from Mahalla," *al-Ahali* (24 September 1986).

93. Magdi Mahanna, "The Fall of the Supply Mafia," *al-Wafd* (15 May 1986).

94. This information was provided by an employee of the company who is also a relative of one of the company's owners. For other details see the lengthy advertisement for ZAS that appeared in *al-Ahali* (11 February 1987). That the ad should appear in *al-Ahali* and stress the point that ZAS is contributing to the national economy is suggestive of the possibility that the company was moving to preempt a campaign against it, possibly by this very paper.

95. Midhat Hassanain of the American University in Cairo claimed in *al-Ahram al-Iqtisadi* (16 December 1985) that the underground economy, which he defined as contraband trade, commissions in land speculation, customs and tax evasion, circumvention of laws, currency trading, the black market for subsidized goods, and leakage from the Port Said free zone, amounted to one-half of the national economy. According to him, comparable figures for Europe and North America range between 7 and 20 percent. Cited in *al-Sharq al-Awsat* (31 January 1986).

96. Magdi Sirhan, "The Story of Baidani with al-Wafd," *al-Wafd* (16 October 1986).

97. Omar Saad El Din Mahmoud, unpublished M.A. thesis, American University in Cairo (May 1984), p. 27. Ali al-Din Hillal, "The Last Page," *al-Ahram al-Iqtisadi* (21 July 1986).

98. Nahed Dajani, "Corporatism Within the Egyptian Context: A Profile of Business and Professional Politics in Egypt." Unpublished M.A. thesis, American University in Cairo (July 1982), p. 65.

99. Hillal estimates that the state has invested £E2 billion in joint ventures, of which it has lost a sizable amount. "The Last Page." *Al-Ahrar* reported that the Ministry of Finance had become so alarmed about the losses of these joint ventures that it has prohibited several public-sector and bureaucratic organizations, including the Ministry of *Awqaf* (Religious Endowments) from entering into any more of them. "The Public Sector Participates in *Infitah* Companies," *al-Ahrar* (27 January 1986).

100. The best source on the scandal involving the Arab-African International Bank is Gallal al-Hammamsi's series of articles that appeared in his column, "Smoke in the Breeze," in *al-Akhbar*. The first piece appeared on 24 August and the last, the eighteenth, appeared on September 15. See also Nimat Ahmad Fuad's articles in *al-Shaab* on 2, 9, 16, 23, and 30 September; and Imam Ahmed, "Banks Under Fire in Egypt for Corruption, Mismanagement," *Middle East Times* (14–20 September 1986).

101. Osman Ahmad Osman, *Pages from My Experiences* (Cairo: Modern Egyptian Library, 1981) (in Arabic). For insightful comments on this book and Osman more generally, see Mohamed Sid-Ahmed, "Sadat's Alter Ego," *Merip Reports*, 107 (July-August 1982), pp. 19–20.

4

THE MILITARY

THE LEGACY OF CIVIL-MILITARY RELATIONS

Husni Mubarak succeeded Anwar al-Sadat at a time of troubled civil-military relations. Sadat's pursuit of a separate peace with Israel in the wake of the October 1973 war raised important questions about the military's future role, size, and sources of weapons. If Egypt was no longer to be at war with Israel, the huge Egyptian military establishment, which peaked in 1973 at almost 900,000 men, was not required. Accordingly, a systematic shedding of military personnel commenced almost immediately after the cessation of hostilities, reducing the total military force by almost one-half during the course of the following decade.[1] No longer charged with the task of preparing for total war with the region's superpower, the military began the process of conversion into a rapid strike force that could intervene in the reasonably proximate areas of the Horn of Africa, the Gulf, or Libya. Western arms suppliers, by far the most important of which was the United States, replaced the Soviet Union as Egypt's chief source of weaponry.[2]

Changes of this magnitude were bound to elicit mixed feelings from the officer corps. Under the slogan of "everything for the battle" they had established first claim on the nation's resources—the fate of the military and the nation had been inseparable. But the changes set in motion after the partial victory over Israel suggested that the military was to become just another bureaucratic claimant for a share of available funds and that Israeli military strength, long the benchmark against which Egypt's abilities were measured, was to be allowed to leap ahead.

Alterations in the size, mission, and weapons inventories of the military were accompanied by a profound downgrading of its political role, a trend that commenced at the inception of Sadat's presidency and rapidly gathered pace after 1973. Declining ratios of former officers to civilians at various levels of the state structure attest to this trend. Under Nasser more than one-third of all cabinet ministers had military backgrounds. By comparison, after Sadat's Corrective Revolution of May 1971 those with exclusively military backgrounds constituted less than 4 percent

An earlier version of this chapter appeared as an article entitled "The President and the Field Marshal" in *MERIP Middle East Report* 17, 4 (July-August 1987).

of all ministers, although an additional 9 percent of ministers were officers who had further technical training.[3] In the final Sadat cabinet only the portfolios of Defence and Foreign Affairs were held by those with military training. Sadat engineered a similar demilitarization of governorships, of which fewer than 5 were held by the military by 1980, compared with 22 of 26 in 1964.[4] Although no figures comparable to Ayubi's for the bureaucracy in 1967 are presently available, impressionistic evidence suggests a decline in the ratios of former officers, which had in 1967 been 6 percent of all those at the *mumtaz* (highest) level in the civil service and 8 percent of all public-sector company chairmen.[5] Declining ratios resulted from retirement claiming officers whose posts were then filled by Sadat with civilians. This was noticeable, for example, in the Ministry of Foreign Affairs, of whose staff over 9 percent had been drawn from the military in 1961 but to which Sadat permitted the military virtually no further access.

The changing trend in civil-military relations suggested by the reduced percentages of former officers in the political and administrative elites is confirmed by the historical evidence. From 1952 until 1967 the military was indisputably the strongest institutional element within the political system. Not only did it supply the core members of the inner elite, including from 1964 to 1967 the First Vice President in the person of Field Marshal Abd al-Hakim Amer, but it successfully defended itself from all attempts to impose external control, including that launched by civilianized former members of the Revolutionary Command Council in the wake of the 1961 Syrian secession from the United Arab Republic. The official party, the Arab Socialist Union (ASU), was never able to operate within the military. Indeed, when ASU activists attempted to steer the country leftward in 1966, the army, in the person of Field Marshal Amer, rather than the ASU, was put in control of the potentially crucial Higher Committee for the Liquidation of Feudalists.

The disastrous performance of the military in the June 1967 war and the subsequent purge of Amer and his network of officer-clients significantly reduced the political role of the military, but given that Egypt was still very much in a state of war with Israel, that most former officers who had made the transition to the political and administrative elites remained at their posts, and that no serious competitors for political power emerged in the turbulent wake of the defeat, the military's political leverage persisted, albeit at a reduced level. Widespread civilian protests and demonstrations in 1968 sparked by lenient sentences meted out to those in the air force high command convicted of negligence for their contribution to the 1967 debacle resulted in retrials and harsher sentences, but that was a palliative intended to placate the population while protecting the military and its role. A truly significant demilitarization of the political order had to await the arrival of Sadat and his consolidation of personal power.

While Sadat's policy of peace and *infitah* worked ineluctably against a preeminent role for the military, just as Nasser's policy of war coupled to a command economy had tended to support it, demilitarization had to be forced on the military. A political backlash was forestalled by constant reshuffling of the high command. Before it became clear that Sadat intended to bring about fundamental strategic changes, he had already displayed his willingness and ability to purge those who opposed him. He jailed Minister of War Muhammad Fawzi in 1971, after having previously secured the support of General Muhammad Sadiq, who then replaced Fawzi.[6] A year later Sadiq was himself placed under house arrest after Sadat had ensured the loyalty of Chief of Staff Saad al-Din Shazli, who in turn was chased into exile once Sadat was assured of the loyalty of Minister of War Ahmad Ismail and Shazli's replacement, General Abd al-Ghani Gamasi. Gamasi, who took over as Minister of Defence after the death of General Ismail in December 1974, and Gamasi's Chief of Staff Muhammad Ali Fahmi were then replaced in 1978 as a result of the former's opposition to Sadat's seeking a peace treaty with Israel and the latter's dissatisfaction with the downgrading of the military and the redirection of its mission away from the eastern front and toward Libya.[7] Any potential reaction within the ranks against the removal of Gamasi and Fahmi was preempted by Sadat's relationship with Husni Mubarak, whom he had promoted from Commander of the Air Force to Vice President, and with Kamal Hassan Ali, the head of Military Intelligence who was promoted to Minister of Defence in Gamasi's place in the Mustafa Khalil cabinet formed on 5 October 1978. Ali's successor, the popular Ahmad Badawi, died along with twelve senior officers in a helicopter crash in March 1980. He was replaced by Egypt's military attache in Washington, Abd al-Halim Abu Ghazala.

Given this record, which suggests tension and distrust between Sadat and his high command, to say nothing of the predictable resentment caused in the military by its downgrading after 1973, it is not surprising that much speculation by the end of the Sadat era centered on civil-military relations. Many sections of the articulate public refused to believe that the crash that killed Badawi and his advisers was an accident, their hypothesis being that Sadat had murderously preempted a move against himself. Some pundits even connected this incident, and the more general dissatisfaction in the military, with Sadat's assassination. They argued that the soldiers in the parade had to pass through three separate gates at which inspections by three different branches of intelligence were undertaken to prevent live ammunition from being carried into the parade grounds.[8] Sharpshooters of the Presidential Guard, who were to have been on the roof of the reviewing stand, were not there. And the real brains behind the outfit, Abbud Zumr, was a colonel in Military Intelligence. To conspiracy theorists, of whom there are no small number, this evidence is sufficient to prove that the military killed Sadat.

Whatever the truth in these matters, Mubarak definitely inherited a restive military. Not only had its size and role been reduced, but the debate about additional duties the military might perform as its defense role contracted had produced few tangible results. Inflation associated with the *infitah* ravaged military salaries, such that in 1982 it was remarked that "a good secretary in a foreign oil company can now earn more than a full colonel."[9] Earlier that year air force technicians had gone on strike at four bases in protest against a change of regulations that required senior noncommissioned officers to wait twelve rather than eight years to qualify for a commission. Strike leaders were arrested, but the demands were met and the Air Force Commander retired prematurely.[10] Mubarak's strategy for coping with the overall crisis in civil-military relations was soon to restore the military's self-esteem and much of the status and influence it had lost in the Sadat era, but at a price to his personal power that has become far higher than he must originally have anticipated.

MUBARAK AND ABU GHAZALA

It is entirely consistent with Mubarak's background and personality that he would seek to restore the military's eroded sense of purpose and some of its political influence when he replaced Sadat. Very much a military man in upbringing, outlook, and demeanor, Mubarak must have been discomfited by Sadat's ceaseless manipulation of the officer corps and by the ambiguity that had come to surround its new role in a state no longer at war. Sadat, who from his youth had been an eccentric, radical nationalist, who among the Free Officers had spent the briefest time on active military duty, and whose close friends were almost invariably civilians, had chosen not to control the military through relations of trust with the high command but through the manipulation of it. By contrast, Nasser, also a radical nationalist but much more a true product of the military, placated this crucial institution of power by indulging it and by relating to it through his comrade Abd al-Hakim Amer. Mubarak demonstrated within months of coming to power that in at least this regard he was a Nasserite. Not only did he set about reassuring the officer corps that there would be no further cutbacks and that the military's "peace" role would be enhanced, but he also opted to permit a latter-day Amer to emerge in the person of Abd al-Halim Abu Ghazala.

Abu Ghazala, whose stable and attractive personality is the very antithesis of Amer's eccentricity, was the ideal candidate to become Mubarak's man in the military. Despite the fact that Mubarak and Abu Ghazala were classmates at the Military Academy from 1947 to 1949, the two-year age gap between the two facilitated and underlined Mubarak's authority. Abu Ghazala and Mubarak had not been in competitive positions in the armed forces, because the former is an artillery specialist while the latter is a bomber pilot. Both had trained in the Soviet Union, their tours there actually overlapping briefly in 1961. From 1976 until 1979 while Abu Ghazala was Defence Attache in Washington and

Mubarak was Vice President, the two worked closely in developing the military aid program with the United States. On the death of Chief of Staff Ahmad Badawi Mubarak urged Sadat to appoint Abu Ghazala to that key post. That their personal relationship is comparatively intimate is suggested by the frequency with which their families exchange visits. Mubarak's passion for squash is paralleled by Abu Ghazala's dedication to tennis, and in most other regards the two men are entirely typical products of the military system. That Abu Ghazala's career was to parallel that of Amer's was signaled in 1982 when in addition to holding the portfolio of Defence and Military Production he was elevated to Field Marshal and subsequently to Deputy Prime Minister, posts that he has retained until this time.

But while Mubarak and Abu Ghazala possess personal characteristics and shared experiences that facilitate this sensitive and politically crucial relationship, in fact the two men are as unlike as chalk and cheese. Abu Ghazala is an articulate, forceful, ambitious figure who impresses those around him. His off-the-record meetings with U.S. reporters, in contrast to those with Mubarak, leave the audience impressed with his grasp of facts and figures, receptivity to ideas, and ability to address points directly and concisely.[11] Whereas Mubarak is a man who gives the impression of having had the presidency thrust upon him and having out of a sense of duty resolved to do the best job possible, Abu Ghazala gives every sign of thirsting for the position and wanting to use it to put a program into effect. Abu Ghazala cuts a dashing figure compared to Mubarak's thickset physique. In the immediate aftermath of Sadat's assassination the contrast was highlighted before world television audiences. Abu Ghazala stood erect, pointing his baton at the fleeing assassins and yelling orders to give chase. Mubarak had crawled under chairs and was extricated by bodyguards who bundled him away unceremoniously. In addition to radiating dynamism, Abu Ghazala seems blessed with good luck. He and the President frequently rotate attendance at important soccer matches, Mubarak having the ill fortune of being present at an embarrassingly large number of defeats. This association, which began not long after Mubarak became president, persisted and intensified until by 1986 it had become a joke gone sour. Miraculously, in the summer of that year, the Egyptian team won the Africa Cup as Mubarak cheered them on, an occasion that was seized upon to lay to rest the image of Mubarak as a loser. The competition was immediately renamed the Mubarak Cup.

The political beliefs and behavior of the President and his Minister of Defence also differ substantively and stylistically. Mubarak, a managerial type by temperament, has sought to integrate various trends in Egyptian politics, or at least to prevent long-standing hostilities from making a mockery of appeals for political harmony, and to restore some balance in Egypt's foreign relations.[12] Abu Ghazala, on the other hand, is an outspoken conservative and fervent anticommunist. At the outset of the Mubarak presidency Abu Ghazala declared that "The primary goal of the Soviets is to reclaim Egypt"; that "If Egypt is lost the entire Arab World will fall under Soviet feet"; and that "The one way to secure the Middle East and Africa together is to expel the Soviets from the region."[13] He is correspondingly pro-U.S. He has asserted that Egypt's security is inseparable from that of the United States and NATO and argued that Arab forces should be coordinated with the U.S.'s Rapid Deployment Force (now the Central Command) so that the latter could pose a credible threat to Soviet expansionism.[14] He strongly favors the participation of U.S. multinational corporations in the Egyptian economy. The Field Marshal, for example, was the Chairman of the Higher Committee for the Egyptian Passenger Car, a post from which he directed the effort to terminate the quarter-century relationship between Fiat and the public-sector firm NASCO, which assembled various of the Italian carmaker's models. Abu Ghazala succeeded in replacing this arrangement with a contract tying NASCO to General Motors and giving the latter a monopoly on new-car sales in Egypt. In contrast to Mubarak's unhesitating preference for secularism, Abu Ghazala has cultivated an image of devoutness and is popular within many religious circles. His wife, almost alone among those of cabinet ministers, wears the *hijab* (Islamic headgear) on public occasions.

The Mubarak–Abu Ghazala relationship, like that of Nasser and Amer before it, has been subjected to stress and strain since 1981 as the President has intermittently sought to restrain his ebullient Minister of Defence. Invoking the provision of the Constitution promulgated under Sadat that prohibits military personnel on active duty from joining political parties, Mubarak removed Abu Ghazala from the Political Bureau of the National Democratic Party in November 1984. Unlike Nasser, Mubarak has not given his Minister of Defence a free reign when making high-level appointments. The President is able to draw on his numerous personal connections within the military elite to monitor the ebb and flow of alliances there. The reshuffle of the senior officer corps in the autumn of 1983 has been interpreted as an attempt by Mubarak to place officers loyal to him in positions of greater influence and to give a warning to any that doubted his authority.[15] A critical indicator of the balance of power between Mubarak and Abu Ghazala concerns the appointment of Chief of Staff. Abu Ghazala has been able to resist the appointment to that key post of a figure who could easily succeed him, although he has not been able to put one of his loyalists into the post either. Mubarak's first Chief of Staff, General Abd al-Nabi Hafiz, was popular with fellow officers but was not a highly respected figure and was in fact sacked after mysteriously vanishing for two weeks, a period he was rumored to have spent in Alexandria with his mistress. Hafiz's replacement, General Ibrahim Abd al-Ghaffur al-Arabi, is a rather dour person who had no conspicuous personal following in the ranks, although his background of training in the Soviet Union, his continued preference for Soviet-style military strategy, his poor relations with U.S.

advisers, and the fact that he was allowed some key appointments as well as occasional press coverage suggest that he was intended by Mubarak to be a partial counter-weight to Abu Ghazala and to the pro-U.S. tendency in higher ranks.[16]

Personnel changes in the civilian elite suggest that Abu Ghazala has been able further to expand his influence since 1985. Mubarak's first two prime ministers, Fuad Muhyi al-Din and Kamal Hassan Ali, were both strong figures who competed in the cabinet with Abu Ghazala, had their own connections into the military, and therefore restrained the Minister of Defence, albeit with difficulty.[17] But with the replacement of Kamal Hassan Ali in September 1985 by the economist Ali Lutfi, the way was thrown open for Abu Ghazala and, at a lower level, two or three other ministers to carve out substantial domains in the cabinet and beyond. Ali Lutfi's low public profile automatically elevated Abu Ghazala's public exposure. For the first time in the Mubarak presidency the Minister of Defence could be seen more frequently in the daily press than the Prime Minister.

Mubarak lost yet another round to Abu Ghazala in the wake of the Central Security Force (CSF) riots of 25–26 February 1986, when he was obliged to dismiss the Minister of Interior, Ahmad Rushdi. An efficient, honest, if uncompromising and stubborn person, Rushdi had been inserted into Kamal Hassan Ali's government, in part as an additional counterweight to Abu Ghazala. His function in that capacity was further accentuated with the replacement of Ali by the much weaker Ali Lutfi. Rushdi had a clean image and was seen by Mubarak as a tool with which to whittle down the power of various pernicious elements, such as drug dealers and their protectors in the security apparatuses. But the CSF riots were Rushdi's Waterloo, prompting many wags to comment that the disturbances had been fomented by the military and its leader in order to remove another obstacle to their aggrandizement. Rushdi's successor, Zaki Badr, is a throwback to the pre-Rushdi era, his name being widely associated with illegal activities, especially drug dealing. He is a highly contentious figure as a result of his undiscriminating attacks on the political opposition. And his appointment caused serious divisions within the Ministry of Interior itself. Badr, despite his readiness to use heavy handed methods, lacks the image, finesse, and unified base of support to counterbalance Abu Ghazala.[18]

Just as Mubarak's juggling of personnel has failed to hem in Abu Ghazala, so did the catastrophic riots of February 1986 reveal that the Ministry of Interior was incapable of maintaining public order, to say nothing of counterbalancing the military. The CSF, composed largely of potential army recruits who fail the military's increasingly strict entrance requirements, had been created in the wake of the 1967 defeat to obviate military involvement in riot control. By Nasser's death it numbered 100,000 and under Nabawi Ismail, Sadat's Minister of Interior, it mushroomed to over 300,000. The military looked upon this motley collection of illiterate peasants with very mixed feelings. On the one hand it did not want to be involved in suppressing public disorder, but it did not favor resources being allocated to another barracked force. This accounts in part for the monthly pay of CSF soldiers being the outrageously inadequate sum of £E6. When the CSF rose in revolt, only to be crushed by the army, it destroyed the illusion that the Ministry of Interior could guarantee public security, underlining the reality that the real protector of the regime was the military. This of course further elevated Abu Ghazala, raising the President's indebtedness to him.

Unable to rely on military or cabinet personnel or even on the Ministry of Interior as significant restraints on Abu Ghazala, Mubarak likewise could not count on the unwavering support of his chief foreign backer, the United States, in the event of a showdown with the Minister of Defence. This was made evident in October and then again in November of 1985, when Mubarak and Abu Ghazala differed over how to resolve the Achille Lauro affair and the subsequent Egypt Air hijacking. Mubarak, not wanting to jeopardize Egypt's reintegration into the Arab World, decided secretly to give safe passage aboard an Egyptian plane to the Achille Lauro hijackers. Abu Ghazala, on the other hand, who is more sensitive to the Reagan Administration's preoccupation with terrorism, wanted to apprehend them.[19] Interceptors from the Sixth Fleet duly forced the Egyptian plane to land in Sicily not long after Mubarak's dissimulation before a global television audience. The upshot of the affair was unruly student demonstrations at Ain Shams University, opposition-sponsored protests at al-Azhar mosque, and a quick visit by U.S. Deputy Secretary of State John Whitehead to repair the damage.

The following month an Egypt Air flight was hijacked and diverted to Malta, where it was detained until a plane carrying Egyptian commandos and three senior U.S. military advisers, including the head of the U.S. military mission in Egypt, arrived. In the "rescue" operation that followed more than half the passengers on board were killed. A public relations disaster ensued when Minister of Information Safwat al-Sharif gave orders for the mission to be portrayed as a success. That effort unraveled in the face of the unpleasant facts that filtered quickly into Egypt through the BBC and other world media sources. The articulate public did not blame Mubarak for this debacle, however, it being virtually universally assumed that the "rescue" mission was ordered and organized by Abu Ghazala.

There is evidence that at this point Mubarak attempted to remove the irrepressible Abu Ghazala from the Ministry of Defence. Aware that the Field Marshal possessed a substantial base of domestic support and had the confidence and respect of key decision-makers in Washington, Mubarak dangled the Vice Presidency in front of him in the hope that it could induce him voluntarily to take his finger off the trigger. Abu Ghazala reportedly accepted the offer on the condition that he retain the Defence portfolio.[20] Before events moved to a showdown the U.S.

Embassy let it be known that it would look unfavorably on the transfer of Abu Ghazala from his current post.[21] There the matter remained until the CSF riots some three months later, which forced Mubarak to fall back on the military and its chief and so abandon the effort to pry Abu Ghazala out of his post.

The abortive move against Abu Ghazala, which began in October and ended in February, was accompanied by efforts to trim his influence by various ways and means. One report claims that Mubarak ordered editors to reduce considerably Abu Ghazala's press coverage—and indeed during this period his photograph appeared less frequently than it had previously or it has since February 1986.[22] Moreover, Chief of Staff Arabi's photo appeared several times while the behind-the-scenes struggle was in progress, but rarely again after its conclusion. On the policy front Abu Ghazala was also losing ground. A project to reclaim some 10,000 *feddan*-s in West Nubariya, for which tenders had been invited by the military but against which a rearguard action was being fought by civilian technocrats in the General Authority for Reclamation and Development of Agricultural Projects in the Ministry of Land Reclamation, was suddenly and inexplicably, after three years of dueling, transferred from the military to civilians. The message received by those who monitor such events was that Mubarak was moving against Abu Ghazala.[23]

As events transpired, however, Abu Ghazala bounced back stronger than ever and began immediately after the February riots to demonstrate that in future he and the military would play an even larger role. In the following year his picture appeared in the press almost as often as Mubarak's and in some weeks even more frequently. Crucial new responsibilities were added to his long list of duties. Particularly noteworthy was the fact that in June and November 1986, he headed missions to the United States to discuss mutual relations. Although the military debt was a critical feature of those negotiations, they also encompassed a much wider range of economic issues, including the sensitive "reforms" that Washington and the IMF have long sought to impose on Egypt. On Abu Ghazala's return from Washington in June the entire cabinet was marshaled at the airport to greet him, Prime Minister Ali Lutfi conspicuously in the background. The drumbeat of announcements of new tasks to be undertaken by the military, from treating civilians in military hospitals to cleaning the polluted beaches, grew at such a pace Egyptians were left wondering what, if any, civilian activities were to be left untouched. As if to add insult to the already injured civilian sector, the opening ceremonies for new military undertakings, including chicken farms and new cities in the desert, became in 1986 occasions on which the appropriate ministers had to tag along behind Abu Ghazala to give their blessings to the latest encroachments into their domain. In the fall of 1987 the military leaked the findings of its "secret" study of the 1973 war, which laid the blame for the defeat with the "political leadership."[24]

The relentless assault by the military and its leader clearly transcends what would result from only a personal connection between the President and the Minister of Defence. While that relationship has facilitated the expansion of the political role of the military, it conceivably could reverse the process in the event of a contretemps. But the possibility of that occurring may already have passed, for the paradox of the sultan, described by Weber as the process whereby the ruler's increased reliance on the military gradually transforms him from superior to subordinate, has begun to take shape.[25] The military's new defense role, including its drive for "self-sufficiency," its expansion into economic enclaves that had been recivilianized under Sadat, and its ability to forge coalitions with key elements of the bourgeoisie, including its political representatives, indicate that Mubarak is caught up in a process from which escape may be impossible.

MILITARY SELF-SUFFICIENCY
AND THE EXPANSION OF PATRONAGE

Abd al-Hakim Amer extended his clientage network down into the military during a time of institutional expansion, whereas Abu Ghazala has accomplished the same during a period of personnel contraction. The "professionalization" of the military has facilitated his achievement. The shrinkage of the military to between 300,000 and 450,000 men[26] has been accomplished by shedding a disproportionate number of lower-ranking and ill-qualified soldiers while retaining commissioned officers, resulting in a top-heavy military.[27] Of the five categories of conscripts, the lowest, being the illiterates, have been foisted off onto the CSF. Other recruits have had their period of conscription reduced from two years to one.[28] Abu Ghazala has applied constant pressure in the cabinet for salary raises for his officers and has met with regular success.[29] Increasing military cooperation between Egypt and the West has provided various benefits for Egyptian officers. Up to 200 per year are trained in the United States on direct government-to-government contracts.[30] Considerably more train on weapons systems purchased from U.S. suppliers. Military facilities, vehicles, and even uniforms have been significantly upgraded. The constant flow of state-of-the-art weaponry, even if in quantities considerably less than those being obtained by Israeli or even Saudi forces, provides a basis upon which military self-esteem can comfortably rest.[31]

An even more critical ingredient in the growth of Abu Ghazala's patronage system has been the provision of a wide range of new benefits to officers, the consequence of which has been to create a neoMamlukian military elite that lives in virtual isolation from civilian society. Nasr City, adjacent to Heliopolis and its military academy, large base, and military factories, has become a modern version of tenth-century Fatimid Cairo, which was constructed alongside the commercial metropolis of

Fustat to house the army and retinue of the Caliph Muizz. Thousands of relatively sumptuous flats have been built along Nasr City's wide boulevards for purchase at highly subsidized prices by officers, for many of whom this becomes a second, third, or fourth source of rental income. Due almost entirely to construction for the military, Nasr City has become the fastest-growing district in Cairo, its population having leapt to a quarter of a million in 1986 from less than 100,000 ten years earlier.[32] Nasr City is not the only location at which housing for the military is springing up. In 1985–86 almost 5 percent of all housing constructed in the country was built by and for the military.[33] A substantial percentage of this is in the new military cities scattered in the desert, principally around Cairo. Two such cities were inaugurated in November 1986, while ten others are scheduled for completion by July 1988. Reported plans call variously for 17 to 30 of these self-contained cities, each of which is ultimately to house 50,000 to 150,000 residents.[34] The facilities therein are intended to provide officers and their families with a standard of living equivalent to what they would expect in Nasr City, as the following enticing newspaper report promises: "Permanent officers have special family apartments in separate quarters . . . equipped with nurseries and primary, preparatory and secondary schools."[35] All of this is to be provided at no apparent cost to the state, which may indeed be the case if Abu Ghazala's creative bookkeeping provides the reckoning of debits and credits. He has authorized the selling for development of land belonging to the military that formerly provided the main sites for camps immediately adjacent to Egypt's largest cities and that is therefore now exceedingly valuable. Another credit to the military's account is to come in the form of sales of land in military cities to civilians who want to escape to the desert to avoid the trials and tribulations of life in the congested Nile Valley.[36]

A chain of military consumer "cooperatives" caters to the day-to-day requirements of officers and their families. They sell a range of domestic and imported goods generally unavailable elsewhere in Egypt, or only to be had at much higher prices. These pleasant shops, which cast the civilian consumer cooperatives into absurdly negative relief, are concentrated in the Heliopolis—Nasr City—Abbasiya area of Cairo where officers are congregated and presumably will in future also be found in the new military cities. Having a friend in the military who can provide access to these "cooperatives," hence to such basic goods as sugar and rice that are elsewhere in chronic short supply, is now a mark of distinction for struggling civilians. Officers and their families also benefit from military hospitals that serve their health needs, a chain of military resorts providing for their holidays, and a military travel service operating in Egypt and overseas.

Entrance into this neoMamlukian, autonomous military world is regulated by an increasingly separate and exclusive educational system. Access to the Military Academy in Heliopolis requires a combination of examination results and influence. The prestige that this institution has attained is reflected in the behavior of Cairo taxi drivers, who invariably stop for military cadets, in their distinctive West-Point style uniforms, while passing civilians by. Proud to have the cream of Egypt's youth aboard, they provide the ride gratis with surprising frequency. The Military Technical College has also been significantly upgraded since 1981 and has been assigned a wide variety of new research tasks for which resources have been readily forthcoming at a time when universities are being starved of funds. The operation of the increasingly complex military empire requires considerable administrative expertise. For that purpose Abu Ghazala called for the creation of a Military Academy for Administrative Sciences, enabling legislation for which was passed by the People's Assembly on 14 June 1986. The staff in military hospitals are now being trained in the Academy of Military Medicine.[37]

While the entire officer corps has access to the housing, educational, health, consumer, and recreational facilities provided by the military, a more select number are directly engaged in procurement of military hardware and other commodities. The opposition claims that illegal commissions paid to these officers vastly inflate prices for military equipment. In one case an alleged $12 million was paid to unnamed members of the high command by the Canadian company that successfully marketed its Buffalo aircraft.[38] Another notorious deal involved the initial arms shipment from the United States to Egypt following the signing of the Camp David accords. For the purpose of shipping the $300 million consignment, a company was formed by President Sadat's brother Ismat and several generals, who are alleged to have charged some four to five times the Pentagon's estimate for shipping costs.[39] Ismat Sadat was subsequently tried for other offenses, but not in the regular court system, which may well have investigated this matter. He was instead brought before the special "Court of Ethics," which was set up by his brother to deal with rising dissent after he signed the peace treaty with Israel and which paradoxically provided Mubarak a convenient forum within which to discredit and convict a handful of prominent *munfatihun*, while containing the scope of judicial inquiries, so that the entire edifice of the regime not be shaken.

Another allegation about the involvement of officers in lucrative and corrupt practices concerns operation of the Port of Alexandria, a veritable gold mine. Among the various irregularities unaccountably escaping the notice of Port Director General Faruq al-Zawil is an insurance rip-off, which was reduced to acceptable proportions by the intervention of Lloyds of London after the greed of those responsible reached truly alarming proportions.[40] Normal pilferage and the extraction of bribes for services rendered have not, however, been affected by this intervention. Nor has the operation of the Alexandria Stevedore Company been curtailed despite howls of protest from the stevedores' union and the opposition. They allege various illegal practices, including monopolization of access to warehouse facilities. This company, formed in 1984 by officers who formerly worked for the Port Authority, is one of several similarly constituted private-sector firms that were authorized in 1978 to compete in an area that previously had been a public-sector monopoly.[41]

HORIZONTAL MILITARY EXPANSION

Military Manufacturing

The vertical integration of the military structure, which has converted it into an almost entirely autonomous enclave of middle-class modernity in an increasingly impoverished and marginalized Third World economy, has been paralleled by a vast proliferation of its activities, facilitating access to patronage resources and, in so doing, reinforcing Abu Ghazala's grip on the institution. Horizontal expansion has occurred in the three basic areas of manufacturing, especially weapons production; agriculture and land reclamation; and construction and service industries.

Both Nasser and Sadat attempted to establish significant weapons and munitions manufacturing capabilities, but neither succeeded. Nasser's efforts were foiled by a shortage of funds, erratic commitment, and by the ill-advised use of former Nazi experts, whose expertise was questionable and whose presence in Egypt stimulated Israeli sabotage efforts.[42] Sadat sought to invigorate the arms industry through the creation in 1975 of the Arab Organization for Industrialization (AOI), which was to draw on Arab capital and Western technical assistance to facilitate the manufacture of weapons in Egypt, whose capital share in the undertaking was provided in the form of four military factories. AOI foundered when the Gulf states withdrew their capital in the wake of Camp David. There were also persistent rumors about the financial improprieties of Ashraf Marwan, Nasser's son-in-law and the AOI's main contact with the Europeans and the Saudis.[43]

But the organizational shell of the AOI, renamed the Egyptian Organization for Industrialization, the physical infrastructure already in place, and the additional resources of the newly created Military Production Industries provided a base from which assembly and manufacturing operations were to be rapidly expanded after 1981. The achievements of this effort far exceed those of previous regimes. By 1984 Egypt had reached self-sufficiency in the manufacture of small arms, mortars, and most calibers of ammunition and was nearly so in rockets and howitzers.[44] The Saqr factory, in Heliopolis adjacent to the airport, employs more than 5,000 and has shifted from the production of Katyushas to making infrared-seeking portable surface-to-air missiles based on the Soviet SA-7. Britain's Westland, which withdrew from an agreement to produce Lynx helicopters once Arab funds were no longer at Egypt's disposal, was replaced in 1983 by France's Aerospatiale, which is cooperating with Egypt in the production of Gazelle helicopters. The first locally assembled Franco-German Alpha jets were handed over to the air force in November 1982. For several years Egypt has been negotiating a coproduction agreement with Dassault for the Mirage 2000, and at one stage there were reports that some coproduction would be involved in the F16 deal, eventually signed in January 1987, which will boost Egypt's inventory of these advanced fighters from 80 to 120. Over 100 Tucano trainer jets from Brazil are now being assembled. In addition to the expansion of small arms, artillery, and aircraft manufacture, military electronics capabilities have also been upgraded. The Benha Electronics factory alone employs over 2,500 workers and currently produces various military electronic systems. It is scheduled to be the company that assembles Westinghouse radar equipment, when and if that long-delayed deal ever comes off.

The endless stream of new weapons systems emerging from military factories provides innumerable occasions for public self-congratulation by the military brass. With the unveiling of a new night-vision range-finder in early 1987, for example, the project's director, Major General Midhat Mustafa, chronicled the sending of Egyptian experts to Britain, Singapore, West Germany, and the United States for training and the building of an ultramodern factory in sterile desert conditions. He concluded by observing that Egypt is now improving on original designs, begging questions of credibility and of cost efficiency.[45] An impartial estimate of the net rate of return on such an investment would likely reveal these to be among the world's most expensive range-finders.

In addition to providing for some 60 percent of the Egyptian military's needs,[46] the arms industries export significant quantitites of weapons and ammunition, their best customer being Iraq. The proceeds from such exports are, however, a military secret and are not included in national accounts or reported to parliament. There is, consequently, confusion about the exact volume of these exports. In 1984 it was claimed that the gross figure already exceeded $1 billion,[47] while at the end of 1986 it was stated that exports had climbed to $800 million.[48] Paul Jabber stated in 1986, however, that exports to Iraq alone in 1983 exceeded $1 billion,[49] so all that can be said with certainty is that arms exports are substantial. The secrecy that surrounds the subject has given rise to controversy over the destination of those arms. When the U.S. press reported in the midst of the unfolding Iran arms scandal that Egypt had sent eleven planeloads of arms to Iran, the Egyptian government flatly denied it. A week later al-Gumhuriya reported that foreigners, including Adnan Kashoggi, had made three attempts to buy Egyptian arms, but that they were rejected when it was revealed the arms were intended for Iran.[50] Abu Ghazala himself reiterated denials of secret deals with Iran before a student audience in February 1987.[51]

Even more confusion surrounds the profitability of military industries. Despite a persistent clamoring in the summer of 1986 by the opposition for the accounts of such enterprises to be brought under the jurisdiction of the Central Auditing Organization (hereafter CAO), Egypt's equivalent of the U.S. General Accounting Organization, no action was taken, although some relevant information was brought to light. *al-Ahrar*, mouthpiece of the conservative Liberal Party, alleged that one factory alone had lost £E20 million in two years.[52] According to this source, a report of the Directorate of Supervision (*al-Raqaba al-Idariya*) describes General Abbas Abd al-Gawad, chairman of the board of military factory 360, as having abused his position by misappropriating funds, conducting secret deals with Italian firms, and distributing company property "to high officials in various sectors of the state."[53] Amin Huwaidi, who had served as Minister of Defence and Director of Intelligence under Nasser, claimed in the National Progressive Unionist Party's *al-Ahali* that Egypt could not compete with similar arms manufacturing nations, such as Israel, Brazil, Argentina, and Taiwan, and that the United States and other Western countries would regulate the flow of technology to ensure their own domination of world markets. He estimated that of the annual defense budget, which he claimed to be £E7 billion, at least £E1 billion could be saved were the armed forces to disengage from their various nonmilitary activities and from arms manufacturing.[54] Hilmi Murad observed in the organ of the Socialist Labor Party, *al-Shaab*, that in the absence of accounting or other control over these enterprises, misappropriation and misallocation of funds were likely.[55]

But accurate cost accounting might not in any case come to terms with the underlying structural distortion of the military receiving manufacturing inputs, including energy, at subsidized prices. All enterprises manufacturing for export are by law to be charged so-called world rates for their inputs, and while that law is not uniformly enforced, only the military is absolutely and permanently exempted. The resulting difference in cost structure is appreciable. Electricity, for example, is provided at a subsidized rate of well less than one-half the world rate, while petroleum products are around a quarter of their world market price. Egypt, in short, is subsidizing its military exports, payment for which goes directly to the military and not into national accounts. On paper, therefore, these industries could well appear profitable, while in fact constituting a large net loss in national income.

Nonmilitary Manufacturing

Having established a manufacturing base in weapons production, the military is now beginning to branch out into other areas of industry, a process that can antagonize civilians but that can also cement the shared interests of civilian and military managers and those between the military and the bourgeoisie more generally. The Benha Electronics Company, for example, has been selected by the military to assemble various gadgets of electronic warfare. Benha's management has mastered the technique of extracting commissions from Western appliance suppliers, a lesson that can be readily applied to its military operations.[56] Just as the military has created its own *infitah*, so is its alliance with public and private sector enterprise and its proliferation of arms industries creating a class of military, and military-dependent, *munfatihun*.

The most prominent example of military intervention into civilian industry was the General Motors deal, which after two years of negotiations was finally signed in June 1986. As Chairman of the Higher Committee for the Egyptian Passenger Car, Abu Ghazala worked closely with the U.S. Embassy, in particular the Commercial Counselor, Ted Rosen, and Ambassador Nicholas Veliotes, in preparing a package that could compete with bids from Fiat, Peugeot, and Japanese car manufacturers.[57] GM, originally reluctant to come to the party, was enticed with a pledge by USAID that up to $200 million of its aid budget for Egypt would be channeled to GM in order to guarantee profitability.[58] This redirection of aid funds was forced on the USAID Cairo office by Rosen and Veliotes, Abu Ghazala's personal involvement and his commitment to GM being used to persuade reluctant USAID officials to take up an opportunity that they should not, out of obligation to U.S. national interests, allow to be passed up. Several USAID staffers objected strongly, arguing that this diversion made a mockery of the aid program, that the planned operation could not achieve economies of scale so would yield a strongly negative net economic return, and that Abu Ghazala's real interest was the construction of an engine plant from which military vehicles could be outfitted. These staffers were transferred to other duties. GM, which had privately informed USAID that it had no intention of ever building an engine plant in Egypt, told Abu Ghazala that it was interested in establishing an engine plant but that it would delay that phase until the assembly operation was properly up and running.[59] Apparently unsure as to whether Abu Ghazala had enough clout on his own to secure the contract for them, GM executives retained the services of Niyazi Mustafa, one of Egypt's wealthiest entrepreneurs, with interests in hotels, construction, agriculture and land reclamation, and who years earlier had acted as GM agent for a large locomotive deal. The GM-NASCO agreement embodied the alliance of the military and the bourgeoisie and its linkage to international capital.

The deal immediately confronted howls of protest, not only from the opposition but from prominent figures in the regime, not the least of whom was Adil Gazarini, the former head of NASCO and, together with former Prime Minister Aziz Sidqi, the architect of the almost 25-year-old NASCO-Fiat partnership. U.S. officials responded with hints that Gazarini had grown rich pocketing kickbacks from Fiat over the years. The GM deal, they claimed, constituted an offer simply too good to refuse.[60]

The opposition did not see it this way. In addition to a host of criticisms centered on allegations of corruption and chicanery, the estimated high price of the product, redirection of USAID funds, and so on, Abu Ghazala's intimate involvement in the affair caused them to believe much more was afoot. The editor of *al-Shaab* alleged that the GM deal was part of a larger scheme cooked up between the United States government and the Egyptian military, whereby the latter was trading rights to use Egyptian bases for access, through GM, to U.S. technology for arms and nonmilitary manufacturing.[61] This assessment was echoed by the leftist *al-Ahali*.[62] According to the *al-Shaab* editor, another reason why the U.S. Embassy pushed GM so hard is that it was a tool of the "normalization" process with Israel. GM's Israeli operations would be called upon to supply technical expertise and components, thus giving Israel access through the back door that it so far has been denied at the front. According to this view Abu Ghazala is not averse to the "normalization" process and seeks only to turn it to his and the military's advantage.[63]

What is indisputably true about the GM deal is that Abu Ghazala played the most important role in steering its acceptance through the labyrinthian approval process, thereby demonstrating his and the military's encroachment into civilian manufacturing. Indeed, that process is more appropriately termed colonization, for instead of military industries emerging from the civilian manufacturing sector, as was their history in North America, Europe, and Japan, they spring to life in Egypt as a result of bilateral agreements between the Egyptian military and foreign arms manufacturers. Egyptian nonmilitary industries that can provide inputs into weapons manufacturing, such as Benha Electronics, are incorporated into this system. The managerial elites of these companies become in a very real sense part of the military-industrial complex, although in a far more subordinate role than their U.S. counterparts. A related aspect of the military's colonization of the industrial sector is its increasing production of civilian goods, which in 1985–86 amounted to a total value of about £E250 million.[64] In sum, the expansion of armaments and civilian goods manufacturing in military factories and the militarization of domestic industry have grown at a remarkable pace since 1982. In the meantime, the domestic nonmilitary industrial sector has stagnated. If the figure of $1 billion for arms exports is correct, Egypt now exports approximately three times more weapons and ammunition than it does all other noncotton-based industrial products combined.[65]

The consequences for domestic and foreign policy of the growth of the arms industry under the military's tutelage are wide-ranging, for which one example will presently suffice. Egypt is exporting annually, according to Paul Jabber, $1 billion worth of arms and ammunition to Iraq. The Egyptian Ministry of Foreign Affairs, among whose primary goals is the reintegration of Egypt into the Arab World, for several years sought to use the leverage of arms shipments to force Saddam Hussein to recognize Egypt and thus pave the way for other Arab states to follow suit. In that effort Foreign Affairs was frustrated by the military, which argued that its highly profitable business should not be jeopardized by the meddling of civilian bureaucrats.

Agriculture and Land Reclamation

The *Gihaz al-Khidma al-Wataniya,* designated in English as the National Service Projects Organization (NSPO, as shown on the shiny black badges sported by its members), was created by the military in 1978 to undertake projects in what were, at that time, exclusively civilian sectors of the economy. It remained more or less dormant until Abu Ghazala, in the wake of Sadat's death, seized on it as the principal organizational vehicle for broadening military activities. It suited his purposes admirably in that it was a semimilitary authority, which meant that he could appoint its staff from within the military without regard to normal considerations of rank, seniority, or civil service regulations. More importantly, it has its own budget and bank account and is not subject to the CAO.

Justifying its move into agricultural production and land reclamation by the argument that national security, for which the military is officially responsible, depends on "food security," the NSPO in 1982 plucked responsibility for those activities from the army's veterinary corps, in whose care they had been placed in 1974 when the idea of the military engaging in civilian pursuits was first initiated. The activities were deposited with a new Food Security Division (FSD), headed by General Muhammad Assam al-Din Gohar. The FSD was charged by the military high command with the task of making the military 100 percent self-sufficient in foodstuffs.[66]

General Gohar, like his fellow officers in the NSPO, has nothing but contempt for civilian bureaucracies and public-sector companies involved in his sphere of competence. He argues that Egypt's problems since Nasser are due to the fact that *ahl al-thiqa* (people of trust, i.e., cronies) have been put in charge, while real experts have been ignored entirely or not promoted. The military, according to Gohar, is a performance-oriented organization that is able to break through deadlocks that have hampered production in the civilian sector.[67] He is, in short, a contemporary version of the irrepressible Magdi Hassanain, the Free Officer who Nasser placed in charge of the showcase Tahrir Province land reclamation scheme and who came to symbolize the military's impatience with the civilian sector,[68] and to represent the arrogance, spendthrift ways, and, ultimately, corruption of the military.[69]

With the ample financial resources of the NSPO behind it and virtually limitless supplies of personnel provided gratis from the military, the FSD became almost overnight the single largest agro-industrial organization in Egypt. Concentrating in high-value, high-technology areas, by 1985 the FSD had blanketed the country with dairy farms and milk processing facilities, integrated poultry complexes, fish farms, and cattle feedlots. In 1986 it launched a drive into fruit and vegetable production and marketing, opening ceremoniously under Abu Ghazala's watchful eye on the day of its name the 6 October Agro-Industrial Complex, which was designed to produce 30,000 tons of fruits and vegetables, much of it in plastic houses, on 7,500 *feddan*-s.[70] Three weeks later Abu Ghazala again personally inaugurated an FSD project, this one an automated vegetable wrapping and packing plant that was to accomplish with 300 conscripts what 2,000–2,500 had been doing in the past. Like most of the FSD agro-industrial complexes, this one was to provide the military with the bulk of its output, the remainder being sold to the civilian sector at "40 percent below market price," or allocated to hospitals and universities.[71] The previous month the FSD had announced that it would soon begin production in its new dairy factory, which was to absorb one quarter of Egypt's milk production and produce enough dairy products to satisfy the entire local market.[72]

The £E488 million worth of food produced by the FSD in 1985–1986 was some 18 percent of the total value of food produced in Egypt that year.[73] It also makes food production the single most important activity undertaken by the NSPO, which in the same year produced £E347 million of manufactured nonmilitary goods, spent £E174 million on constructing buildings and installations, and provided additional services worth £E144 million. The FSD produced between 3 and 4 percent of all white and red meat and fish consumed in the country in 1985.[74] While no figures are available on the operating costs, fixed capital, or workforce of the FSD, or of the NSPO for that matter, it is clear that the FSD's annual budget is in the hundreds of millions and that it employs a labor force in the tens of thousands.

The military has also once again begun to reclaim land. Precisely because this had become during the Nasser period a preserve of the officer corps that was then progressively civilianized and even privatized under Sadat, the resurgence of activity in this area by the military has rekindled old fears and hostilities. Moreover, by the 1980s it was not just the bureaucracy and public-sector land reclamation companies that stood to lose by the military's involvement. Large private-sector concerns, innumerable cooperatives formed of investors and individuals working the land, private individuals, foreign companies working on contract for landowners, and last, but by no means least, Osman Ahmad Osman's Arab Contractors Company, which is responsible for the 56,000 *feddan* showcase Salhiya project, had all entered the field during the Sadat period and did not want to be brushed aside by the military. Erecting agro-industrial complexes did not impinge so directly on other interests. But anything to do with land, its ownership and utilization, contains the potential for heated conflict in Egypt, where its scarcity value is understandably ingrained in the national psyche. At a more mundane level the economic return through buying and selling wholly or partially reclaimed land or land simply earmarked for such work in the future has become, during the 1980s, one of the most profitable areas of economic speculation. That profitability was one of the reasons why Minister for Land Reclamation Hassab Allah al-Kafrawi, almost immediately after Sadat's death, reinstituted the dominant role of public-sector companies in this activity, for their profits accrue to his ministry. By designating an area for reclamation, installing a minimal amount of physical infrastructure, planting some windbreaks and maybe a few trees or vines, the land can be sold to private buyers for many times the cost of the bare land and improvements.[75]

So Abu Ghazala and the military had to tread warily in this area. They adopted two separate approaches. With regard to areas that were highly desirable, particularly for possible use as retirement or holiday sites by officers or because of proximity to urban areas, and for cases in which ownership was in any way disputable the military adopted a technique perfected by the Israeli military to dispossess Palestinians. Soldiers would arrive in such an area, declare it as designated for military maneuvers, and simply chase out any occupants.[76] In this way, for example, they seized six kilometers of prime beachfront at Sidi Khrair, west of Alexandria, in the summer of 1986.[77] Shortly thereafter the military police sealed off a large area on the outskirts of Nasr City that had been sold by a land company to private individuals. The officers claimed that the transaction by which the land company had acquired the parcel was illegal and that it belonged to them.[78] Needless to add, possession in such cases is well more than 90 percent of the law.

To obtain rights to reclaim very large tracts of land for which the state held indisputably valid title, the military worked out compromises with the Ministry of Land Reclamation and the public companies under its authority. This, however, was fraught with difficulties, for while Minister Kafrawi or the chairman of the board of a company might agree to specific proposals, employees further down in the system could, out of a variety of motives, impede the military's access. One such case was in Nubariya. Abu Ghazala had approached various foreign companies and governments within weeks of Sadat's death to assist the military in reclaiming this area. In the meantime the General Authority for Reclamation and Development of Agricultural Projects, one of the bureaucratic enclaves under the Minister of Land Reclamation, set to work to derail Abu Ghazala. Its top-ranking employees, invited to assess the proposals solicited by the Field Marshal (who at this stage was, along with the NSPO, trying to curry support within the bureaucracy) nitpicked their way through numerous proposals and managed to consume almost three years.[79] In the late fall of 1985 their delaying tactics paid off when the project was abruptly switched from the military to the Ministry of Land Reclamation, probably as a punishment for Abu Ghazala's meddling in the Achille Lauro and Egypt Air hijacking incidents.

But just a few months later, in the wake of the CSF riots, Abu Ghazala turned the tables. He gathered under his chairmanship in the cabinet a ten-member committee to decide land reclamation policy. He informed the committee that the *kataib* (regiments) that the NDP had formed of party youths for a general clean-up in the wake of the riots were such a good idea that the military henceforth would copy them, creating from among its ranks of conscripts "development regiments" that would number 30,000. They would be provided additional training in development after they completed boot camp.[80] On 16 May it was announced that this committee had decided to spend £E732 million on three reclamation projects, including £E600 million in Wadi Natroun.[81]

Abu Ghazala and the army had shown everyone who was boss. The money for these endeavors was now to come directly from the state treasury without interference by the Ministry of Land Reclamation or, for that matter, anyone else. This prompted opposition watchdog Hilmi Murad to complain that not only was the military now in control of a very large slice of public funds without any oversight by the CAO, but that the army lacked the requisite technical capability to reclaim and plant large tracts of desert.[82] This and other opposition condemnations were to no avail, for Abu Ghazala and the military were, in the wake of the CSF riots, indispensable. This was underlined during the train drivers' strike of July 1986, when the military again stepped in, this time by providing buses to transport stranded passengers.

Now in the driver's seat as chairman of the Policy Committee, Abu Ghazala could not only award the NSPO land for reclamation, but he could withhold it from his enemies. The latter include the public sector companies under the Ministry of Land Reclamation with whom the NSPO struggled from 1982 until 1986. Conversely, he has also been able to help his friends in this area, who are primarily former officers with interests in private-sector investment companies, as well as their counterparts from the civilian bourgeoisie. In February 1987, for example, Abu Ghazala announced that his committee was awarding 50,000 feddan-s in al-Awniyat in the western desert to such companies. He added that during the coming year research would be undertaken at the site on utilization of solar and wind power for water purification to allow reclamation of 2,000 feddan-s. That research would be conducted by the Military Technical College.[83]

The intentions of Abu Ghazala and the military with regard to land reclamation have now become manifest. Their dissatisfaction with what they perceive as the bureaucratic malaise that infects the public sector, combined with their desire for access to resources, has caused them to develop an autonomous capability, the management of which is concentrated in the NSPO, the personnel for which is drawn from the ranks of conscripts, and the necessary supplementary technical expertise solicited from various branches of the military, including the Technical College. Additionally, the military favors the private sector, not only because it perceives it as more dynamic and possessing superior resources, but also because of its ability generously to reciprocate favors granted. Unlike the patronage network within the land reclamation sector during the Nasser period, which was constructed in the nexus that linked the military to public sector companies, the system now being established rests on the principle of farming out patronage to the private sector which, like its public-sector predecessor, is to be the military's junior partner in these activities.

Infrastructural Development

Since 1981–1982 the military has taken on a series of physical and human infrastructural development projects worth in excess of £E300 million.[84] The motives behind this new departure—for even under Abd al-Hakim Amer the military did not spread its net so widely—are mixed. The principal justification is that the service currently is inadequately provided to the military and/or civilian sectors. This covers virtually any activity in the country.[85] Unstated motives include the desire to gain popular support, or at least to alleviate hostility toward the military for laying claim to the lion's share of the country's scarce resources; to absorb redundant military personnel; to provide the employment, foreign contracts, and goods and services that underpin the patronage network spreading downward from the high command and the Field Marshal himself; and to cement ties to the private sector while simultaneously undermining the civilian bureaucracy. A few examples are suggestive of the military's creative application of these guiding principles.

Among these high-profile projects of use to the military and to the civilian sector and with substantial public relations value are the Ramses overpass in central Cairo, which the military never tires of pointing out was constructed in record time (even faster than Osman's Arab Contractors' equivalent efforts), and the installation of new telephone lines, of which the military's share in the five-year plan of 1981/82–1985/6 was over 40 percent.[86] This accomplishment is likewise frequently claimed as proof of the military's abilities and its commitment to the general welfare. Privately, officers smugly compare the scandal that surrounded the government's acquisition of a new telephone system under Prime Minister Mustafa Khalil with their own probity and efficiency.[87]

Other projects are intended to glorify the military and its traditions. The new museum opened in Cairo's Citadel in 1986, for example, is devoted to "5,000 years of Egyptian military history" and is, in comparison to virtually any other museum in the country, lavishly appointed and equipped. The former naval vessel Mahrusa, which served as King Faruq's private yacht and on which he sailed into exile in July 1952, was restored by the navy on orders from Abu Ghazala, fitted out with appropriate antiquities, and designated a "floating world museum for antiquities carrying Egyptian artifacts to the ports of the world." The Egyptian Antiquities Organization, headed by a retired officer, gave its blessing and some of its collection for this novel undertaking.[88]

Abu Ghazala has a keen sense of public relations and in fact competes with Mubarak in the number of inaugurations and similar events he attends. His timing in these matters is impeccable. During the continuing controversy over the pollution of Egypt's Mediterranean beaches Abu Ghazala announced that military helicopters would spray along the northwest coast to combat oil pollution, "especially in regions where the pollution comes from outside Egypt's territorial waters" (i.e., the military is protecting Egyptian beaches from Libya's pollution).[89] While the controversy over the declining quality of health care in Egypt's hospitals was raging, Abu Ghazala directed that the hospital operated by the Islamic Society for Charity and Guidance in Abu Zaabal be given a £E250,000 kidney machine.[90] He also declared that military hospitals would henceforth treat those who had requested the government finance their treatment abroad.[91] This pledge was given while Abu Ghazala was opening a £E33-million military hospital in Alexandria and as the squalid civilian hospital in Cairo, Qasr al-Aini, deteriorated yet further as the wrangle over its reconstruction ground on.

The civilian service sector of the economy was also targeted by the military as an area into which it could profitably expand. In 1986, after extracting approval from Minister of Economy Sultan Abu Ali, who assured the civilian competition that he had "perused the constitution" and found no contradictions, the NSPO, together with the Armed Forces Evacuation Bank, formed under the provisions of the Arab, Foreign and Free Zone Investment Law a jointly owned travel agency that they named Dahab (Gold). The venture was capitalized at £E2 million, of which 50 percent was in convertible currencies. In addition to undertaking virtually all the standard tourist activities within Egypt, for which it was to have a chain of offices and a fleet of tourist buses, Dahab was also authorized to contract agency agreements overseas.[92] The chronic overcapacity of the Egyptian tourist industry caused many in the business to wonder if the real motive behind this step was to open a conduit for the movement of ill-gotten hard currency gains out of the country.

The tourist agency initiative, which has potential for causing friction between the private sector and the military, is not representative of their relations more generally, which are characterized by cooperation. The military awards contracts to the private sector, domestic and foreign, worth hundreds of millions annually for its ventures in nonmilitary areas. Moreover, it actively seeks cooperative arrangements whereby military technicians gain access to advanced technologies found in the private sector, such as those in food production and processing. These developments and others are suggestive of the possible emergence of a Latin American style corporate state based on an alliance of the military with the upper bourgeoisie. Such a coalition is personified by the relationship between the military and Osman Ahmad Osman, labeled the *eminence grise* of the *munfatihun* by David Hirst[93] and simply the Godfather by the Egyptian opposition.[94] Osman, according to Hirst and confirmed by the most cursory review of the Osman empire, employs "scores of generals at ten times their former salary."[95] Such rewards presumably result from services rendered. One allegation is to the effect that massive quantities of cement destined for bunkers at military airports were rerouted by conniving officers to Arab Contractors, which poured it into various of its profitable projects. Circumstantial evidence certainly supports the hypothesis that Osman had a private channel through which he obtained cement: Not only did Arab Contractors appear to be unaffected by the chronic shortage thereof, but Osman played a key role in sabotaging the expansion of Egypt's cement industry, an act that guaranteed massive profits for importers and a competitive edge to any operator (e.g., Osman) who had access to the product through back channels.[96]

A manifestly political aspect of the Osman-military relationship is the support provided by engineer-officers to Osman in the syndicate of engineers. Not only did they back his first two successful candidacies for president of the syndicate, but they also provided a key base of support for his campaign in late 1986 to amend the bylaws so that he could run for a third term.[97] This small example of reciprocity, in itself of no great moment, is, however, indicative of the much larger network of connections that frustrate efforts by both the President and by the opposition to curtail the increasingly powerful alliance between the military and the *munfatihun*. The political aspect of these efforts is mirrored in the struggle between Mubarak, Abu Ghazala, and the opposition, a contest that the Field Marshal is gradually winning.

MUBARAK, ABU GHAZALA, AND THE OPPOSITION

Abu Ghazala's military juggernaught, whose power has been enhanced by linkages to the *infitah* bourgeoisie, has forced most politicians of the regime and even of the opposition either to seek an accord with it or to be increasingly circumspect in their criticism. Civilian cabinet ministers who, prior to the rapid accumulation of power by Abu Ghazala and the military in the wake of the CSF riots, had diligently protected their fiefdoms from the military, were after that date left with little alternative but to give way to military demands. Even the most powerful of those ministers, including Yusuf Wali (the Minister of Agriculture, Deputy Prime Minister, and Secretary General of the NDP) and Hassab Allah al-Kafrawi (Minister of Development and, until November 1986, of Land Reclamation), who have served in all of Mubarak's governments, were subjected to the humiliation of tagging along behind Abu Ghazala as he opened military projects that impinged on their portfolios. These events are splashed across the front pages of the government daily newspapers, the ministers and clusters of dignitaries often being caught in obsequious poses.[98]

Confirmation of Abu Ghazala's new status was also afforded by the United States government, which elevated his visit of June 1986 beyond the level normally reserved for a Minister of Defence. He was received not only by Secretary of Defense Caspar Weinberger but also by the Secretary of State, the National Security Adviser, Vice President George Bush, and several senators and congressmen. That his influence over policy now extends well beyond the area of defense was indicated by the fact that he initiated discussions not only on reduction of interest on the military debt but also on general economic issues. Civilian members of the delegation, including Minister of Planning and Foreign Cooperation Kamal Ganzuri, Minister of Finance Salah Hamid, and Minister of State for Cabinet Affairs Atif Ubaid, were left to sort out the technicalities after Abu Ghazala and the U.S. administration had come to an agreement on principles.[99] Abu Ghazala had secured his warm welcome in Washington by roundly condemning the Soviet Union in an interview in the Egyptian government weekly *Mayo* just prior to his departure. He alleged that the Soviets were trying to dominate the petroleum-producing regions of the Gulf, especially Saudi Arabia, which caused Tass to retort that the Field Marshal "seemed more concerned with political than military matters."[100] Appearing as it did just as the Egyptian Ministry of Foreign Affairs was working with the Czechoslovakian and East German governments to prepare for a visit by Butrus Ghali, Minister of State for Foreign Affairs—a visit that was intended to improve relations with the East bloc more generally—the Field Marshal's interview struck many of those in the Ministry the same way it did Moscow, and they could not but agree with the Tass assessment.

At precisely this juncture a campaign was launched in the opposition press to subject the military to greater civilian control. There is reason to believe that the attack on military profligacy, which shaded off into criticism of Abu Ghazala himself, was encouraged by Mubarak. That virtually the entire opposition press latched onto this issue simultaneously and then just as suddenly at the end of July dropped it is suggestive of a hidden hand at work. Mubarak's public statements were in all cases supportive of the military, including rejection of claims that commissions were being paid on weapons purchases, a line echoed in the columns of Ibrahim Nafa and other of the regime's editorial defenders.[101] However, Mubarak sent a clear message to the articulate public that he was following this debate with interest and possibly approval. After Adil Hussain, editor in chief of *al-Shaab*, wrote widely read and much discussed editorials on 2 June and 1 July in which, among other criticisms, he called into question Abu Ghazala's assertion that he had not given in to U.S. pressure during his negotiations in Washington, Hussain was invited for a first-ever meeting with Mubarak, who had during the year been lambasting the opposition press and refusing to meet with its editors. Hussain was received politely by Mubarak, who encouraged him to expound his point of view. On 15 July Hussain's column included a stinging attack on the military for having discarded Egypt's personnel advantage in its search for technologically advanced and expensive weapons systems and for not having attempted to achieve balance in its weapons inventories between East and West. A further indication that an attempt had been initiated at the highest level to rein in Abu Ghazala may be found in a headline that appeared on page one of *al-Shaab* on 10 June, which declared that for the first time the CAO was going to supervise the military budget, a claim for which no source was given but that suggests a government leak to bring pressure to bear on Abu Ghazala and the military.

If indeed it had been Mubarak's intent in the summer of 1986 to curtail Abu Ghazala and the military's rapidly expanding powers, by the fall that attempt had failed. The drumbeat of military "victories" (completion of projects) as recorded in the dailies and weeklies quickened pace. Abu Ghazala's visage appeared in the press virtually as frequently as Mubarak's. In November Abu Ghazala returned to Washington to resume negotiations, whereas Mubarak's trip for the same purpose was postponed due to U.S. hesitancy to receive him before an economic reform package was agreed upon. And in early 1987 the government press commenced an active defense of the Field Marshal's most exposed political flank, which is the public perception of him as being "soft on Israel." Ibrahim Saada, editor in chief of *Akhbar al-Yom*, indignantly reported in his front page column of 7 February, suitably adorned with a portrait of Abu Ghazala that took ten years off his age, that Israel was conducting a propaganda campaign against Egypt and, more specifically, its Minister of Defence. The fact that Abu Ghazala had testified to a People's Assembly committee on the need for a strong military defense provided, according to Saada, the pretext for the Israeli smear. The ultimate proof of Abu Ghazala's nationalist credentials was gleefully offered by Saada in reference to an interview published in France earlier in the week, in which Israeli Prime Minister Yitzak Shamir launched an attack "against Egypt, against its policies, and against its Minister of Defence!"[102]

Much more remarkable than the favorable coverage of the Field Marshal in the government press was that in the opposition press, which almost in unison did an about-face in its treatment of him. As late as 21 August *al-Wafd* was still adhering to the previous line that the military had to be subjected to more controls. One of the paper's regular columnists, Galal Kishk, under the title "Yes to Building a Strong Army . . . But for Egypt," recalled the glorious tradition of the Egyptian military from the mamluks to the anticolonial struggle and then lamented how it had been subverted under Nasser by Abd al-Hakim Amer, Shams Badran, and others from its ranks who used it for "power games" and to "strike at and torture civilians." But, according to Kishk, the army was put back on the right track under Sadat. Moreover, it is absolutely necessary for Egypt to have a strong military and one that manufactures as much of its armaments as possible. The danger, however, is that the military will be tempted to play its "power games" once again. To prevent this Kishk called for the military, its budget, and policies to be placed under the supervision of the nation in the form of a national security council composed of civilian representatives or under a specialized committee within the People's Assembly.

Less than a month later *al-Wafd* abruptly signaled that the line exemplified in the Kishk editorial was no longer operable. Instead, Abu

Ghazala and the military were now to be seen to be saviors of the nation from the twin perils of the civilian bureaucracy's incompetence and the Minister of Interior's maliciousness. On 18 September in a front page article headlined "The Government Ignores the Abu Ghazala Plan to Finally Solve the Housing Crisis," Galal Abd al-Fattah reported that civilian ministers had, out of petty motives, "put into their files" a plan proposed by Abu Ghazala whereby the army would provide building materials and train workers to construct thousands of apartments. Abu Ghazala, according to Abd al-Fattah, had already secured the consent of three European countries to contribute to building the three cement plants necessary to put the plan into effect. That *al-Wafd* should suddenly be condemning civilian politicians for standing against military intervention into their domains and that the tone of a lead article was openly supportive of Abu Ghazala came as quite a surprise to the paper's readers.

It was, however, not long before *al-Shaab* followed suit. On 9 September Hilmi Murad's column contained an indictment of the military's excesses and of the lack of supervision of its expenses. But on 14 October, Muhammad Abd al-Quddus, son of the prominent writer Ihsan Abd al-Quddus and son-in-law of the prominent Moslem Brother Muhammad al-Ghazali, "saluted the Marshal" in his column. His praise of Abu Ghazala came in response to a television debate that did not go to air but the content of which rapidly became public knowledge. In this "Meet the Press" program that was to have been broadcast on the anniversary of the outbreak of the October war, Abu Ghazala was interrogated by four leading journalists closely associated with the regime, including the widely detested Musa Sabri of *al-Akhbar*. Muhammad Abd al-Quddus described the session as one in which these journalists of the regime were trying to prod the Field Marshal into attacks on the opposition, but he steadfastly refused to be provoked. He resolutely defended the opposition's patriotism and loyalty, saying that enemy bullets did not discriminate between supporters of the government and its opponents. He asserted that there was no conflict between himself and the opposition because "I am the leader of the armed forces which represent all the people of Egypt, those of the opposition and government loyalists alike." He also conceded that there may well be radical Islamic activists in the ranks, explaining that the military is a composite of all elements of society. Abd al-Quddus further burnished Abu Ghazala's Islamic credentials by drawing to his readers' attention the fact that the Field Marshal's wife was one of the very few spouses of high officials to wear the *hijab*. Abd al-Quddus closed the column with a demand for clarification from Minister of Information Safwat al-Sharif as to why the program was censored. Lest doubt remain about the new attitude toward Abu Ghazala in the Socialist Labor Party, a week later Ibrahim Shukri, President of the Party, appeared in a picture on the front page of *al-Ahram* on the right side of the Field Marshal as he is clipping a ribbon to declare a new military project open.[103]

al-Wafd was simultaneously instructing its readers on the fine example set by Abu Ghazala in refusing to strike the name of the son of a prominent Wafdist from the list of those admitted to the Military Technical College as a result of their having passed the examination. This exemplary behavior was compared to that of Minister of Interior Zaki Badr, who, it was reported, ordered his underlings to scratch the very same name from the list of successful applicants to the Police Academy.[104] Abu Ghazala was also congratulated for inviting the leaders of the opposition parties to attend the celebration of Armed Forces Day and for ordering his subordinates to reply to questions that the opposition might raise.[105]

Al-Ahali refrained from effusive praise of the military and Abu Ghazala, but in the fall of 1986 it toned down its earlier strident criticism. Moreover, under its "Secrets of the Week" column, it carried the story of the censored "Meet the Press" program, interpreting it in a way that cast as favorable a light on Abu Ghazala as Muhammad Abd al-Quddus had done in *al-Shaab*.[106] This remarkable turnabout in the opposition's interpretation of the Field Marshal and the military clearly requires comment.

One explanation is that the editors and party bosses had decided to heap praise on Mubarak's chief opponent in order further to divide the two and thus precipitate a clash that would weaken the regime and pave the way for the opposition to acquire more power. This view, favored by many in the rank and file of the opposition parties, is probably incorrect. Not only have the parties repeatedly demonstrated an inability to coordinate strategy,[107] but this explanation ignores the fact that the government press likewise enhanced its favorable coverage of the Minister of Defence and that cabinet ministers, who formerly kept their distance from Abu Ghazala and his innumerable projects, were now clambering over one another to be associated with them. A more likely explanation is that Abu Ghazala himself, in the wake of the February riots that may have saved him from political oblivion, set about systematically to expand his power base and improve his public image. His control over a sprawling empire and ample funds gave substance to this public relations exercise. A prominent opposition journalist, for example, has intimated that his counterparts in other opposition papers have changed their line on the Field Marshal because he has made it worth their while to do so.[108] He leaves unanswered, however, the question as to why his paper has moved in a similar direction, suggesting complicity in the crime of bribery, fear of retaliation by the military, or the more likely explanation that Abu Ghazala has in fact won considerable support from opposition elements.

The opposition had yet another motive for giving favorable coverage to the military and its chief, which was to cast the Minister of Interior and his increasingly draconian methods into an even more negative light. Abu Ghazala had cleverly distanced himself and the military from the repressive policies of Zaki Badr and had further refused to join in the chorus of condemnation of Islamic activists. He implied by his and his wife's behavior that he, in comparison to Badr and most other high officials, understood the Islamic impulse in Egyptian society and politics and was willing to come to terms with it. The opposition could therefore fruitfully contrast this indulgent style with the punitive alternative offered by the Minister of Interior and hope in so doing to relieve themselves of some of the pressure Badr was exerting. Such relief was, however, won at the price of the military and Abu Ghazala further legitimating their assumption of economic and political power.

THE FUTURE OF CIVIL-MILITARY RELATIONS

The opposition has been drawn into the thus far peaceful but potentially deadly game of maneuver between Mubarak and Abu Ghazala, that is, between semicivilian rule and outright military control. In part this results from Mubarak's search for a counterweight to the ambitious Field Marshal outside his weakening regime, for within the military, the cabinet, the bureaucracy, and even the NDP, Abu Ghazala has been able to overcome personnel and policy obstacles placed in his path. By expanding the political dialogue to include legitimate opposition forces, Mubarak has sought to contrast his tolerance of democratic forms of government with the possibility of a return to military rule. His decision to dissolve parliament in February 1987 and call for new elections under a modified election law that is much more favorable to the opposition than that which Fuad Muhyi al-Din imposed for the 1984 election is indicative of the enhanced importance the opposition has assumed in Mubarak's strategy to contain the military. It is, however, an approach that causes concern within the officer corps, some elements of which simply oppose anything more than marginal civilian political partici- pation. Others fear that the removal of controls over political expression at a time of deepening economic crisis will result in a breakdown of political order à la Iran. Sensitive to these apprehensions, Mubarak paid a much-publicized and lengthy visit to the commanders of the Second and Third Armies on 5 February 1987, the very day that the results for the referendum on the dissolution of parliament were scheduled to be announced.

Having multiplied the forums from which the opposition parties make their cases, Mubarak can orchestrate opposition campaigns that reflect negatively on Abu Ghazala, the military, or other individuals or insti- tutions that he seeks to undermine. The example of the debate over the military budget has already been mentioned. Similar use has been made of the opposition over the General Motors deal, a cause celebre that has not dropped out of the pages of the opposition papers since it first caught their attention in 1985. That the government itself condones this campaign is suggested by the many leaks from key agencies to opposition reporters and by the fact that since the deal was signed in June 1986, responsible officials, including the very Minister of Industry who signed the contract, have periodically stimulated further debate on the issue by announcing their dissatisfaction with one or another aspect of the deal and their desire to have it renegotiated.[109] Minister of Industry Muhammad Abd al-Wahhab could not take these initiatives independently, and while there are several reasons underlying Mubarak's handling of this matter, Abu Ghazala's close identification with the project may be foremost among them.

Mubarak is not so foolish as to put all of his eggs in the opposition basket. He manipulates elite politics to the same end of containing challenges. It is highly probable that elements of his foreign policy likewise derive from the preoccupation with presidential power. Abu Ghazala's close identification with the United States is at once a source of strength and weakness, for U.S. patronage is at times useful, at others essential, but the deterioration in Egyptian-U.S. relations simultaneously reflects more negatively on the Field Marshal than on Mubarak. The military debt of $4.5 billion for which interest of some 13 percent was being charged through 1986 was as heavy a political burden for Abu Ghazala as it was a financial liability for the country as a whole. Mubarak's systematic courting of the USSR may suggest a desire not only to restore balance in Egypt's foreign relations but also to provide a counterweight to Abu Ghazala and his U.S. backers.

Abu Ghazala has, however, been able to parry most of Mubarak's thrusts. He has brought the potentially pesky opposition almost completely to heel, probably through a mix of sanctions and inducements as well as by his political astuteness and sheer personal charm and presence. The traps that have been laid for him—such as the "Meet the Press" program in which Musa Sabri sought to demonstrate before the Egyptian public a detestation of the opposition by the Field Marshal as great as his own—failed to snap shut. Abu Ghazala has also avoided dealings with opposition politicians that could be interpreted as attempts by him to undercut presidential authority and thereby provide justification for a move against him. He refuses to grant personal interviews to opposition spokesmen, but is punctilious in responding to written questions about points of fact. His major potential liabilities, which are his connections to the United States and to corrupt practices and persons, are paradoxically also important sources of his strength. The patronage network that he has established in the military and that tails off into the public and private sectors, for example, makes it very difficult for anyone to undermine his authority. Presumably it would require a much broader move against elements of the *infitah* bourgeoisie to ensnare Abu Ghazala, but the continued strength of that group/class and the military and of the alliance between them militates against such a move. By tying his fate not only to the military but also to the fate of a sizable socioeconomic group or class, Abu Ghazala has raised the stakes to such a level that anyone who wants to move against him has to contemplate a "corrective revolution" of at least the magnitude of the one that Sadat launched in May 1971.

The opposition is much the weakest player in this three-handed game. First of all it is not united. The Wafd and the NPUP, for example, both profoundly distrust the military, but their stands on virtually all other issues are poles apart. A concerted, self-motivated move by the opposition against an opponent as powerful as Abu Ghazala is inconceivable. This reality reduces the opposition's options in the power game between the President and the Minister of Defence to selling their services to the highest bidder, the inducements being in the form of preferential policies or just cash; to voluntarily throwing their weight behind one or another in the hopes of affecting the outcome; to attempting further to aggravate the split between the two and thereby precipitate an open confrontation; or to ignoring the clash and pursuing other interests. Whichever option is selected—and the evidence thus far suggests vacillation among them—the opposition, individually and collectively, is at this point still marginal to the outcome, although its potential contribution may assume greater weight in the future.

But even if Mubarak were fully to commit himself to the very risky strategy of rapid and thorough democratization in order to escape the paradox of the sultan, a possibility that is highly unlikely, the odds are stacked against him. In the inevitable race that would ensue and that would pit the military against civilians for the accumulation of power, civilian politicians would be fatally handicapped by their inexperience and divisions and by the fact that the most powerful social class, the bourgeoisie, would be divided in its loyalties. When and if push ever comes to shove between Mubarak and Abu Ghazala, civilian politicians will be left on the sidelines to cheer whoever emerges victorious.

NOTES

1. On the reduction of the military over this period see Ibrahim Nafa, "Quietly," *al-Ahram* (11 July 1986). The military announced in October 1987 that it had shed 45 percent of its personnel since October 1973. *Middle East Times* (11–17 October 1987). The figure 900,000, which appears repeatedly in the Egyptian press, must have included mobilized reservists and those in noncombatant roles.

2. But armed forces of this size cannot be transformed overnight. By 1986 only 5 of Egypt's 12 divisions had been converted to U.S. arms and order of battle, while approximately one-third of the air force was similarly equipped. Colonel William Oldes, Head of Land Forces Program in Egypt, interview (26 May 1986).

3. Mark N. Cooper, *The Transformation of Egypt* (Baltimore: Johns Hopkins University Press, 1982), p. 144. See also Mark N. Cooper, "The Demilitarization of the Egyptian Cabinet," *International Journal of Middle East Studies*, 14, 2 (May 1982), pp. 203–225; Raymond A. Hinnebusch, Jr., *Egyptian Politics Under Sadat: The Post-Populist Development of an Authoritarian–Modernizing State* (Cambridge: Cambridge University Press, 1985), pp. 100–105; and Shahrough Akhavi, "Egypt:

Diffused Elite in a Bureaucratic Society," in I. William Zartman, et al., *Political Elites in Arab North Africa* (New York: Longman, 1982), pp. 237–242.

4. Nazih N. M. Ayubi, *Bureaucracy and Politics in Contemporary Egypt* (London: Ithaca Press, 1980), p. 351. The figure for 1980 was obtained through interviews with local government officials at the Conference on the Decentralization of Local Government, Fayoum (January 1980).

5. Ayubi, *Bureaucracy and Politics in Contemporary Egypt*, pp. 345–352.

6. Sadiq has published his version of these events. They provide an interesting insight into Sadat's techniques of manipulation. See his *Military Pages*, published in Saudi Arabia in February 1987 and reviewed in the *Middle East Times* (1–7 March 1987).

7. Hinnebusch, *Egyptian Politics Under Sadat*, p. 130.

8. In the trial of the conspirators it was claimed that the ammunition was smuggled into the parade ground in the duffel bag of Lieutenant Khalid al-Islambuli.

9. Charles Richards, "Defence Forces Seek a Role," *Financial Times* (7 June 1982).

10. *Ibid.*

11. Several reporters in attendance at an off-the-record question and answer session with Abu Ghazala at the *Washington Post* in June 1986, made these observations to the author.

12. Robert Springborg, "Egypt," *Current Affairs Bulletin*, 62, 5 (October 1985), pp. 25–30.

13. Cited by Philip Gallab, "Marshal Abu Ghazala and Non-Alignment," *al-Ahali* (19 May 1982).

14. *Ibid.*

15. Middle East Research Institute, University of Pennsylvania, *Egypt* (London: Croom Helm, 1985), p. 18.

16. On 19 May 1987 *al-Shaab* reported that the government had become aware of a large secret revolutionary organization in the military. The article also stated that Mubarak had appointed Chief of Staff Ibrahim al-Arabi and not Abu Ghazala to investigate the organization, thereby implying that Mubarak had no confidence in his Minister of Defence. The government press immediately refuted the allegation of the existence of the organization, and Arabi himself denied that he had been appointed to investigate one. The speed and vehemence of the response and the attention given to the alleged appointment of Arabi indicate the sensitivity of the Mubarak–Abu Ghazala relationship. See the statement by Arabi on the front page of *al-Ahram* (20 May 1987) and that by Mubarak in *al-Ahram* (25 May 1987). For a further refutation of the report see Hamdi Lufti, "What Is Behind the Communique About General al-Arabi?" *al-Musawwar* (22 May 1987).

17. Fuad Muhyi al-Din, from the powerful family that provided the Free Officer conspirators Zakariya and Khalid, as well as a smattering of top-level bureaucrats, was trained as a doctor but from his student days pursued a career in politics. He was one of the few civilians who served as a governor under Nasser, while under Sadat he was governor of the key provinces of Alexandria and Giza prior to entering the cabinet as Minister for Local Government in 1973. He remained in the cabinet during the rest of the Sadat years, serving as Minister for Health, People's Assembly Affairs, and finally as Deputy Prime Minister. A tough, forceful politician, the act for which he is best remembered was his modification of the electoral law prior to the 1984 parliamentary election

in such a way as to guarantee a victory for the NDP. He died eight days after the election and his controversial law was finally struck down in early 1987. An indication of Muhyi al-Din's influence is provided by the list of contributors to a *festschrift* in his honor published in 1985 by al-Ahram Publishing Company. It is a veritable who's who of Egyptian politics over the last four decades. See *Fuad Muhyi al-Din: Forty Years of Struggle* (Cairo: al-Ahram, 1985) (in Arabic).

18. Zaki Badr's appointment as Minister of Interior was due to Mubarak's need to send a message in the wake of the CSF riots that he could and would get tough in the face of provocations. In his previous post as Governor of Asyut, Badr had demonstrated a willingness and ability to confront Islamic activists in that strife-torn province. But his extremely aggressive, outspoken nature makes him a political liability. In a meeting with the board of directors of the syndicate of journalists on 18 November 1987, for example, he became engaged in a shouting match with the opposition journalist Muhammad Abd al-Quddus, referring to him as a "liar and son of a liar." Obscenities were then exchanged. Syndicate members were outraged and demanded a general meeting in which they could censure Badr. See Imam Ahmed, "Row over Alleged Strong-Arm Tactics Pits Egyptian Ministry Against Press Syndicate," *Middle East Times* (29 November–5 December 1987).

19. That Abu Ghazala actually informed the United States that the hijackers were being given safe passage to Tunis was claimed by the American ABC television network on 10 June 1986. The following day it was denied by State Department spokesman, Bernard Kalb. On 12 June *al-Akhbar* carried Kalb's denial on the front page accompanied by a statement from its military reporter that "the subject arises within the context of a rumor campaign against Egypt and its leadership." Shortly after the hijacking *Le Monde* reported that Abu Ghazala had tipped off the United States because Mubarak had not allowed the Field Marshal to order his commandoes to apprehend the hijackers. Cited by Anthony McDermott, *Egypt From Nasser to Mubarak: A Flawed Revolution* (London: Croom Helm, 1988), p. 88. Egyptian military sources flatly deny these allegations. They say that Abu Ghazala presented his ideas to the crisis management team initiated by Prime Minister Lutfi and supervised by the President and that while those ideas differed from Mubarak's, Abu Ghazala did not then pursue an independent course of action. Indeed, these sources claim that the Field Marshal was furious with the U.S. for forcing down the Egyptian plane. Bob Woodward claims that the CIA interrupted a phone conversation between Mubarak and his Foreign Minister that indicated the Egyptian President was lying to the United States. *Veil: The Secret Wars of the CIA 1986–1987* (New York: Simon and Schuster, 1987), pp. 414–415. This interpretation appears closest to the truth.

20. This account of the minuet between Mubarak and Abu Ghazala over the Vice Presidency was circulating in Cairo in early 1986. Its veracity was attested to by informed Egyptian observers and Western embassy sources. A similar interpretation is offered by McDermott, *Egypt From Nasser to Mubarak*, pp. 77–78. As late as the end of July 1986, Abu Ghazala was still being questioned about his refusal to accept the Vice Presidency. His standard reply when denying that he harbored political ambitions was "I find that I am only a soldier." See *al-Shaab* (29 July 1986).

21. This viewpoint was widely dispensed through various channels, including nominally off-the-record briefings by embassy officials, including those given by the Political-Military officer, John Michael Davis.

22. The source of this report is an exceptionally well-informed Egyptian press officer in a Western embassy.

23. On this incident see Robert Springborg, "Aid for Egypt Hits a Sandbag," *Financial Review* (1 August 1986).

24. See Hamid Lufti, "Official Egyptian Study Criticizes Political Conduct of October War," *Middle East Times* (1–7 November 1987).

25. Max Weber, *Economy and Society*, vol. 2, ed. Guenther Roth and Claus Wittich (Berkeley and Los Angeles: University of California Press, 1978), pp. 1006–1069.

26. These are the lower and upper limits of estimates from various sources. Richards claims that the army comprises 200,000 men, the air force about 40,000, air defence about 85,000, and the navy 17,000. Reserves, according to him, take the total figure to 1 million. "Defence Forces Seek a Role." Jabber, on the other hand, states that Egypt has 445,000 men under arms (320,000 army, 80,000 air defense, 25,000 air force, and 20,000 navy). See Paul Jabber, "Egypt's Crisis, America's Dilemma," *Foreign Affairs* (Summer 1986), p. 970. *The Arab Strategic Report 1985*, also gives the figure of 445,000 men in active service with reserves of 380,000, for a total of 825,000. See *The Arab Strategic Report 1985* (Cairo: al-Ahram, 1986), p. 402 (in Arabic). The U.S. Head of the Land Forces Program in Egypt estimates Egypt's military manpower at 300,000. Oldes, interview.

27. Oldes, interview. Ibrahim Disuqi Abaza, in a seminar organized by the Egyptian Society of Economists in July 1986, called attention to the manpower imbalance in the Egyptian army, comparing it unfavorably to the ratio that prevails in the Israeli Defense Forces. See Hassan Amer, "Former Government Leaders Examine the Ills of the System," *Middle East Times* (3–16 August 1986).

28. This reduction applied to university graduates and to products of the religious educational system who could demonstrate that they had memorized the Koran. Graduates of the higher technical institutes had their periods of service reduced to one and a half years. *al-Akhbar* (20 October 1986) and *al-Ahram* (4 February 1987).

29. For details of the most recent salary rise, see *al-Wafd* (22 January 1987).

30. Oldes, interview.

31. For the most recent comprehensive survey of weapons acquisitions by the Egyptian military, see *The Arab Strategic Report 1985*, pp. 409–416.

32. *Eyptian Gazette* (19 September 1986).

33. Masbah Qutb, "Military Infitah," *al-Ahali* (4 June 1986).

34. *al-Ahram* (22 October 1986); and *Middle East Times* (14–20 December 1986).

35. *Middle East Times* (2–8 November 1986).

36. *Ibid.*

37. On this and other aspects of the military's vertical integration of its own educational system, see *The Arab Strategic Report 1985*, pp. 425–429.

38. See the interview with Amin Huwaidi in *al-Ahali* (25 June 1986); and Hussain Abd al-Raziq, "We and the President," *al-Ahali* (9 July 1986).

39. I am indebted to P. J. Vatikiotis for providing the details of this transaction, which he in turn obtained from contacts in the military and political elite.

40. Lloyds became suspicious of the inordinate amount of claims for damaged goods passing through the Port of Alexandria and hired a local agency owned by two expatriate Irish brothers to investigate. Shortly thereafter the Egyptian government revoked the residence and work permits of the Irishmen. Lloyds responded by informing the Egyptian government that if these men were not allowed to continue their investigations, no further insurance would be written for ships discharging cargo at Alexandria. A compromise was eventually reached

whereby the Lloyds representatives undertook their assessments in the presence of an Egyptian admiral.

41. For accounts of the Alexandria Stevedore Company and others operating at the port and of the consequences for labor of operations being shifted to the private from the public sector, see Ahmad al-Husri, "The Private Sector Besieges the Public Sector in the Work of Loading and Unloading," al-Ahali (2 April 1986); and Abd Allah Abd al-Ghani Ghanim, The Immigration of Laborers: A Study in The Social Anthropology of the Social Structure of the Porters in the Port of Alexandria (Alexandria: Modern University Press, 1982) (in Arabic). al-Wafd (2 April 1986) connects corruption at the Port with the formation of various stevedore companies by retired naval officers. In November the head of one of these companies was removed amidst allegations of embezzlement. See al-Ahrar (7 November 1986).

42. For a colorful account of Israeli espionage directed at these efforts, see Wolfgang Lotz, The Champagne Spy: Israel's Master Spy Tells His Story (New York: St. Martin's Press, 1979).

43. Ashraf Marwan, from a wealthy Egyptian family and whose father was a general, married Nasser's daughter Mona and went to work in General Intelligence. He became a confidant of Sadat and at age 27 was appointed as his private secretary responsible for information and public relations. Through Sadat he became acquainted with prominent figures in the Arab World, including Qadhafi, Adnan Khasoggi, Kamal Adham, and so on. At age 30 he was appointed head of the AOI, which at that time employed more than 18,000 and was capitalized at a level of $1 billion. Rumors began shortly thereafter about his financial improprieties and side deals with Jihan Sadat and Kamal Adham. He resigned in 1978 and in 1981 went into business with the British entrepreneur Tiny Rowland. See the article on Marwan in Rigal Ummal (March 1987), cited in al-Wafd (2 April 1987).

44. Robert Bailey, "Armed Forces Modernization Spurs Growth of Arms Industry," International Herald Tribune (14 June 1984). For a more current discussion of this aspect of armaments manufacturing, see the interview with the Minister of State for War Production, General Gamal Sayid Ibrahim, in al-Ahram (3 February 1987).

45. See Hamdi Lutfy, "Local Production of High Tech Military Hardware Comes on Line," Middle East Times (4–10 January 1987).

46. Jabber, "Egypt's Crisis," p. 971.

47. Bailey, "Armed Forces Modernization."

48. Middle East Times (30 November–6 December 1986).

49. "Egypt's Crisis."

50. See al-Gumhuriya (18 December 1986); and Middle East Times (21–27 December 1986 and 28 December–3 January 1987).

51. al-Ahram (8 February 1987).

52. al-Ahrar (4 August 1986).

53. "Big Deviations in the Military Factories," al-Ahrar (15 September 1986).

54. al-Ahali (25 June 1986). Huwaidi's estimate of £E7 billion is very high. Other informed sources estimate the defense budget at £E2.6 billion. Sawt al-Arab, a Nasserist weekly that first appeared in August 1986, reported on 2 November 1986 that the Minister of Finance's report for 1985 revealed that 47 percent of governmental revenue was allocated to cover military expenses. Some of the confusion over figures may have to do with varying definitions of

"military," with some including industrial and agricultural products and others not.

55. *al-Shaab* (9 September 1986).

56. This company imports semifinished televisions that require little more assembly than bolting the case on to the chassis. Since "components" attract a much lower tariff than finished sets and since Benha enjoys a monopoly over television assembly, it has a guaranteed market for its output. This attraction it dangles in front of Japanese television producers, who compete for supply contracts by offering generous commissions to Benha's management.

57. Ted Rosen, interview, Cairo (19 June 1986). Rosen, who is Jewish, was previously posted to Israel and was formerly married to a Jewish woman now resident in Israel. He married while in Cairo the daughter of Mustafa Kamal Murad, the head of the Liberal Party.

58. According to Rosen this figure was scaled down to as little as $40 million as private investors pledged investment funds for the project. *Ibid.* In principle, however, GM still has USAID's approval to draw up to $200 million.

59. This information was provided by various employees of USAID, Cairo, on the condition that they not be identified.

60. Rosen, *op. cit.* William Clark, Deputy Chief of Mission, U.S. Embassy, Cairo, interview (17 June 1986).

61. Adil Hussain, interview, Cairo (10 November 1986).

62. Muhammad Sid Ahmad, "Liquidation of the Manufacture of the Nasr Car on Account of General Motors," *al-Ahali* (2 July 1986).

63. Hussain, interview. Spokesmen for the Egyptian military claim that Abu Ghazala and the military have been made scapegoats for the project's failure which, according to them, was due to various economic factors and to conflict between NASCO and GM.

64. Qutb, *op. cit.* Since 1982 the military has constructed factories for the production of optical instruments, wooden doors and windows, boxes and tin cans, and various engineering goods. *The Arab Strategic Report 1985*, pp. 426–428.

65. In 1983–1984, for example, Egypt exported $300 million of industrial goods other than yarn and textiles. *Egypt: Country Report*, Economist Intelligence Unit, no. 2, 1986.

66. *al-Ahram* (13 April 1982).

67. General Gohar, interview, Cairo (2 June 1986).

68. By distributing land to various categories of beneficiaries and ensuring that they would receive adequate support from the state, Hassanein built up a substantial personal following in Tahrir Province. He sought to capitalize on that following in the April 1987 parliamentary elections. He offered his candidacy in the third Buheira constituency, which includes Kom Hamada, where Tahrir Province is situated. Although in February it was anticipated that he would win the election in the event he did not. See *Akhbar al-Yom* (21 February 1987).

69. Robert Springborg, "Patrimonialism and Policy Making in Egypt: Nasser and Sadat and the Tenure Policy for the Reclaimed Lands," *Middle Eastern Studies*, 15, 1 (January 1979), pp. 49–67.

70. *al-Ahram* (7 October 1986).

71. *al-Ahram* (30 October 1986).

72. *Middle East Times* (7–13 September 1986).

73. Percentage calculated from figures in Qutb, *op. cit.*, and "Economic Profile of Egypt," U.S. Embassy, Cairo, 9 March 1986.

74. Qutb, *op. cit.*

75. On the inflation in land prices see Amal Alam, "Despite the Increase in Area Offered Demand Is Still Three Times Supply," *al-Ahram* (February 1987). The author personally attended several auctions of reclaimed land held by public sector land reclamation companies in the summer of 1986. Bidding on plots of less than 100 *feddan*-s was invariably highly competitive, with the average price being somewhere between £E4,000 and £E5,000 per *feddan*. Large tracts with considerable infrastructure in place were occasionally passed in, as the highest bids did not meet reserve prices.

76. This technique was first brought to my attention by Ambassador Tahsin Bashir, interview, Cairo (21 May 1986).

77. *al-Ahrar* (4 August 1986).

78. *al-Ahrar* (29 September 1986).

79. Dr. Rifqi Anwar, former Director of the General Authority for Reclamation and Development of Agricultural Projects, interview, Cairo (28 May 1986).

80. Ghada Ragab, "Military to Employ Conscripts in Desert Reclamation Plan," *Middle East Times* (20–26 April 1986).

81. *al-Ahram* (16 May 1986).

82. *al-Shaab* (27 May 1986).

83. *al-Ahram* (4 February 1987).

84. The scope of these activities is increasingly difficult to discern, for in 1985 the military responded to opposition criticisms of its expansion into nonmilitary areas by adopting a policy of very selective announcement of its endeavors. See *The Arab Strategic Report 1985*, p. 429. As of that time its human infrastructural development projects included training courses for various construction and manufacturing trades, including spinning and weaving, Egypt's oldest and best-established industrial undertaking; basic literacy courses; and professional training in medicine and engineering. *Ibid.* pp. 427–428.

85. A semiofficial list of the goals of the military "in the area of national service" includes eight justifications, the sixth of which legitimates the self-indulgence of the neoMamlukian military caste. It is as follows: "Providing the requirements of individuals in the armed forces and their families at reasonable prices a sort of compensation for the lowering of their income in comparison to the income of workers in many other sectors." *Ibid.*, pp. 426–427.

86. Qutb, *op. cit.* Between 1981 and 1983 the military completed installation of telephone facilities worth £E43 million. In 1984 it installed 5 telephone networks in Cairo and Alexandria. *The Arab Strategic Report 1985*, p. 428. In early 1987 it announced completion of 4 new exchanges in Alexandria worth £E93 million. *al-Ahram* (6 February 1987).

87. Other projects completed by the military in the area of transport and communication include construction of two-thirds of Alexandria's new international airport; installation or upgrading of various rail lines, including the Helwan metro; construction of several thousand kilometers of new roads; provision of water pipes linking various outlying areas, including Mersa Matruh, to the national water grid; and the construction of innumerable bridges and pedestrian overpasses. *The Arab Strategic Report 1985*, pp. 426–427.

88. *al-Akhbar* (21 October 1986).

89. *al-Ahram* (27 September 1986).

90. *al-Ahram al-Iqtisadi* (9 November 1986).

91. *Middle East Times* (18–24 May 1986).

92. *al-Ahali* (20 August 1986).

93. *The Guardian,* (8 April 1986).

94. Talat Ramih, "The Godfather," *al-Shaab* (16 September 1986).

95. Among them are Adil Gabrial, former *wakil* (deputy director) of the National Security Council, who was, immediately upon retirement, appointed to the Ismailiya Poultry Company; Hassan Taha, former *wakil* of the security department in Ismailiya, who was given a post in the Nasr City branch of Arab Contractors; Yunis al-Ansari, former director of the Cairo Airport; and Ali Wasfi, who was Magdi Hassanain's adviser at Tahrir Province and who has now turned up at Salhiya as a consultant to that Osman satrapy. *Ibid.*

96. The Suez Cement Company, which was incorporated in 1979 when Osman was Minister of Housing, was to be the vehicle to overcome the chronic shortage of cement. It was a mixed venture, with 20 percent of its shares offered to Egyptian private investors and the remaining 80 percent taken up by 11 banks and companies, at least one of which is part of the Osman empire. USAID contributed $100 million. The contract for construction was awarded to Arab Contractors. Four years later, despite massive cost overruns, the Suez Cement factory was still not operating, causing Ibrahim Shukri, leader of the Socialist Labor Party, to raise the issue in parliament and demand that the "public sector firm responsible" be fined. Nothing of the sort occurred, despite the fact that after three more years the installation was still not operating. For Shukri's testimony before parliament on 19 April 1983, see Galal al-Sayid and Sami Mahran, *The Egyptian Parliament* (Cairo: The General Organization for Books, 1984), pp. 343–344 (in Arabic). See also *Middle East Times* (20–26 October 1985). *al-Wafd* (2 April 1987) provides further information on how the "cement mafia" has forestalled the expansion of local production. In the meantime the military, in 1983, commenced construction of 7 new cement plants that were to have an output equivalent to that of the entire installed capacity in the civilian sector. See *The Arab Strategic Report 1985,* p. 427. Spokesmen for the military are extremely critical of what they term the "cement mafia."

97. *al-Shaab* (16 December 1986).

98. See, for example, *al-Ahram* (22 October and 30 October 1986 and 6 February 1987); and *al-Akhbar* (30 October 1986).

99. For a semiofficial account of this visit, see the article by *al-Ahram's* Washington reporter, Hamdi Fuad, "The American Administration Affirms It Is Striving to Solve the Problem of Military Loans to Egypt as Quickly as Possible," *al-Ahram* (25 June 1986).

100. Cited in Sid Ahmad, "Liquidation of the Manufacture of the Egyptian Car."

101. See, for example, Nafa's column in *al-Ahram* (11 July 1986).

102. This incident was also reported by Muhamed Abd al-Monaim, "Marshal Abu Ghazala . . . and a Storm in Israel," *al-Ahram* (5 February 1987). The Israelis claim that in this closed committee meeting Abu Ghazala testified that Israel was Egypt's chief enemy. See Tom Porteous, "Brief Encounter," *Middle East International* (6 February 1987).

103. *al-Ahram* (22 October 1986).

104. *al-Wafd* (16 October 1986).

105. *al-Wafd* (30 October 1986).

106. *al-Ahali* (15 October 1986).

107. The most recent example of that is the collapse of the all-party coalition that was to have contested the April 1987 parliamentary elections.

108. Ali Hussain, interview, Cairo (10 November 1986).

109. In October 1986, for example, it was reported that NASCO had put 19 new conditions on its willingness to cooperate with General Motors. Mahmud al-Hadari, "General Motors Refuses All Egyptian Requests to Protect Its Interests," *al-Ahali* (29 October 1986).

5

THE SYSTEM OF POLITICAL CONTROL

The control of autonomous political expression in Egypt is being relaxed simultaneously with the implementation of a policy of economic austerity. This is a risky course of action. With the military on one side and volatile street politics on the other, Mubarak is in danger of being squeezed out of his controlling position. Whether the military would again return to the barracks, as it did after putting down the CSF riots of 25–26 February, 1986, is an open question. It is further complicated by the fact that the threat is not just from anomic violence in response to specific austerity measures, as occurred, for example, in January 1977.[1] Since that time the Islamicist tendency and maybe other movements have attained considerable organizational depth and coherence. They provide both cause and justification for military intervention.

Why then is Mubarak jeopardizing his and Egypt's future? Would it not be safer and easier to reinvigorate the institutions of control, both state and corporate, at least until some basic economic reforms have been implemented?

There are at least three possible answers to this mystery. The first is that the President lacks sufficient power to reverse the process of fragmentation and degeneration of the control system first erected by Nasser. The private sector has sucked too many resources away from the state for it to serve unequivocally as the ruler's sword. The transformation of corporatist into pluralist groups and the gradual expansion of political participation are processes difficult if not impossible to contain in the absence of imposed ideological imperatives and accompanying mobilizational structures. Accordingly, Mubarak confronts the dilemma of witnessing a continued erosion of the system of control or intervening with what could easily prove to be insufficient resources in an attempt to halt the process.

A second explanation is that Mubarak has purposely sought to synchronize the relaxation of political control with the tightening of economic screws. By permitting autonomous political expression and organization and by challenging the opposition to provide reasonable alternatives to his economic strategy, he has opened the political safety valve that permits a relatively high level of economic pressure to be exerted. The trick is to equilibrate the two processes. This explains the stop-start nature of both the political liberalization and the economic rationalization. It is far too risky for Mubarak to move boldly and decisively on either front. Tactical retreats are frequently necessary. Austerity measures are announced and then canceled, aspects of press censorship loosened and then reimposed. Implementation of the austerity program requires fastidious fine-tuning. Price rises, such as those for utilities, school fees, energy, and so on, are put into effect without having been announced out of the calculation that such policy declarations can and have stimulated riots, whereas individuals confronted at different times with mysteriously higher bills are unlikely to take collective action.[2]

Mubarak, in short, is "boiling the frog," gradually increasing the heat under the pot but not so fast that the frog will jump out. In economic terms this takes the form of a gradual reduction of subsidies coupled with inflation calculated to outrun salary increases. Politically it suggests that the weakening of the system of control is intended to facilitate the absorption and deflection of political protest across a broader front. Once the frog is boiled (i.e., economic austerity measures adopted) Mubarak can either liberalize further or tighten up political controls once again. In either case, he self-consciously is playing the difficult role of political maestro, orchestrating potentially conflictual economic necessities and political demands.

A third perspective is that Mubarak is presiding over the transition from "inclusionary" to "exclusionary" corporatism that was begun during the Sadat era. The former phase, which was coterminous with the import substitution period of the Nasser era, was characterized by an expanding welfare system that accommodated what the regime termed "popular forces," ranging from national capitalists to workers and peasants. A strategy of export-led growth, on the other hand, which Sadat initiated and which Mubarak, according to this view, is likewise pursuing, demands economic retrenchment, which may have to be accompanied by selective exclusion, or "demobilization," principally of the working classes.[3] Evidence for this proposition is that Mubarak's economic rationalization is affecting the poor more adversely than the rich and that the relaxation of the system of political control has been uneven. While the bourgeoisie have been granted ample measure of political liberties, as evidenced by their formation of interest groups and political parties and by the expression of their views in the media, the working class, peasants, and the urban and rural lower middle classes continue to confront serious obstacles to political participation. Unions, unlike business associations, have not been transformed from corporatist to pluralist structures.[4] Strikes elicit immediate repressive reactions by government. Agricultural cooperatives, especially those in agrarian reform areas, whose members are exclusively small peasants, have been stripped of functions and depoliticized. The regime's party has been colonized by the bourgeoisie and closed off to those of the lower strata, who had in the Nasser era joined the ASU.[5] Radical Islamic *gama'at* (societies), comprised largely of marginal elements drawn from the *ezba*-s (slums) that surround the major cities,[6] are harassed mercilessly by the authorities, whereas the Moslem Brotherhood, which represents bourgeois Islamicists, is permitted to offer candidates for parliament and is granted regular access to the media. In sum, the system of control has been focused on those strata the regime wants to demobilize as it seeks to "sweat" them in order to accumulate capital.

In this and the following chapter evidence will be presented that may aid determination of which, if any, of these explanations of the cause of the deterioration of the system of political control is correct. First to be examined will be the carrot—the inducements that the regime manipulates to recruit and retain loyal followers. Then the stick will be considered. Two crucial instruments of control, the Ministry of Interior and the National Democratic Party (NDP), will be analyzed in some detail, while the role of the Ministry of Insurance and Social Affairs will be highlighted as an example of the control functions that many of the ministries perform.

THE CARROT

The most significant inducement for general public subservience to the state is the offer of employment within it. Commenting several years ago on the administration and public sector, John Waterbury noted that they "hold a vast salariat in occupational and material thrall," and are, therefore, "preeminent instruments of political control."[7] The temptation to buy compliance from successive generations of graduates has proven too much for Egypt's leaders to resist. In 1950 about 2.2 percent of the Egyptian population was employed in the civil service, a comparatively and distressingly high ratio according to the British public administration expert of the day, A. P. Sinker, who had been hired by the Ministry of Finance to report on personnel issues.[8] In retrospect that appears as a veritable golden age and one that would require a revolution to restore. Total employment in the public bureaucracy mushroomed from 350,000 in 1951–1952 to 1.2 million in 1969–1970, at which time it accounted for 3.8 percent of Egypt's total population of 32–33 million.

After almost a decade of Nasser's Arab Socialism such expansion is hardly surprising. But what is startling is that under Sadat and Mubarak, two proponents of economic liberalization and expanding the role of the private sector, the pace of growth of employment in government administration and the public sector quickened yet again. In the summer of 1986 the Minister of Planning and International Cooperation announced that 4.8 million Egyptians were on the public payroll, or almost 10 percent of the entire population and some 35 percent of the labor force of 13 million.[9] This quantum leap had occurred despite the fact that Mubarak had extended the lag time between graduation and government employment, so that in the summer of 1986, graduates from 1981 were just being assigned their bureaucratic sinecures. Two days prior to the 6 April 1987 parliamentary elections it was announced that the 1982 graduating class from universities, the 1985 and 1986 classes from al-Azhar, the 1983 and 1984 classes from teachers colleges, and the 1981 class from higher institutes would receive appointments. For an allocation of £E100 million in the new five-year plan Egypt had bought 200,000 more souls. Since the government was already paying over £E4 billion annually in salaries to bureaucrats, this was a comparatively trifling sum.[10]

But life in the bureaucracy is not what it used to be. Waterbury graphically and humorously illustrated the plight of civil servants in the Nasser and Sadat years.[11] Their remuneration and general conditions of work have deteriorated yet further in the 1980s. For the system of control to remain effective, additional inducements must increasingly be dangled before the state's employees. Promotion is one such enticement and it has been used unstintingly. The Central Agency for Organization and Administration reported in late 1986 that there were almost 7,000 undersecretaries in the government.[12] By comparison in 1967 there had been 975 civil servants above rank two, of which not more than one half could possibly have attained the rank of undersecretary.[13] Promotion above grade three is on the basis of "merit," hence easily manipulated for the purposes of control. Open support for an opposition party disqualifies a bureaucrat for promotion to top levels.

But the wages and emoluments associated with even the highest rungs of the bureaucratic ladder are increasingly inadequate. A counselor in the Ministry of Foreign Affairs earned in 1987, prior to the 20 percent salary increase announced in June of that year, around £E200 per month, and a minister's salary, including allowances, was £E375, while some £E500 per month was required to maintain a nuclear family's comfortable middle-class existence. So another layer of inducements has been laid on top of the employment structure. A major portion of these are redeemable only on retirement, presumably not only because they are needed to top up pensions, but because they serve as significant incentives for loyalty and perseverance by those under age 60. The posts held by Muhammad Abdu, a retired former Vice Minister of Finance, are illustrative. In the summer of 1986 he received remuneration for the following duties: adviser to the Ministry of Planning; representative of the Ministry of Planning in the general society of Egypt Air; member of the board of directors of the National Investment Bank; representative of the Ministry of Planning on the board of directors of the Akadema Drug Company; member of the board of the National Organization for Military Production; member of the board of the General Organization for Drugs; and member of the advisory committee to the Ministry of Finance.[14]

Various public bodies exist partly if not exclusively to top up the salaries or pensions of their members. Frequently these are organizations that in the past were intended to play some administrative or political role but that events subsequently passed by. Among them are the National Production Councils, which were originally created shortly after the 1952 coup d'etat and which were resuscitated by Sadat as advisory bodies, assigned the top floor of the old ASU building (which was incongruously modeled on the neighboring Nile Hilton Hotel), and placed under former Minister of Information Abd al-Qadir Hatim. Although turning a deaf ear to advice tendered by the National Production Councils, Mubarak has expanded their membership so that most retired ministers, prominent undersecretaries, and other notables can reasonably anticipate appointment to the appropriate council if they resist the temptation to join an opposition party or speak critically in public of government policy. The same is true for the manifestly political *Maglis al-Shura* (Consultative Council/Assembly, or upper house), which is a retirement haven for burned-out top-level bureaucrats, ministers, and politicians, including those who formerly served in the *Maglis al-Shaab* (People's Council/ Assembly, or lower house). Encouraging opposition parties to boycott the *Shura* Council elections of October 1986, prominent columnist Fathi Radwan commented:

> Since the beginning the *Maglis al-Shura* was intended as a means to group together some of the politicians who the state was unable to employ in top jobs, or was intended to compensate some of those who lost their seats in the ministries. In the final instance it is a council without purpose or influence and does not participate in nor direct the affairs of the state.[15]

The list of perks that are doled out to the faithful is lengthy. Lucrative posts are made available in joint-venture enterprises in which the state holds a stake. Similar although generally less remunerative appointments are available in the plethora of projects financed by bilateral and multilateral public and private aid organizations. As Egypt is the Third World's largest aid recipient, the number of consultancies, training positions, and full-time jobs in this area is by no means negligible. Virtually all require approval by the government. Opportunities entirely within the administration and public sector also exist. They possess a staggering number of boards and councils, appointment to which entitles the member to a fee for each meeting attended. A senior official in the Ministry of Agriculture, for example, is known for several years to have attended on average five such meetings a day during the six-day work week, with the fees averaging some £E20 per meeting.[16] A convention in many ministries is to post 59-year-olds to the provinces for the last year of their working lives so that they will earn the pension associated with the higher-ranking job that is available there but not in Cairo. Permission to undertake the *hagg* (pilgrimage) is used in the bureaucracy and party to reward the faithful.[17] Most ministries also provide perks for their employees out of the sectors that they administer, including access to tourist facilities for those in the Ministry of Tourism and inexpensive food in the Ministry of Agriculture. Through its markets adjacent to its headquarters, the Ministry of Agriculture in 1986 took the novel step of providing 4,000 sheep at reduced prices to its employees for the Feast of the Sacrifice.[18]

At middle and lower levels of the bureaucracy rewards necessarily have contracted as numbers have swollen, but employment itself remains a considerable inducement for those of more humble status. In the countryside in particular and especially in Upper Egypt, where there are comparatively few employment opportunities, a job in a cooperative or ministry is still valued by upwardly mobile youths of peasant origins. The control over scarce resources associated with government employment is in turn used to extract side payments from administered clienteles. But the overall attractiveness of rewards provided by the civil service is undeniably deteriorating. A government job for £E60 per month is meager compensation for an Egyptian who until recently may have been earning ten times that much in the Gulf or even in private-sector employment at home. A possible indication of broader disaffection is the significant percentage of civil servants who have been found to be members of the various radical Islamic groups that have from time to time been rounded up. The state, in short, lacking sufficient carrots, has also to rely on the stick. But it, too, is showing signs of deterioration.

MINISTRY OF INTERIOR

Relations with the Military

Competitors for the potential or actual use of coercion to contain domestic dissent, the Ministry of Interior and the military are jealous of one another's prerogatives and are mutually hostile, as are the security services under the jurisdiction of both.[19] Sadat's demilitarization and his suspicion of his generals worked to the advantage of Interior. Mamduh Salim, for example, an officer in *Mabahath Amn al-Dawla* (semiautonomous State Security Agency that reports directly to the Minister of Interior), was a key figure in Sadat's May 1971 "Corrective Revolution." He then became the first prime minister and head of the ruling party to be recruited from the State Security Agency (SSA). The domestic strongman after Salim's political eclipse was another former officer of the SSA, Nabawi Ismail. Civilians and police officers also replaced those with military backgrounds as governors of most provinces during the Sadat era. The Ministry of Interior's Central Security Force (CSF) was built up to obviate the need to call in the military to contain domestic violence and to serve as a counterweight to the armed forces. Similarly, military intelligence, which had encroached on the civilian security and intelligence services' turf during the Nasser era, was under Sadat made to comply with a more restricted, strictly military definition of its role.

The resurgence of the military under Mubarak has increased tension between it and Interior. Prior to the CSF riots, top-ranking army generals were openly complaining about the quality and trustworthiness of this force.[20] When the military had to be called in to put down the insurrection, care was taken by Field Marshal Abu Ghazala to select units that were well disciplined to forestall the inclination of some officers and soldiers to perpetrate a bloodbath at the expense of the CSF. The military's contempt for Interior is not limited to the CSF but includes virtually the entirety of that ministry's branches and leadership. In the early stages of the train drivers' strike of 7–8 July 1986, Abu Ghazala is reported to have called his counterpart in Interior, Zaki Badr, to ask what was happening. When Badr could not provide satisfactory answers, Abu Ghazala ordered the military to take charge of the situation and provide military buses as alternative transportation.[21] Abu Ghazala has been careful to distance himself from Badr's ceaseless attacks on the opposition and on Islamic activists and has conveyed the impression that he finds the minister's remarks unhelpful and impolitic. As if to underscore Badr's and his ministry's shortcomings, following the assassination attempt on former Minister of Interior Hassan Abu Basha in May 1987, Abu Ghazala appeared for a photo session with the presiding doctor, whereas Badr's visage was nowhere to be seen in the press.[22]

For their part those in the Ministry of Interior resent the privileges and ever-expanding duties of their counterparts in the military. While Interior has sought to emulate the military in constructing opulent facilities for its officers, including handsome clubs in prime locations along the Nile, it is clearly a second-best effort. Normal policemen's pay and conditions have deteriorated in comparison to those of enlisted men in the military. While Egyptians in general take pride in the military, even the opposition press being circumspect in criticism of it, the Ministry of Interior is roundly condemned, with the exception of traffic policemen, who generally earn and truly deserve the public's sympathy. Responding to the widening and potentially dangerous gap between the two institutions, the Ministers of Defence and Interior seized upon the thirteen anniversary of the October "victory" to stage a particularly widely publicized meeting between themselves and their respective commands. Zaki Badr, leading a delegation from his ministry to Abu Ghazala's office, congratulated the Field Marshal on the military's accomplishment in 1973 and stated that "Egypt is proud of its armed forces and considers them the armour of the nation." Abu Ghazala responded by praising the "big role which the police played in the October War in securing the rear of the armed forces in the internal front."[23] Similar meetings and exchanges of compliments were held between governors and commanders of military units in Alexandria, Port Said, Ismailiya, Suez, and Beni Suef. But the more flowery the mutual compliments, the more it suggested that antagonism between these competing guardians of public order might itself become a threat to the very stability each was claiming to defend.

Declining Effectiveness: Inadequate Resources

The constituent elements of the Ministry of Interior are all confronting increasing challenges in their areas of responsibility without commensurate enhancements of their capabilities. The CSF, which the President, Prime Minister and Minister of Interior promised would be overhauled in the wake of the February riots, remains substantially the same, other than a 10 percent reduction in its numbers that was achieved in the wake of the riots when the rebels themselves were dropped from the ranks.[24] According to a report that appeared on the first anniversary of the insurrection, the living conditions of recruits remain appalling. Camps have been provided with some but insufficient toilet facilities. Soldiers are still without beds and sleeping on the ground. Salaries of enlisted men were doubled to £E12 per month, but inflation has nullified that increment. According to the report soldiers continue to work virtually as officers' domestic slaves, carrying home their purchases from shops, cleaning their houses, tending their gardens, looking after their children, and so on. The report concludes that the CSF is a bomb ticking away.[25]

Other evidence suggests persisting tension in the CSF's officer corps. In August 1986, Zaki Badr extended the appointments of three generals who had previously been identified by the public prosecutor as bearing considerable responsibility for the insurrection.[26] In the following month the commanding officer of the CSF traveled to London for medical reasons. No temporary replacement was named, apparently because of a dispute between the "old guard" that had been in command at the time of the riots and a group of new officers who had subsequently been promoted.[27] Still lacking resources commensurate with its size and duties and torn by internal dissension, the CSF has nevertheless been thrown into numerous affrays since the disastrous riots. It has been called upon to subdue demonstrating students on several university campuses; to intimidate strikers at industrial centers in the Delta; to confront Islamic activists at pray-ins, seminars, and large gatherings in various parts of Upper Egypt; to deal with peasants demonstrating against interruption to irrigation water supplies throughout the countryside; and its poor conscripts are still obliged to stand twelve-hour shifts at countless strategic and not-so-strategic installations around the country. That reform has not progressed further in the CSF suggests that the military is strong enough politically to prevent its opponent from being upgraded and that the Ministry of Interior possesses enough clout to prevent the CSF from being disbanded.

The police are similarly confronting difficulties—in their case an escalating crime rate without adequate resources to combat it. The opposition, particularly the Wafd Party, argues that the inability of the police to contain the spiral of theft, murder, and other crime is due to the Ministry of Interior devoting too many of its resources to the surveillance and containment of opposition political activities rather than to the apprehension of common criminals.[28] Minister of Interior Badr has refuted those claims, asserting that the arrest rate in major crimes is 80 percent.[29] A revelation following the use of a stolen police car in the assassination attempt on Hassan Abu Basha that 350 police cars had "recently been stolen" suggested Badr's figure might well be on the optimistic side.[30] Whatever the case it is indisputably true that the police, like the CSF, are suffering from neglect. Pay and conditions have so seriously deteriorated that in late 1986 there were 40,000 unfilled vacancies, or almost one third of the existing force size of 122,000 policemen.[31] This is due less to an insufficiency of funding support for the Ministry of Interior as a whole than to the misallocation of resources within it. The budget of the ministry was £E91 million in 1977, £E260 million in 1981, and £E348 million in 1985, almost a fourfold increase in eight years. The bulk of these appropriations, however, was earmarked for the purchase of new equipment to be used by the CSF in riot control. A typical policeman in mid-career was in 1986 earning some £E60–70 monthly, a salary that over the decade had fallen far behind the rate of inflation.[32] The police officer corps has also seen its salaries significantly reduced in real terms, which has caused some to complain bitterly to opposition reporters. Moreover, police under the Ministry of Interior have lost authority as other law enforcement agencies have been created or expanded by other branches of government, such as the Ministries of Supply, Finance, Transportation, and the customs service. By 1986 Egypt had 34 separate police forces.[33]

Not surprisingly, those charged with enforcing the law have succumbed to the temptation to break it in order to make ends meet. At the bottom of the scale traffic police routinely extract "tolls" from drivers against the threat of issuance of a ticket or for favorable treatment in traffic snarls.[34] This writer, for example, while waiting on a Cairo street corner, witnessed a large truck laden with bags of sugar (then in scarce supply) rumble through an amber light and then brake abruptly. The driver, having seen the officer at the light pull out his notebook to report the infringement, jumped out, grabbed one of the bags off the back of the Ministry of Supply's truck, trotted over to the policeman, and dropped the bag under the sunshade next to him. A closer look revealed a substantial collection of merchandise stacked up under the sunshade, presumably acquired in similar fashion earlier in the office's shift.

Turning a blind eye to infringements of the law or actively participating in them in order to supplement salaries is not confined to humble police officers flicking switches on traffic lights. The most lucrative activity is the drug trade, so it has sucked in protectors and participants from the minister on down. The U.S. Embassy in Cairo estimated in 1986 annual retail sales of soft and hard drugs to be in excess of £E2 billion, while other sources put the figure at £E3 billion.[35] Countless stories have appeared in the media of fishermen, waiters, attendants at sporting clubs, and others of modest means amassing millions in the drug trade. The really big fish though are those who have bought protection at the very highest levels. Rashid Osman, prior to his arrest during the purge by Mubarak of the most notorious of the Sadatist *munfatihun,* made tens of millions in drug deals and acquired extensive influence in the NDP, parliament, and the President's entourage. According to reports in the opposition press, a host of similar although more modest operators have sprung up since Osman's removal. A typical report cites the 28-year-old son of a deceased former minister exploiting his father's connections to the families of Osman Ahmad Osman and Sadat and his employment of no fewer than twelve ministerial undersecretaries as "consultants" to amass a fortune in drugs.[36] Another report refers to the case of a millionaire car dealer with close connections to the leadership of the NDP who was arraigned before the Qasr al-Nil court on charges of dealing in drugs.[37] That illicit drug trafficking has a profound effect on the economy is another of the opposition press's standard charges. *Al-Ahali,* for example, claimed in April 1986 that the sudden devaluation of the pound was due to a drug deal for which the principal had to seek urgent loans of hard currency from Egypt's banks.[38]

While many of these reports may be substantially incorrect, there is no question that the drug trade is enormous, that it has a serious negative effect on the economy, and that it enjoys the protection of some in officialdom. The increase in heroin trade and consumption supports these contentions. In 1981, as in most previous years, no heroin was seized by the narcotics authorities. In 1982 just less than half a kilo was found in Alexandria. But in 1983, 243 kilos of heroin were confiscated, of which 233 were said to be in the process of being transshipped from Thailand to Europe and North America. In 1984 and 1985, 20 and 49 kilos respectively were seized.[39] The significance of the increase in heroin seizures, and undoubtedly therefore its usage, is that heroin consumption more than that of any other drug requires the complicity of authorities. Addicts simply must have immediate access to the drug, so its distribution has to be at least semipublic. Egypt's use as a transit point in the heroin trade may also suggest high level complicity.

Other evidence confirms the existence of police corruption. Arrests of officers involved in drug rackets occur intermittently. In October 1986, for example, Colonel Assam al-Din Aissa Mansur of the security directorate of Sohag Governorate in Upper Egypt and, according to *al-Wafd,* a close associate of the Minister of Interior, and some of his men were remanded for trial on the charge of having imported £E25 million worth of hashish, of which the major portion mysteriously disappeared after its seizure.[40] According to informed sources drug smuggling gangs are so large and well organized that in the provinces most directly affected, governors stand no real chance against them so almost invariably come to terms with the gangs. One route is across northern Sinai into Sharqiya, then down the Red Sea coast and across to Asyut. In 1983 an Egyptian-Lebanese gang landing hashish on the north Sinai coast paid the border guards a bribe of £E1 million, but were nevertheless apprehended.[41] In 1985 a gang of north Sinai bedouin smugglers was attacked and overwhelmed by the troops of the Anti-Narcotics General Administration, who seized 2,143 kilos of hashish from a single cache.[42] Smugglers can clearly be powerful friends or tough enemies of those charged with enforcing the law.

Zaki Badr, when governor of Asyut, was one of those officials who most appreciated the useful role drug gangs can play, partly because he was most in need of assistance. He had been appointed governor of Asyut immediately after the Sadat assassination and subsequent rebellion in Asyut in which 90–100 members of the CSF were killed. His predecessor, Muhammad Osman Ismail, was a close Sadat associate who had been made governor of Asyut in 1973, largely for the purpose of building up the Islamic gama'at against the left.[43] In Ismail's nine years as governor he had created a Frankenstein, which Badr was in 1982 charged with destroying. Wisely avoiding a two-front war, Badr made peace with the drug bosses of Asyut, who, according to reliable reports, assisted Badr in his crackdown on fundamentalists. This relationship prospered right up until the time Badr was promoted to Minister of Interior after the CSF riots in February 1986.

As if to confirm the public's worst suspicions about the degree to which drug usage has permeated society and negatively affected the economy, the government announced in the wake of the IMF-inspired reforms of May 1987 that it had arrested 221 drug dealers and importers to prevent them from speculating against the pound.[44] Many Egyptians wondered why, if the government could so easily identify the drug bosses then, they had not previously been arrested on drug-related charges.

Internal Factionalization

Progressive debilitation of the system of control of both political and criminal activities is further suggested by indications of increased rivalry and tension between the organizations and individuals that compose it. The case of the former governor of Alexandria, Fawzi Muaz, is illustrative. A tough-fisted, aggressive man, he became mired in controversy over alleged involvement in various illegal rackets at the port and for his unique innovation of selling off the municipality's land to private interests for the purpose of housing construction. As high rise apartments began to sprout around the city in 1983–1984, some half dozen members of the Alexandria branch of the NDP ventured to criticize Muaz for having profited from these land and construction deals. The chairman of the Alexandria parliamentary delegation, Ahmad Abdilla, supported the move against Muaz and helped facilitate the preparation of a parliamentary committee report in 1985 implicating Muaz in the mishandling of public funds.[45] al-Wafd had in the meantime joined in the campaign against Muaz, who in response demanded that the parliamentary immunity of al-Wafd's editor, member of parliament (MP) Mustafa Shurdi, be lifted. More importantly, the fact that NDP deputies had made common cause with Wafdist MPs against the governor provided him the opportunity to charge them with disloyalty to the party. He arranged with NDP Secretary General Yusuf Wali and Assistant Secretary General Kamal Shazli to submit NDP MPs Gabrail Muhammad and Ahmad Izzat to the party's disciplinary committee. Subsequently they were struck from the list of NDP parliamentary candidates. But al-Wafd continued its attack on Muaz until his sudden death by heart attack in May 1986, while he was still serving as governor.[46]

His legacy to Alexandria was a highly divided NDP and a discredited provincial branch of the Ministry of Interior. The struggle within the NDP and between it and the Ministry of Interior continued through the following year. Those in the NDP who had opposed Muaz attempted unsuccessfully to gain control of the branch of the party in the wake of the death, also by heart attack, of the branch's head, Mahmud Dawud, who was a former Minister of Agriculture and longtime associate of Yusuf Wali. But the dominant NDP faction aligned with the Ministry of Interior did not have it all its own way either. The new governor of Alexandria, Sayid al-Gusaqi, was a former Air Force lawyer and Mubarak loyalist. He immediately began to try to undermine the old Muaz power base in the NDP and the Alexandria branch of Interior, in part by bringing into his office those with whom he formerly had worked closely in upper Egypt.[47] While it was unlikely that Gusaqi, lacking direct ties to the security agencies, could over the long haul induce the branches of Interior in Alexandria to submit totally to his will, he at least forced a measure of relaxation of the iron grip that those around Muaz had previously held on various activities in the city.

The Ministry of Interior is subjected to increased pressure as a result of political liberalization, which not only permits vociferous criticism of its role by the opposition, but also causes it to have less than the 100 percent backing of the President for some courses of action its employees might choose. Having to be more responsive to political demands, Mubarak, as he indicated with Muaz's replacement, may not support his security specialists if the political price is too high. This, for example, may have been the reason underlying the indictment of over forty officers on charges of torturing members of the al-Jihad Islamicist organization in September 1986. Included was the former director of the SSA, General Fuad Alam. Coupled with this element of equivocal political support is the continued deterioration of the pay and conditions not only of police on the beat but of those in virtually all branches of internal security as well.

Not surprisingly, the commitment of those responsible on a day to day basis for intimidating the regime's opponents, especially the Islamic activists, is weakening. While some members of the CSF, the police, and even the SSA undoubtedly sympathize with the activists, there are additional calculations that militate against a sustained, effective policy of repression. The regime itself follows an erratic line, sometimes seeking to placate activists and at other times cracking down on them. Those charged with applying force have found themselves left high and dry when a shift is made or tactical retreat ordered. This occurred, for example, in the case of the SSA plainclothes agents who accosted a youth in Asyut in Spring 1986 who was pasting a poster on a wall announcing a meeting to be held in a local mosque. A revolver belonging to one of the agents discharged during the struggle, seriously wounding the youth. With the situation in Asyut threatening to explode, Mubarak ordered the youth to be flown to Cairo for emergency medical treatment and the agents to be interrogated. With a state of near-insurrection prevailing in Asyut and elsewhere in Upper Egypt periodically since 1981, Mubarak's refusal to provide carte blanche to his security forces and his occasional slap on their wrists has caused consternation in the ranks. This, combined with their apprehension that in the not too distant future many of those whom they are currently intimidating will assume positions of authority either by invitation from a weak and vacillating government or simply by taking them, has caused some in the security forces to hedge their bets.[48]

Pressure on the Ministry of Interior is reflected in the comparatively rapid turnover in that cabinet portfolio, in increasingly public disagreements between cabinet-level security specialists over issues and personalities, and in factionalization within the ranks of security organs. Mubarak has had four Ministers of Interior—Nabawi Ismail, Hassan Abu Basha, Ahmad Rushdi, and Zaki Badr. For the five-year period from October 1981 until November 1986, when the Atif Sidqi government was formed, Ministers of Interior enjoyed an average tenure in office of just over 15 months, which is about half the average length of service of those in other cabinet positions. Mubarak values stability in the cabinet and top-level positions generally. Discounting the government formed one week after Sadat's assassination, by October 1987 five cabinets had served under Mubarak, for an average of one a year. By comparison, Nasser on average also formed one a year, whereas the average term of cabinets under Sadat was around eight months. But turnover in portfolios has occurred at a much slower pace. In Mubarak's first five cabinets, a total of 163 portfolios were occupied by 58 individuals. In this period Mubarak averaged 9.5 cabinet ministers per year, compared to 7.2 for Nasser and 20.6 for Sadat.[49]

Egyptian commentators have assigned considerable political significance to the relatively rapid turnover rate for the Interior portfolio. The leftist Hussain Abd al-Raziq, for example, considers it the natural consequence of the politicization of the role—of making the minister of interior the prime defender of the ruler and his party.[50] Saad al-Din Ibrahim, a prominent political sociologist, commenting on the high turnover rate in both the Interior and Economy portfolios, suggested the analogy of a sociopolitical thermometer. As the temperature rises, the turnover rate increases. He also noted a relationship between civil unrest and ministerial turnover. If, following the announcement of economic rationalization measures, protests and demonstrations are widespread and violent, then the Minister of Interior goes. If, on the other hand, not too much blood is spilled, it is the turn of the Minister of Economy.[51]

Ministers of Interior, however, resent the role of sacrificial lamb. Their successors attract much of their hostility, a problem aggravated by Mubarak's tactic of replacing hard-liners with moderates and vice versa. Mubarak inherited Nabawi Ismail from Sadat but took the first opportunity, which was the formation of the Fuad Muhyi al-Din cabinet of January 1982, to kick Ismail downstairs to Minister of Local Government, a sort of junior Interior portfolio. His replacement was Hassan Abu Basha, an uncompromising man who unleashed the full force of his ministry's powers on the regime's opponents. He, along with Nabawi Ismail, was subsequently accused by members of the *al-Jihad* organization when they gave evidence to the public prosecutor in the fall of 1986 of torture or threats to torture them. Abu Basha denied their allegations and added that he had issued strict instructions to all police "and especially those in the *Gihaz Mabahath Amn al-Dawla* (SSA) not to use cruelty or violence with any accused during the investigation or interrogation of him whether in prison or the station house."[52] But the negative image of Abu Basha could not easily be squared with Mubarak's desire to embark on a more liberal course following the 1984 elections and he, like his predecessor Ismail, was booted downstairs to the Ministry of Local Government and replaced by Ahmad Rushdi. Although personally severe, Rushdi was a keen reformer who preferred dialogue with rather than intimidation of the opposition. Mubarak's only Minister of Interior not to be implicated by prisoners testifying in the "torture case" of 1986, Rushdi vigorously directed his ministry's efforts to such mundane but important tasks as improving the traffic flow in Cairo, as well as to the important and politically sensitive matter of rounding up drug dealers. For these efforts he earned the grudging admiration of the opposition and the enmity of various powerful forces and personages, not the least of them being his successor, Zaki Badr.[53]

In the wake of the CSF riots Mubarak jettisoned Rushdi and called on Badr, who for more than three years had been keeping the lid on potentially explosive Asyut Province. An ambitious person who thought his predecessor too soft and who bore a personal grudge against Abu Basha, who had opposed his appointment as governor of Asyut, Badr immediately set about reversing Rushdi's conciliatory approach to the opposition. While Islamic activists bore the brunt of Badr's security crackdown, opposition parties were also hounded and harassed much more actively than they had been since early 1984. They retaliated by launching an anti-Badr campaign in their newspapers, during which innumerable accusations of torture, protection of drug dealers, forging of elections, violations of civil rights, and so on were made. *Al-Ahali* took delight in pointing out how Badr expunged Rushdi's name from the annual report of the Ministry of Interior for 1986.[54] *Al-Shaab* reported that Rushdi, piqued by his succesor's insults, voted not for the NDP candidate for Minufiya in the 1987 parliamentary election but for the Socialist Labor-Liberal-Moslem Brotherhood Alliance candidate.[55]

Disagreement over policy issues and personal matters at the highest levels of the Ministry of Interior and associated security organs contributes to factionalization further down in the system. The surprising degree of discord became particularly evident following Badr's appointment as minister. It appeared to be triggered by an editorial by Ibrahim Saada in *Akhbar al-Yom* on 15 March 1986, in which this prominent editorialist closely associated with the President attacked the SSA. Saada confirmed an unpleasant reality already well known to most Egyptians—namely, that the SSA has agents in every government department and public-sector company who provide information for pay. He also accused it of knowing about the CSF riots in advance but not informing the governor and chief of police in Giza, implying that at a minimum the SSA wanted to bring down Ahmad Rushdi. Moreover, he claimed, it had a large file on Badr's illicit and immoral dealings when he was governor of Asyut, suggesting that it would use that information to blackmail the new minister to prevent him from establishing his authority over this semi-autonomous agency.[56]

The Saada editorial provoked a torrent of commentary and signaled that Mubarak was intending to use his new Minister of Interior to reduce the power of the SSA. Subsequently it became apparent that he was enlisting other members of the political elite in this cause. Secretary General of the NDP Yusuf Wali entered the fray in late March by demanding that the SSA not embark on any new investigations of party members without prior approval from him.[57] His justification was that further corruption cases would be politically destabilizing. This move could not have been made by Wali without presidential backing, even though it dovetailed with Wali's bid to consolidate his hold over the party and to enhance his influence more broadly, in part through cementing an alliance with the new Minister of Interior.

That Mubarak chose to trim the wings of the SSA in the wake of the CSF riots suggests at a minimum that he had been waiting for an opportunity to reshuffle its leadership and possibly that he was seeking to reduce its role more generally. Although the SSA had roots in the *ancien regime*, when it was known as the political police, and was one of the many security and intelligence agencies active during the Nasser era, of which the more important was the *Mukhabarat Amma* (General

Intelligence) that reported directly to Nasser, the SSA emerged as the dominant domestic intelligence agency only under Sadat. He gave it access to the portfolios of Prime Minister, Interior, and Local Government and to top positions in the ruling party. At lower levels officers from the SSA were given key posts in the police force under the Ministry of Interior and were made provincial governors. According to Hussain Abd al-Raziq they also became entrenched in the economic organizations, including public-sector companies, in unions, the media, the political parties, and even the parliament. Accordingly, "as we can speak about the state of the *mukhabarat*, i.e., the Nasser era, so we can speak about the state of *Mabahath Amn al-Dawla.*"[58]

Mubarak had several reasons to move against the SSA. It still had many Sadatists in key positions, although in the four-year period prior to the CSF riots Mubarak had changed the commanding officer of the agency four times.[59] It was a potential threat to his autonomous exercise of power for, as discussed below, its influence over policy ranged virtually across the board. It was extremely unpopular with the public and increasingly hard to justify in a "state of institutions." It had either not done its job in heading off the CSF riots or had sought to use those riots for its own purposes. Yet despite these and other problems with his main security organ, Mubarak did not seek to liquidate it. Rather, his strategy was to reduce its power vis-à-vis other key institutions and individuals, chief of whom were the Minister of Interior, Secretary General of the NDP, and General Intelligence. Abolishing the SSA might have served as an unwanted stimulant to opposition political activity, and it would have deprived Mubarak of an important counterweight to the military and the Field Marshal.

Between March and August 1986, the new Minister of Interior retired, promoted, and transferred hundreds of officers in his ministry and the SSA. In addition, an order was issued in mid-March restricting the distribution of payments to informants and agents of the latter.[60] But from the outset it was clear that these shake-ups were not to presage a broader liberalization and that many were for the purpose of establishing Badr's authority. General Muhammad Tantawi, the commander of the SSA sacked immediately after the riots, had been a close associate of Ahmad Rushdi and was known to believe in dialogue with rather than oppression of the legal opposition.[61] His replacement, General Mustafa Kamal, a Zaki Badr loyalist, had been supervisor of the Cairo branch of State Security during Sadat's roundup of the opposition in September, 1981, and clearly had not revealed any liberal tendencies previously in his career.[62] Colonel Mamduh Kadwani, head of the SSA in Asyut, was, within two days of Badr becoming minister, transferred to the general administration of the agency in Cairo, where Badr could keep an eye on him. Kadwani had compiled the Badr file in Asyut and was clearly a threat to his nominal boss.[63]

Several groups of officers from the Ministry of Interior and the SSA, who opposed Badr either because he transferred them from their sinecures, because they disagreed with his harsh tactics against the political opposition, or for other reasons, leaked news of their discontent with Badr to the public.[64] In April 1986 pamphlets labeled "Communique Number One of the Committee of Police Officers for Democracy" appeared in Cairo and elsewhere. They claimed the committee was composed of almost 300 officers who were opposed to Badr, his repressive methods, and to the fact that in his previous posts he had engaged in various corrupt activities.[65] While these and other allegations that surfaced could be exaggerations, there is no doubt that the Ministry of Interior and the SSA were wracked with dissension as a result of the measures taken by Mubarak and Badr in the wake of the CSF riots. This, in turn, may account for their poor subsequent performance, as indicated by their inability to nip the July 1986 train drivers' strike in the bud or to prevent a sudden and dramatic increase in assassination attempts on U.S. and Israeli diplomats and on Egyptians, including not only Abu Basha, but also the prominent editorialist Makram Muhammad Ahmad, who spoke out against Islamic radicals.

Another negative consequence for political and public security of these personal and institutional conflicts was the disorder that occurred in Asyut in the spring and early summer of 1986. On accepting the portfolio of Interior, Badr demanded that his personal friend and former detective in Alexandria, Sami Khudair, be his replacement. Badr could rely on Khudair to suppress information about his previous activities in Asyut and to support him in the move against the Asyut branch of the SSA. Khudair reportedly was so thorough in pursuing these tasks that he neglected the more important one of containing the various radical Islamic groups in his province. By summer 1986 they were getting out of hand and Khudair was transferred to Port Said. His replacement, Mamduh Salim Zaki, began immediately to crack down on the now-confident activists, who responded by blowing up one of the pylons of the almost-completed bridge linking the two banks of the Nile in Asyut. The bridge was of strategic importance, for when finished it would provide immediate access to Asyut city for the large CSF camp on the other side of the river. Badr responded to the challenge by flying to Asyut and taking personal control of operations there. On 29 August al-Akhbar signaled that the crisis was coming to an end by carrying a story that the central square of Asyut had been renamed Zaki Badr Square, with the minister himself in attendance at the ceremony. Four days later a small cable of congratulations to President Mubarak from the director of security for Asyut appeared on one of al-Ahram's back pages. That was the only public reference, vague as it was, to the fact that Badr and his ministry had finally succeeded in dealing with the emergency. No mention was made in the media of the sabotage of the bridge. While some of what occurred at that time may have taken place in the absence of disarray in the Ministry of Interior and the SSA, there is no doubt that internal divisions seriously hampered the regime's ability to deal with Egypt's least easily governed province and the problem of Islamic activism more generally.

Relations with Semiautonomous State Organizations

In competition with the military, suffering from declining rewards and status, and embroiled in personal and organizational disputes, the key security agencies are confronted with yet another problem. Under Mubarak several of the state's organizations that also play a role in determining the permitted level of political expression and participation have gained a greater degree of autonomy. Most important of these are the courts, which resist governmental pressure with remarkable success. The list of decisions judges have taken in support of a more liberalized political system is impressive and growing. A court granted the Wafd Party permission to reestablish itself in 1983; a favorable decision on an appeal to the Supreme Court against the electoral system fashioned for the 1984 election led to its modification; an appeal against a government decision to try Islamic activists in military courts resulted in the trials being transferred to civilian courts in 1987; and so on. The courts, in short, have become one of the chief battlegrounds on which political conflicts are fought. Although not immune to intervention by the components of the control system, that is not for want of effort on the part of judges and the legal profession more generally.

The response of security agencies to the expanding autonomy of courts has been to attempt to circumvent them by using the provisions of the Emergency Laws, enacted at the time of Sadat's assassination, which allow security to hold suspects without filing charges for sixty days "on suspicion" and which delegate further powers to the Minister of Interior if he has information that suggests suspects are a potential security threat. The Emergency Laws were renewed again for two years on 21 April 1986. In the wake of assassination attempts in May and June 1987, the government requested a further broadening of their scope.

Another strategem of the Ministry of Interior is simply to ignore court decisions in "security" cases. Just prior to the 1987 parliamentary elections, for example, the SSA arrested four professors and several tutors who are members of the Cairo University faculty club and who were opposing prominent university administrators, including the president, Hilmi Nimr, who were standing as NDP candidates. Following the election the public prosecutor ordered the faculty members released from jail, but the Ministry of Interior refused. The academics' freedom was eventually won by threat of strike action by their colleagues.[66] This is not an isolated case. In the previous year Zaki Badr had rejected a ruling by the supreme state security court that blind theologian Omar Abd al-Rahman and fifty-five other Islamic activists be released from prison. Instead Badr ordered them moved from Aswan, where they had been arrested on 30 April, to a penitentiary in nearby Qena.[67] Also in

1986 Badr refused to honor a court order obtained by activist cleric Hafiz Salama to permit prayers in Abdin Square on *Aid al-Fitr*, the celebration that ends Ramadan. Badr claimed such a prayer would create traffic problems and ordered the SSA to flood the square from fire hoses.[68]

The courts provide political activists only limited protection from intimidation and incarceration by internal security forces. Their effectiveness in any given case depends most heavily on the attitude and measures taken by the President. Nevertheless, this constraint on the Ministry of Interior's arbitrary exercise of power contributes to the complexity of the task of political control and undoubtedly to disagreements in the Ministry of Interior over how best to proceed.

There are at least three additional semiautonomous governmental organizations that are involved in the investigation of potential criminal activities that may have strong political overtones. *Al-Raqaba al-Idariya* (Administrative Supervision) reports to the Prime Minister and is intended to investigate acts of malfeasance and misfeasance by public servants. During the 1960s it was directly involved in highly contentious political activities, such as tracking down violations of agrarian reform laws. At that time it coordinated its activities closely with the ASU and security organs.[69] Under Sadat its semiautonomy, indicated by its numerous reports on corrupt activities by high-ranking officials, annoyed the President. He was on the verge of abolishing it when he was assassinated. Having escaped that fate, Administrative Supervision emerged in the Mubarak era as an energetic investigator of abuses. Its reports are regularly leaked to the opposition media, presumably in most instances with presidential approval, for such reports provide to Mubarak a means with which to maintain control over the sprawling bureaucracy and public sector. A move in the spring of 1986 by members of the NDP politbureau to abolish Administrative Supervision did not succeed, principally because Mubarak did not support it.[70]

The Central Auditing Organization plays a similar role, and its reports have frequently served as the basis for muckraking campaigns by the opposition. Its power and status under Mubarak were attested to by the appointment of its director and his deputy, Atif Sidqi and Yusri Mustafa, respectively, as Prime Minister and Minister of Economy in November 1986. Similarly, the Socialist Prosecutor, a sort of Grand Inquisitor created by Sadat in 1975 to intimidate his political opponents, was transformed under Mubarak into another watchdog over abuses by public officials and private citizens. Because of its association with oppression in the Sadat era and because it is still subject to few controls, although in theory it reports to parliament, the opposition continues to call for its abolition. A certain ambivalence, however, now surrounds those demands as the Socialist Prosecutor has turned its attention to the misdeeds of those in high places.[71]

Increasing fragmentation and even pluralization of the political system have provided the courts and these three agencies of financial and administrative oversight both cause and opportunity to pursue semiindependent paths. Their renaissance under Mubarak is also due to the fact that they are useful tools of presidential control over the administration, the public, and the "joint" sectors. For reasons of efficiency of control, political image, and political balance, Mubarak has enhanced their roles in comparison to those of the SSA and other organizations under the Ministry of Interior. The price Mubarak has had to pay for their change is a deterioration in the coherence of and coordination within the system of control, which formerly was indisputably at the command of the security services. Now the Ministry of Interior is no longer above the political fray and must seek allies from among the state structures and within the political elite to preserve and to seek to extend its power. Its principal partners have been the ruling party and various ministries, which, locked into their own political struggles against various opponents, are receptive to alliances with powerful actors.

Political Influence

While the capability of the Ministry of Interior to control autonomous political participation has under Mubarak deteriorated, its leverage over policy making has not so noticeably eroded. The political elite, attempting to implement an economic austerity program in the absence of an effective political party, has had to rely on domestic security forces to provide information on the public's receptivity to specific measures, as well as to provide the necessary backstop against negative reactions. It is routine practice to use the extensive network of agents to gauge reactions to trial balloons prior to officially declaring policies. So, for example, after it had been widely announced in the early spring of 1986 that a series of austerity measures would be implemented on 25 March, agents reported back that if the measures were to be implemented as rumored, riots could easily occur. The regime backtracked, so much so that the public was amazed at the leniency of the reforms. Specific proposals for price increases put forward by ministers or from various departments and agencies are likewise screened by security. When in September 1986 the Ministry of Education proposed hiking university fees for the new academic year, the Ministry of Interior reported that its security agents recommended postponing the increase "because of the danger of beginning studies under the shadow of a fee increase."[72] The government concurred in this assessment.

The input of security agencies into decision making is not restricted to vetoing price increases or other potentially destabilizing economic austerity measures. Indeed, the Ministry of Interior and especially the SSA became involved in personnel and policy matters throughout the state apparatus, where their agents are widely entrenched. Civil servants who have connections to them, whether through kinship, friendship, or otherwise, employ those links to advance their careers or influence policies. Wily operators in Egypt's games of bureaucratic politics consider it standing operating procedure to preempt interventions by security. Directors of private voluntary associations, many of whose activities are regarded suspiciously by security precisely because they lie outside the state's direct control, are particularly sensitive to this dimension. Samuel Habib, head of the Coptic Evangelical Church, which runs the extremely active Coptic Evangelical Organization for Social Services (CEOSS), meets periodically with Mubarak to inform him of CEOSS's activities. Over the years he learned that if he did not take this precaution, the inevitably negative reports on CEOSS's activities filed by security agents would result in orders to suspend programs.[73]

Organizational initiatives resulting in new behavior patterns immediately attract, as the CEOSS example suggests, the unwanted attentions of security agents. That fact alone is enough to discourage policy innovation, except by the naive or by those sufficiently committed and powerful to take on the security agencies in bureaucratic power games. Nevertheless, the increasing proportion of economic activities in the private sector, coupled with features of the general liberalization, including such seemingly minor ones as relaxation of restrictions over internal travel, has increased the complexity of tasks confronting security agencies and has begun to impose certain constraints on their intervention into policy making and implementation. No longer a law unto themselves, they seek political allies, of which the regime's party is a favorite.

THE NATIONAL DEMOCRATIC PARTY

Relations with Security Services

It is difficult to determine the precise demarcation line that separates the party from the security agencies. The Ministers of Interior and Local Government, both of whom are usually members of the party's polit-bureau, the NDP's chief executive body, are publicly and intimately involved in all of the party's activities, from selecting candidates to speaking at the party's public rallies. During the campaign for the *Shura* Council elections in the fall of 1986, for example, Zaki Badr spoke to numerous meetings of the party's provincial leaders, railing against the opposition and lauding his audience for their activities in cementing the alliance between the party and "popular bases."[74] Governors did likewise. Badr's replacement in Asyut, Mamduh Salim Zaki, lectured NDP members of that province on the conspiracies of the opposition and the need for integrating the efforts of "political and administrative bodies."[75] During this and the subsequent People's Assembly election campaign in the following spring, the opposition press reported innumerable instances of intervention by the Minister of Interior, governors, and even SSA agents in the selection of NDP candidates and subsequent support for them. *Al-Ahali* reported, for example, that General Atif Zaki, the director of security in Giza, had been pensioned off after one month in that job because he refused to ignore the illegal appropriation of some state land by two prominent NDP members of parliament who had the Ministry of Interior's backing.[76]

The NDP also has a foothold in the Ministry of Interior. The integration of the two organizations has become more noticeable as both have weakened and so increasingly sought one another's support. The head of the NDP since the formation of the Ali Lutfi government, Yusuf Wali, has forged a close working alliance with the Minister of the Interior. This not only provides Wali an extremely valuable ally in intraparty struggles, but it has resulted in his being permitted to nominate several of his clients to key posts either in the security system or in organizations over which they exert power. In 1986, for example, Ahmad Goueli and Yahia al-Hassan, both of whom had been Wali's subordinates at the Ministry of Agriculture, were appointed as governors of Damietta and Minufiya, respectively. Another former undersecretary of the Ministry of Agriculture whose career has benefited from Wali's patronage, Osman al-Khuli, was made president of Minufiya University. These and other appointments gave Wali a substantial base in the Ministry of Interior and in the politics of several key provinces.

The operational style of the NDP and the security services has also become similar. The party has developed its own corps of *bultagi*-s, or young toughs, whom it calls out to intimidate opposition supporters and candidates and to provide protection against retaliation. This recourse to physical intimidation and the general tightening of relations between the NDP and security services suggest the control function is gradually displacing others that the NDP's predecessors performed, albeit never very effectively.

Mubarak and the NDP

The key factor that explains the ebb and flow of Egypt's dominant parties over the past three decades has been presidential attitudes toward them. Periodically Nasser and Sadat felt the need to upgrade the control, communication, and mobilization functions of their parties, and they did so, but they did not sustain their commitment. Mubarak has had an ambivalent attitude toward Sadat's legacy of the NDP, which had been formed out of the failure of the liberalization experiment of 1976–1978. The Party was closely associated with the increasingly desperate and heavy-handed measures of the final months of the Sadat presidency. Presidential support for the NDP, therefore, could not easily be reconciled with a reintegration into the nation's political life of the semilegitimate opposition, much of the leadership of which was in prison in October 1981.

Mubarak chose to fudge the issue. When he was requested by Fuad Sirag al-Din, the leader of the Wafd, and other prominent members of the opposition to personally keep aloof from the NDP and become a President "above politics," he is reported to have responded that he was favorably disposed to that idea but would remain a member of the party during a transition period.[77] In the event, he did not follow that course of action, but neither did he throw his full weight behind the NDP either. His equivocal stance toward it has been its most fatal weakness, for only if he were to be personally strongly identified with it, to imbue it with some identifiable ideology, and to devote a larger measure of the state's resources to it could the NDP aspire to even the relatively limited importance that the ASU had under Nasser.

Mubarak had several reasons for not wanting to breathe much life into the NDP. Were he vigorously to do so the opposition, which he has courted from the first moment he became President, would loose its effectiveness as a counterbalance against the military, the parasitic bourgeoisie, the state apparatus generally, and the NDP itself. Also, Mubarak's personal style does not dovetail with the requirements of being party leader. His emotional austerity, preference for bureaucratic management through a chain of command, and only occasional, halfhearted efforts to float some slogan that might serve as a substitute for a more elaborate ideology are all incompatible with the demands of successful leadership.

The NDP that Mubarak inherited was paradoxically both fragmented and a vehicle for the interests of Sadatist elements of the bourgeoisie. Its three main factions were the residue of elements who had joined Nasser's ASU and for want of a better term are commonly called Nasserists; even more conservative elements who had jumped on board during the Sadat era in order to make their careers; and the most powerful of the parasitic bourgeoisie, including Osman Ahmad Osman. The last faction was the strongest, so Mubarak, who was trying to reduce the power of that class segment, could not simply throw his weight behind the NDP. His strategy was to select members of the first fragment—conservative Nasserists—and push them forward, while simultaneously attempting gradually to squeeze members of the other factions out of positions of influence. That process is still not complete, and the conservative Nasserist faction is itself hampered by fatal weaknesses, including the existence of more attractive, independent organizational manifestations of that movement. So the best Mubarak may be able to hope for from the NDP is continued fragmentation and weakness.

A final reason why Mubarak did not give the NDP a bigger push is that he did not want it to develop a will of its own or to serve as a platform on which talented, aspiring political leaders could demonstrate their abilities. For reasons discussed in Chapter 2 he has preferred to delegate authority to individuals who pose no threat to his image or position of power and who are, for the most part, gray, nonideological, bourgeois apparatchiks. This has become a more pronounced tendency as he has consolidated his hold on the presidency. Mustafa Khalil, whom

Mubarak inherited as head of the party, was closely associated with Sadat and Osman and was jettisoned a year later and replaced by Fuad Muhyi al-Din, who was independent of Osman and who possessed the personality and connections to be a force in his own right. Muhyi al-Din's death in 1984 marked the real transition to the Mubarak era, for it paved the way for the rise to power in the NDP of Secretary General Yusuf Wali, Assistant Secretary General Kamal Shazli, and various other apparatchiks, none of whom had substantial political careers prior to that time or disposed of resources comparable to those of Muhyi al-Din's. Seven of the 13 members of the politbureau were replaced at this time, as were 16 of the 23 members of the general secretariat and nine of the 15 chairmen of the party's standing committees.[78] Similar transitions occurred in the People's Assembly, where the Speaker, Kamal Laila, was succeeded by the unpopular and dogmatic Rifat al-Mahgub. This position is also a key one within the party, for it is in parliament that the NDP must do battle with the opposition. Neither Laila nor Mahgub could compare in talent or breadth of political experience to Sayed Marei, who had served Sadat in that capacity, or even Marei's deputy speaker, Gamal al-Utaifi. These and other appointments suggest that Mubarak is intent on elevating his stature by choosing to surround himself by those who do not themselves command attention.

The consequence for the NDP of Mubarak's treatment of it has been an inability effectively to recruit new and active cadres, to serve as a channel of two-way communication, to articulate the President's desires and spell out specific policies, or even to keep the opposition at bay with superior political performance as opposed to intimidation. The indicators of these shortcomings are to be found in the internal structure of the party, its performance in elections, and in the continued dominance of it by the numerically restricted but politically powerful parasitic bourgeoisie.

NDP Weakness

Structural Indicators. Since the NDP succeeded the Socialist Party of Egypt as the President's choice in the summer of 1978, it has had but four general congresses, despite the fact that clause 64 of the party's bylaws requires them to be held annually. The first two were held during the Sadat era. The latter of these, convened in late September 1981, provided the occasion for Sadat's last full-blown tirade against his domestic and external enemies, real and imagined.[79] The desire not to revive memories of this unpleasant event may have contributed to Mubarak's reluctance to convene a national congress, and he did not do so until in office for almost two years. There are, however, additional reasons for the dearth of party activity at this and other levels. A conference tentatively scheduled for the late summer of 1985 was called off when conflicts between factions threatened to break into the open.[80] Also, congresses under Nasser and Sadat were occasions on which elections were held "from the base to the top" of the party, but Mubarak has never held an election within the NDP.[81] All its posts are filled by appointees, a sure recipe for the triumph of opportunistic elements and the gradual atrophy of the party structure itself. Some of the party's newly successful candidates in the 1984 parliamentary elections demanded that elections be held to "renew party leadership," but that demand was successfully resisted by the incumbent party elite.[82]

Proceedings of the 1986 party congress confirmed the organization's inability to play a leadership role. The deliberations of the committee on religion, one of the twenty subcommittees, are particularly instructive. The recommendations of this committee were the only ones not released in full to the government press. Instead, the party announced a single recommendation from this committee—that the NDP supported the supervision of private mosques by the Ministry of Religious Endowments. The committee's chairman and link to the large Islamicist constituency, Dr. Abd al-Munaim al-Nimr, irritated that his efforts had been studiously ignored, explained after the congress that the committee had passed twenty-one additional recommendations within three major categories: "Purification of existing laws which are in contradiction with provisions of the *Sharia;* roles of the media in spreading religious values and morals; and the dedication of efforts to spread the Islamic message internally and externally."[83] Within the first subcategory the committee had recommended that the government move with alacrity to review existing legislation in light of the *sharia.* The recommendations were subsequently published in full, but not by the NDP or government press. Instead they appeared in the religious weekly of the Liberal Party, *al-Nur.*[84] The incident itself suggested that the party might have failed to manipulate the committee's proceedings in the desired direction, that it was undoubtedly divided on religious issues, and that it lacked the ability and will to take the lead in attempting to resolve these thorny issues across a broader front. By trying to finesse the issue of the relationship between Islam and politics in Egypt's semisecular polity, the NDP congress confirmed the status of the party as rearguard rather than vanguard of public opinion.

Preference for the use of the list system in elections is another indicator of the internal fragmentation and overall ineffectiveness of the NDP. Prior to 1984 Egyptian elections had always been conducted on a single or dual member, first past the post constituency system. (The dual-member provision was introduced during the Nasser era in order to fulfill the requirement of 50 percent membership of workers and peasants in the parliament). While the borders of constituencies were occasionally adjusted to suit the personal predilections of those supervising elections, they had remained fairly static since 1923. But the 1984 election law reduced the number of constituencies from 176 to 48. The average Delta or Upper Egyptian province that had previously had some 15–20, now had 3 to 5 constituencies. Moreover, voters were called upon to vote for party lists, with independents banned from offering their candidacies and those party lists not obtaining 8 percent of the votes losing those votes they had obtained to the list with the greatest number.

Many commentators have interpreted these changes to electoral law as a means by which a majority was ensured for the NDP, which is true. The additional importance of these dramatic changes for the internal structure of the NDP has, however, received little comment, despite outcries against it by the NDP rank and file.[85] The new electoral law destroyed the bargaining power of notables with the ruling party, for not only could they not run as independents, but the constituencies were now so large that those whose power bases virtually guaranteed success in the old, relatively small ones now had to sail in broader, uncharted waters and in competition with other local notables. Those in charge of selecting candidates to serve on the NDP's lists, which included the party's leaders, representatives of the security agencies, the President himself, and various ministers, could, once they resolved their conflicts, impose their choices on constituencies.

The cost of this innovation was that a large number of prominent figures refused to have truck with this system and simply opted out, so the party was left with generally inferior candidates. While the law was partially revised in 1987 as a result of a court ruling that the 1984 electoral law was unconstitutional, in its key respects it remained much the same. In the 1987 elections many prominent political figures once again refused to offer their candidacies on NDP lists, and less prominent members of the party grumbled very audibly about the dictatorial methods of the party leadership and its use of the list system to manipulate potential candidates. A device to ensure centralized control at the cost of excluding capable politicians, the list system also militates against recruitment of young, energetic political activists. When Yusuf Wali spoke in 1986 of invigorating the NDP by bringing youths into the Shura Council, he was referring to those in the 50-plus age group. Wali's youths are those who were not active in politics in the Sadat era and who were willing to sign on with the NDP on the Secretary General's terms.[86]

The porosity of the NDP is suggested by the lack of a rigorous definition or test of membership. Those who defeat NDP-endorsed candidates are regularly invited by the party to join it, a practice that has negative consequences for party loyalty. When a prominent member of the party argued in the politbureau that the NDP should remain committed to those candidates it had endorsed, whether they won or lost, he found himself in a small minority.[87]

Powerful figures who have built their careers on the solid foundations of control over important organizations in the state apparatus and who are backed by leading members of the parasitic bourgeoise have been able to ignore the NDP, although there are signs that such independence diminished as Yusuf Wali tightened his control over the party in 1986–

1987. Saad Hagrass, for example, built up a substantial personal power base as director of the agrarian reform organization under Sayed Marei, and over the years he cemented his personal tie to Osman. He joined the ASU in 1972 and was elected to the People's Assembly in 1976. In 1979 he shifted to the *Shura* Council, which, according to his account, was the biggest political mistake he ever made. Like other ambitious politicians, he thought that Sadat intended it, rather than the People's Assembly, to serve as the major parliamentary body. In 1984 he shifted back to the People's Assembly and was then elected as chairman of its agricultural committee and, subsequently, as president of the syndicate of agricultural engineers. He had, of course, to offer his candidacy in 1984 as an NDP member. But when asked about his relationship with the party, he denied any connection to it.[88] Neutral observers pointed out that much of his popularity was due to the fact that he was seen as being independent of the party. He studiously avoided participation in the NDP agriculture committee and indicated his distaste for its chairman and for the Secretary General of the party as well. This was a challenge the latter preferred not to ignore. In the 1987 parliamentary elections Wali prevented Hagrass from obtaining a place on the NDP list from his home province of Daqahliya. This was made possible because Hagrass was long-retired from the agrarian reform organization and because Wali, working as Mubarak's loyal political bureaucrat, was charged with thinning out the ranks of Osman clients in the party structure. Hagrass's outspoken disloyalty to the party and its boss made him an ideal target. But other prominent NDP members, such as Ahmad Abdilla, chairman of the foreign affairs committee in the People's Assembly, continued to voice sentiments very similar to those of Hagrass, suggesting that it was probably the Osman connection that cost Hagrass his job rather than his questionable loyalty to the party.

Another factor that has weakened party discipline and loyalty is the party's practice of trying to bribe members of opposition parties to defect to the NDP. Inducements offered include top posts in the regime's party. Politicians who are being vilified by leaders of the NDP have found themselves virtually overnight in leadership positions within it. Hilmi Hadidi, for example, was in 1985 attracted out of the Socialist Labor Party by the offer of the post of assistant secretary general. From the outset, however, he and Wali conflicted, possibly as a result of the harsh words they had previously exchanged. Although Wali eventually got the better of Hadidi, the conflict further debilitated the NDP and the practice of enticing opposition deserters into the NDP continues.

Finally, structural weakness in the NDP is suggested by the virtually total absence of branches of it, whether in urban or rural areas. Other than the headquarters building along the Nile in Cairo, there are very few physical manifestations of the party's presence. A social scientist who has spent over two years in Upper Egypt claims never to have seen a party office there nor encountered any behavioral manifestation of party life, whether governmental or opposition, in villages and towns.[89] A survey of 200 residents in a Delta province turned up 33 who claimed to be members of the NDP and 1 who indicated membership in an opposition party, or 17 percent of the sample as a whole. None, however, had ever attended a village or town party meeting.[90] A survey of Cairo University students revealed similarly apathetic attitudes and the absence of effective party activity on that crucial campus.[91] The party newspaper, *Mayo* was found to be read occasionally by 6 percent of a sample of newspaper readers, compared to 34 percent for *al-Wafd*, 8 percent for *al-Ahali*, 6 percent for *al-Shaab*, and 4 percent for *al-Ahrar*.[92]

Elections. Because of the party's weakness it does not play a major role in the control of elections. That task is handled by various branches of the state apparatus, including the Ministries of Interior and Local Government. In the countryside the agricultural bureaucracy, including cooperatives, the extension service, and the Principal Bank for Agricultural Development and Credit, through which all subsidized inputs are distributed and which is virtually the sole source of agricultural credit, are used to provide the appropriate carrots and sticks. Their equivalents in urban areas, principally the administration and the large public-sector companies, do not dominate urban economies or the lives of their clients as totally, hence the NDP regularly records poorer results in cities.

The process of candidate selection is complex and conflictual precisely because the party is but a weak arm of the state and one in which various powerful personages feel they have a right to intervene. As the NDP struggled to put together its lists of candidates in February-March 1987, *al-Ahali* reported that presidential adviser Usama al-Baz had refused to meet with the governor of Daqahliya because that official had rejected the candidacy of Baz's nephew; that the SSA had vetoed the names of several NDP candidates for the "independent" seats in Daqahliya and instead offered them jobs in local administration; that the *shilla*-s (small groups of friends and allies) of Wali, Mahgub, Osman, and others were in amoebalike fashion forming and dissolving coalitions to secure nominations for candidates in various constituencies; and of course that the Minister of Interior was intervening across the length and breadth of the country.[93]

Voters do not display the same enthusiasm as candidates, suggesting that the heated contests over nominations are not a sign of political vigor but an indication that patronage is the central concern of the organization and its members. Despite the claim by Wali a month before the 1987 election that he was commanding a force of 42,000 party cadres who were mobilizing voters behind the NDP, the evidence suggested this was either wishful thinking or those cadres were sorely deficient in organizational skills.[94] Despite the usual backing of the state apparatus the NDP's rallies were very poorly attended. The opposition press published photos of vast marquees with few other than the candidates and their staffs in attendance at scheduled rallies.[95] When the votes were finally tabulated the government announced that 7.7 million of the country's 14.3 million voters had cast ballots, for a turnout rate of 54 percent, of which the NDP obtained 76 percent. The turnout rate in the 1984 election had been 42 percent, while the government claimed that in the 1986 *Shura* Council election the turnout was 80 percent, of which the NDP took 97 percent of votes.

All of these figures are exaggerations of a significant magnitude, particularly those for the *Shura* Council. A well-informed source at the U.S. Embassy estimated that for this election the government had simply added a zero to the actual rate of about 8 percent. Other sources claimed that 5 percent would be an overestimate.[96] The Vice President of the Wafd Party, Wahid Rifat, claimed that in all these elections more than two-thirds of the registered voters do not cast ballots and that 90 percent of voters in cities do not go to the polls. He further claimed that the electoral register lists only 55 percent of those actually eligible to vote.[97] In a speech to a labor rally after the 1987 election, Mubarak lamented that only 20 percent of Cairenes had voted.[98] The *Economist* stated that less than 25 percent of registered voters in Cairo, Giza, and Alexandria had voted in the 1984 election.[99] A firsthand observer of those elections claims that in the urban and rural polling stations he visited, the turnout "nowhere exceeds 20 percent."[100] The general secretary of the NPUP's central committee estimated the turnout of the 1987 election at 30 percent, arguing that the electoral list contained 3 million Egyptians abroad and 2.5 million who have died, leaving a real total of 9 million, of whom around one-third went to the polls.[101] Probably the most accurate official reports on an election were those issued for the Alexandria by-election of 4 January 1984, for the government was attempting to induce the opposition to participate in general elections scheduled for later that year. The NPUP candidate won by 189 votes. Less than 10 percent of registered voters went to the polls.[102]

A study of political participation of university students conducted in 1980–1981 revealed extremely low rates of political involvement. Of the sample of over 500 students of voting age from Cairo University, 81.2 percent had not registered to vote. Of those who had, 54.3 percent did not vote in the previous election. Of those who did vote, 27.9 percent explained they did so because of personal and family connections to the candidate.[103] A prominent Egyptian political scientist, when asked to explain the low level of voter turnout responded that "The Egyptian people realize that the political balance is already calculated ahead of time in favor of a given party."[104]

The NDP, in combination with the state apparatus, has contained oppositional participation more or less effectively, but it has not attracted voters to say nothing of dedicated cadres to its ranks. That discontent with the party may be growing is indicated by the unusually high number of "spoiled" ballots, or those with no preference indicated, cast in the 1987 election. It was reported that there were over 400,000 such ballots, compared to 221,000 in 1984, for a 122 percent increase. The relative uniformity of the rate of spoiled ballots across constituencies suggested that it was not a function of illiteracy. While it could be due to various factors, it might well be a protest vote.[105]

Another idiosyncrasy of the 1987 election was that for the first time since 1952 an incumbent cabinet minister was defeated. Gamal al-Sayid, who had entered the cabinet in November 1986 as Minister for War Production, lost in Cairo's southern district to Shaikh Yusuf al-Badri, the candidate of the Alliance and a longtime activist cleric who had built up a personal following in the industrial suburb of Helwan. While Sayid was a newcomer to his portfolio, the fact that the Ministry of War Production has several large factories in the constituency that employ over 30,000 workers, of whom 18,000 are registered to vote locally, would normally be sufficient to guarantee a victory for virtually any Minister of War Production. While the difference between the two was but 282 votes out of over 213,000 total and Sayid had, instead of courting workers, taken a tough line on several employment issues after becoming minister, commentators on the election interpreted the failure of the NDP candidate as a result of infighting and laxity in the NDP. After the party hierarchy had imposed an unpopular list of candidates on the constituency, the party apparatchiks either ceased activity altogether or went to work behind the scenes for the Alliance. One of the prominent candidates on the NDP list, the Minister of Religious Endowments, slept in on the morning of the election until 11:00 instead of mobilizing his supporters and supervising at polling booths, as is typically done. The NDP failed entirely to coordinate its efforts with the union associated with the military factories. In short, the party apparatus fell apart.[106]

This begs the question of why the Ministry of Interior did not "correct" the results once they were in its controversial computer, a practice alleged to have been commonplace in the 1987 election, the first in which a computer was used to tabulate results.[107] While that would have caused a strong reaction, as it did in the Sharqiya constituency where former Minister of Economy Mustafa al-Said was first declared elected before the computer changed its mind, discontent could have been contained, as it was in the Said case. The real explanation might be that Mubarak himself ordered that Sayid go down to defeat, not only as a demonstration of the fairness of the elections but possibly also as a warning to Sayid's patron, Field Marshal Abu Ghazala. Nevertheless, even if Mubarak's intervention was the real cause of Sayid's defeat, the fact of the party's disarray and lassitude remains. All that might be different is that such incompetence is absolutely typical and that it was simply latched onto in order to explain this particular loss.

Dominance of the Bourgeoisie. Sadat contracted the social base of the Nasserist single party, shedding lower strata and concentrating control in the hands of the bourgeoisie. Mubarak has not reversed that process.

He has, however, gradually replaced NDP members who rose to prominence under Sadat with other members of the bourgeoisie who were not directly politically involved with the Sadat regime. In so doing he has eroded some of the influence of the previously dominant parasitic bourgeoisie. By 1987 there were signs that he was attempting to overcome the problem of fragmentation within the NDP by concentrating an increasing amount of power in the hands of its Secretary General, but the centrifugal forces are probably too strong for Wali ever to weld the personalities and factions into a cohesive whole.

Even Sadat, who staged the Corrective Revolution of 1971 that purged his opponents in the state apparatus, did not achieve a transformation of the single party's membership overnight. While a significant change of party leadership was effected in the 1971 elections, the exclusion of other elements proceeded only gradually, finally culminating in a thoroughgoing housecleaning when the Socialist Party of Egypt was transformed into the NDP in 1978. At that time virtually the entirety of the nonbourgeois local-level leadership was purged. In Sharqiya, which exemplifies predominantly rural Delta provinces, not a single representative of peasants who had been active in the ASU or the Socialist Party of Egypt was appointed to any of the NDP district or provincial committees at that time.[108]

Nor have peasants made a comeback under Mubarak. In Sharqiya, not only is the NDP still lacking peasant members in its district and provincial committees, but their representation in the *Shura* Council and People's Assembly has declined even further than the already low levels of the Sadat period. In the 1987 People's Assembly elections three NDP candidates running in the peasant category in Sharqiya won election, compared to five in the 1976 elections and four in the 1979 elections. In 1979 another peasant representative running as a member of the NPUP also won, whereas in 1987 none of the opposition parties succeeded in electing a member in the peasant category from Sharqiya. *Shura* Council election results reveal a similar trend. In the 1980 elections one peasant representative was elected from Sharqiya. In the 1983 half-renewal elections he was joined by another NDP peasant representative. But in the 1986 election none of the eight seats from Sharqiya was taken by a candidate running in the peasant category. In the 1984 elections 12.7 percent of NDP candidates were "peasants," whereas for the population as a whole more than one-third truly are peasants.

The replacement of Sadatist NDP leadership at the national and provincial levels is suggested by the high turnover rates in recent elections. In the 1986 *Shura* Council elections, 31 of the 70 NDP candidates were new. In the 1987 People's Assembly elections, 42.5 percent of NDP candidates had not previously been in parliament. Moreover, turnover rates were in the 1987 election very high in the two provinces where influence of Sadatist *munfatihun* in the NDP had most persisted. In Alexandria 74 percent and in Port Said 80 percent of the NDP candidates were new. Only Ismailiya, which also had an 80 percent turnover rate, was at all comparable. Although all new members in Alexandria and Port Said were of the bourgeoisie or the labor "aristocracy," they were not the wealthy importers who had dominated both delegations previously. In Port Said those *munfatihun* shifted their allegiances to the Wafd Party, as they did, although to a lesser extent, in Alexandria.

Profiles of first-time candidates on the NDP lists for Alexandria in 1987 illustrate the preferred social bases of recruitment to the NDP under Mubarak. New candidates in Alexandria's first district, which spreads eastward from the city along the Mediterranean coast and includes numerous fishing villages and extensive agricultural land, included a client of the party's secretary general who served as chairman of the Alexandria NDP's committee on rural development and who offered his candidacy in the peasant category and an executive from the provincial federation of the union running as a worker. A second close associate of Yusuf Wali, a professor at the faculty of agriculture of Alexandria University, was likewise placed on the list. The upper bourgeoisie in this district was represented by the chairman of the party's industrial committee who is president of three large paper companies. This district also included one of the few woman candidates on NDP lists. She is chairman of the women's committee in the Alexandria branch of the NDP and a member of the al-Dib family, one of Alexandria's wealthiest mercantile-industrial families. The "independent" candidate nominated by the NDP for Alexandria's first district is chairman of the board of several large construction companies and one of the city's most successful businessmen.

New NDP candidates in Alexandria's second district included the assistant secretary of the party's provincial branch, who is also president of the Alexandria Chamber of Commerce and of the United Club of that city, which plays a leading role in the life of Alexandria's bourgeoisie. The new worker representative nominated from the second district is an employee of the Sporting Club, which if anything is even more prestigious than the United Club. The head of the party's list for the third district, which extends from the middle of Alexandria all the way to the border of Matruh Province on Egypt's northwest Mediterranean coast, is the president of yet another well-known club and chairman of the board of a large manufacturing company. This list also included two prominent lawyers and the president of a leading agricultural company. The party nominated for the "independent" seat in the third district the prominent chairman of several petroleum companies.[109] The backgrounds of these new candidates suggest that the NDP was increasingly closely associated with the old business establishment of Alexandria as opposed to the parasitic bourgeoisie that had emerged under Sadat, and that Mubarak was encouraging the Secretary General of the NDP to build up a considerable network of clients within this and no doubt other provincial branches of the party.

A sample of 23 of the 31 newly elected members of the 1986 *Shura* Council confirms the expansion of Secretary General Yusuf Wali's power base.[110] Ten of them were employed in the sprawling agricultural colleges and universities or in agricultural labor unions. It can safely be assumed that all of them are beholden in one way or another to Wali, who as Minister of Agriculture since January 1982 has worked assiduously to consolidate his control over the various bureaucratic elements that together constitute the agricultural sector. Moreover, another 10 candidates in the sample indicated involvement in agricultural activities, such as participating in the establishment of cooperatives or "facilitating mechanization of agriculture" (presumably by selling agricultural machinery), or listed as their main political objective some aspect of improving agricultural production. The latter suggests at a minimum that candidates perceived the wind to be blowing in Wali's direction, and at least in some cases these phrases were intended to indicate the candidate's association with the Secretary General and his concerns. Eleven of the 23 had, like Wali, begun their political careers in the ASU prior to 1971, whereas 10 had entered politics during the Sadat era. In establishing his personal power base, Wali, who had spent much of the Sadat period out of Egypt, was collecting around himself an appreciable number of those who like himself could, because of their organizational memberships if not political beliefs, be called Nasserists.

Ahmad Abd al-Akhar, who has served as chairman of the NDP agriculture committee since the party was formed, exemplifies the type of bourgeois apparatchiks who now constitute the dominant element in the party. After graduating from Cairo University's faculty of agriculture in 1947, this scion of a landowning family from Upper Egypt worked until 1961 in various bilateral and multilateral agricultural and rural development aid programs. When his patron, Minister of Agriculture Sayed Marei, lost his post in that year, Abd al-Akhar devoted his efforts to a commercial onion dehydration project in his native province of Sohag. When Marei bounced back into the cabinet after the 1967 war, Abd al-Akhar's political career once again took off. In 1968 he won election to parliament from Sohag and became chairman of that province's ASU committee. In 1971 he, like Marei, cast his fate with Sadat against the leftist tendency represented by Ali Sabri, Sami Sharaf, and Sharawi Gumaa and was subsequently rewarded. When Sadat appointed Marei secretary general of the ASU, the latter picked Abd al-Akhar to be assistant secretary for Upper Egypt. Two months after Marei was transferred from his post to the presidency in 1973, Abd al-Akhar followed his patron. In November 1974, he was promoted to the powerful post of governor of Giza, where he served for four years, after which time he became director general of Sadat's office for the NDP as well as chairman of its agricultural committee. Abd al-Akhar became one of the beneficiaries of the process of privatizing presidential patronage when, in 1982, he was made chairman of the Giza Company for Food Security, which is a food producing and processing conglomerate. Although Marei and Wali are competitors in both political and professional life, Abd al-Akhar managed to establish a sufficiently close connection with the latter to prevent his ouster from the chairmanship of the agricultural committee. He is, in sum, a typical representative of the second layer of leadership in the NDP, although he enjoyed greater political success under Sadat than most.[111]

That the NDP remains a vehicle of bourgeois interests, despite the prevalence of leadership elements who did their political apprenticeship in Nasser's ASU and despite sloganeering about "protecting the interests of those with limited incomes," is revealed by the party's policy recommendations. These emerge from time to time from various of its 15 committees and are generally intended to serve as the bases for legislation or for ministerial decrees. The economy and finance committee, for example, convened a conference on 14 January 1987 to discuss means of "reforming the public sector." The proceedings degenerated into a virulent attack on that sector orchestrated by the committee's chairman, culminating in recommendations for public-sector enterprises to be converted into limited liability companies of which 49 percent of shares should be offered for purchase by private investors; for the management to be made completely independent of government control; for "social pricing" to be abolished; for various laws favorable to workers to be repealed; and for more of the state's investment capital to be allocated to the private sector. Reform, in sum, to those in the NDP responsible for policy formulation meant dismantling the public sector.[112]

Ahmad Abd al-Akhar's agricultural committee has worked consistently to undo what provisions remain of the agrarian reform laws of the Nasser era. In 1975 that committee, when part of the ASU, backed legislation that increased land taxes (hence rents) and abolished committees that had been established by the agrarian reform laws to hear disputes between landowners and tenants, which thereby obviated the expensive necessity of going to court. In 1986 the committee recommended further dilution of the agrarian reforms in the following ways: more than doubling rents from 7 to 15 times the land tax; canceling rental contracts in cases of subletting; returning land to owners on the death of lessees who do not have heirs working the land; and granting lessors the right to sell rented land in two installments over a five-year period, with compensation to lessees of about 10 percent of the land's value. All of the committee's other recommendations were also favorable to bourgeois interests in agriculture. Purchase of reclaimed land was to be simplified; agricultural cooperatives transformed into limited liability companies; producer organizations modeled on joint-venture enterprises created; cooperative marketing abolished for some crops; and a greater share of the profits of cooperatives given to their shareholders rather than to their employees.[113] In 1987 the committee also supported draft legislation in parliament for the payment of compensation to those whose land had been confiscated by the agrarian reforms.[114]

While all of these proposals are inimical to the interests of small peasants, NDP "peasant" representatives, who are uniformly of the rural bourgoisie, are even more likely to support such changes than are other members of parliament. In a survey of MP's attitudes and voting behavior the Strategic Studies Center of *al-Ahram* found that a higher percentage of peasant members (57 percent) supported the provisions of Law 67 for 1975 that penalized peasant lessees than did the membership of parliament as a whole (48 percent). Of the peasant representatives, 72 percent supported the proposal to increase rents; 62 percent were in favor of dissolving the *muassassat* (public sector holding companies), compared to an overall average of 53 percent.[115]

The composition of committees of the NDP, its policy recommendations, and the behavior of its peasant representatives in parliament support the proposition that the party has severed its links to the peasantry. Rural political mobilization, which occurred fitfully under the auspices of the ASU during the Nasser era, has given way entirely in the NDP to the priorities of control and demobilization of the peasantry combined with the consolidation of power by the bourgeoisie. Erosion of the single party's base in the labor movement has also occurred as independent labor activists have deserted the NDP for opposition parties. "Worker" candidates nominated by the NDP are either members of the labor union bureaucracy, which for all intents and purposes is an integral branch of the state, or are relatively high-ranking employees in the administration or public or joint sectors.[116]

The evidence suggests that Mubarak's intent toward the NDP has so far not been to transform the class character of the party he inherited from Sadat. He has allowed it to remain an enclave of bourgeois exclusivity. His more limited goals have been to rid the leadership ranks of the party of some of the more notorious *munfatihun*, such as Rashid Osman; to build up a clientage network of bourgeois apparatchiks, a task that has been executed on his behalf by Yusuf Wali; and to isolate the most powerful of the old Sadat entourage, chief among whom are Osman Ahmad Osman and Mustafa Khalil. While these men are still chairmen of the NDP popular development and foreign affairs committees, respectively, and enjoy reasonably good relations with Wali, their influence within the party has been reduced although by no means eradicated. Osman did not head the Ismailiya list for the NDP in the 1987 elections and instead ran as an NDP "independent." The turnover rate in that governorate was 80 percent among NDP candidates, which suggested the government was removing several of Osman's clients.

So while Mubarak may have made some headway in subjecting the NDP to his personal will, he has yet to even begin, if he ever will, to make the party more representative of social forces in the country or even responsive to the narrow class interests it now represents, as opposed to the interests of bourgeois party activists themselves. The last elections in the NDP were in 1980, a year prior to Sadat's death.

Mubarak appears content to order affairs within the party on the model of chain of command, while employing his security agencies to impose the NDP on the electorate. As a result, both institutions are weakening, leaving the President without a substantial base of support outside the decaying state apparatus. While the elections of 1987 paved the way for his second term as President because the NDP majority in parliament guaranteed his nomination, those elections, precisely because they were rigged to ensure an NDP victory, did nothing to enhance his legitimacy. In that regard he has made virtually no progress since coming to office and may, therefore, have to rely increasingly heavily on the stick to maintain control.

MINISTRY OF SOCIAL AFFAIRS

Various of the ministries also perform important control functions over their clienteles. Many ministries, including transport, education, supply, tourism, and others, dispose of their own police forces in addition to utilizing the normal bureaucratic leverage. The Ministry of Education is the first line of defense against student protests; a major task of the Ministry of Agriculture is to ensure political quiesence in the countryside; the Ministry of Transport is responsible for preventing strikes in that critical industry, and the Ministry of the Labor Force and Training has the same responsibility over a broader front; the Ministry of Religious Endowments (and/or Religious Affairs) oversees activities in mosques, including Friday sermons, which are subject to its censorship; and the Ministry of Insurance and Social Affairs regulates private voluntary associations. Like other elements in the control system, the ministries are confronting increasingly pluralistic activities with stagnant or declining resources and in the absence of effective coordination between the system's constituent parts. Operations of the Ministry of Insurance and Social Affairs (MSA) under Mubarak illustrate these trends.

The rising prominence of the Minister of Insurance and Social Affairs is a good indicator of the growing importance of that portfolio. Assigned that post in the wake of Sadat's trip to Jerusalem, Amal Osman, a specialist in international law, has remained minister until this time. She is the longest-serving minister currently in the cabinet. A friend of Jihan Sadat's, she was one of the few figures closely associated with the previous president or his wife to make the transition successfully to the Mubarak era. This was due in part to her utility to Mubarak in the early days of his presidency, when he needed a ceremonial "first lady" but, with the role of Jihan Sadat fresh in his and the public's mind, was reluctant to push his wife Suzy into the limelight.[117] But Amal Osman's political longevity is probably due more to the compatibility of her image with Mubarak's desire to shed the more objectionable authoritarian aspects of his predecessor's regime. The MSA is the first point of contact between the government and associational activity, which was bound to increase as a consequence of the policy of liberalization. The MSA is also an organizational mainstay with which foreign aid agencies, government and private, must deal. Mubarak thus required a minister with a politically benign and progressive image but who could apply the iron fist, particularly with radical Islamicists, when necessary. Having performed her role admirably, Amal Osman is, after Mubarak's wife, the most powerful woman in the country. Among other indications of that prominence is her preeminent role in choosing women candidates for NDP lists.[118]

The MSA employs several techniques in controlling private voluntary organizations (PVOs). All of them must, according to the provisions of the Law of Associations (Law 32 of 1964), register with the MSA and have their bylaws approved by it. Attending meetings of unregistered organizations is a criminal offense. Private fund-raising activities are strictly regulated, both in order to limit organizational autonomy and to provide a source of income for employees of the ministry. It routinely rejects requests by PVOs to raise funds independently, demanding that they participate in the ministry's centralized collection campaign, Winter Aid (a sort of United Way). Collectors in the Winter Aid campaign are the staff of the MSA. They receive 3 percent of donations. Bigger rake-offs are secured by high-ranking employees, who accomplish that while simultaneously participating in control functions. The favored mechanism is to force PVOs to accept these bureaucrats, frequently on their retirement, as members of their boards or even as their presidents, both of which are typically paid positions. These plums in turn provide inducements for loyalty in the ministry and to the minister herself.[119] According to a report in the opposition press, members of Amal Osman's *shilla* in the ministry are particularly well rewarded. In 1986 the first undersecretary, Mustafa Muhammad al-Mahi, was a president or member of the board of 18 PVOs, from one of which, the Society of the Day of the Hospitals, he was accused by the public prosecutor of having embezzled funds. Another member of the *shilla*, al-Mahi's predecessor, was paid as a consultant to the ministry and served as a member of the board or president of 31 PVOs. The legal adviser to the ministry, Ramzi al-Shair, who was simultaneously the dean of the college of law at Ain Shams University, was a member of 11 PVO boards.[120] A poll conducted in 1985 by a consultant to the Ford Foundation of 180 members of boards of PVOs found that virtually without exception they identified the MSA and its employees "feeding off the PVOs" as the greatest obstacle to the successful operations of their organizations.[121] In this sentiment they were joined by the principal theoretician of *al-Jihad*, the Islamicist organization whose members assassinated Sadat. Abd al-Salam Farag, in his *The Hidden Imperative*, condemned Muslim charitable associations "because these associations are subject to state control, registered and directed by it."[122]

The MSA's system of control, which might be labeled "passive" as opposed to the "active" control exerted by the Ministry of Interior, is not applied equally across the galaxy of PVOs. Those with more substantial political and financial resources are much more able to defend themselves from the depredations and control of the ministry. PVOs composed largely of the urban poor or of the peasantry, for example, which receive backing from international aid agencies, are far more likely to be able to squirm out from under the ministry's heavy hand than are their counterparts lacking such connections. Well aware of this, the ministry works assiduously to curtail the activities of such international agencies. Similarly, Christian PVOs, backed by the considerable financial and political resources of the church, enjoy more autonomy than Moslem ones. Associations composed of high-status professionals are able to win more independence than those composed principally of individuals with fewer skills and resources. The Businessmen's Association, for example, commenced activities in 1985 with the government's blessing without having registered with the ministry, a novel event in Egypt's recent organizational history and one that caused considerable speculation and comment.

A group of Harvard graduates, attempting to emulate the success of the Businessmen's Association, ran into difficulty with the MSA. This may have been due to the fact that the ministry had been locked in a battle with the faculty club of Cairo University since 1984 and therefore perceived the founding of the Harvard Club as an end-run strategy by some of the ministry's antagonists. But the faculty club has for the most part been able to keep the ministry at bay. Its success is illustrative of the expansion of pluralism more generally and the decreasing ability of the MSA to contain those, such as professors and businessmen, who have the ability to defend their interests. Increasingly the MSA is a watchdog over the activities of the politically semiarticulate and financially handicapped, as associations composed of those of higher status escape its network of control and enter the domain of the next layer of the control system, which is the Ministry of Interior and the security agencies.

The MSA also employs its tools of passive control in conjunction with the more aggressive activities of the security agencies, but coordination between the two levels appears to be problematical because of the increasing complexity of their tasks and because of differences inherent in passive and active systems of control. The MSA cannot be too closely associated with direct means of political repression or it would lose its credibility altogether and possibly stimulate a plethora of challenges to its passive control activities. Its behavior in the train drivers' strike of 7 July 1986 illustrates this dilemma. The strike was organized not by activists in the union or opposition political parties but by the president and leading members of the *rabita*, (association of train drivers), a registered PVO with the MSA, the nominal purpose of which is to look after the social welfare of its members. When the drivers abandoned their trains on the night of 7 July, they gathered at the *rabita* building in a poor quarter of Cairo and issued a series of demands for improved pay and reforms of the dangerously dilapidated railway system. The military responded by organizing alternative transport, while the Minister of Interior declared a state of emergency and ordered CSF troops to assault the *rabita* headquarters and seize everyone within.

At some point in these proceedings the Minister of Social Affairs is reported to have dissolved the *rabita*, thereby paving the way for the sequestration of its funds and so assisting the strike-breaking. But some two weeks later, once the government had the situation well in hand and the troublemakers in jail, Amal Osman denied having dissolved the *rabita*, although confirmed that its board of directors had been dismissed. Presumably she took this position because of the considerable negative publicity that surrounded the act of dissolving the *rabita*, which was a symbol of self-help welfare among a category of workers who, by common consent, had over the past few years received a very raw deal indeed.[123] Confused governmental accounts of precisely who had done what and who was actually responsible for supervising and dissolving the *rabita*'s board of directors—the governor, the Minister of Interior, the Minister of Labor, or the Minister of Social Affairs—suggested both disagreement and poor coordination between the various control agencies. Subsequent accounts also revealed that drivers had been meeting in the *rabita* headquarters for weeks prior to the strike, issuing complaints and inviting the authorities to hear them out. That no one did may be due because it was not clear who, in this complex and overlapping system of control, bore ultimate responsibility.[124]

Similar problems beset the systems of control over students, journalists, Christian and Moslem community welfare workers, and virtually all other clienteles as their levels of activity have increased. The gradual loss of authority of the MSA over voluntary associations comprised principally of the articulate bourgeoisie, of whatever political outlook, is indicative of a more general trend. The Ministry of Agriculture similarly exerts much less control over wealthy landowners than poor peasants. The Ministry of Religious Endowments is far more concerned with religious activities of those drawn from the poor quarters on the peripheries of the major cities than with those of the Moslem Brotherhood, which has evolved into a bourgeois, conservative expression of the Islamicist tendency. Passive elements of the system of control, in particular, are increasingly targeted on the relatively uninfluential and the poor.

EXCLUSIONARY CORPORATISM?

Is uneven pluralization of the polity an intended or unintended consequence of regime policy? If it is the former, it suggests the government is following the third strategy outlined in the introduction to this chapter— that is, it is seeking to impose exclusionary corporatism by demobilizing workers and peasants in order to achieve economic competitiveness demanded by a strategy of export-led growth. If, on the other hand, the pluralization of bourgeois associational life has proceeded more rapidly than that of collective activity among the lower social strata simply because in the liberalized political climate the resources of the bourgeoisie are much more easily mobilized, it suggests that over time increasingly effective political participation may seep further down in the social structure. The latter prognosis is consistent with the interpretations of pluralism emerging either because the deterioration of the system of control leaves Mubarak no realistic alternative or because Mubarak is skillfully equilibrating political and economic liberalization in order to prevent the pressure from unmet demands blowing the lid off the system.

Evidence presented in this chapter does not permit an unequivocal answer, although it lends some support to the proposition that Mubarak has tentatively embarked on a course of exclusionary corporatism. In his second presidential term, he has done nothing to expand the narrow social base of the NDP. He has instead pursued the more limited goal of replacing a Sadatist faction within it with one loyal to himself. That, however, could be a necessary first step in the expansion of participation, with it to spread downward as Mubarak consolidates his authority. On the other hand, the opposition political party with most support among organized labor and the peasantry, the NPUP, has been more harshly and consistently repressed than any other. Also, the system of passive control has become so markedly uneven and discriminatory in application that it points to design rather than accident. Finally, the regime without question perceives its major enemy to be Islamic activists grouped within underground organizations and comprised mainly of socially marginal elements. While not capable of overthrowing the system single handedly, they could serve as the mobilizational nucleus of a mass movement, and of course they can assassinate political leaders. For these reasons the government has enticed conservative Islamicist elements, including the Moslem Brotherhood, into the formal, legal political opposition and ensured that their economic interests are protected at least as well as those of the secular bourgeoisie. Toward radicals the repressive apparatus is being granted a longer leash, for as austerity continues to bite deeper negative reactions are anticipated. But whether the system of control— seriously weakened by having to respond to mixed signals and to make increasingly sophisticated differentiations between legal and illegal activities, favored and disfavored clienteles, and at the same time suffering from an eroded presence among precisely those elements most likely to rebel—can ultimately impose exclusionary corporatism remains to be seen. The various challenges it confronts are the subject of the next chapter.

NOTES

1. According to a recent crossnational comparison of the political impact of anomic disorder stimulated by consumer subsidy cuts, such violence rarely has

significant long-term political effects. This can be but cold comfort though to political elites attempting to maintain stability. See Henry S. Bienen and Mark Gersovitz, "Consumer Subsidy Cuts, Violence, and Political Stability," *Comparative Politics*, 19, 1 (October 1986), pp. 25–44.

2. For a humorous description of mysteriously rising water, electricity, telephone, and gas bills and for the government's response, which is to deny any increase in charges, see Ahmed el Mahdi, "The Mystery of Rising Utility Rates," *Middle East Times* (22–28 March 1987).

3. For a brief review of the literature on inclusionary and exclusionary corporatism and the application of these concepts to Egypt, see John Waterbury, *The Egypt of Nasser and Sadat: The Political Economy of Two Regimes* (Princeton: Princeton University Press, 1983), pp. 309–310.

4. Robert Bianchi, "The Corporatization of the Egyptian Labor Movement," *The Middle East Journal* 40, 3 (Summer 1986), pp. 429–444. That pluralization has proceeded unevenly and to the advantage of the bourgeoisie is a theme common to most analyses by Egyptian social scientists of liberalization under Mubarak. For a sample of that literature see note 7, Chapter 2.

5. On the change of the class base of the dominant party from the Nasser to the Sadat era, see Raymond A. Hinnebusch, Jr., *Egyptian Politics Under Sadat: The Post-Populist Development of an Authoritarian-Modernizing State* (Cambridge University Press, 1985).

6. The use of the term *ezba* to describe the country's most appalling slums reveals something of the wry sense of humor of Egyptians. The term literally refers to the semifeudal estates of the landed notability, which were typically composed of manor houses surrounded by mud huts of peasant retainers.

7. Waterbury, *The Egypt of Nasser and Sadat*, p. 349.

8. Cited in Nazih N. M. Ayubi, *Bureaucracy and Politics in Contemporary Egypt* (London: Ithaca Press, 1980), p. 240.

9. The minister's report is cited in "Ten Percent of Egyptians on State Payroll," *Middle East Times* (22–28 June 1986). See also Imam Ahmed, "Major Changes in Managers of Public Sector Expected," *Middle East Times* (2–8 March 1986). Almost a year later *al-Ahram* published the figure of 3,849,582 government employees, suggesting that the statistic released in the previous year may have included the military. *Al-Ahram*'s figures were stated to include employees in all grades in the ministries, general organizations, units of local government, and the public sector. The ministries were said to account for 400,502 employees, the general organizations 598,058, local government organizations 1,559,703, and the public sector 1,291,319. Ahmad Nasr al-Din, "Salaries of Four Million Civil Servants on the Discussion Table," *al-Ahram* (28 May 1987).

10. "Allocation of £E100 million to Employ 200,000 Graduates in a Few Days," *al-Ahram* (4 April 1987).

11. Waterbury, *The Egypt of Nasser and Sadat*, pp. 347–349.

12. Cited in *Middle East Times* (21–27 December 1986).

13. "The Workers at Leadership Levels," Central Agency for Organization and Administration, 1967, cited in Clement Henry Moore, *Images of Development: Egyptian Engineers in Search of Industry* (Cambridge: MIT Press, 1980), pp. 117–118.

14. This case was described in the most widely read of the opposition newspapers' gossip columns, "The Sparrow," which appears in *al-Wafd*. This particular piece appeared on 3 July 1986.

15. "Thoughts of the Week," *Sawt al-Arab* (19 October 1986).

16. I am indebted to Otis Kedrick, a consultant to USAID on training programs, for this information.

17. In May 1986, for example, it was reported that the Prime Minister had agreed to a proposal from the NDP that each NDP MP be allowed to nominate 15 people to undertake the *hagg*. Previous practice had been that MPs of the ruling and opposition parties had been granted 5 nominees each. See *al-Ahali* (21 May 1986).

18. *al-Shaab* (12 August 1986).

19. It should also be noted that the security and intelligence agency directly under the president, *Gihaz al-Mukhabarat al-Amma*, or General Intelligence, also known as *Gihaz al-Amn al-Qawmi*, or National Security Agency, is a third competitor in the struggle for supremacy among the state's security organs. Nasser relied heavily on it, whereas Sadat preferred the *Gihaz Amn al-Dawla*, or State Security Agency, also known as *Mabahath Amma* or *Mabahath Amn al-Dawla*. Mubarak appears to be attempting to balance the two. In October 1986 it was revealed that the political opposition would be subjected to supervision by General Intelligence rather than the SSA, which had supervised the opposition in previous election campaigns. "General Intelligence to Supervise the Parties' Activities," *al-Ahrar* (27 October 1986). General Intelligence and Military Intelligence received a further vote of confidence in June 1987 when Mubarak transferred responsibility to them from the SSA for investigating assassination attempts on Abu Basha and Makram Muhammad Ahmad. See *al-Shaab* (2 June 1987).

20. I am indebted to diplomatic sources for this information.

21. *Ibid.*

22. *al-Ahram* (7 May 1987).

23. *al-Ahram* (7 October 1986).

24. *al-Ahrar* (30 June 1986).

25. Aiman Nur, "A Year After the Events of the CSF," *al-Wafd* (26 February 1987).

26. "Secrets of the Week," *al-Ahali* (6 August 1986).

27. "Secrets of the Week," *al-Ahali* (3 September 1986).

28. See for example Nur, "A Year After the Events of the CSF."

29. Izzat al-Saadni, "Investigatory Report with the Minister of Interior," *al-Ahram* (31 January 1987).

30. "Report on Abu Basha Attack About Ready," *Middle East Times* (14–20 June 1987). It likewise undermined Badr's claim when his predecessor's flat was broken into and his bed, among other things, stolen. See *al-Shaab* (19 May 1987).

31. Adil al-Gawgari, "The Budget of the Ministry of Interior Doubles Four Times in Ten Years," *Sawt al-Arab* (9 November 1986).

32. *Ibid.*

33. This figure was provided by the prominent Wafdist lawyer Ibrahim Disuqi Abaza. Cited in Hassan Amer, "Former Government Leaders Examine the Ills of the System," *Middle East Times* (3–16 August 1986).

34. Mirvat al-Said, "Police Officers Have Problems That Require Investigation," *al-Wafd* (13 March 1986).

35. Interview with Charles B. Jacobini, first secretary, economics section, U.S. Embassy, Cairo (23 January 1986). For estimates in the £E3-billion range, see "Arrest of Drug Dealers . . . Why?" *Akhbar al-Yom* (23 May 1987); Imad al-Din Adib, "Egypt in 1986," *al-Sharq al-Awsat* (31 January 1986); and "The Emperor of Bataniya," *al-Akhbar* (18 April 1987).

36. "May the Lord Protect Us, My Son," *al-Shaab* (23 September 1986).

37. "Millionaire Before the Qasr al-Nil Court," *al-Shaab* (13 January (1987).

38. "Big Drug Deal Behind the Raising of the Dollar Against the Pound," *al-Ahali* (23 April 1986). See also Adil Hussain, "The Drug Dealers and the Banks in Egypt," *al-Shaab* (9 September (1986).

39. These figures are taken from Riad Mohamed Hashim, Assistant Minister of Interior, *Narcotics Problem in Egypt,* (Cairo: Anti-Narcotics General Administration of the Ministry of Interior, 1986). In early 1988 it was estimated that there were one quarter of a million heroin addicts in Egypt. See Mahmoud Abdullah, "Egypt's Heroin Addicts," *Middle East Times* (14–20 January 1988).

40. Ali Khamis, "Police Colonel Imports Three Tons of Drugs," *al-Wafd* (23 October 1986).

41. Hashim, *Narcotics Problem in Egypt,* p. 7.

42. *Ibid.,* p. 8.

43. Gilles Kepel, *Muslim Extremism in Egypt: The Prophet and the Pharaoh* (Berkeley and Los Angeles: University of California Press, 1986), p. 134.

44. *al-Ahram* (18 May 1987). According to a report in *al-Ahram*, the 221 drug smugglers and merchants were arrested and charged under the Emergency Decrees. Two days later *Akhbar al-Yom* claimed the Decrees had not been invoked. See Abd al-Aziz Mahmud, "The Drug Kings Fall," *al-Ahram* (21 May 1987); and "Arrest of Drug Dealers . . . Why?" *Akhbar al-Yom* (23 May 1987). When asked why they had not been arrested previously, General Abd al-Wahid Ismail, Director of the Anti-Narcotics Bureau, replied that if they had seized the known dealers and smugglers, the big fish would have escaped. *Ibid.* On 29 May an article appeared in *al-Musawwar* under the title "Who are the Drug Dealers?" It identified many of the 221 under detention by their colorful nicknames and stated they were the biggest dealers and smugglers in the country, accounting for 90 percent of all trade in drugs. This suggested the authorities had been aware of their identities for some time. In sum, the arrests were mandated by the government's decision to devalue the pound, for it was feared the financial muscle of drug dealers could scuttle the reform. Their normal protection by police and politicians in the face of this priority was overridden.

45. Interview with Ahmad Abdilla, Cairo (18 February 1986).

46. The mystery of why the government continued to stand behind Fawzi Muaz may have been answered by Hilmi Murad, who reported in his weekly column in *al-Shaab* on 4 February 1986 that Muaz had a cousin in the presidential palace.

47. They were brought up from Beni Suef. See "The Conflicts Continue in Alexandria Governorate," *al-Ahali* (13 August 1986).

48. Information on prevailing attitudes and morale in the internal security services responsible for dealing with Islamic activists was provided by a former official of the presidency and by first-hand observers of events in Upper Eqypt.

49. Data on the Nasser and Sadat periods are from Hinnebusch, *Egyptian Politics Under Sadat,* p. 88; and Mark N. Cooper, *The Transformation of Egypt* (Baltimore: Johns Hopkins University Press, 1982), p. 147. Data on the Mubarak period were compiled from Egyptian press reports. Calculations are the author's.

50. "The State of Investigations," *al-Ahali* (26 March 1986).

51. "The Ministers of Interior and Economy . . . Why?" *al-Ahram al-Iqtisadi* (16 June 1986).

52. Cited by Izzat Badawi, "News of the Week," *al-Musawwar* (19 September 1986). Three years later Abu Basha was seriously wounded in an assassination

attempt by three members of *al-Jihad* in front of his Cairo home. The government maintained that the attempt was not directed at Abu Basha because of his alleged involvement in the torture of members of *al-Jihad* in the wake of the Sadat assassination, but was part of a larger plot to destabilize the regime. See *al-Ahram* (29 May 1987 and 30 May 1987) and *Middle East Times* (7–13 May, 1987).

53. The prominent opposition editorialist Muhammad Abd al-Quddus, for example, compared Rushdi favorably to his predecessors and successors. See his column, "Children of the Country," *al-Shaab* (25 March 1986). For a similar viewpoint see *al-Wafd* (26 June 1986).

54. *al-Ahali* (13 August 1986).

55. "Ahmad Rushdi Votes for the Star," *al-Shaab* (14 April 1987).

56. For a summary of this article in English see Imam Ahmed, "State Security Agency Criticized," *Middle East Times* (23–29 March 1986).

57. "Secret Ministerial Meeting under the Chairmanship of Wali at the State Security Agency," *al-Wafd* (20 March 1986). As far as can be determined the SSA never complied with Wali's demand. It was widely rumored that representatives of that organization later met with Wali and warned him off. They are also rumored to have told Wali they had video tapes of Ibrahim Saada in a tryst with a "foreign woman" at the Mina House Oberoi Hotel, during which large sums of money were exchanged, thereby implying Saada's involvement in security breaches, to say nothing of his moral turpitude.

58. "The State of Investigations," *al-Ahali* (26 March 1986).

59. *al-Ahali* (5 March 1986).

60. *al-Wafd* (20 March 1986).

61. *al-Ahali* (5 March 1986).

62. *Ibid.*

63. "The Sparrow," *al-Wafd* (20 March 1986).

64. "Secret Organization in Interior Calls Itself 'The Free Officers'," *al-Ahali* (8 May 1986).

65. *al-Ahali* (16 April 1986).

66. "The Classroom, Arbitrariness and Arrest," *al-Wafd* (7 May 1987). The SSA's relative autonomy from the courts is enhanced by the fact it runs its own prison system. In the 1985 parliamentary session the Wafd tried but failed to raise this as an issue in order to force the government to transfer responsibility for these prisons away from the SSA. See *The Arab Strategic Report 1985* (Cairo: Al Ahram, 1986), p. 332.

67. *al-Ahram* (8 May 1986).

68. *al-Nur* (11 June 1986).

69. Hamied Ansari, *Egypt: The Stalled Society* (Albany: State University of New York Press, 1986), pp. 38, 251–254.

70. Imam Ahmed, "Egypt Opposition Claims Plot in Government to Shield Corrupt Officials," *Middle East Times* (27 April–3 May 1986).

71. Spokesmen for opposition parties, aware of the dilemma posed by the office of the Socialist Prosecutor, continue to emphasize the principle of due process of law over the importance of apprehending lawbreakers. See "Socialist Public Prosecutor's Office Under Fire," *Middle East Times* (28 July–4 August 1985).

72. "Government Retreats from Its Decision to Raise University Fees," *al-Wafd* (18 September 1986).

73. For accounts of interventions by security agents into the activities of private voluntary organizations and for the organizations' response, I am indebted to Roger Hardister, a consultant to the Ford Foundation.

74. *al-Akhbar* (11 September 1986).

75. *Ibid.*

76. "Outcry in Interior After Atif Zaki Pensioned Off," *al-Ahali* (6 August 1986).

77. I am indebted to Ahmad Abaza, chairman of the Wafd Party's economic committee and a close associate of Sirag al-Din, for this information.

78. *The Arab Strategic Report 1985,* p. 332.

79. On this congress see Waterbury, *The Egypt of Nasser and Sadat,* pp. 386–387.

80. Mahmoud Nafadi, "NDP National Congress May Be Postponed After Intra-Party Discord," *Middle East Times* (11–24 August 1985).

81. This is despite the fact that elections are required by the NDP's bylaws. The first clause specifies that "democratic elections are the way to form committees." Clause 63, paragraph two, stipulates that the general congress shall elect members of the political bureau of the party. For other bylaws and a discussion of the violation of them in practice, see "Is the National Democratic Party Democratic?" *al-Shaab* (13 May 1986).

82. Nafadi, "NDP National Congress May Be Postponed."

83. *al-Nur* (30 July 1986).

84. *Ibid.*

85. "Members of the NDP Refuse the List System," *al-Ahrar* (28 July 1986).

86. The average age of 23 of the candidates identified as "youthful elements" by Wali and about whom information is available was 54. Calculated by the author from biographical details provided in *al-Akhbar* (8 September 1986) and *Mayo* (8 September 1986).

87. Interview with Ahmad Abdilla, Cairo (18 February 1986).

88. Saad Hagrass, interview, Cairo (3 February 1986).

89. Richard Adams, interview, Cairo (16 October 1986).

90. Salah Mansi, *Political Participation of Peasants* (Cairo: Dar al-Mawqif al-Arabi, 1984) (in Arabic) p. 69.

91. In a sample of over 500 Cairo University students interviewed in 1981, about 80 percent demonstrated total apathy toward politics generally. While four-fifths of those who had a party preference expressed support for the NDP, less than 20 percent of the sample had any preference. The interviews were conducted prior to the formation of the Wafd Party, which, given the bourgeois social origins of the majority of the sample group, would have significantly affected the results. Saad Ibrahim Gumaa, *Youth and Political Participation* (Cairo: Dar al-Thaqafa lil-Nashra wal-Tawziya, 1984), see especially pp. 157–158.

92. Bahira Mukhtar, "The Egyptian People . . . and Their Preferred Newspaper," *al-Ahram* (28 May 1986).

93. See reports in *al-Ahali* of 11 February, 18 March, and 11 April.

94. "After the Declaration of Lists . . . What's Going on in the Parties," *Akhbar al-Yom* (7 March 1987).

95. See for example *al-Ahali* (21 March 1987).

96. This was the general consensus among close observers of Egyptian elections from the press and the universities.

97. Mahmoud Nafadi, "Voter Apathy at the Heart of Low Turnout in Egyptian Elections," *Middle East Times* (26 April–9 May 1987).

98. Imam Ahmed, "Fear Moves Egyptians to Back Emergency Laws on Terrorists," *Middle East Times* (14–20 June 1987).

99. *Economist* (2 June 1984).

100. Bertus Hendriks, "Egypt's Elections, Mubarak's Bind," *Merip Middle East Report* 129 (January 1985), pp. 11–18.

101. Nafadi, "Voter Apathy."

102. David B. Ottaway, "Egyptian Party Politics Showing Signs of Revival," *Washington Post* (25 January 1984).

103. Gumaa, *Youth and Political Participation.*

104. Ali al-Din Hillal, cited in Nafadi, "Voter Apathy." For a discussion of electoral participation in Egypt since 1952, see Ali al-Din Hillal, *Democratic Development in Egypt* (Cairo: Maktaba Nahda al-Sharq, 1986) (in Arabic).

105. Hassan Amer, "Spoiled Ballot Party Makes Impressive Showing in Elections," *Middle East Times* (19–25 April 1987).

106. The best analysis of al-Sayid's defeat is by Mustafa Bakri, "Why the Minister of War Production Did Not Win," *al-Musawwar* (24 April 1987).

107. Hassan Abu al-Ainan, "The Computer of the Ministry of Interior . . . Innocent of the Accusation of Forgery," *al-Ahram* (14 April 1987). For a typical allegation of election fraud perpetrated by computer, see *al-Shaab* (12 April 1987).

108. Mansi, *The Political Participation of Peasants,* pp. 117–22.

109. These profiles are drawn from various press sources, the most useful of which is Sultan Mahmud, et al., *"Oktober* Follows the Election Battle," *Oktober* (15 March 1987).

110. This sample was compiled by the author from profiles contained in *al-Akhbar* (8 September 1986) and *Mayo* (8 September 1986).

111. I am indebted to Ahmad Abd al-Akhar for information on his career, provided in an interview, Cairo (4 March 1986).

112. Ghada Ragab, "Economy at the Crossroads: How to Reform the Public Sector," *Middle East Times* (1–7 February 1987).

113. For information on the agriculture committee's recommendations and activities more generally, I am indebted to its chairman, Ahmad Abd al-Akhar.

114. This legislation called for the payment of £E267 million to over 6,000 former landowners. *al-Ahram* (27 May 1987).

115. Cited in Mansi, *The Political Participation of Peasants,* pp. 63–84.

116. Bianchi, "The Corporatization of the Egyptian Labor Movement."

117. Earl L. Sullivan, *Women in Egyptian Public Life* (Syracuse: Syracuse University Press, 1986), p. 101.

118. See *al-Ahali* (11 February 1987).

119. For information on the relationship between PVOs and the MSA, I am indebted to Roger Hardister and Barbara Ibrahim, the former a consultant and the latter a program officer of the Ford Foundation, Cairo.

120. Mamduh Qassim, "Kings and Playboys of the Societies and Projects," *al-Shaab* (28 January 1986).

121. The poll was conducted in 1985 by Roger Hardister with support from the Ford Foundation.

122. Cited by Kepel, *Muslim Extremism in Egypt,* p. 200.

123. When in April 1987 the court dismissed the case against 37 drivers accused of having organized the strike, it stated: "This strike would not have

happened from workers who were a model of conscientiousness and sacrifice, if they hadn't felt they were being discriminated against and really suffering to get the necessities of life." Cited in *Middle East Times* (8–26 April 1987).

124. For accounts of the role of the *rabita* in the strike, see *al-Shaab* (15 and 29 July 1986), and *al-Ahali* (30 July 1986).

6

SECULAR AND ISLAMICIST OPPOSITION

In the calculus of political control, repressing or balancing off the opposition are interchangeable. Mubarak, as compared to his predecessors, has emphasized the latter. The key constituencies that he has sought to pair off in opposition to one another are secular versus Islamicist political activists and, among the religious, radicals against conservatives. For the first five years or so of his presidency Mubarak achieved considerable success with these tactics. The immediate threat posed by violent Islamic *gama'at* (societies) in the wake of Sadat's assassination was countered in part by cultivating secular politicians whom Sadat had tired of and thrown in jail or otherwise barred from effective political participation. Mubarak's relationship with the secular opposition flourished in the following two years and was given an official stamp of approval in the 1984 parliamentary elections when the Wafd Party was permitted to emerge as the leader of the opposition. Its junior coalition partner in those elections, the Moslem Brotherhood, the organizational manifestation of the conservative Islamicist movement, was hamstrung by various constraints imposed by government, including prohibition of its forming an officially recognized, independent political party. Thus the balance between secular and religious was tilted by the regime in the former's favor.

With regard to the Islamicist movement itself, the regime facilitated the dominance of moderate over radical elements. Restrictions were lifted on politically relevant Islamic "call "(propagation) activities by conservatives, while radicals remained incarcerated or under strict surveillance. Writing in the summer of 1985, Gilles Kepel proclaimed the success of this effort.[1] Mubarak's tolerance of Islamicist discourse had, in Kepel's view, undermined the appeal of apocalyptic radicals and encouraged moderates to believe that if they abided by the regime's rules their battle cry, "Islam is the solution," would by peaceful means prevail. But just as Kepel was congratulating the government on its success in defanging the dangerous *gama'at*, Mubarak's strategy of divide and rule began to founder. Later in that very summer Islamic activists undertook systematically to probe the limits of permissible political behavior. They challenged university administrators for control of campuses, burned video shops that dealt in "decadent" films and grocery stores that sold alcoholic beverages, and in various other ways tested the capabilities of the security forces. Less than two years after Kepel had concluded that the Islamicist threat had been contained by a policy that encouraged a proliferation of views and groups, the iron fist had to be used in an attempt to crush a movement that had again turned to assassination. In the summer of 1987 hundreds and possibly even thousands of militants were rounded up, the emergency laws declared at the time of Sadat's assassination were amended to make them yet tougher, and the populace was seized with a sense of foreboding.

It was not violence per se, however, that posed the greatest threat to government. Rather, this chaos indicated the failure of the strategy of neutralizing Islamicists through reconciliation and the use of countervailing forces. The relative density of the Islamicist trend had made it impossible for Mubarak to find the precise point that maybe only hypothetically divides radicals from conservatives. Those at either end of the Islamicist spectrum chose not to vilify one another, but to close ranks behind the accusation that the government's repression and commitment to secularism was the cause of violence. Together they proclaimed that the one solution is to apply the *sharia*.[2] Unable effectively to exploit internal divisions within the Islamicist movement, the government's strategy of bolstering secular forces as counterweights to the Moslem Brotherhood and other organizational manifestations of the establishment Islamicist tendency had, by 1987, likewise broken down. In the parliamentary elections of April 1987 the Brotherhood demonstrated that it possessed the most broadly based, lavishly financed, and well organized opposition electoral machine in the country. It established itself as the core of the opposition to government in parliament.

It is conceivable that the 1987 elections reflected a change of strategy by Mubarak. He may have decided, at least temporarily, to cease using secularists to counterbalance Islamicists and instead to bring the latter onto center stage to expose their weaknesses, just as he had previously done to the Wafd Party. If indeed that was Mubarak's thinking in the spring of 1987, it would attest both to the comparative strength of the Islamicist movement and to the frailties of secular political organizations. But whatever Mubarak's intentions were, the question remains as to why secularists in the comparatively liberal climate of the Mubarak era could not broaden and deepen their appeal. Although most of the opposition parties only commenced their activities in earnest at the time of the 1984 elections, it was evident after three years that none had expanded significantly beyond the class base of the bourgeoisie, nor had any successfully aggregated the demands of the newly invigorated interest groups that had sprung up, principally within that same social class. These groups tended to compete with rather than contribute to the appeal and capabilities of the political parties.

The comparative failure of secular opposition political parties can be explained at both the abstract level of Egypt's political culture and at the prosaic level of the cut and thrust of contemporary politics. The deterministic, cultural explanation, which is proffered by Islamicists, is that since secularism is a foreign implant into Egypt's quintessential Islamic society, it is bound to provide insufficient stimulus for political mobilization. Apparent historical contradictions of this dictum, which were the Wafd Party between 1923 and 1952, when it led the nationalist movement, and the Nasserist experiment, which in its basic thrust was also secularist, can be explained variously. The old Wafd can be dismissed as a traditional notable party, the base of support for which was provided by peasant retinues of landowner patrons. Since the *latifundia*-style agriculture that provided the social base on which the Wafd and other *ancien regime* parties relied was destroyed by Nasser's agrarian reforms, such parties will, in this view, never reestablish their power. As for Nasserism, its support among the masses is alleged to have rested squarely on its manipulation of the resources of the state over which it presided. Nasserism, accordingly, was not an autonomous political movement but a populist dictatorship. It therefore has no future independent of the state. The Moslem Brotherhood, on the other hand, is pointed to by most Islamicists as the only broadly based, durable political movement in twentieth-century Egypt that has demonstrated an autonomous mobilizational potential that crosses many of the class, regional, and other cleavages that impede the expansion of secular organizations. This reading of modern Egyptian history is proffered as proof of the argument that when the rules of the political game are fair, religiously based political organizations inevitably will overwhelm their secular competitors.

Another interpretation of the inability of the neo-Wafd Party, the National Progressive Unionist Party (NPUP), the Socialist Labor Party (SLP), and others to mobilize large numbers of followers and effectively aggregate interests of preexisting, semiorganized constituencies is that various aspects of Egypt's political culture favor face-to-face, small-group interaction rather than abstract loyalties to organizations and causes. Large, formal institutions are little more than aggregates of kinship, friendship, and other personalistic networks, hence prone to fragmentation and vacillation.[3] Secular organizations are particularly vulnerable to such fissuring for they lack the abstract appeal of membership in the community of the faithful and the organizational backbone provided by the religious structure itself, whether of the establishment or the opposition. The contemporary state, which imitates its colonial predecessor in dividing and ruling the plethora of political fragments that make up the system, gradually undermines secular political organizations, leaving only the more tightly knit Islamicist tendency, which cannot so easily be divided and ruled.

But one does not have to have recourse to generalizations derived from interpretations of Egypt's political culture and the behavior of its weak state to explain the changing balance of power between the secular and religious oppositions. The appeal of Islamic activism may be simply that it has not yet been discredited, precisely because the state has, out of fear, precluded it from the formal, legal political system. If this interpretation is correct, Mubarak's decision (if that is what it was) in 1987 to permit the Islamicist tendency to emerge as the chief opposition to government should demonstrate that the Moslem Brotherhood and its fellow travelers have no better answers to Egypt's pressing problems than he does and that the slogan "Islam is the solution" reflects not a coherent plan to tackle problems but an evasion of political responsibility. By bringing Islamicists in from the cold of political isolation, Mubarak will expose their weaknesses, just as he did to secularists. Moreover, the price of admission to the game of politics will be closer supervision by the system of control. That system has been deteriorating, but retains sufficient capability to contain the secular parties because of their inherent weaknesses and because the opposition parties tarnished irrevocably their credibility when they chose to scramble for political spoils. Once the Islamicist tendency is in the same position, the system of control can be brought to bear on it. Then its organizational fissures, ideological inconsistencies, and programmatic deficiencies will become manifest, or so Mubarak's reasoning may go.

Speculation that equates the political strength of secularists and Islamicists may, however, be incorrect. The Islamic tendency is, according to some, a sociopolitical movement, replete with the ideological and organizational infrastructure to guide personal and societal transformation, whereas opposition political parties are essentially status quo oriented seekers of power.[4] There is no guarantee that the security forces will be able to subdue the Islamicists as it has the secularists, even now that the Moslem Brotherhood has agreed to enter the political game on the President's home grounds and according to his rules. It may prove to be the case that the system of control was strong enough to destroy the political hopes and chances of secularists and in so doing open the door to Islamicists. It is the investigation of this scenario that will provide the central focus for this chapter. The various weaknesses of and the means by which the secular opposition has been contained will be reviewed in the first section. Then the nature of the sprawling and as yet almost entirely unorganized constituencies other than the bourgeoisie will be briefly described, for it is only when those constituencies are at least partially mobilized that truly dramatic political change can occur. Finally, an attempt will be made in the last section to determine whether the resilience of the Islamicist tendency under Mubarak has been due to its inherent strength or to its having benefited from the regime's miscalculation in simultaneously legitimating its oppositionist credentials and undermining the appeal of the secular counterbalance.

The Secular Opposition

THE LIMITS TO DEMOCRACY

Having legitimated opposition political parties, the government ensured their weakness by restricting their recruitment to the same constituency the government itself cultivates—the bourgeoisie—and by preventing the parties from aggregating the interests of the various organized and semiorganized interest groups whose membership is drawn from that same class. Opposition parties' inability effectively to appeal to nonbourgeois constituencies results from the economic dependence of peasants and a large proportion of workers on the state and from the fact that the parties' leaders, almost exclusively drawn from the bourgeoisie, have neither the will nor ability to appeal beyond the class of their origins. The General Confederation of Trade Unions, public-sector companies, local government bodies and the agricultural bureaucracy centered on cooperatives and village banks, the security services and the NDP, have so far proven equal to the task of isolating workers, peasants, and much of the civil service from the appeals of the opposition. By imposing a political quarantine on these social forces, the state has created a political vacuum that manifests itself in the apathy described in the previous chapter. It is this vacuum, however, that also nurtures anomic disorder and attracts the attention of Islamicist activists, who have the organizational skills and ideological commitments that the secularists lack.

With regard to the politically dominant constituencies of the upper and middle classes, the regime could not hope to impose absolute quarantines, so instead it places obstacles in the path of hopeful opposition politicians. It utilizes the state's resources to underwrite the preponderance of the NDP, and it limits the appeal and effectiveness of opposition parties by fragmenting the pluralist infrastructure. The government ensures that demands for political participation are channeled into as many voluntary associations as possible, so a plethora of such groups has emerged. But the real test of pluralist democracy is not the number of interest groups present, but whether the demands articulated by them can be freely aggregated by political parties. This test Mubarak's Egypt fails. Through a variety of strategems the government impedes access of parties to pressure groups and vice versa. Its reaction to the 1984 election for the governing board of the faculty club of Cairo University defined the narrow limits of its tolerance. When candidates opposed to the NDP won a majority, the Ministry of Insurance and Social Affairs stepped in to invalidate the elections. For the most part, however, the government has not had to assert itself to sever such connections. Opposition parties have rarely succeeded in "colonizing" voluntary associations. Access to government and its resources is for such groups

a significant inducement for compliance and independence from opposition parties. Only very highly committed, politicized groups, such
as those representing university faculty members, are willing to risk
access to government and invite retribution by associating closely with
opposition parties.

Professional syndicates, which group an overwhelming majority of
Egypt's doctors, lawyers, engineers, dentists, agronomists, actors, journalists, teachers, and other professionals into their separate organizations,
provide through their elections a good indication of the balance of power
between government and the secular and religious oppositions. Since
1985, candidates identified with the Islamicist movement have won
pluralities or absolute majorities on the boards of the doctors, engineers,
dentists, and teachers syndicates and have established strong minority
positions in several others. By comparison, candidates associated with
opposition secular parties have fared well only in the lawyers syndicate,
which has had a longstanding connection with the Wafd Party. Even
there, however, Islamicists won sufficient seats on the board in 1985 to
force the creation of a special committee on the application of Islamic
law. Elections for the presidency of the comparatively highly politicized
syndicate of journalists in March 1987 provide an indication of the upper
limits of support for the secular opposition in professional syndicates.
The incumbent president and editor in chief of *al-Ahram*, Ibrahim Nafa,
a Mubarak loyalist with the backing of the NDP, received 1,043 votes,
while Gallal al-Hammamsi, an *al-Akhbar* editorialist backed by the Wafd,
garnered 309. Mahmud al-Maraghi, deputy editor in chief of *Ruz
al-Yusuf*, was supported by the NPUP and obtained 292 votes. Since
many of the votes for Hammamsi and Maraghi were cast by their personal
friends and supporters in their places of work, the opposition parties
could not have mobilized a third of the eligible voters to cast ballots
for their candidates.

Because of the government's efforts to fragment political participation
and/or because of cultural preferences for small groups rather than large,
impersonal organizations, pressure groups compete with rather than
provide support for political parties. In this competition groups have
fared better than parties, for by focusing on the narrow interests of
their members they have enhanced their perceived utility. Also, because
they constitute less of a threat to government, they suffer less from
coercion. Moreover, they possess a certain measure of leverage with
government by virtue of the threat, real or implied, to throw their
support behind the opposition. One close observer of the Egyptian
political process equates interest groups with large families and tribes,
for they all seek to sell their support to the NDP and deal with the
opposition only to improve their bargaining position.[5] Even university
student organizations, among the most politicized of Egypt's pressure
groups, are remarkably autonomous from the secular opposition parties.
While student government elections are contested between candidates

associated with various political tendencies or even specific organizations, the abiding preoccupation of virtually all student government bodies has been the issue of security forces on campus.[6] The secular opposition parties have not been able to impose their programs or preferences on the agendas of student organizations, nor have the parties been able to take effective action on the issue that preoccupies students.

Competing for recruits from more or less the same bourgeois constituency that the government considers its own, and hobbled by restrictions on attempts to aggregate pressure group interests, the secular political parties are reduced to the status of contestants in a semidemocratic political game in which the vast majority of citizens are spectators. All the parties can hope to accomplish is to demonstrate their superior skills before this audience and in so doing win its tacit support. But even in this restricted context there are serious constraints on partisan activity. The key arenas within which the parties can demonstrate their acumen and skills are parliament, parliamentary elections, and the media. All are carefully and, after 1984–1985, increasingly regulated.

CONTROL OF ELECTIONS

The electoral success of the NDP is not the result of its popularity or organizational structure. Just before the 1984 elections 35 political scientists associated with either *al-Ahram's* Strategic Studies Center or the prestigious Faculty of Economics and Political Science at Cairo University were asked why the NDP would win; only one listed the popularity of the party as a cause.[7] Thirty-three responses referred to the power of the state apparatus and its ability to control the dissemination of information, while 12 political scientists identified election fraud as a reason. The ratio of 33/12 may in fact reflect the comparative importance to the NDP of the two key factors of utilization of state resources and outright fraud. Within the former category the list of rewards and punishments is almost endless. It includes various forms of distribution of governmental largesse, including salary and pension increases, bonuses, relaxation of mandatory crop deliveries required of producers, appointments to public bodies, the discretionary granting of licenses and permits, and various other inducements offered in the weeks and days prior to elections.

The large and powerful families that dominate electoral politics in rural constituencies are the primary conduits through which patronage is delivered. In preparing for the 1984 election in Sohag Province in Upper Egypt, for example, the government supervised the division of seats in the People's Assembly, *Shura* Council, and Sohag Provincial Council between representatives of the six families that dominate Sohag. When in late April of that year it was announced that the shaikh of the Awlad Ali, a prominent tribe in Matruh Province, was going to be nominated on the NPUP list, the government moved immediately to forestall that threat by offering the shaikh and his tribe various rewards, including positions on the provincial council. Within twenty-four hours the Awlad Ali and their leader publicly associated themselves with the NDP.[8] In the summer of 1986 the Socialist Labor Party accused the Ministry of Interior of siding with the Abu Aqil tribe in the town of Gahina in Sohag against the 8,000-strong Bani Ramad, who had supported the SLP in the 1984 elections. According to al-Shaab, government troops confiscated the weapons of the Bani Ramad, leaving them defenseless in the face of their tribal enemies.[9] During the 1987 election campaign the prominent journalist Yahia Gamal, who was offering his candidacy in Giza, complained to an al-Ahram reporter that it was no use trying to convene popular conferences and rallies there, for Giza's big families totally dominate the province's politics.[10]

Intimidation and election fraud by the government likewise embrace a wide range of activities. Parties are prohibited from holding open-air rallies, so they must seek enclosed premises in which to gather. Public installations such as government schools are typically denied them. When a private school outside of Alexandria rented its premises to the Wafd for a rally organized in support of the boycott of the 1986 Shura Council election, its headmaster, according to reports by Wafdist organizers, was interrogated by security officers. CSF troops are routinely dispatched to constituencies where the opposition parties enjoy support, their purpose being to intimidate voters and party poll watchers. Ballots are not secret.[11] Journalists sympathetic to opposition parties are frequently prevented from covering meetings and rallies held by those parties.[12] If these and other measures have not secured the desired outcome, results are forged. While in the 1987 election this was facilitated in various traditional ways, such as by preventing party observers from monitoring vote counting, that election also witnessed the introduction of computerized tabulation, which appears to have fully automated the process of election fraud and in so doing provided ample grist for Egypt's satirists, as suggested by Mustafa Amin's postelection analysis:

> The computer in charge of the law on election by party lists is well behaved. It speaks when we want it to speak and shuts up when we tell it to. At first it announced the election of Khaled Muhyi al-Din, leader of the NPUP, but an official glared at it, whereupon it announced the failure of Mr. Muhyi al-Din after he had won. The computer remembered that it is an official of the Ministry of Interior and announced that all candidates of the National Democratic Party had won and all opposition candidates had lost. Curses poured down on the head of the poor computer, which was only obeying orders. Then it announced that the Moslem Brotherhood and the Socialist Labor Party had won 40 seats but the Wafd was finished as it had not won a single seat. Some candidate digged (sic) the computer in the ribs, whereupon the computer said 40 Wafdists had been returned, then it brought down the figure to 35.[13]

While the 1984 elections witnessed more irregularities than those of 1976, which were the most free of any held since 1952, by comparison to the *Shura* Council elections of 1986 and the People's Assembly elections of 1987, the 1984 elections stand as a high-water mark of electoral democracy in Mubarak's Egypt. Within two years of those elections Mubarak became exasperated with attacks on his policies, supporters, and even his person by the opposition parties. He obviously decided to use the electoral process to cut them down to size.

PARLIAMENT

The tendency to tighten up on the opposition also became manifest in parliament after the 1984 elections. Rifat al-Mahgub, the first speaker of the People's Assembly ever to have been appointed rather than elected to parliament, became increasingly dictatorial in the speaker's chair. Opposition MPs walked out as a body in protest against his rulings a record nine times in the 1986 session. Despite his having alienated numerous NDP parliamentarians and his lack of support among the party's leaders, he was elected to the parliament in 1987 and then reelected as speaker, obviously as a result of direct presidential support. In June 1986, Mahgub caught the opposition off guard when he suddenly announced the termination of the parliamentary session. Opposition members had expected several more meetings to be held. In this way Mahgub headed off debate on issues the government preferred not to subject to public scrutiny, including the role of the Islamic investment companies and the contract it had recently signed with General Motors.

But it was not just the premature closure of the 1986 parliamentary session that indicated the government was moving to downgrade the legislative body's role, hence that of the opposition parties. The 1985–1986 session had only 67 sittings, compared to 100 in the 1984–1985 session. Some 1,400 speeches were given in 1985–1986 compared to 1,650 in the previous year. Only 84 bills were debated in the 1985–1986 session compared to 277 in 1984–1985. While 149 agreements were concluded in 1984–1985, only 76 were agreed upon the following year. The number of questions dropped from 372 in 1984–1985 to 317 in 1985–1986, and committee reports declined from 414 to 305. In the 1985–1986 session 364 MPs spoke, of whom 36 were members of the opposition parties. In the previous session 45 of the 222 MPs who addressed the parliament were from the opposition, so the proportion of opposition MPs speaking in parliament dropped from over 20 percent to less than 14 percent. On the crucial issue of the budget only 33 members were allowed to speak in 1986, as compared to 124 MPs in 1985.[14] The parliament, which according to article 92 of the 1971 constitution was to run until 1989, was dismissed in February 1987. Following the 1987 elections the new parliament convened on 23 April 1987. It went into recess on 9 July and only resumed on 31 October after members of the opposition threatened to stage a sit-in strike in protest against the unprecedented three-month interruption.[15] On Mubarak's reelection on 5 October 1987, three parliaments had served during his six-year presidency, for an average duration of two years. Sadat's parliaments averaged 44 months and Nasser's 31.

Although the People's Assembly does provide an arena in which the opposition can attempt to display its parliamentary skills and embarrass the government, the latter enjoys such an overwhelming preponderance of resources that the opposition has little chance of making serious inroads at the government's expense. The NDP guarantees the government an automatic twothirds majority, which can be used to terminate debate, pass legislation virtually without comment, reject opposition demands for investigation of alleged improprieties and illegal activities, and so on. In July 1987, for example, the NDP rejected a call from the opposition to investigate allegations of torture of those arrested in conjunction with the assassination attempts on Hassan Abu Basha and Makram Muhammad Ahmad. The speaker can invoke a clause that bars debate of cases under police or judicial investigation, a tactic that was used repeatedly early in the 1987 session. Although MPs, including those of the opposition, are permitted to ask questions, they have no right of follow-up. While MPs may demand to interrogate ministers, in recent sessions those demands have resulted in ministers presenting themselves to parliament to confront less than half the requested interrogations.

Parliamentary standing committees, which performed important functions prior to 1952, became after that time large and unwieldy. Their functions became restricted almost exclusively to hearing the chairman read the government's annual program for their particular sector. The agriculture committee, for example, has more than 150 members. It has no subcommittees. During an average parliamentary session in the Mubarak era that committee met less than half a dozen times. No desks are supplied to MPs in committee meetings. If they want to speak they have to leave their seats and walk to a microphone at the front of the room. Specialized committees picked up some of the slack left by standing committees during the Sadat period, especially in the 1971–76 parliament, when 17 of them were formed. In the 1977–79 parliament 12 were created, while in the 1979–81 parliament only six special committees were constituted.[16] In the Mubarak period no new special committees have been added to those inherited from the last Sadat parliament.

Indirect but nevertheless significant control is exerted by government over parliament by virtue of the fact that over one third of MPs are employees in the civil service or public sector, whereas prior to 1952 public servants had to resign their post if elected to parliament. Also, since a major purpose of opposition activity in parliament is to appeal to the public by exposing governmental abuses, the manner in which parliamentary debates are handled by the media is crucial. Television coverage is sporadic. The government press provides only very selective transcripts of debates. While the opposition newspapers present the views of their respective parties on issues before parliament, they are read by a significantly smaller percentage of the public.

THE MEDIA

It is in fact the media, and especially the press, that provides the opposition the third arena in which it can demonstrate before the Egyptian public its skill in playing the political game. The government has appreciated that buying and reading an opposition party newspaper is in most cases stimulated by the desire to obtain news not available elsewhere rather than by party allegiance, so it has refrained from attempting to impose a crude censorship. Indeed, its strategy has been a sophisticated one. By denying the opposition newspapers access to officially generated news and by harassing their journalists, the government has sought to induce the opposition papers to go to excess, to report rumors as fact, to disguise advertisements as news stories, and to use intemperate language. In general this strategy has succeeded, for as the novelty value of the papers wore off in the middle 1980s, so did their circulations plateau and their reputations as reliable sources of news deteriorate. Compared to Egypt's largest circulation daily, *al-Akhbar*, which had a circulation of slightly over 900,000 in 1986, and the largest-selling weekly newspaper, *Akhbar al-Yom*, which at that time distributed over one million copies throughout the country, the opposition papers, all of which were weeklies until *al-Wafd* began daily publication in March 1987, are relatively minor.[17] Only *al-Wafd*, much the most professionally produced of the papers and enjoying the best access to politically sensitive information, established itself on a relatively equal footing with the government papers. In various weeks of 1986, as it benefited from the public's keen interest in several prominent scandals it was dutifully reporting, *al-Wafd* achieved circulation figures as high as three-quarters of a million copies.[18] While this placed it behind *al-Akhbar* and *al-Ahram*, it ranked it well ahead of the third government morning paper, *al-Gumhuriya*, and the government's afternoon paper, *al-Misa*.

The various other opposition papers achieved on average from 1984 something less than one-quarter of *al-Wafd's* circulation, with the NPUP's *al-Ahali* generally attaining the widest circulation, averaging some 100,000 copies per week, and the Liberal Party's *al-Ahrar* the lowest.[19] In a panel survey conducted of some 2,200 respondents from July 1985 to January 1986 by six academics sponsored by *al-Ahram*, it was found that 34 percent of the sample regularly read *al-Wafd*; 25 percent *al-Liwa al-Islami* (*The Banner of Islam*), the religious weekly of the NDP that Mubarak created in an attempt to fill the gap left when *al-Dawa*, the Moslem Brotherhood weekly, was banned; 8 percent *al-Ahali*; 6 percent *al-Shaab* and *Mayo*, the latter the party paper of the NDP; and 4 percent *al-Ahrar*. For daily papers the preferences were 48 percent for *al-Ahram*, 35 percent for *al-Akhbar*, 15 percent for *al-Gumhuriya*, and 2 percent for *al-Misa*.[20] These results do not correspond exactly to circulation figures. *al-Akhbar* sells somewhat more copies than *al-Ahram*, and *al-Ahali*, according to its editor in chief, attains a circulation four times that of *Mayo*.[21]

The government strategy of seeking to discredit the opposition press by inducing it to commit excesses is based on the calculation that the commitment to responsible journalism is less than ubiquitous among the country's editors, reporters, and columnists. The history of the press during the *ancien regime* provides ample evidence for this assessment, as does the behavior of journalists working for the government press.[22] The combination of journalistic traditions, the removal of censorship after so many years of strict control, and a persistent, generally subterranean campaign of harassment and intimidation of opposition journalists has succeeded in attaining the objective of shaping a nongovernment press that can reasonably be called irresponsible. The struggle for credibility, which the government was clearly losing when the opposition press still had novelty value, had by 1986–1987 become a much more equal contest.

The range of tactics utilized by the state to instill a siege mentality in the opposition press has been appreciable from the outset. Since 1986 it has been yet further expanded. Denial of access to government news sources; limitation of advertisements in opposition papers by public-sector firms; attacks on the "excesses" of the press by the Minister of Information and, from January 1986, Mubarak himself; implied threats to reimpose strict censorship; assigning inadequate production facilities to the papers; and various other tactics have been used to keep opposition journalists off balance. The leftist *al-Ahali*, which in terms of journalistic quality compares favorably with all other opposition papers, has, because of the potential political threat it represents, been subjected to more harassment than *al-Shaab* or *al-Ahrar*. During the Sadat era it was printed on the modern, high-quality presses of *al-Akhbar*. As its circulation rose that arrangement was terminated by the then-editor of *al-Akhbar*, Musa Sabri, a loyal servant of three presidents. Forced to shift its printing to the old-fashioned and abysmally poor quality presses owned by *al-Gumhuriya*, *al-Ahali* is so poorly produced that it requires a dedicated effort and very good light to read. While the other opposition papers are the occasional beneficiaries of advertisements placed by public-sector companies and obtain substantial revenues from advertisements placed by private-sector firms, *al-Ahali* is boycotted by both. The NDP paper, *Mayo*, distinguished itself from 1984 by attacking *al-Ahali* with such a vengeance that the authors of *The Arab Strategic Report*, who are members of the staff of the *al-Ahram* Strategic Studies Center, felt moved to comment on it.[23]

Mubarak's outbursts against the opposition press in January 1986 signaled a qualitative change in the pattern of harassment of the opposition press and its increasing concentration on *al-Wafd*, which along with the Wafd Party was then posing the greatest threat to Mubarak and the NDP. For the first time, opposition journalists became targets of various techniques of intimidation. A reporter for *al-Wafd* was in the summer of 1986 lured out to the pyramids plateau by an anonymous telephone caller who promised to reveal information about a scandal in one of the ministries. On arrival at the designated location he was physically assaulted, presumably by agents of the SSA.[24] The private car belonging to the editor in chief of *al-Wafd*, Mustafa Shurdi, was rear-ended by a large truck belonging to the CSF in light traffic and in broad daylight on the airport road. Shurdi, who was not in the car, alleged that the Ministry of Interior had bungled a purposeful attempt to assassinate him or to aggravate his chronic back ailment.[25] On 10 October 1986 the Ministry of Interior entrapped the editor of "The Sparrow," the most widely read column in *al-Wafd* and the opposition press generally. Said Abd al-Khaliq, the government alleged, was caught red-handed with two of his colleagues, including the son-in-law of the Wafd's president, Fuad Sirag al-Din, while accepting a £E100,000 bribe from Abd al-Rahman al-Baidani to cease an anticorruption campaign against him and his firm, Egycon.[26] Agents of the SSA began in the summer of 1986 conspicuously to deploy themselves outside of *al-Wafd's* headquarters. Similar although less intensive campaigns were mounted against the other papers.[27]

The net effect of these moves was to unsettle the opposition press. Unsure as to the precise new limits of intimidation, desperate to retain or expand circulation (hence revenues) by exposing scandals and government misdeeds (but finding such scandals increasingly difficult to uncover as potential targets for muckraking took greater precautions), the papers began to waver between truculence and apology in their treatment of officials and between excess and caution in their scandal-mongering. Government allegations that subventions were being paid by foreign governments to the opposition press, including a claim by Mubarak that *Sawt al-Arab*, the Nasserist weekly that commenced publication in August 1986, was on Qadhafi's payroll, began to gain credence.[28] The attempt to circumvent the government's ban on the Moslem Brotherhood's newspaper that had been in effect throughout the Mubarak era by publishing *al-Bashir* in April 1986 was unsuccessful. After two issues were published and immediately seized from newsstands, its publishers abandoned the effort. In order further to dilute the impact of the opposition press on public opinion, the government announced in June 1987 that the highly regarded London based Saudi paper, *al-Sharq al-Awsat*, would be allowed to publish an edition in Cairo. In retrospect it appears as if 1984–1986 may have been the golden age of the opposition press in Egypt.

Media under direct governmental control are not uniformly supportive of all official policies but they are censored, and there are strong disincentives for journalists to criticize in ways that might benefit the opposition. Even the most prestigious of Egypt's columnists are not immune to the censor's scissors. Ahmad Baha al-Din, a confidant of Sadat who since the early 1970s has written regularly in *al-Ahram*, lambasted in a March 1986 column Shams al-Din al-Fassi, chairman of the International Sufi Council and a financial wheeler and dealer with many profitable interests in Egypt. Fassi had been intercepted by customs officials when departing Cairo airport in the company of Muhammad al-Ahmadi Abu Nur, the Minister of Religious Endowments, with a suitcase full of weapons and jewelry. Ibrahim Nafa, editor of *al-Ahram*, refused to run Baha al-Din's expose.[29] Earlier in the year Egypt's most famous columnist and one who poses a significant political challenge to the regime, Muhammad Hassanein Heikal, was offered the opportunity of ending his twelve-year banishment from the Egyptian press by the *al-Akhbar* group, which commissioned him to write a series of articles. After the first few appeared in which Heikal savagely attacked the decision-making process under Mubarak and the accumulation of power by vested interests, the agreement was terminated. Former Minister of Agriculture and prominent political fixture in both the Nasser and Sadat years, Sayed Marei, was requested by the editor of one of the major government dailies to write a piece on contemporary Egyptian agriculture. The article, critical of agricultural policy, was shown to the incumbent minister, Yusuf Wali, prior to publication. Wali insisted that the piece not appear.[30]

Journalists without the reputations of luminaries such as Baha al-Din or Heikal are completely at the mercy of their editors, who hold their positions because they follow presidential orders. It is widely believed that SSA agents are sprinkled liberally throughout the media. The regime has done nothing to dispel that perception. The secretary general in the mid-1980s of the Higher Press Council, which is the controlling body for all papers, was Sabri Abu al-Magd. A former editor of *al-Musawwar* and the NDP weekly *Mayo*, Abu al-Magd began his career with the political police in the 1940s and, according to *al-Ahrar*, maintained his connections to the security apparatus throughout his long journalistic career.[31]

During the April 1987 parliamentary elections numerous journalists were physically assaulted by CSF troops and SSA agents. A week following the elections two journalists and a photographer from *al-Akhbar* were beaten up and had their camera smashed while covering a fire in a gasoline station in Qalyubiya Province. The syndicate of journalists responded to these events by sending a strongly worded letter of protest to the Minister of Interior. The publication of that letter on 16 April in the government dailies and a front-page editorial in *al-Akhbar* demanding an investigation of the major general, major, and lieutenant colonel from the SSA who *al-Akhbar* alleged participated in the assault in Qalyubiya all suggested that the government might be backing away from its policy of the physical intimidation of reporters. But within two months it became clear that the policy was not to be changed. In the wake of assassination attempts on Hassan Abu Basha and Makram Muhammad Ahmad, the Ministry of Interior rounded up as many as several thousand "suspects," including several journalists. Among them was Hamdin Sabahi, who had been head of the Cairo University student union in 1977. He was among those arrested by Sadat in September 1981 and was in 1987 director of the Nasserist Arab Center for Communication and Publication. Despite the fact that the syndicate of journalists has been granted the right to be notified of arrests of its members and to have contact with them while under detention, the police refused to honor those rights in the case of Sabahi and several of his colleagues. The syndicate objected once again but with no effect.

The syndicate itself is subject to manipulation by the government, so the limits of its protests are relatively carefully circumscribed. Some three months before the June 1987 incidents, the government had ensured the reelection of *al-Ahram* editor Ibrahim Nafa as president of the syndicate. Prior to that election the government announced salary and pension increases for journalists of 25 percent, distribution of apartments to the journalists' housing cooperative, payment of an increased governmental contribution to the syndicate's pension fund, and the topping up of the Higher Press Council's severance pay fund. This sudden beneficence caused *Akhbar al-Yom* editorialist Salah Hafiz to comment that "The shortest cut to prosperity in Egypt is not industry, or agriculture, or tourism, or oil. It is elections."[32]

The electronic media is generated from fewer sources and under direct governmental ownership, hence much more easily controlled than newspapers. The directors of radio and television and members of their *shilla*-s supervise programming, staffing, and the distribution of virtually all other significant resources. In a country where *mahsubiya* (nepotism) is endemic, the radio and television organizations are remarkable by their degree of commitment to this principle, which ensures compliance of those on the payroll.[33] Expert analysts, including academics, brought in for occasional commentary are carefully instructed as to the acceptable limits of criticism, and television coverage of parliamentary debates systematically favors the government and the NDP.[34]

The resources of the state remain so overwhelming compared to those of opposition parties that the three main arenas in which limited democratization has occurred, the media, parliament, and elections, are sites of unequal contests. Moreover, the government has since 1985 moved further to reduce the scope of opposition activities. There is little if anything those parties can do to prevent this erosion of the semiliberal environment, except to hope that the government, out of fear of the Islamic tendency or some other calculation, will once again decide to grant more freedoms to the secular opposition.

SOURCES OF OPPOSITION PARTIES' WEAKNESS

While the opposition parties' newspapers, election campaigns, and parliamentary activities are the key targets for governmental harassment and intimidation, the party organizations themselves are also subjected to pressure. The government is well aware of divisions within and between parties and seeks to manipulate them. One technique of exacerbating internal tensions is to license or threaten to license a new party with appeal to a major faction within an existing one. Uncertainty surrounding legalization of a Nasserite party has for several years placed additional strain on the Nasserist-Marxist alliance that is the core of the NPUP. The chief *raison d'être* of the Liberal Party, which was formed with governmental assistance, is to attract some support from the same constituencies cultivated by the Wafd. The Umma Party, licensed in the wake of the 1984 elections, was seen by the government as a vehicle to fragment the bourgeois Islamicist constituency to which the Moslem Brotherhood appeals. By nurturing the hopes of would-be deserters from the six licensed parties operating by 1987, the government has contributed substantially to discord within each. Harassment is also commonplace. SSA agents are occasionally posted in front of party headquarters, telephones are tapped, and those who join parties, particularly the NPUP, are on occasion subjected to various forms of reprisal.[35]

The drumbeat of governmental criticism of the parties also has had an enervating effect. Since the Wafd was the formal leader of the opposition between 1984 and 1987 and the most effective and trenchant critic of government policy, it was the target of most such attacks. When *al-Wafd* berated the government for its dependence on "external sources" (i.e., the United States), the government press retaliated by publishing the allegation that the Wafd had been allowed to reconstitute itself as a party in 1978 because the then-U.S. Ambassador, Hermann Eilts, had exerted pressure on Sadat to that end.[36] The government, which had early in 1986 censored Muhammad Hassanein Heikal's columns on decision making in Egypt, had no such objection to the serialization of his new book on the Suez Crisis, which eulogized Nasser and by implication cast the Wafd's performance in a negative light. As *al-Wafd* was urging its readers to boycott the *Shura* Council election of October 1986 because of the probability that election results would be falsified and because of the general climate of corruption, Musa Sabri retaliated. In a "Letter to the Pasha Sirag al-Din," which appeared on the front page of *al-Akhbar*, he reminded readers that when the current leader of the Wafd had been Minister of Interior prior to 1952, he had shown no hesitation in manipulating elections or in engaging in illegal transactions with Madam Nahhas, wife of the then-party leader, documentation for which Sabri gleefully provided.[37] Usama Khalid in *al-Akhbar* explained how the Wafd, when in government, had supported censorship and emergency decrees.[38] When conflict erupted within the

Wafd in the spring of 1986, the government press devoted unparalleled efforts to describing the jealousies and animosities that divided the party's leaders and provided ample space for opponents of party leader Fuad Sirag al-Din to air their grievances. While government newspapers and magazines also contain much cruder attacks on the opposition parties, by and large they have demonstrated considerable sophistication in selecting and exploiting issues that the Wafd and other parties would prefer not to have as the center of public attention.

After the first blush of enthusiasm as the parties reconstituted themselves and contested the 1984 elections, they then slid into the doldrums. Membership figures and election results reflect this trend. The NPUP's share of votes, for example, slid from more than 4 percent in the 1984 election to less than 3 percent in the 1987 election. In the wake of that election the NPUP engaged in an orgy of self-criticism. Speaking for one of the radical leftist factions, Salah Issa, a member of the NPUP central committee, claimed that the party's problems were due to the fact that it had not determined whether it was a revolutionary or reformist party. "I am one of those who say we must go to the streets to distribute our pamphlets in front of factories and universities. They [the Islamicists] are on the streets, but we are inside."[39]

Ismail Sabri Abdulla, speaking for a more conservative faction within the party, disagreed with Issa, arguing that this strategy would reduce the NPUP to a protest movement and that radical slogans would alienate rather than attract potential supporters. But like Issa, Abdulla was clearly impressed with the tactics of the Islamicists and also recommended that they be imitated. To Abdulla that meant organizational work within factories and universities and involving the NPUP in community self-help schemes.[40] But these were forlorn hopes, for the party lacked sufficient organizational coherence and adequate cadres to compete in mobilizational activities with the Islamicists. Raymond Hinnebusch claims that in 1981 the party had a hard-core membership of some 20,000 and that its membership "was strongest in urban and more modernized areas." For the provinces of Gharbiya and Qalyubiya he provides the figures of 2,000 and 400, respectively.[41] A newspaper investigation of election activities in Ismailiya, which certainly qualifies as "an urban and more modernized area," revealed that in 1987 the NPUP could mobilize less than 30 members in the entire province.[42]

It is not just the left that is suffering from an inability to attract members or voters. The conservative Liberal and Umma parties have never been more than their leaders and their coteries of followers. While Wafdist MP Alwi Hafiz claimed in the fall of 1986 that his party had about two million registered members, that is a very optimistic estimate.[43] A more neutral source and one with an extensive knowledge of all the parties, Sayed Marei, observed in the spring of 1987 "that after eleven years of the multiple party system, adherents to all the parties today do not exceed one million."[44] The very important extraordinary general assembly of the Wafd, which was held on 27 June 1986 and which Wahid Rifat, Vice President of the party, claimed would attract some 2,500 to 3,000 members, in fact brought together less than half that estimate.[45] In both the 1984 and 1987 elections the Wafd captured some three-quarters of a million votes (778,131 and 746,023 in 1984 and 1987, respectively), compared to 3.7 million for the NDP in 1984 and 4.7 million in 1987. By the spring of 1987 it was apparent that none of the secular opposition parties was attracting significant numbers of new voters or members. Indeed, they were struggling to hold on to those they had.

The internal weaknesses of the parties have much to do with the conditions of their creation. They emerged from the vacuum of the Nasser and early Sadat eras in which no new generations of opposition party activists had been trained. The only experienced politicians on the scene by the mid to late 1970s were those who had been active prior to 1952 or who had participated in the Nasserist or Sadatist experiments. All were consumed with a desire to settle old scores and to turn the clock back to precisely the point at which their party and its political philosophy had prevailed. For each the remedy for contemporary ills was to be found in the prescriptions of the past. This preoccupation both impeded cooperation between the opposition parties and enhanced the salience of factional fights that had beset the Wafd, the Nasserist movement, and the left more generally in their heydays.

Abd al-Hamid Yunis, in an extensive analysis of factions within opposition parties, concluded that while there are 6 official opposition parties, there are in reality more than 20, for each of the 6 is divided into several factions that operate more or less independently.[46] The NPUP, the Arabic name of which is *Tagamu*, or alliance, admitted from the outset that it was a coalition of several different factions, including Nasserists, Marxists, Arab Nationalists, social democrats, and even some progressive religious elements.[47] It has held together primarily because those separate factions have not been licensed to operate independently as parties and because the party possesses an ideal conciliatory leader in the person of its secretary general, Khalid Muhyi al-Din. He presides expertly and in a nonconfrontational manner over the party's disunited ranks and would be extremely difficult to replace. Indeed, 15 of the 35 political scientists queried in the 1984 poll indicated the NPUP might not survive if Muhyi al-Din were removed. When asked which parties they thought would continue to exist if there were complete freedom to form parties, positive responses for the Wafd and NPUP were 25 and 17, respectively, and for the NDP and SLP, 10 and 3, respectively. Five political scientists believed that if there were complete freedom to form new parties, the NPUP would fragment into two or three different wings.[48] This poll, moreover, was taken at a time when the NPUP was relatively united, despite a penchant for debating such issues as whether all capitalists were necessarily parasitic or by their size and behavior could be classified as nationalists.[49]

The Socialist Labor Party is the most cohesive of the three major opposition parties because it has been reconstituted from a single *ancien regime* political organization, *Misr al-Fatat* (Young Egypt). Led by Ahmad Hussain, Young Egypt began its life in the 1930s as a neofascist movement. After the war it was transformed into a socialist party with Islamic overtones. Such ideological flexibility continues to be a hallmark of the SLP. When reorganized under Sadat's tutelage in the late 1970s by the former Young Egypt parliamentary deputy, Ibrahim Shukri, the SLP was a left-of-center, predominately secular party. But as secularism appeared increasingly to be a spent force, the SLP identified itself more closely with Islam. By 1987 it had moved into an electoral coalition with the Moslem Brotherhood. This ideological mutation was not without cost. The editor of the SLP's newspaper, *al-Shaab*, has since late 1985 been Adil Hussain, younger brother of the founder of Young Egypt. An economist and journalist, Adil Hussain's adoption of an Islamicist perspective in place of his former commitment to secular neo-Marxism has not only given rise to charges of opportunism, but it has aggravated tension between majoritarian Islamicist and minoritarian secularist wings of the party.[50]

That the party has been divided on various important issues accounts in part for the defection from it of numerous prominent members, including Dr. Hilmi Hadidi and Abu al-Fadl al-Gizawi, both of whom left the SLP for the NDP. Sabahi Awad Allah, a Young Egypt stalwart, was denied the SLP endorsement for the Cairo Sayida Zainab district and left the party for the newly created Umma Party. The government press regularly announces defections from the ranks of provincial party members to the NDP, usually providing accompanying interviews in which the defectors level criticisms at the party's elite. Nevertheless, the core leadership of the party, which includes Shukri, Hussain, Hilmi Murad, and a few others, is knit together by shared experiences in Young Egypt and by extensive kinship connections. As a result of this elite solidarity and the SLP's comparatively small size, it has been able to permit a significantly larger measure of internal democracy than the Wafd. Membership on its various committees is determined by election rather than appointment. Important policy issues are subject to debate and approval by the party's general assembly. In 1984, for example, when the party leadership decided to accept the appointment by Mubarak of four of its members to the People's Assembly after the party had failed to obtain the minimum 8 percent of the popular vote, that decision was approved in the general assembly by the narrow margin of 284 to 224.

In the 1984 election the SLP obtained 364,000 votes compared to the NPUP's 214,000 and the Liberal Party's meager 33,000. The coalition of the SLP, Liberal Party, and Moslem Brotherhood in 1987 attracted more than 1.1 million votes. Salah Muntasir, a leading editorialist, calculated the Moslem Brotherhood's share of the vote in 1987 at 550,000, suggesting that the SLP might have increased its votes by 100,000 or so.[51] Election results are, however, imprecise indicators of party strength. First-hand observers of election campaigns and polling have invariably noted that the NPUP's presence is typically more impressive than that of the SLP's.[52] The superior electoral performance of the latter presumably reflects the government's preference for the SLP, as it constitutes less of an ideological and organizational threat. Certainly Egypt's leading political scientists are not impressed by the depth or coherence of the SLP. As mentioned above, only 3 of 35 believed in 1984 that if there were complete freedom to form parties the SLP would persist. When asked about the party's fate if Ibrahim Shukri were no longer able to lead it, 8 said it would continue, 19 that it would confront a deep crisis, and 7 that it would cease to exist. Only the NDP, according to those polled, would face greater difficulty in the event of the absence of its leader, who is, of course, President Mubarak.

PARTY INFIGHTING: THE CASE OF THE WAFD

Internal factionalization, common to all the opposition parties, was by 1986 contributing substantially to the erosion of the preeminence of the Wafd. As in the other parties the cleavages divided those of older and younger generations and, among the former, memories of conflicts that occurred as much as fifty years ago served to impede elite cohesion. While a semblance of unity was retained until mid-1986, the divisions that erupted then dated back some two years and centered on the formation of lists for the 1984 parliamentary elections. At that time party leader Fuad Sirag al-Din had intervened in selection procedures from Aswan to Alexandria to ensure that his loyalists, dubbed the Siragiyin or Fuadiyin, as opposed to the Nahhasiyin (those associated with the memory of Nahhas Pasha, the Wafd's previous president), obtained the top positions on the party's lists. Sirag al-Din sought in particular to ensure that Saif al-Din al-Ghazali not expand his base of support in the parliamentary wing of the party. Ghazali, leader of the Nahhasiyin, claimed a longer personal history of party activity than Sirag al-Din and was one of several possible alternative leaders of the party. Another was Fuad's brother Yassin, who was chairman of the Wafd's important Cairo Committee. Shortly after the 1984 elections Fuad had moved against his own brother, whose rising popularity in the wake of a widely publicized trip to the United Nations in New York had led to speculation about Yassin replacing his brother. Acting independently, Fuad stripped Yassin of his position and "froze" his party membership, leaving his relationship with the Wafd in a state of suspended animation.

The controversial Islamicist radical Shaikh Salah Abu Ismail, who had been swept into parliament as a result of the Wafdist–Moslem Brotherhood alliance in the 1984 election, also engendered Fuad Sirag al-Din's wrath. Abu Ismail, who had coveted the position of leader of the Wafdist parliamentary delegation and therefore of opposition forces in parliament but who was thwarted when Sirag al-Din awarded that post to the secularist Mumtaz Nassar, sought to force the Wafd and the rest of the opposition to lend support to his call for the implementation of the *sharia*. Sirag al-Din and his secular allies in the party finessed this issue, verbally endorsing the call but doing nothing to effect it. When Abu Ismail tried to force the issue in the summer of 1985 by seeking to align the Wafd with the application of the *sharia* in the Sudan and by publicly criticizing Sirag al-Din for his foot-dragging on the issue, the latter announced to the party's higher committee that the shaikh had submitted his resignation from the party. The committee duly accepted that resignation just as the shaikh himself was protesting bitterly that he had done no such thing. He demanded, to no avail, to see a copy of the letter of resignation Sirag al-Din claimed to have received.[53] The president of the Wafd, who had earned a reputation for uncompromising toughness prior to 1952, clearly had not mellowed even though he had passed his eightieth birthday.

The Pasha, as Sirag al-Din is commonly known, is a masterful political infighter. When the Wafd was reconstituted in 1983–1984, a general assembly in which all authority was to be embodied was convened. It elected the Pasha as president and made him chairman of the higher committee, to which was delegated the authority to implement the general assembly's resolutions. Meetings of the general assembly were to be held each January. Through this higher committee Sirag al-Din exerted his control over the party, with the crucial exception of its parliamentary wing, in which were congregated several of his opponents, including Saif al-Din al-Ghazali. The first public indication of the smoldering feud between the Pasha and his MPs came in the summer of 1985. Wafdist MPs, whose attack on Governor of Alexandria Fawzi Muaz was cut short when Speaker Mahgub adjourned parliament on the grounds that President Mubarak was holding a tea party for parliamentarians and could not be kept waiting, refused to attend the presidential reception. The Pasha, on hearing this news, phoned the opposition room in parliament and instructed Wafdist MPs to go to the reception to prevent the insult to Mubarak being used as a pretext for a crackdown or to discredit the party before public opinion. Most MPs refused Sirag al-Din's direct order. Following this incident the Pasha and Ghazali set about seeking allies in preparation for the final confrontation. Paradoxically Sirag al-Din cultivated the socalled *mustawafdiyin*, or younger elements in the party, chief of whom was former university professor Namaan Gumaa, while Ghazali sought to mobilize the core of the old Wafd to his side.[54]

Maneuvering between the Pasha and Ghazali went on for almost a year. A showdown was finally precipitated when Ghazali and two other Wafdist MPs accepted an invitation from the government to participate in a delegation going to India. This prompted Sirag al-Din to move to force Ghazali and his allies from the party and to bring the parliamentary wing more directly under his control. He utilized the higher committee to "freeze" the membership of Ghazali and his two associates and scheduled an extraordinary general assembly of the party for 27 June 1986 for the purpose of amending the party's bylaws.

The assembly, which had not been convened since the first was held after the party was reconstituted in 1984, provided the Pasha an opportunity to display his skills of political manipulation. In theory some 50,000 members of committees on the village, town, district, provincial, and national levels were eligible to attend and vote, but Sirag al-Din's ally, party Vice President Wahid Rifat, announced that no venue could hold such a large number so that restrictions to limit attendance to some 2,500 to 3,000 would have to be imposed.[55] Admission to the assembly was to be granted only to those possessing green cards identifying the bearer as a fully paid-up party member. These cards were issued by governorate committees that, acting on instructions from the Pasha, systematically withheld them from the Nahhasiyin. On the appointed date some 1,000–1,400 of the faithful were admitted to the meeting, 500 of whom were alleged by reporters from the government press to be from Sharqiya Province and thus part of the machine controlled by the Abaza family, whose patriarch Ahmad is a close ally of Sirag al-Din. Given the decidedly bourgeois character of the party, a remarkably high number of those attending could neither read nor write, as indicated by their use of the ring stamps that substitute for signatures among the illiterate. Many of the party's prominent figures, including Mumtaz Nassar, Yassin Sirag al-Din, Mustafa Shurdi, and others, did not attend.[56]

The meeting was chaired by the Pasha and his assistant, Wahid Rifat. All procedural challenges to proceedings were overruled by the chair. As objections from the floor by Ghazali's supporters became more heated, the Siragiyin encircled the protesters and subdued them. The new bylaws, which provided for an unlimited term for the president, appointment rather than election to the higher committee, and a requirement that Wafdist MPs submit all proposed parliamentary initiatives, including interpellations and questions, to the higher committee for prior approval, were rammed through. Members of the minority faction led by Ghazali, who prior to the general assembly had threatened to create a Democratic Wafdist Front, vented their spleens to the press, accusing the Pasha of using dictatorial methods. They reminded Egyptians that Sirag al-Din had not permitted elections to any party committees since 1984; that the annual meeting of the general assembly required in the party's bylaws had not been held for three years; and that the Pasha, whose chief demand of the government was that it permit more democracy and who claimed that democracy was the solution to virtually all of Egypt's pressing problems, was a hypocrite. Sirag al-Din's Wafd, they claimed, was no more democratic than Yusuf Wali's NDP.[57]

While Sirag al-Din's unrelenting aspiration to control the Wafd with an iron fist stimulated much negative reaction, divisions within the Wafd are so numerous and deep-seated that in the absence of his firm, not to say dictatorial methods, fragmentation may have been even more debilitating. The old Wafdists have not forgotten their previous clashes. Ibrahim Talaat, for example, who had been a brilliant young Wafdist MP from Alexandria in the 1950 parliament, sought a prominent place on the Wafdist list for that city in the 1984 election. But thiry-four years earlier Talaat had opposed Sirag al-Din, who was then Minister of Interior, in his efforts to impose press censorship. That, in combination with Talaat's alignment with the Nahhasiyin, caused him to be excluded entirely from the Wafdist list. He responded by urging voters not to cast their ballots for the Wafd.[58]

Younger Wafdists, well aware that the mantle of leadership will in the near future have to be handed down to their generation, are divided by their personal ambitions. Sirag al-Din's proteges, Dr. Namaan Gumaa and Mustafa Nagi, both of whom since 1978 have been seeking to construct competitive patronage networks in the party, clashed publicly during the traumatic events of June 1986.[59] Others, including the editor of al-Wafd, Mustafa Shurdi; lawyers' syndicate head and claimant to the leadership of the resuscitated Wafdist Vanguard Organization, Ahmad al-Khawaga; Dr. Abd al-Muhsin Hamuda of the Nahhasiyin; Ahmad Abaza's son Mahmud; and several other prominent figures in the younger generation (i.e., 45–65) are engaged in a game of musical chairs that will come to a halt only when the Pasha finally departs the scene. Structural divisions within the party also militate against unity of purpose. Conflict between the parliamentary wing and the higher committee has already been mentioned. The two leading provincial branches of the party, those in Cairo and Alexandria, are now, as they have been since the party was first founded in the wake of World War I, keen rivals.

Whether policy issues only provide the grounds on which factional disputes are fought out or are themselves actually of independent importance is ambiguous. For the most part members are agreed that they want more democracy, economic policies that favor the bourgeoisie, and most of all that the Wafd should come to power. There are, however, some points of contention that are no less fractious for being largely symbolic. An example is the question of the party's attitude toward the Nasser and Sadat legacies. While the former is denounced unequivocally as having "destroyed" Egypt, the latter is more problematical. Although the Wafd during its first reincarnation in 1978 was highly critical of Sadat, by the mid-1980s many members were having second thoughts. Sadat, after all, had initiated the deNasserization of Egypt. Reflecting this new orientation, al-Wafd, which continued to berate Nasserism but ceased its attacks on Sadatism, serialized in early 1987 the biography of Sadat by his daughter and later in the year Jihan Sadat's book.

The reinterpretation of Sadat's legacy was due in part to Mubarak's strategy. As the President sought to revive Nasserism to cover his exposed flank to the left, to mollify the underprivileged, and to use Nasserists to contain Sadatists within the state structure, so did some in the Wafd perceive an opportunity in associating themselves with the Sadatist legacy. The increasingly restrictive economic measures, particularly those regarding imports, had alienated the wealthy Sadatist *munfatihun*, who formerly had been associated with the NDP and the government. Many of them, especially in Alexandria and Port Said, deserted to the Wafd.

The new rightist push to the party manifested itself in conflict over the issue of consumer subsidies. Since its reestablishment the party had been unable to agree as to whether subsidies should be continued, reduced, eliminated, or changed in some other ways. Its two leading economic spokesmen, Ahmad Abu Ismail and Ahmad Abaza, disagreed, with the former arguing against cuts on the grounds of possible food riots and negative voter reaction. Ahmad Abaza, on the other hand, contended that subsidies were too heavy a drain on investment capital and so distorted the economy that they had to be abolished.[60] Imitating Solomon's wisdom, the party made Abu Ismail chairman of the finance committee and Abaza head of the economic committee, thereby providing each a platform from which to air his views.

Similarly, the party's stance toward the public-sector has been problematical and for much the same reasons. Party strategists fear that calling for its abrogation would so alienate its managerial ranks that the party would lose one of its constituencies. During the extraordinary general assembly of 27 June 1986, this was the only policy issue that gave rise to heated debate. A minority faction wanted to amend paragraph five of section one of the new bylaws, which called for the private sector to be permitted to participate alongside the public sector in building the Egyptian economy. The proposed amendment called for the abolition of the public sector. The Pasha called for a voice vote and ruled, in the face of vigorous protests, that the majority opposed the amendment.[61]

Similar considerations underlay the party's stance on the key foreign policy issues of relations toward the United States and Israel. Attracting popular support would appear to dictate a policy critical of both, but the party's strong endorsement of economic liberalization, its condemnation of excessive military spending, its unease with Arab nationalism, and the fact that some of its members have business dealings with the United States and/or Israel have required that the issue be avoided. Of the opposition newspapers, *al-Wafd* provides the least coverage of Egyptian-U.S. and Egyptian-Israeli relations. The litmus test of attitudes about the United States and Israel, which is opinion on the Camp David accords, revealed in a survey of party activists the sharpest division of any single issue.[62] That division, moreover, appears to pit the Siragiyin against other factions within the party. Fuad Sirag al-Din and his close ally, Wahid Rifat, endorsed Sadat's trip to Jerusalem, and as late as October 1985 the latter was still publicly defending the Camp David accords, although after that time political considerations dictated that silence be maintained on this issue.[63]

The Wafd, like all other opposition parties, confronts the divisive issue of the proper relation between Islam and the state and more specifically how, when, and with what thoroughness the *sharia* should be adopted. For the Wafd, however, the Islamic challenge has been comparatively easy to confront, if only because of the party's long association with secularism. The electoral alliance with the Moslem Brotherhood in 1984, the formation of which caused numerous prominent Wafdists to leave the party, dictated that the Wafd endorse the call for the application of the *sharia* and then do as little as possible to pressure the government to that end. That approach to the issue first led to the break with Shaikh Salah Abu Ismail and ultimately to the breakdown of the alliance with the Brotherhood. As that organization began in 1986 publicly to search for a new partner with which it might associate for electoral purposes, the Wafd began to distance itself from the Islamicist tendency. *al-Wafd* ran occasional articles critical of leading figures of the Islamic establishment, including the Shaikh of al-Azhar, whom *al-Wafd* accused of taking over a student hostel for use as his private house.[64] In the 1987 elections the Wafd courted the Coptic vote and stood alone among the opposition parties in deemphasizing the need for the application of the *sharia*. Even some elements of the NDP more closely associated themselves with that demand. This retreat into secularism has so far not led to a reaction within the party, but the question remains as to whether the Wafd can stand against the trend toward greater religiosity.

CLASS BASES OF OPPOSITION PARTIES

A further indication of the weakness of opposition parties is their inability to recruit from beyond the limited fragments of the bourgeoisie upon which all rest. The Wafd, according to a recent investigation of the backgrounds of the elite of that party, is led by the landed, professional, and commercial bourgeoisie, especially those associated with the private sector.[65] When asked what social categories the parties represent, the 35 political scientists who participated in the open-ended 1984 survey referred to above identified the Wafdist constituencies as follows: big capitalists—18; landowners, feudalists, and old families—4; intellectuals and professionals—2; middle classes—2; small bourgeoisie—1; no one specifically—11.

Attitudes of Wafdist MPs reflect these relatively narrow social origins. During the 1985/1986 parliamentary session *al-Ahram* conducted a survey of parliamentarians, asking 211 of the 448 elected MPs, of which 184 were from the NDP and 27 from the Wafd, 25 questions about their attitudes on specific issues. Included in the Wafdist subsample were 9 Moslem Brothers who had been elected to parliament on Wafdist lists, so the responses may have been more heterogenous than would be the case if they were only from Wafdists. Also included in the Wafdist sample of 27 MPs were 10 who had been elected to parliament as workers and 5 as peasants, and they presumbably would be somewhat less conservative than the Wafdist elite of undeniably bourgeois backgrounds. It is equally true, however, that these MPs are not typical workers or peasants either. Of the 27 Wafdist MPs, 3 claimed literacy but no postprimary credentials, while all the rest held university or postgraduate degrees. When asked what the most important problem confronting their electoral districts was, none of the Wafdist MPs referred to agricultural issues, compared to 3.3 percent of the sample of NDP deputies. Nearly 11 percent of NDP deputies most wanted to see legislation introduced in parliament to protect land and raise agricultural production, while no Wafdist deputies indicated this as a primary legislative concern. Over 10 percent of NDP deputies, compared to none of the Wafdist MPs, identified education and the eradication of illiteracy as the major tasks facing Egypt. When asked if the problem of housing should be left to the private-sector, 48 percent of Wafdists compared to 27 percent of NDP deputies agreed. Of the sample as a whole, 43 percent wanted the maximum limit on landownership to be raised, and 93 percent supported the proposition that peasants should be expelled from land for which they have rental contracts if they did not plant that land every season.[66] Although Wafdist and NDP deputies are both supportive of bourgeois interests, the Wafdists, at least as represented by this sample, are noticeably to the right of those in the government's party.

The class bases of recruitment of other opposition parties are more mixed, although those parties generally recruit from lower strata within the bourgeoisie. The SLP is identified by one of Egypt's most prominent lapsed Marxists, Abd al-Azim Ramadan, as "representing no one, for it cannot claim to represent the working class, it cannot claim to represent any segment of capitalism, and it cannot claim to represent the petit bourgeoisie." That, according to Ramadan, is why the government has imposed fewer restrictions on the SLP than on the NPUP or the Wafd.[67] Egypt's leading political scientists agree with Ramadan. Of the sample of 35 of them, who were asked what social category the SLP represents, 18 said none. Seven said it represented the middle class, 3 replied "capitalist," and two said it represented workers.

The core of the leftist NPUP is provided primarily by middle-class intellectuals and professionals, as well as some trade union officials.[68] The appeal of the party to workers and peasants, which showed some promise when the party was first organized, demonstrated a noticeable decline through the mid-1980s, a result both of regime pressure and the inability of the party leadership to fashion appeals and organizational methods to mobilize nonbourgeois constituencies. Also, according to Abd al-Azim Ramadan, the *infitah*, by enriching significant numbers of the working class, by converting large numbers of them into self-employed tradesmen, and by eroding the relative dominance of public-sector industry, undermined the appeal of the NPUP to the working class.[69] According to the same political scientists referred to above, the NPUP represents workers/working class (18 responses); intellectuals (9 responses); petit bourgeoisie (4 responses); and various others. That the NPUP has not yet identified its position was claimed by 11 respondents. In sum, the NPUP is seeking without success to establish a base in the working class in the modern industrial sector. This strategy is unlikely ever to prove successful because of class differences between the party's leadership and those it hopes to recruit, regime pressure, and the economic position of workers, which is a highly vulnerable one.

The political energies of the bourgeoisie are thus channeled in a variety of directions. The NDP can claim the largest current because it most effectively taps into the state administration and public sector and has access to the resources off which the parasitic bourgeoisie feed. The Wafd brings together elements of this same parasitic bourgeoisie who are increasingly disaffected by Mubarak's reforms, as well as the bourgeoisie who have been too far removed from the centers of state power to become parasitic. The NPUP attracts bourgeois intellectuals and those who have fond memories of their days of glory under Nasser, while the SLP is a small coterie of similar types differentiated principally by the fact that they never made their peace with Nasser. With this degree of fragmentation of the principal class base for political organization, it is not surprising that the opposition parties, like the NDP, remain weak.

LACK OF COORDINATION
BETWEEN OPPOSITION PARTIES

Fragmented internally into various competing factions, opposition parties have been unable to devise and implement a collective approach in dealing with the government. Since 1985, the idea of forming some type of national opposition front has been discussed but with no concrete results.[70] When one of the opposition parties champions the idea, as the Wafd did in the summer of 1985, another rejects it, as the NPUP did at that time. In 1987 the NPUP, fearful it would not obtain the required minimum of 8 percent of total votes, threw its weight behind an attempt to form an all-party coalition to contest the parliamentary elections. The Wafd, confident it would cross the 8 percent threshold, objected and persisted in its determination to contest the elections independently. In the summer of 1986 the parties held extensive talks on forming joint lists for the *Shura* Council elections. That they could not accomplish, but they did agree on a joint strategy of boycotting the elections. Immediately following the 1 October election the coalition crumbled, for the president of the Liberal Party, Mustafa Kamal Murad, could not resist the temptation to accept an invitation from Mubarak to serve in the Council.[71]

It is not just the inability to form and maintain a grand coalition that attests to the lack of cohesion among the opposition parties. Even on issues of mutual concern they do not effectively coordinate strategies. When *al-Wafd*'s Said Abd al-Khaliq was arrested on the charge of having accepted a bribe, the opposition parties did not rally around him and portray the incident as a probable frame-up designed to intimidate *al-Wafd* and the opposition press more generally. Instead, they reported the case in a matter-of-fact way, relying heavily on governmental accounts of the incident. *Sawt al-Arab*, the mouthpiece of the quasi-legal Nasserite party, used the occasion to heap scorn on Sirag al-Din and the Wafd.[72] Non-Wafdist opposition politicians were pleased with the discomfort the incident was causing the leading opposition party and privately nurtured hopes that their weekly papers might pick up some of the circulation that *al-Wafd* was bound to lose when its popular column, "The Sparrow," no longer appeared. Had the opposition rallied around the jailed editor, the resulting pressure on the government might have led to the establishment of a larger measure of freedom for the opposition press.

THE POLITICAL VACUUM: EXPLOSIVE OR JUST EMPTY?

Neither the NDP nor the opposition parties have attracted significant followings among the lower-middle class, workers, or peasants. What they have accomplished is further to fragment the bourgeoisie. Divided politically between the government and the opposition and further subdivided into countless corporatist and pluralist groups, the bourgeoisie, although comprising the only politically articulate class, are too lacking in cohesion to dominate the state. Moreover, spreading awareness that the state disposes of political resources more than sufficient to match those of the opposition has enervated the Wafd and other opposition parties and led to widespread cynicism. Realizing that the parties can contest for power but never attain it, the politically articulate are either lapsing into apathy or shifting their allegiances to the Islamicist movement, the one oppositional force that as yet has not been revealed as impotent in the face of the state. The system of political control, having deteriorated since the Nasser and Sadat eras, has nevertheless remained sufficiently strong to contain the comparatively weak secular opposition, but in so doing it has created a vacuum that the more powerful Islamicist opposition threatens to fill.

But the bourgeoisie, even if mobilized by Islam, would not necessarily be united, nor would it be revolutionary. While those struggling to maintain a middle-class existence may succumb to appeals for a radically egalitarian Islamicization, those more firmly established within the bourgeoisie are unlikely to. They see no contradiction between capitalism and an Islamic political and cultural revival. For the political vacuum to become dangerously explosive rather than simply prone to a gradual and largely symbolic Islamicization, the nonbourgeois must be galvanized into collective political action. Is there a chance this could occur among workers, peasants, and the various elements that constitute the lower middle-class?

To summarily dismiss the vast majority of the Egyptian population, which is comprised of peasants and workers, as politically more or less permanently impotent and apathetic would be a mistake. The combined processes of social mobilization and deterioration of the state's control capabilities are unlikely to continue indefinitely without stimulating some sort of political challenge, although it may very well not be an organized one. As much as one-quarter of the entire population has since 1970 been directly affected by the experience of working abroad, either because they or a close member of their family did. At any given time since the late 1970s, some 2 million to 3 million Egyptians have been working abroad. Egypt now has scores of cities with more than 50,000 inhabitants. The countryside itself has been urbanized in a variety of ways. Transportation and communication facilities have been vastly upgraded, particularly since the United States Agency for International Development program was launched in 1975. U.S. aid has also supported the construction of thousands of classrooms throughout the country. Subsidization of basic commodities, especially foodstuffs, has contributed to the replacement of the "productive" village (one that is more or less self-sufficient) by the "consuming" village (one that imports much of what it consumes from nearby cities). It is cheaper for peasants to buy bread from government bakeries than it is for them to bake it from their own wheat. If bakers strike, even peasants are affected. More than 50 percent of the average farm family's income is now derived from nonagricultural sources, for family members are forced to augment their incomes by seeking off-farm employment, generally in proximate urban areas. As a result, the performance of the national economy has an immediate impact on rural areas.

Villages no longer even appear as they did twenty years ago, when virtually all consisted exclusively of one or two story mud brick residences. The inflow of worker remittances combined with locally generated capital has resulted in construction in villages of red brick dwellings and apartment blocks that are architecturally indistinguishable from those in urban Egypt. As these changes have occurred, the government's control over the agricultural sector has declined. Compulsory delivery of crops to agricultural cooperatives has gradually been relaxed, both by removing more crops from the list of those affected and by nonenforcement of sanctions. Mechanization has contributed to the exodus of the rural labor force, a process further stimulated by the education of children of peasants. Rural Egypt, in short, has undergone massive social and economic change since the death of Nasser in 1970. Paradoxically, that has taken place stimultaneously with a government-engineered political demobilization of the peasantry. Logic would suggest that an increasingly socially mobilized rural population is bound sooner or later directly to seek satisfaction of political demands.

There are indications that political apathy among peasants is giving way to intermittent rebelliousness. By the mid-1980s peasant demonstrations and protests were occurring throughout the country on an average of one every few weeks. A report on peasant movements (*taharruk*), including strikes, *itisam* (resistance) and protests, revealed that in 1986 there were 20 such events.[73] The majority were protests against the government's inability adequately to provide irrigation water, a problem resulting from poor maintenance of drains, overusage, and inadequate Nile discharge as a result of low rainfall in the river's catchment area. Partly as a result of these manifestations of peasant restiveness, the Egyptian government, with support from USAID and the World Bank, has since 1985 allocated substantial sums for the upgrading of the country's irrigation system. Assuming that water delivery problems will gradually be ameliorated, discontent stimulated by that problem should similarly abate. But while peasant rebelliousness may not develop into a significant political factor, the countryside is increasingly an economically diversified and politically complex area. Children of peasants are being educated and they seek employment outside of agriculture. Many commute on daily and weekly bases to nearby towns and cities. Marginal elements suspended between rural origins and urban comforts, they are a potential source for recruitment into radical political organizations.[74] They are not being absorbed into governmental political structures.

Indications that the unmet demands of the urban working class are contributing to a willingness to use direct action also became increasingly numerous in the mid-1980s. In 1985, 50,000 workers participated in 44 *taharruk*-s, which took the form of strikes, sit-ins, protests, and confrontations with authorities. In 1986 the number of participants in such activities more than doubled and the number of incidents increased to 75. Fifteen of Egypt's 22 governorates were affected.[75] The largest strikes occurred at the Esco textile mill, where 10,000 workers succeeded in closing it down on two occasions in the spring of 1986, and at the public-sector spinning and weaving companies in Mahallat al-Kubra, where 45,000 workers struck at various times during the year, including 3,500 employees who closed down the largest carpet factory in that industrial city. While most protest action was for the purpose of obtaining improved pay and conditions, strikers at Mahallat al-Kubra in April 1986 demanded that the government stop placing SSA agents in their midst and assigning those agents workers' flats.

Rumors of industrial sabotage were widespread in Egypt by the mid-1980s. The first arrests on such charges were made in June 1987, when the government announced it had indicted 5 workers in the Helwan Company for Spinning and Weaving for setting fire to the company's warehouse and destroying £E1.5 million worth of merchandise.[76] Whether this is the tip of an iceberg or an isolated incident is unknown. What is unambiguous is that confrontational action of various sorts is much more commonplace in Mubarak's Egypt than it was under either Sadat or Nasser. Moreover, vital installations and services are being affected. Railway workers closed down most of the country's trains in July 1986, and threatened to do so again in February 1987. Bakers ceased production of bread, the country's nutritionally and politically vital foodstuff, in a series of wildcat strikes in November 1986. In these instances the military was immediately called upon to assist. In the railway strike it provided bus transportation, and when the bakers went out the military bakeries produced loaves for consumption by civilians.

But workers, like peasants, are not yet on the verge of revolutionary or even very widespread rebellious activity. Their disruptions of industrial production to date have been designed to achieve specific economic goals rather than general political ones. While Mubarak's Egypt is much more prone to labor unrest than was Sadat's or Nasser's, that is a consequence in part of the more difficult economic circumstances of the mid-1980s. It is, however, also true to say that worker disturbances result from governmental efforts to hold down labor costs. Worker protests at the Esco spinning and weaving company, for example, resulted in part from the government's nonimplementation of a court order requiring the company to calculate the payment of bonuses in a manner favorable to employees. Moreover, the elaborate system of unions backed up by the single party that Nasser put in place but that began to decay under Sadat has eroded so much further under Mubarak that it indicates a conscious effort by the regime to demobilize workers. The government appears to believe that wildcat strikes and industrial sabotage are a price that can be afforded in the general campaign to impose greater discipline and reduce costs. Insurance against truly disruptive action against industry is provided by the system of control described previously and out of the sheer conditions of workers, who are dependent on government and public-sector companies for their housing and other basic services and who in virtually all cases have meager savings to draw on in support of strike efforts. In these circumstances the attitude of sullen apathy that characterizes a large share of the modern industrial labor force is understandable and predictable. But so, too, is the fact that some workers have been attracted to radical opposition groups, of which much the most numerous and active are those comprising part of the highly variegated but nevertheless influential Islamicist movement.

The social background characteristics of those recruited into the radical underground Islamic *gama'at* in fact provide a good indication of the relative mobilization of various classes and social forces. Such data generally confirm the above observations on the political apathy of the peasantry and, to a lesser extent, the modern industrial labor force. Members of the so-called Video Group, for example, an offshoot of the *al-Jihad* organization that assassinated Sadat and was responsible for burning numerous video shops between November 1985 and June 1986, have backgrounds similar to those of other radical Islamicists arrested in the Sadat and Mubarak eras. Of the 73 members of that group rounded up in July-August 1986, only one was a peasant. Another was a factory worker and a third a construction worker. The remainder of those in menial occupations were virtually all self-employed, worked in small concerns, and/or were traditional artisans. Over 41 percent of the group, for example, were furniture makers, blacksmiths, gunsmiths, tilers, painters, folk musicians, waiters, drivers, or those with modern skills such as electricians. Various others were clerks or junior employees in large public- or private-sector firms or the civil service. Six were merchants who owned small shops.[77]

In sum, over half of the arrested members of the Video Group were from the urban traditional working class or the traditional or modern lower-middle classes, which have for over half a century been the major sources of recruitment into Islamicist political organizations. Whereas the peasantry and the modern industrial working class are not socially marginal, many members of these other classes are, especially those who have recently been urbanized. Moreover, artisans and those working in small, mostly traditional concerns constitute a vital element of the economy. A World Bank mission reported in 1980, for example, that "Despite the uninviting climate, small-scale industries (i.e., those employing between 10 and 50 workers) have managed to hold their own and even grow, accounting for about one-third of total value added generated in industry and 54 percent of total industrial employment."[78] In addition, at that time the artisan sector—defined as including those working in establishments with from 1 to 9 employees (of which 72 percent had only 1 and 98 percent fewer than 5 workers)—employed, according to the World Bank mission, around one-third of a million workers.[79] Artisans, like those in small, private industrial firms, have continued successfully to defend their economic activities from possible inroads by modern, highly capitalized ventures. But there are indications that in order to remain competitive these traditional and/or small-scale producers have had to absorb reductions in remuneration and deterioration in working conditions. They work longer hours and for less pay than those in modern, large industrial plants, and their rate of underemployment is high. They have suffered disproportionately from government economic policy that restricts their access to credit and raw materials and in other ways discriminates in favor of the modern, capital-intensive sector.[80] In sum, despite their contribution to the economy and their sizable numbers, those in the traditional working and lower middle classes have not benefited from the modernization process to the degree that those employed in modern industry have, to say nothing of their relative deprivation vis-à-vis the *infitah* bourgeoisie.

Under constant economic threat and largely ignored by the government, these socially marginal but economically productive subclasses pose a greater potential threat to political stability than either peasants or modern industrial workers. Paradoxically, they are unlikely to engage in the type of protest activity, such as demonstrations and strikes, that the modern industrial labor force favors. The division between those who work with their hands and those who perform clerical functions or are merchants, the isolation that results from employment in small workshops, and the kinship and other primordial relations that frequently tie employers to the employed all militate against the sort of collective protest behavior that can lead to incremental policy adjustments by government. Equally, however, while their life situations inhibit participation in large, impersonal social collectivities, the relative intimacy of their work and frequently of their residential environments combines with their overlapping kinship connections to provide the bases on which small groups of dedicated members can easily be formed. Those groups, in turn, can be integrated into a larger movement, as has occurred with numerous of the Islamic *gama'at* that have sprung up in the past fifteen years.

Thus, while those of the traditional urban working class and the traditional and modern petit bourgeoisie may by aggregate measures of collective social behavior appear to be as or even more apathetic than peasants and industrial laborers, in reality they may be more politicized and pose much more of a threat to political stability. A major source of recruitment into the Islamicist movement, they could provide the shock troops that the bourgeois, secular political parties lack. Whether that Islamicist movement has the coherence and strength to actually contest for ultimate power or whether it is fragmented like the opposition parties is the question to be taken up in the next section of this chapter.

The Islamicist Opposition

THE REEMERGENCE OF ISLAMIC ACTIVISM IN MUBARAK'S EGYPT

For the first three years of the Mubarak presidency Islamic activists and issues were conspicuous by their absence from the national political limelight. The assassination of Sadat and the accompanying uprising in Asyut sapped the energies of radicals and caused moderates to lay low to avoid being implicated in those cataclysmic events. Islamicists, moreover, were using this period to assess the new President and his attitude toward Islam generally and the implementation of the *sharia* more specifically before making their first move. But this lull after the storm came to an end with the 1984 parliamentary elections. For the first time since 1944 the Moslem Brotherhood contested seats, although under the banner of the Wafd Party. The consequence of the electoral reemergence of the Brotherhood was to thrust the issue of the proper legal status of the *sharia* onto the national political agenda.

With expectations of Islamicists having been raised as a result of the election of nine Moslem Brothers to the People's Assembly, their call for the implementation of the *sharia* could no longer be ignored. While the government sought to finesse the issue by promising much but doing little, others chose to confront Islamicism head on.[81] Farag Fuda, a Wafdist who had deserted the party in protest against its electoral alliance with the Brotherhood, published a book entitled *Before the Fall*, in which he lambasted the claims of Islamicists that their religion provided a suitable framework for government. Fuda was immediately answered by a leading Islamicist scholar, Muhammad Yahia, whose *In Answer to Secularism* reasserted the Islamicist claim that Islam is not parallel to Christianity for it has no church, no clergy, and does not admit of the separation of state and religion.

Other luminaries joined in the debate and by the summer of 1985, following the parliament's rejection of demands for the immediate application of *sharia*, the public had become visibly agitated by the issue. Bumper stickers with verses from the Koran or the Bible and pictures of Coptic Pope Shanuda III began to proliferate in a "stickers war." It was brought to an abrupt halt in early July when the Ministry of Interior imposed a ban on the display of pictures and writing on automobiles. A "Green March" (green being the favored color in Islam) on Mubarak's Cairo office scheduled for mid-June and promoted by the radical Shaikh Hafiz Salama was intended to force the President to decree the implementation of the *sharia*. The march did not occur because the Moslem Brotherhood ordered its members not to participate in a demonstration for which the government had refused to issue a permit and because security forces detained more than 500 activists prior to the scheduled commencement of the march and sealed off al-Nur mosque, from which the parade was to have commenced. On 5 July the government moved to curtail the influence of Hafiz Salama, Omar Abd al-Rahman, and other radical *imam*-s who had attracted large followings at various mosques in Cairo, Alexandria, Fayum, and Upper Egypt. A decree was issued that called for the replacement of these *imam*-s by others appointed by the Ministry of Religious Endowments. At various mosques this imposition of government control was resisted, so a week later the Ministry of Interior arrested Salama and 44 other activists. Most of them, including Salama himself, were released later in the summer, but only after a series of confrontations between Salama's supporters and the police and the closure of al-Nur mosque. Although the government eventually managed to contain what in June and July had promised to be a very long, hot summer of Islamicist discontent, the problem did not go away. Student demonstrations at al-Azhar University in the fall caused the government to close that institution for two weeks.

The next cycle of activism commenced with the CSF riots of February 1986 and has not yet abated. The riots themselves, which were initiated by mutinous CSF troops, provided the opportunity for radical Islamicists in the Giza area to vent their rage. Scores went on the rampage literally in the wake of the rampaging soldiers who had surged down the Pyramids Road. These activists torched numerous establishments that had been left unscathed by the soldiers and that attracted the wrath of Islamicists because they sold alcoholic beverages and/or catered to Western or Westernized clienteles.[82] The riots also had a profound effect on Upper Egypt, not only because they seemed to inspire radical Islamicists there, but because deserters from the CSF sold or gave their weapons away, most of which were acquired by gun-loving *Saidi*-s (Upper Egyptians), a significant percentage of whom were radical Islamicists. The price of a Kalashnikov automatic rifle, which had risen from about £E1,000 in 1980 to £E4,000 by early 1986, plummeted on the black market to £E600–£E800.[83] Within a matter of weeks student activists were clashing with security forces on campuses throughout Upper Egypt. In the spring and early summer a wave of arson attacks on video and grocery shops in Cairo, Alexandria, and Fayum only came to halt when in July some 75 members of an offshoot of *al-Jihad* were apprehended.

With the commencement of the new academic year in October 1986, the government signaled it was going to adopt a tougher stance toward student radicals. It authorized the rector of Cairo University to forbid the wearing of *galabiya*-s, the traditional robe favored by male Islamicists, and the *niqab* (veil) by female students. This led immediately to heightened tension and a series of incidents on campus. On the first day of classes at Asyut University 35 students were arrested following demonstrations against the presence of security forces on campus.[84] In November student union elections were conducted in what approached a state of siege as the government sought unsuccessfully to engineer the defeat of Islamicist candidates.[85] Asyut remained tense throughout the fall. In early November clashes erupted there between radicals and security forces during protests against the replacement by the Ministry of Religious Endowments of the popular radical *imam* of Asyut's main mosque by Imam Abu al-Ala, a progovernment cleric.[86] Just prior to the end of the year violence erupted again in Asyut, where Islamicists demonstrating against the detainment of their colleagues and in support of the application of the *sharia* were set upon by security forces, who injured scores of activists and arrested over 100 of them. This incident, in combination with preparations for the April parliamentary elections, stimulated an increase in religious tension that resulted in the most widespread religiously inspired violence to affect Egypt since the summer of 1981.

The trouble began in early February in Beni Suef Governorate, where a disputed border between a Coptic monastery and adjoining properties owned by Moslem villagers led to a violent confrontation. Shortly thereafter rumors began to spread throughout Upper Egypt that small crosses were appearing on the garments of Moslem women after they were washed, the result, it was alleged, of Christians having sprayed those fabrics with a mysterious substance. On 25 February Coptic-owned shops in Beni Suef were attacked by rioting Moslem students. Violence quickly spread to Asyut and Sohag, in the latter of which a church and mosque were set afire by rival gangs of young Christians and Moslems. Security forces restored order after four days of disturbances, but less than a month later trouble flared again, and this time it also occurred in Lower Egypt. In the Delta village of Shabasi al-Shuhada there was at least 1 death, numerous injuries, and some 50 arrests were made in the wake of a Moslem-Christian confrontation that resulted in the burning of several houses, both Christian and Moslem.

The election campaign, which was in full swing at this time, clearly had escalated religious animosities. It witnessed the greatest public displays of pro-Islamicist sentiment in the history of Egyptian parliamentary elections. The Brotherhood blanketed the country with posters carrying such messages as "Give your vote to Allah, give it to the Moslem Brotherhood." Even the NDP and the secular opposition parties attempted to associate themselves with a revitalized, politicized Islam. The Moslem Brotherhood emerged the clear winner from the elections. It captured 38 seats compared to the Wafd's 35. This result, satisfying to Islamicists, combined with the termination of the election campaign itself and activities by leaders of the Moslem and Christian communities to pacify their followers, resulted in a month's relative peace.

But just less than thirty days after the election an assassination attempt was made on former Minister of Interior Hassan Abu Basha. The timing and the target suggested an attempt to keep the caldron of religious conflict boiling. On 26 May shots were fired at two U.S. Embassy employees as they drove through Old Cairo, and on 4 June the outspoken secularist editor in chief of *al-Musawwar*, Makram Muhammad Ahmad, was shot at as he drove through the crowded square behind the American University in Cairo. The government responded by arresting as many as 3,000 Islamic activists and others and by amending the emergency decrees to make them yet tougher.[87] But the failure of the government dragnet to apprehend those behind the assassination attempts was made evident on 13 August, when gunmen narrowly missed killing former Minister of Interior Nabawi Ismail. Two days later the government identified the three gunmen as members of yet another splinter group of *al-Jihad*. The following day they were surrounded at their hideout in a village north of Cairo, but in the ensuing gunbattle they escaped, leaving three wounded and one dead policeman. Minister of Interior Zaki Badr subsequently announced that the ringleader of the group was in custody, but he provided no further details.[88]

This sequence of events indicates that since 1984 Mubarak has been confronting a rising tide of Islamic activism. The events themselves, however, neither corroborate nor disprove propositions about the strength or coherence of the movement. They can, for example, be taken as evidence of the relatively peripheral nature of Islamic radicalism. Assassinations can be interpreted as the desperate acts of the weak and politically isolated. Violence in traditional rural areas remote from the capital can similarly be seen as posing little if any threat to the national political order. Indeed, Upper Egypt has been infamous for the propensity of its residents to engage in violence, so the present manifestations should not be overemphasized.

But the events just outlined also lend themselves to a more alarmist interpretation. That violence has become so commonplace and widespread, that the Moslem Brotherhood performed so well in the elections, and that radical groups can repeatedly fire on prominent figures with apparent impunity can be interpreted to mean that the contemporary semisecular political order is under real threat. Moreover, these events, in combination with the remarkable growth of the "Islamic economy" (of which the Islamic investment companies are a part) and the proliferation of social services provided by Islamicists (clinics, schools, and so on) are suggestive of a sociopolitical transformation in which violence could trigger the collapse of the regime and pave the way for the establishment of Islamic government. In this view the Islamicist movement consists of a continuum, ranging from the most radical of the *gama'at* to the most conservative factions of the Moslem Brotherhood. The various elements arrayed along that continuum complement rather than contest one another, making the regime's task of containment of the trend an almost impossibly difficult one.

ARE ISLAMICISTS PRACTICING *TAQIYA*?

The Islamicist movement, according to some close observers, is a seamless web, the various elements of which despite appearances to the contrary are parts of an integrated whole. That the coherence of the movement is not manifest is, according to this view, due to the practice of *taqiya* (dissimulation) by Islamicists themselves. Self-interest requires Islamicists to mislead opponents and to induce underestimates of the true strength and organizational integration of the Islamicist movement. In reality, radical *gama'at* implicated in assassination attempts and other acts of violence, less radical *gama'at* that group together university students or those who are involved in community work, the Moslem Brotherhood, Islamic investment companies, and significant sections of the *ulama* are all united in the desire to replace the semisecular government with a truly Islamic one. They are, moreover, agreed that each segment has a particular role to play. Radicals are to apply pressure by engaging in spectacular acts that enervate the state apparatus and undermine public confidence in it. Moderates are to present the legal face of the movement by participating in the political system and exploiting its channels of communication further to spread the Islamicist message. Moderates are also to reassure a public wary of the excesses of radical Islamicists and, ultimately, to accumulate sufficient power to be recognized as an alternative government when the semisecular regime reaches the point of collapse. Both radicals and moderates are supported by the increasingly wealthy Islamic sector of the economy.

A precedent for this broad-based assault on secular government is to be found, according to some, in the activities of the Moslem Brotherhood in the post–World War II period, when it combined social welfare work, Islamic "call" activities, and political moderation and respectability with a secret organization that engaged in assassination and even guerrilla war. Said Ashmawi, President of the State Security Court, in response to a question as to whether contemporary relations between radical *gama'at* and the Moslem Brotherhood are characterized by cooperation or conflict, drew on this precedent when providing an assessment of the Islamicist movement:

> In my opinion there is no difference between the segments of the Islami-
> cist tendency—either the *gama'at* or the Brotherhood—for all of these seg-
> ments are based on one thought, which is to overthrow the system of
> government and establish what is called Islamic government. . . . As to
> the claim by the old trend (i.e., the Moslem Brotherhood) that it is fin-
> ished with violence and it desires to integrate into political life, that is a
> type of deception which is known in Islam by the name of *taqiya*.[89]

Ashmawi's viewpoint is by no means confined to functionaries in the state apparatus charged with the task of containing Islamicists. Dr. Ali al-Maligi, for example, a political scientist whose Sorbonne Ph.D. thesis is on the *gama'at*, uses Clausewitz rather than the notion of *taqiya* to describe what he believes to be intimate, secret linkages between segments of the Islamicist movement. Islamicists, according to Maligi, turn Clause-witz's famous dictum on its head, for to them politics is an extension of war by other means. They are engaged in a life and death struggle against secularism and are using all available resources, including par-liamentary politics. When asked about relations between the Moslem Brotherhood and the *gama'at*, Maligi replied that the latter is *al-ibn al-shari* (the legal son) of the former. This is so because Hassan al-Banna, who founded the organization in 1928, understood that con-verting and organizing mobile and educated youths was of far greater political value than bringing even entire villages, geographically and politically isolated as they are, under the banner of the Brotherhood. The *gama'at* are the present organizational embodiment of this time-tested Brotherhood strategy.[90]

Numerous foreign observers have also interpreted the Islamicist move-ment as an integrated whole. Israel Altman, writing during the Sadat era, claimed that the Moslem Brothers' coexistence with the regime was a "temporary tactic dictated by considerations of the limits of their actual strength." Their connections to university campus-based *gama'at* were to Altman evident from sympathetic coverage of *gama'at* activities in the Brotherhood's *al-Dawa*, from the participation of prominent Brothers in *gama'at* activities, and from the similarity of their stated ideologies.

Altman further suggested that the Islamicist movement in Egypt has connections throughout the Arab World and in particular has received support from Libya and the Palestine Liberation Organization (PLO).[91] Several Western journalists have chronicled the establishment of parallel health, educational, and financial services by Islamicists, suggesting they are manifestations of an overall strategy to undermine the foundations of the state.[92]

Statements by Islamicists themselves can indeed be interpreted as manifestations of *taqiya*. Members of various radical *gama'at* were in 1982 in fact explicitly accused of practicing *taqiya* by leading *ulama* from al-Azhar, who had been taken aback during a seminar conducted in prison when young radicals expressed complete agreement with their religious interpretations.[93] Following the Moslem Brotherhood's very impressive performance in the 1987 elections, its leading spokesmen took a remarkably moderate, conciliatory line, suggesting they were trying to put the public at ease and to avoid provoking a confrontation with the government. In the first interview after the election the new Supreme Guide of the Moslem Brotherhood, Muhammad Hamid Abu al-Nasr, instead of demanding the immediate application of the *sharia*, said that it could only be applied gradually.[94] Yusuf al-Badri, the Islamicist associated with the Liberal Party who had defeated the Minister of War Production in the South Cairo constituency, responded similarly. Instead of pointing to his remarkable victory as evidence of popular demand for the rapid and wholesale application of the *sharia*, he said that 80 percent of the *sharia* was already in effect and that the remaining 20 percent should be implemented gradually.[95]

Immediately after members of the splinter group from *al-Jihad* were arrested in July 1986 and charged with setting fire to video shops and with various other offenses, *al-Shaab* columnist Muhammad Abd al-Quddus, who is closely associated with the Moslem Brotherhood, launched an attack on the government for permitting decadent Western videos to be sold and rented in Egypt. While he did not go so far as to explicitly condone the acts of arson, he implied that members of *al-Jihad* had been inspired by understandable and even laudable motivations.[96] When asked point-blank if they have secret relations with radical *gama'at*, spokesmen for the Brotherhood and other moderate Islamicists provide stock replies that appear to have been well rehearsed and that never really answer the question. An interview published in *al-Hawadeth*, a weekly London-based magazine, with Supreme GuideAbu al-Nasr is typical. When asked about his and his organization's relations with the *gama'at*, he responded that Nasser's methods and the very nature of his regime had driven the radicals to understandable excesses. The Brotherhood had itself, according to Abu al-Nasr, sought to lead the radicals back on the right path. He asserted that the best way to deal with them was not through torture and intimidation but through dialogue. Asked about the relationship between the Brotherhood and

Islamic investment companies, he replied that these companies are doing an excellent job of financial management in accordance with the provisions of the *sharia* and that they do not interfere in Brotherhood affairs.[97]

Salah Abu Raqiq, a senior figure in the Brotherhood who was elected to parliament in 1987, answers such questions in much the same fashion. Asked about connections between the Brotherhood and the radical *gama'at*, he responded by saying the members of the latter represent a very small group of former Brothers who in prison fell under the influence of the Qutbiyin, the followers of Sayid al-Qutb, the charismatic Moslem Brother executed by the Nasser regime. In recent years, Abu Raqiq claimed, the Brotherhood has been working with the government to rehabilitate these radicals. For this purpose former Supreme Guide Omar Tilmisani conferred with Ministers of Interior Nabawi Ismail and Hassan Abu Basha.[98] To a skeptic, these answers represent evasions and justifications. They are offered as proof of the proposition that the Brotherhood, the radical *gama'at*, and the Islamic investment companies are part and parcel of the same movement and are all dedicated to the overthrow of the semisecular government.

There are, however, other opinions about relations between the various segments of the Islamicist movement. One is that allegations of *taqiya* are made in order to discredit the movement. Some Islamicists, for example, argue that this misinformation is disseminated by Zionists, Western news reporters, and others who are seeking to present the Arab World as caught up in a frenzy of ever-increasing religious fanaticism that will inevitably pit it militarily against the West.[99] A more benign interpretation is that assumptions of Islamicist unity are based on analyses at the ideological, not organizational, level. Fadwa al-Guindi, for example, claims that while the bulk of Islamicists agree on the goals of Islamicization, they are highly fragmented organizationally, in part because of disagreement on tactics.[100] In Guindi's view statements that are interpreted as manifestations of *taqiya* by observers hostile to Islamicism are really intended by those Islamicists to cover up organizational factionalization and to avoid further exacerbating internal tensions. Dissimulation, in other words, is a sign of weakness, not strength. There is also an empiricist perspective, which is that the available evidence is insufficient to permit a determination of whether or not the Moslem Brotherhood has succeeded in forging organizational linkages with the Islamic student movement and radical *gama'at*. This was the conclusion reached after several years' study by one of Egypt's bestinformed students of the Islamicist movement.[101] Still other observers dismiss the entire issue of the organizational integration of the Islamicist movement as irrelevant. To them it matters not whether radical and conservative Islamicists are coordinating their efforts, for they are working for the same objectives. In that sense the various organizational fragments should be seen as composite elements in a social movement, whether or not they are in direct contact with one another.[102]

In the absence of conclusive new data, assessment of these interpretations is problematical. There clearly are communications between Islamicists of different political persuasions. Shukri Mustafa, for example, the leader of the *Takfir wal Hijra* (Redemption and Holy Flight) group that assassinated the Minister of Religious Endowments in 1977 and who was himself apprehended and executed, was for several years prior to that time in regular communication with conservative Islamicists, including those associated with the group that went on to form the Socialist Labor Party in 1978.[103] Nevertheless, because radical and conservative Islamicists talk with one another does not prove that they conspire together. In fact, there is considerable evidence to suggest that the Islamicist movement is highly pluralistic, consisting of hundreds of relatively small collectivities organized around an individual or small nucleus of activists who are enamored of a particular ideology and/or activity. While these semiformal organizations could be hammered into a more coherent whole, that has not yet happened and there are substantial obstacles in the path of those who would attempt it. In the meantime relations between these many fragments are obviously not invariably harmonious. So while the Islamicist movement may appear on first glance to be so strong as to be virtually irresistible, a more thorough investigation reveals serious liabilities that will continue to plague the movement.

STRENGTHS OF THE ISLAMICIST MOVEMENT

The size, diversity, and organizational capabilities of the Islamicist movement are undeniably impressive. Structurally the movement consists of several distinct categories of groups, which range from those more or less supportive of the status quo to those that lie outside of and reject the existence of the established order. At the former end is al-Azhar, consisting of its attendant institutions for education, research, and control over mosques and religious endowments. At the radical end of the spectrum are those underground *gama'at* willing to use force to overthrow the regime that they believe to be illegitimate. According to Adil Hamuda of *Ruz al-Yusuf*, there are some 36 of these *gama'at*, each of which has its own *imam* (leader), call to prayer, and internal regulations.[104] Muhsin Muhammad of *al-Gumhuriya* puts the number of such *gama'at* on university campuses alone at 40,[105] while John Kifner of the *New York Times* estimates that there are some 50 "schismatic organizations" with ideologies forged in prison camps and operating in underground cells.[106] Mustafa Kamal Murad, leader of the Liberal Party, claims there are at least 200 *gama'at*.[107]

That there is so little agreement on precisely how many such groups there are results not only from their shadowy nature but from the conceptual confusion surrounding the term *gama'at*. Used by some to refer only to violent underground groups, the term *gama'at* normally also refers both to nonviolent campus-based organizations of Islamicists and Islamic voluntary associations that engage in a wide variety of self-help and charitable activities. Like the radical *gama'at*, these other types also proliferated in the 1970s. Although not secretive, some of these *gama'at* have not registered with the Ministry of Insurance and Social Affairs and are therefore, strictly speaking, illegal. Also to be found on the spectrum of Islamicist organizations are Sufi orders, which have been relatively closely controlled by the government throughout this century, and various populist *imam*-s and their followers. These latter groupings are typically centered on individual mosques situated in lower- and lower-middle-class urban quarters.[108]

Paralleling the organizational diversification of the Islamicist movement is the increasing variegation of its membership. While lower-middle-class youths are the largest single element within radical *gama'at*, these organizations also include professionals and occasionally military officers. Additionally, more conservative components of the Islamicist movement, including voluntary associations of all sorts and the Moslem Brotherhood, have much more diverse memberships, for they include substantial numbers of even the wealthiest of the bourgeoisie. Hamid Abu al-Nasr, who succeeded Omar al-Tilmisani as Supreme Guide in May 1986, is from one of Asyut's most wealthy and powerful families. Omar al-Tilmisani was himself from an Algerian family that migrated to Alexandria in 1830 and by the turn of the century had acquired substantial wealth, including seven houses and 300 *feddan*-s. The magnate Osman Ahmad Osman, who hails from Ismailiya, the city situated along the Suez Canal where Hassan al-Banna founded the Moslem Brotherhood and where it remains strong, has long had close connections with that organization. In the early Sadat era he played the key mediating role that led to the tacit alliance between the President and the Brotherhood.[109] Another example is that of Muhammad Abd al-Quddus, son of Ihsan Abd al-Quddus, the writer who thirty years ago was the *enfant terrible* of the Egyptian literary scene, shocking and delighting his readers with frank accounts of sexual escapades. The son, however, has renounced the path favored by his father of emulating Western cultural norms. Married to the daughter of the prominent Moslem Brother Muhammad al-Ghazali, whose sister Zainab has long been associated with the radical wing of the Brotherhood, Muhammad Abd al-Quddus is himself active in that organization. His weekly editorial in *al-Shaab* is written from the perspective of an *ibn al-balad* (literally, son of the country, or simple person). Despite Abd al-Quddus's residence in his father's sumptuous Nile-side flat in one of Cairo's wealthiest districts, he adopts a simple, almost ascetic style. Countless other less well-known but nevertheless very wealthy members of the bourgeoisie are also associated with Islamic voluntary associations, the Moslem Brotherhood, and/or other mani-festations of the Islamicist movement.

The Islamic financial sector, consisting of Islamic banks and investment companies, as well as organizations that collect *zakat* (Islamic personal income tax), has contributed to the growth of an Islamic social sector, which includes facilities for the provision of health, educational, and welfare services. Although these were initiated in the 1970s, the concept behind them is not novel among Islamicists, for in the 1930s the Moslem Brotherhood constructed a similar network. Currently the proliferation of organizations providing social services is extremely impressive. The Islamic Medical Society, for example, operates seven clinics in Cairo, at one of which alone some 50,000 patients were treated in 1986. Like other Islamicist-run clinics, those of the Islamic Medical Society are clean, well provisioned, and able to provide medical services virtually free of charge, for they obtain financial support from wealthy Moslem contributors, from imposition of the *zakat* on their members, and possibly from Islamic investment companies.[110] A related phenomenon has been the proliferation of social, health, and educational facilities in association with private mosques, of which the most successful and well known is the Mustafa Mahmud mosque in Muhandisin, a Westernized, middle-class suburb of Cairo. Constructed in 1978 as a result of the efforts of the prominent writer, television personality, and former secular leftist of that name, the Mustafa Mahmud mosque has an associated hospital that employs 36 doctors and technical staff and performs a wide variety of surgical operations, for which patients are charged a nominal fee. The mosque also runs a social center that supplies monthly donations to poor families and stipends to needy university students. In 1986 the mosque received donations of some £E500,000.[111] The majority of such mosque complexes, however, are much more humble and situated in less well-to-do quarters. The General Islamic Center for Propagation of the Unity of God and the *Sunna* (traditions of the Prophet) in Zaitun, for example, in addition to operating a school for Koranic learning, also teaches English, French, and German and runs a small hospital. It collects *zakat* and provides alms for the poor. In its structure and activities it is similar to scores of other such associations to be found throughout Cairo and other major cities in the country.[112]

In providing alternative social, health, and educational facilities the Islamicist movement is challenging the state structure, hence the credibility and even legitimacy of the government. The Islamic social sector also serves as a conduit through which clienteles are absorbed into the Islamicist movement. Schools associated with Islamic voluntary associations, for example, actively propagate an Islamicist political message. In one such school in Asyut a sign in a classroom includes a sketch of the Koran and a sword with the accompanying phrase "This is what the Prophet Muhamed brought to us." Another sign says "We need Islam . . . Neither East nor West" and is accompanied with flags of the United States and the USSR with lines drawn through them. The organizer of the school, a professor of civil engineering, claims that its purpose is to challenge the government by providing an example of the Islamic way.[113] Islamicist activists also engage in highly visible public campaigns designed to contrast their commitment and efficiency with the lack of

interest and general incompetence of civil servants. In the summer of
1986, for example, teams of young Islamicists systematically combed
through poor neighborhoods of Suez, ridding them of accumulated
garbage.[114] Supervision of public rallies, meetings, and outdoor prayers
by Islamicist organizations is also conspicuous in its efficiency. Monitors
dressed in clean, conservative attire, identifiable by special armbands,
direct proceedings in polite but firm fashion and are well drilled and
expertly coordinated. The police force, by comparison, is much less
professional in its handling of crowd control. Whatever the area in which
the comparison is made, governmental capabilities are declining while
parallel services provided by Islamicists are expanding vertically and
horizontally. To an increasing number of Egyptians this is tangible proof
of the claim that "Islam is the solution."

A further indication that the Islamicist movement is large, diverse,
and powerful is that even the radical elements within it, who constitute
a small minority of the total movement, are to be found almost everywhere
in the country. Radical *gama'at* are firmly entrenched in all provinces
of Upper Egypt. Even Fayum, an overwhelmingly agricultural, relatively
isolated province some 100 kilometers southwest of Cairo, has been the
scene of attacks on video shops and grocery stores by Islamicist activists,
and its mosques have provided venues for radical *imam*-s. The adjoining
province of Beni Suef was wracked with violence in early 1987 as radical
Islamicists confronted local Christians. The poorer outlying areas of Giza
and some of the villages of that province, now being overgrown by
Cairo's urban sprawl, are breeding grounds for Islamic activists. Members
of the Video Group, the bulk of whom were arrested in Cairo in July
1986, were still being rounded up in Alexandria in the fall of that year.[115]
Periodically, brief articles in government dailies announce arrests of
radicals in the Delta and Canal provinces.[116] The gunmen who attempted
to assassinate Nabawi Ismail in August 1987, went underground in nearby
Minufiya Province, which suggests they had connections there. The Delta
province of Kafr al-Shaikh was the scene of violent religious conflicts
in the spring of 1987. Other than in the sparsely settled frontier provinces
of Matruh, North and South Sinai, Red Sea, and the New Valley, there
has been evidence of radical Islamic activism virtually throughout the
country.

Islamicists' assertiveness can be charted by tracing their electoral
performance and general influence within secondary political institutions,
including university student unions, faculty clubs, professional syndicates,
and even the secular political parties. Despite concentrated governmental
efforts to undermine the strength of Islamicists and to defeat their
candidates in student union elections, they have managed to remain
dominant on campuses since Sadat facilitated their rise to power in the
mid-1970s. In the 1985 student union elections, for example, the government, working through the NDP, university officials, and the security
agencies, redoubled its efforts to defeat Islamicist candidates. Yusuf Wali,

Secretary General of the NDP, personally coordinated the party's efforts. Even on the crucial battleground of Cairo University, however, victory eluded the majority of NDP-backed candidates. Wali was forced to concede to the Islamicist activist Issam Sultan, who was elected head of the Cairo University union: "We have done much this year, but your organization was better."[117] Members of campus-based Islamic *gama'at* had offered their candidacies in 19 of the 26 Cairo University faculties and won in 12 of them. These faculty representatives then elect the university's union secretariat. In that contest at Cairo University in 1985 Islamicists were able to deliver 35 votes compared to the NDP's 17. The secular opposition was completely without representation. At Cairo's second university, Ain Shams, where the Islamicist movement has traditionally been weaker, *gama'at* candidate Hani Zaghlul won the chairmanship of the student union in 1985 with 16 votes, against 5 for the NDP-backed candidate and 1 for the leftist nominee. At al-Azhar University the NDP incumbent was defeated by the Islamicist Muhammad al-Bultagi 25 to 13. At Helwan University the government-supported candidate won by 1 vote. Islamicists won every seat in the faculties of education, commerce, dentistry, science, and agriculture at Alexandria University and went on to elect a slate of Islamicists to the union secretariat.

At provincial universities the November 1985 student union elections produced similar results. At Mansura University Islamicists captured the entire secretariat, while at Zagazig the election resulted in a tie, which through allegedly illegal activities the NDP-backed candidates for the secretariat then won. At Suez University Islamicists won control of 4 of the 9 faculties and the position of assistant general secretary. At Minufiya and Minya Universities students sued the government for striking from the lists of nominees a large number of Islamicists, as a result of which elections were postponed. Amidst charges of police intimidation NDP-supported candidates won at Tanta University, whereas in Asyut and Aswan Islamicists won all positions on the secretariats. At all of Egypt's universities Islamicists attracted the highest percentage of votes in the most selective faculties, including those of science, engineering, medicine, dentistry, and pharmacy, and the lowest percentages in the faculties of social science.[118]

Although the power of student unions was reduced by the 1979 law that transferred authority and functions to faculty members and administrators—a measure designed by Sadat to counter the Islamicists with whom he was then struggling—student politics nevertheless still serve as a useful barometer of Islamicist strength. The government's inability in the November 1986 student elections to make inroads into Islamicist control of student unions, despite the yet more vigorous efforts of the NDP to attract votes away from Islamicists (including forcing its candidates to run under the name of "The Moderate Islamic Group") indicates that Islamicists remain the overwhelmingly predominant political force on university campuses. Results of a straw poll on the campus of Cairo University just before the April 1987 election further support this conclusion. The poll revealed that two-thirds of students supported the Moslem Brotherhood—Socialist Labor Party—Liberal Party Alliance.[119] Undergirding this electoral support is a highly articulated network of Islamicist *gama'at*, which consists of small groups organized around individual *amir*-s (princes, i.e., leaders). Fifteen such *amir*-s constitute an organizational unit at a higher level, which in turn is presided over by a "grand *amir*."[120]

Because of the relative breadth and depth of their support and because of their unequaled organization, Islamicists are able to exert considerable influence over university policy. In the wake of the shooting by two members of the State Security Agency of a student Islamicist at Asyut University in the spring of 1986, the *amir*-s of the campus-based *gama'at* decreed a boycott of classes for one week, a command that was duly executed.[121] On all campuses Islamicist demands for provision of suitable locations in university buildings for prayers have been acceded to. In many faculties, especially in the Upper Egyptian universities, sexually segregated seating is officially sanctioned. Student Islamicists have allies among academic and administrative staffs. The most active faculty club in the country, for example, is that at Cairo University. In its past two board elections, held in 1984 and again in 1986, all twelve seats were won by Islamicists, despite the fact that in the second of those two elections leftists and candidates supported by the NDP forged an alliance in a vain attempt to block Islamicists.[122] On most university campuses Islamicist faculty are well organized. They systematically recruit new members, in part by offering them various useful services. They actively canvass for votes prior to faculty club elections and organize transportation to and from polling places, as well as baby-sitting. By comparison, secular leftist and progovernment faculty are woefully ill-prepared.

Islamicists have also penetrated university administrations. The ballot box has been a key tool in this process, for in faculties that have twelve full professors, deans are elected. Many are Islamicists. Another means by which Islamicists have assumed administrative posts is for students and faculty to pressure government, typically through provincial governors and the educational bureaucracy, to appoint Islamicists who, according to their argument, better understand students and can, therefore, win their respect and obedience. Top administrators at Asyut University, for example, including President Abd al-Raziq Hassan, are Islamicists. Their response to student activism has been to placate, if not to encourage it. They terminated mixed-sex classes and reduced female enrollments as a percentage of total students.

The Asyut University administration has been noticeably reluctant to impose disciplinary measures sanctioned by law on Islamicists. Dr. Mustafa Shamakh, a professor of education, and his wife were in the spring of 1986 standing together on the campus when they were assaulted by students who objected to any male-female interaction in public. The University took no punitive measures against the perpetrators, its president claiming that the University was unable to cope with the threat posed by Islamicists. In March of the same year two fourth-year male students, who had been chatting with two of their female classmates, were assaulted on their way home. One received nearly fatal knife wounds. The following day a sizable number of students refused to attend classes unless they could have an appointment with the University's president. Eventually Dr. Hassan, who is also the NDP's Secretary General for Asyut and is married to an American woman, acceded to this demand and promised that the incident would be thoroughly investigated. Three days later, when as yet no steps had been taken, relatives and friends of the wounded students arrived on the campus of 41,000 from their villages, armed with shovels, hoes, and other crude weapons. Under this threat University authorities informed police of the identities of the assailants and they were arrested.[123]

On the one recent occasion on which a university administrator has openly challenged Islamicist students, his action received only equivocal support from colleagues and the government. Dr. Hashim Fuad, Dean of the Faculty of Medicine at Cairo University, who declared he would uphold the ban on wearing the *niqab* that had been declared in the wake of Sadat's assassination but only loosely enforced, reacted to a challenge to his decree by stripping a veil off a female student. Immediately surrounded by Islamicists who struck him on the chest and threatened to cut off his hand and tongue, he managed to flee to safety. The government-controlled press initially ignored the incident, but as news of it filtered through the country, editorialists announced their support of the dean, although with varying degrees of intensity. In the meantime the syndicate of doctors, on the board of which Islamicists have a majority, referred the dean to an ad hoc investigatory committee for possible disciplinary measures. Five thousand students demonstrated in support of the right to wear veils, and the faculty and articulate public divided on the issue and the dean's handling of it. Eventually the Cairo University Board of Trustees ruled that students were forbidden to cover their faces. In this complex situation all that was perfectly clear was that university administrators who are willing to take a hard line against Islamicists, such as Dr. Fuad, do so largely at their own risk.[124]

Patterns of political recruitment suggest there are direct linkages between campus-based *gama'at* and the polity beyond. Numerous student activists have graduated into Islamicist politics in the Brotherhood and elsewhere. Two well-known such individuals are Issam al-Arian and Hilmi Ghazzar, both of whom were leaders of *gama'at* in the Cairo University Faculty of Medicine in the late 1970s. They were among the over 1,500 persons arrested by Sadat in September 1981. On their release both became active in the syndicate of doctors, eventually winning seats on the board of that organization. In 1987 they were elected to parliament as candidates for the Alliance.

The strength and organizational diversity of Islamicists is attested to by their dominant position on university campuses, by their ability to operate an impressive network of social services, and by their strong electoral performances in professional syndicates. Another indicator of their substantial weight in quasi-political settings is their ability to turn out and control very large crowds. At the 23 May 1986 funeral of Moslem Brother Supreme Guide Omar al-Tilmisani, as many as half a million mourners appeared to pay their respects. Crowd control was expertly managed by hundreds of well-trained monitors. Police were conspicuous in their absence. At the end of Ramadan in June 1986, the government banned public prayers in Cairo's sprawling Abdin Square, but Islamicists managed to congregate over 100,000 of the faithful in the less accessible square adjacent to the Sayida Zainab mosque. The following year the government relented, and public squares in major cities were filled with those praying and in so doing conveying an unmistakable political message. Again public order was maintained by well-organized Islamicists.[125]

Within the political arena itself there are also unambiguous signs of Islamicist power. For all intents and purposes the Moslem Brotherhood "alliance" with the Liberal and Socialist Labor parties in the 1987 elections amounted to a takeover of them, especially with regard to the weaker Liberals. While the SLP retains some of its identity and autonomy, unlike the Wafd it ultimately may not be strong enough to defend its separate existence. Its newspaper, *al-Shaab*, has had to make way for Moslem Brother editorialists and reporters, and its editor in chief, Adil Hussain, has been conspicuous since early 1987 in toeing the Brotherhood line. He has even defended the Islamic investment companies, a curious position indeed for a staunch critic of the policy of *infitah* and law 43, under which the Islamic investment companies operate. The Umma Party, which was brought into existence as part of a government strategy to draw support away from autonomous Islamicist organizations, was by 1986 still without any following and seeking to "sell" itself to the Brotherhood.[126] The electoral performance of the Brotherhood in 1987 surpassed that of any of the opposition parties. Its campaign rallies were better organized and attracted more supporters than did those of the Wafd or even the NDP. It garnered almost 10 percent of the total vote, or about 2 percent more than the Wafd.

All of the above evidence suggests that the mobilizational capabilities of Islamicists are resilient in the face of government attack and are growing. But it is premature to conclude that Islamicists will inevitably triumph in their struggle against secularism. In fact, there are indications not only of considerable fragmentation within the movement but also of its relative weakness when measured against the power of the state, subjects that will now be explored.

WEAKNESSES AND VULNERABILITIES
OF THE ISLAMICIST MOVEMENT

The diversity of the Islamicist movement is at once a source of strength and of weakness. Its appeal across class lines, combined with its inclusion of both radical and conservative ideological and organizational formations, has facilitated its recruitment of comparatively large numbers of Egyptians. On the other hand, the lack of class homogeneity may lead to debilitating factionalization. Except for some of the radical *gama'at*, the Islamicist movement is not committed to a socioeconomic transformation that would fundamentally alter relations between different classes and status groups. It is not a movement committed to uprooting the present social order and establishing a new, radically egalitarian one. That it is not transformational in character is reflected in hierarchies that obtain within component elements of the movement itself. External status, wealth, and/or power rankings are translated directly into equivalent orderings within Islamicist organizations. Those bodies have not created autonomous hierarchies dependent on the personal commitment and relevant skills of individual members. The reproduction within the Islamicist movment of society wide status and power rankings has facilitated the rapid growth of the movement, for by refraining from challenging the social order and demanding radically altered power and status relations, it has kept the threshold for membership low. The persistence of highly inegalitarian relationships within the movement, however, is a source of weakness. Leadership of the Islamicist movement is exercised by the bourgeoisie, while the great bulk of membership is drawn from the lower-middle classes. As Islamicists are drawn more closely into the political system and forced to take specific positions on issues, their movement will be bedeviled by the conflictual economic interests that set its leaders apart from their base of support.

The *al-Ahram* survey of attitudes of parliamentarians cited previously in this chapter highlights the conservative nature of the leadership of the Islamicist movement. Nine of the 27 Wafdist deputies questioned by *al-Ahram* were in fact members of the Brotherhood. Although that subsample was not separately analyzed, because of the almost unanimous responses of its members it is clear that Moslem Brother deputies were every bit as conservative as their former Wafidst allies and noticeably more so than NDP deputies. Virtually all of them wanted to alter tenancy laws in favor of owners; none of them demonstrated any significant interest in rural Egypt in general or the problems of peasants specifically; none saw illiteracy as a critical problem; and a higher percentage of Moslem Brothers than NDP deputies appear to prefer that the private rather than the public-sector be entrusted with the responsibility of resolving the housing crisis.

In these views Moslem Brother deputies reflect prevailing attitudes of the leadership of their organization and of the Islamicist movement more broadly. Shaikh Yusuf al-Badri, for example, during his 1987 election campaign and then on entering parliament, called for selling the public-sector to private investors.[127] The serialized review of the Islamicist movement by Adil Hamuda that appeared in *Ruz al-Yusuf* in the summer of 1986 included references to various programmatic statements by principal figures in the Brotherhood. All of them emphasized the organization's commitment to the defense of private property.[128] A comparative analysis of the program of the Brotherhood before and after the Nasser era revealed that the organization's leadership has abandoned its commitment to social reform and increasingly associated itself with property rights.[129] The "neoconservatism" of the Brotherhood may be a reaction to Nasser's Arab Socialism and the association of the state with the repression of the Brotherhood, or it may be the consequence of the embourgeoisment of the Brotherhood's leadership, benefiting as it has from connections to the Arab oil-exporting countries and from the *infitah*. Whatever the explanation may be, the contemporary Brotherhood, which might better be described as the neo-Brotherhood, has unquestionably shed the economic component of the populist message of its forerunner.

The structure of the Islamicist movement, far from being radically egalitarian, is in fact that of a classical patronage organization. The resources to sustain it are provided by the Islamic financial and social service sectors. Like other patron-client networks, such as the Wafd Party in its heyday, the Islamicist movement is vulnerable in ways that radical egalitarian movements are not. Opponents, of which the most important is the state, can move to dry up the sources of patronage and thereby undermine the movement. The government's redoubled efforts in 1987 to rein in Islamic investment companies must be seen partly in this light. Alternatively, the state or other antagonists can seek to attract clients from Islamicist patrons by delivering competitive goods and services, or they can drive a wedge between patrons and clients by enhancing the salience of underlying class differences. These techniques are now being employed by the Mubarak government.

Although the various tendencies in the Islamicist movement are all committed to the goal of establishing an Islamic government, whatever that may in fact mean, it is also true that there is much factionalization within and between them. The notion of *taqiya* notwithstanding, there is evidence of ideological and organizational splits between the radical *gama'at* and the Moslem Brotherhood. Members of the former do denounce Brothers as collaborators with the corrupt, heretical regime. Brotherhood leadership has been visibly frightened by the *gama'at* and the challenge they pose and have attempted to counter their appeal to youths by supporting alternative moderate *gama'at*.[130]

FACTIONALIZATION OF THE MOSLEM BROTHERHOOD

A pattern of dissension and factionalization that is at once more surprising and critical for the future of the Islamicist movement is the one that prevails within the Brotherhood itself. Although that organization seeks to render its internal affairs opaque to outside observers, shadows of competititve factions can be discerned. The struggle over the choice of successor to Supreme Guide Omar al-Tilmisani aroused the animosities of members of competitive factions to the point they were willing to take their cases to the public and to state openly their indignations. In so doing, they provided useful information about the internal workings of their organization.

Initially the transition went smoothly. Within hours of Tilmisani's death on 22 May 1986, it was announced that his successor would be Hamid Abu al-Nasr. But shortly thereafter it became evident that the succession had been rammed through by one of the four major factions in a fashion described by one observer as tantamount to a coup d'etat.[131] The first indication of dissent was that the new Supreme Guide was referred to by some of his colleagues as *al-Murshid al-Muaqqat* (Temporary or Provisional Guide) without clarification. This term had never been applied to any of Abu al-Nasr's three predecessors. On the announcement of his ascension it was declared that Abu al-Nasr had been selected because, as the Brotherhood constitution required, he was the oldest member of *al-Haia al-Tasisiya* (Founding Organization), having been born in March 1913. Several days later Dr. Hussain Kamal al-Din, a former professor of engineering at Cairo University, announced to the press that he had been born in February 1913 and should, therefore, be the new Supreme Guide. At this juncture Abu al-Nasr inexplicably departed Cairo not for the Gulf or Europe, where many anticipated he would travel to rally behind him powerful Moslem Brothers living abroad, but to his family home in Manfalut in Asyut Province. It appeared as if he were going into self-imposed exile. In the meantime Salah Shadi, a prominent Brotherhood figure who was known to have been seeking the leadership position, disappeared entirely from public view and by so doing indicated publicly his refusal to support Abu al-Nasr. By the end of May the press began to regale its readers with sordid details behind these curious events. Suddenly, as if a dike had broken, the participants themselves began to pour out their tales of the struggle for power.

As a result of these revelations it is clear that the Brotherhood, like the secular opposition, is fragmented in stair-step fashion according to the era in which members of each respective faction exercised power. Accordingly, there are factions based on the periods of incumbency of Hassan al-Banna (1928–1949), Hassan al-Hudaibi (1949–1972), and Omar al-Tilmisani (1972–1986). Leaders of those factions are in virtually every case individuals who were advisers to those Supreme Guides. In addition, the faction based on the al-Banna period remains divided, just as the Brotherhood was at that time, between moderates and those willing to employ violence to attain their objectives, the latter of whom were members of the so-called private or special organization that was involved in numerous incidents of political violence.

Stair-step factionalization transcends personal factors, for each era was associated with particular social, political, and economic configurations that shaped elite perceptions. The moderate al-Banna faction is comprised principally of *Ashab al-Fadila* (Masters of Erudition, i.e., accomplished Islamic scholars), including Shaikhs Muhammad al-Ghazali, Abd al-Sitar Abd al-Maaz, Sayid Sabiq, and, most notably, Abd al-Rahman al-Banna, the younger brother of the founder of the Brotherhood. All of these men enjoy reputations as devout Moslems, and most are ascetic scholars who possibly as a result of the hostile political climate of the Nasser period more or less eschew political activism. Their contemporaries with radical inclinations are those who provided the shock troops of the Brotherhood in the 1940s and early 1950s. Their leader is Salah Shadi, a former police officer who became one of the chief organizers of the secret organization that did battle with British and Israeli troops and Egyptian politicians. The Hudaibi group, reflecting the personal beliefs and political style of that Supreme Guide, who had the unenviable task of accommodating the organization to Nasserism, are conciliators who believe in cultivating ties with government and renouncing radicalism and violence. It includes Salah Abu Raqiq, who was elected to parliament in 1987, Ahmad al-Malat, who has accumulated sizable wealth and influence through his good connections in the Gulf, and Muhammad Kamal Abd al-Aziz, a former judge and close associate of Hudaibi.

The triumphant faction was the one that emerged during Tilmisani's tenure. While it naturally possessed advantages by virtue of incumbency at the time of the transition in 1986, its resources are clearly superior to those of its competitors. Tilmisani, like Hudaibi, was a moderate but a rather more flamboyant and independent one, possibly reflecting the impact on his personality of his independent wealth, as opposed to the conservatizing effect on Hudaibi of a lifelong career in the judiciary. More to the point is that Tilmisani was at the helm during Sadat's *infitah* and the great Arab oil boom. The economic resources made available to prominent figures in the Brotherhood were enormous in comparison to any previous period, while Sadat's strategy of bolstering Islamicists to contain leftist secularists provided the Brothers leverage and comparative independence. As a result the Tilmisani faction is comprised of men of means and connections. Its leader, Mustafa Mashur, who managed Tilmisani's affairs and directed his office, was appointed Deputy Supreme Guide by Tilmisani well before his death. He personifies the type of individual who rose to power in the Brotherhood under Sadat. From a wealthy landowning family in Sharqiya Province, Mashur dabbled profitably in business and finance while other members of his family capitalized on Mashur's good relations with Sayed Marei, Sadat's close confidant, and Sadat himself; one relative entered parliament and Mashur Ahmad Mashur became director of the prestigious Suez Canal Authority. Mustafa Mashur developed close relations with Gulf Arabs and with the Islamic financial institutions they backed. These resources were brought into play by him and his allies as Tilmisani's health began to fail and the question of a successor became salient. Having access to telecommunication facilities, they moved quickly to mobilize their supporters in Kuwait, Saudi Arabia, and elsewhere in the Gulf, as well as in Europe, particularly Munich, where wealthy and powerful Brothers reside. But despite the financial and organizational resources and undeniable ambitions of members of this faction, they did not attain their precise objective when Tilmisani finally died, which suggests that the other factions retain appreciable residual powers.

Mustafa Mashur sought to succeed Tilmisani in his own right, claiming within hours of Tilmisani's body being laid to rest in a burial plot owned by the Mashur family that his designation as Deputy Supreme Guide meant that he should automatically be elevated to the top spot. Mashur made this claim in an emergency meeting not of the Founding Organization, which includes some 100 to 150 of the organization's senior figures, but in the Guidance Bureau, which with a membership of 15 became under Tilmisani the real decision-making body within the Brotherhood. Subsequently the choice of venue became a point of contention with leaders of the other factions, especially the moderates of the Banna period, for they still possess a majority within the Founding Organization as there have been no additions to its membership since 1954. Constitutionally all power still resides with the Founding Organization, not the Guidance Bureau. In any case Mashur did not have everything his own way even in this restricted arena, for Salah Shadi, who enjoys the support of many younger, radical Brothers, objected vehemently to Mashur's proposal and nominated himself as an alternative. Mashur backed skillfully away from this challenge by putting forward Abu al-Nasr as the constitutionally correct choice by virtue of seniority. Abu al-Nasr is known to be a rather passive individual and one over whom Mashur has a great deal of influence. This, in addition to the fact that Mashur continued to refer to Abu al-Nasr as Provisional Supreme Guide long after his selection, was taken by virtually all observers to indicate that Abu al-Nasr was not only controlled by Mashur, but will be succeeded by him. Subsequent events have confirmed this assessment. Abu al-Nasr has not imposed his identity on the role or the organization, while Mashur, who continues to exert organizational control from the Guidance Bureau, has become the one member of the Brotherhood to have regular media access through a weekly column in *al-Shaab*.

There was, however, a considerable cost to the Tilmisani faction in imposing Abu al-Nasr on the organization. Not only was Shadi so outraged that he refused to pay his respects to the new Supreme Guide, but the other factions also resented the proceedings and their outcome. The moderate Banna group had supported Hussain Kamal al-Din as their standard bearer out of the same calculations that caused Mashur to back Abu al-Nasr—namely, that he was the oldest member of their faction to be a member of the Founding Organization. The principle of seniority had been established in practice if not constitutionally at the time of the succession from Hudaibi to Tilmisani, so both factions had clearly groomed their oldest member for the job. That the conflict degenerated into conflicting claims of legality of birth certificates was not only undignified and irrelevant to more critical leadership qualifications, but it also led to the revelation that Abu al-Nasr, with Mashur's backing, had in fact misrepresented himself as the oldest member. Abd al-Rahman al-Banna and his allies, who are generally of scholarly dispositions and committed to the defense of moral rectitude, were clearly outraged by these underhanded tactics. The Hudaibi group was similarly alienated by the outcome of the succession struggle, for they believed that their nominee, the moderate judge Kamal Abd al-Aziz, was ideally suited to moderate the debilitating dispute between the Tilmisani and Banna factions, just as almost forty years previously Supreme Guide Hudaibi had as a successful compromise candidate sought to reconcile the moderate and radical factions of the Brotherhood. The Hudaibists saw victory by one of the strongly opposed factions as a dangerously destabilizing outcome.

Leadership squabbles can occur in even relatively coherent, united organizations and need not necessarily indicate chronic factionalization or presage organizational decay. In this case, however, personal rivalries are not autonomous phenomena, but reflect deep-seated divisions within the Brotherhood. Those currently in control are of the Islamic *infitah* bourgeoisie. It can reasonably be claimed that they "bought" the organization with resources acquired through collaboration with the Sadat regime. That, naturally enough, has gravely antagonized many older Brothers who see "their" organization as having been kidnapped by upstarts. As far as the future of the Brotherhood is concerned, that would pose no particular problem if the Banna and Hudaibi factions could be dismissed as products of bygone eras and the faction currently led by Mashur could be seen as the wave of the future. The problem with this analysis, however, is that the group now in control has less credibility and legitimacy among youth than do the other factions. The moderate Banna and Hudaibi factions have legitimacy by virtue of their historical associations and struggles, while the radical Banna faction is much admired by youth for its activism. It is widely rumored that Shadi and other former members of the Brotherhood underground have direct contacts with campus-based and other *gama'at*. Critics of the Tilmisani faction within the Brotherhood have argued that as many as 90 percent of the young men so much in evidence at public events, including not only prayers in public squares but even at Tilmisani's funeral, are not in fact members of the Brotherhood but of the *gama'at*. These youths are said to be disaffected from the Islamicist *infitah* bourgeoisie, who in their view have distorted the purpose of the organization as intended by its founding fathers. Additionally, young radicals as well as the old guard deeply resent the influential role played in Brotherhood affairs by wealthy, generally conservative, non-Egyptians. The proposal that the Founding Organization meet in Mecca during the pilgrimage in the summer of 1986 to confirm the selection of Abu al-Nasr was vehemently rejected by Abd al-Rahman al-Banna and others of the old guard as entirely inappropriate.

Gaps between factions on various issues remain wide. Much of the old guard believes it is a mistake for the Brotherhood to seek to become a fully fledged political party or to ally itself with semisecular parties for election purposes. The faction in control is firmly committed to transforming the organization into a party. Radical youths want the Brotherhood to push more strongly for the adoption of the *sharia* and for segregation of the sexes in public settings, while more conservative, generally older, Brothers urge caution on such issues. There are no suitable intraparty arenas in which such disagreements can be aired, possibly reconciled, and then hammered into a coherent platform.[132]

It is possible that the factionalization and organizational disarray that currently beset the Brotherhood will be overcome through compromise or by the triumph of one faction over all others and then its broader legitimation. While that seems unlikely given the incumbency in the Brotherhood elite of scores of individuals who deeply distrust and resent members of other factions, a younger generation will be taking control in the not too distant future. Indeed, Saif al-Islam al-Banna, the son of Hassan al-Banna, is already in the wings, having been elected to parliament as a Brotherhood candidate for the Alliance in 1987. Having served his political apprenticeship in prison under Nasser like so many other Brothers, Banna is not strongly identified with any faction. But he is thought of as being relatively conservative, and he seemed to cultivate the image of himself as a future Supreme Guide at Tilmisani's funeral, where he acted conspicuously as host, greeting those dignitaries who came to pay their respects.[133]

The Brotherhood, however, does not have the luxury of time. It has, maybe unwisely, allowed itself to be drawn directly into the political arena while it is still fragmented and has not resolved many of the fundamental organizational and ideological issues that would enable it to unite. Even the constitutional role of the Guidance Bureau remains very much at issue, which suggests that as the pressure mounts serious questions as to the legitimacy of decision-making procedures may well arise. One observer has predicted that the Brotherhood will soon resemble the radical *gama'at*, which are known by the names of their *amir*-s, implying that it is going to fragment into small groups oriented around individual leaders.[134] Whether that eventuates or not, it remains the case that divisions within the organization make it highly susceptible to manipulation by the state. The example of the Wafd Party may be instructive. When in the wake of the 1984 election it appeared to mount a serious challenge to the regime, it was confronted with a systematic campaign to exacerbate those divisions within and between the older and younger generation of Wafdists, a campaign that ultimately seriously weakened the party and paved the way for the Brotherhood's electoral triumph of 1987. Organizational analogies between the Wafd and the Brotherhood, including an inability of those of the older generation to reconcile their differences, to say nothing of their failure to accommodate and recruit youth, are too striking to be ignored. The Brotherhood, in short, in its current configuration is not a threat to even the regime's NDP party, much less to the regime itself.

WEAKNESSES OF *GAMA'AT*

That the radical *gama'at* pose a mortal threat is also improbable. Although they pop up throughout the country and regularly commit audacious acts, they are in reality little more than a nuisance to the state and, in fact, are in a way an assistance to it. As Ajami has noted, Egyptians by and large abhor violence and pride themselves on having a stable, reasonably civil culture.[135] The radicalism and violence of some Islamicists is shocking and repulsive to the great majority of the population, a fact that the government exploits to discredit Islamicists more generally. The wide coverage given to various outrages, the frequent publication of the radical and even heretical views of members of *al-Jihad*, *Takfir wal Hijra*, and other *gama'at*, and the regular sermons of the Minister of Interior, who warns the public of the fanaticism of Islamicists while simultaneously comforting them with assurances of the vigilance of his men,[136] all contribute to the desired effect of causing Egyptians to rally around the state for protection from the threatening unknown of Islamicist terror.

The violent *gama'at*, while having recruited thousands of members, are led primarily by a relatively small group of former Moslem Brothers who were heavily influenced by the radical ideologue Sayid al-Qutb, who was executed by Nasser in 1965. Shukri Mustafa, head of the *Takfir wal Hijra* group, Khalid Islambuli and Abd al-Salam Farag of *al-Jihad*, and Taha al-Samawi, the *amir* of the Video Group, who were arrested in 1977, 1981, and 1986, respectively, all interacted with one another.[137] The radical *gama'at* that have been dredged up to the surface by the security forces are tied together by threads of personal interaction and kinship that can be traced to specific common roots. This suggests that the phenomenon is not one proliferating beyond control into all segments of society and regions of the country, but is in fact a conspiracy organized by a relatively limited number of fanatics. It is, in other words, more akin to Europe's Red Brigades than to Iranian revolutionaries. Moreover, it is a conspiracy that security forces ultimately will contain, precisely because it is interconnected through individuals and because it is operating on the margins of society. Taha al-Samawi, who was arrested in 1986 for masterminding arson attacks from October 1985 to June of 1986, had first been rounded up as far back as 1977 and was frequently the subject of surveillance and investigation. That is suggestive not only of a protracted game of cat and mouse between underground terrorists and the security apparatus, but also of the possibility that the regime has been willing to tolerate a certain amount of such activity. Clearly the Ministry of Interior computers have a thorough list of suspects who can be rounded up within a reasonable period if the order is given.

The relative success of Islamicists in voluntary associations, including those based on university campuses, can also be interpreted less as a reflection of their strength than as an indication of the weakness of the competition and the general apathy that is the result of many years of authoritarian government. The great majority of students and faculty do not vote in elections in unions and clubs. Even in the relatively hotly contested student elections of 1985, for example, quorums of 50 percent of students were not obtained in the first rounds of voting in numerous faculties. In the second rounds, when the quorum requirement drops to 20 percent, many classes and faculties still could not muster quorums.[138]

The politics of professional syndicates are likewise more accurately characterized as apathetic than hotly competitive. Annual general meetings of branches of the teachers, agricultural engineers, and other syndicates with large memberships typically attract less than 10 percent of total members. In most, Islamicists are virtually the only opposition force well enough organized to canvass actively for votes and to possess the infrastructure required to ensure that their voters actually are present at elections. If the impressive performances by Islamicists in elections in voluntary associations and for parliament had been achieved in conditions of intense competition with other political forces and with the participation of a significant percentage of those eligible to vote, it would indicate the unquestioned existence of a broad base of support. That such victories have been won in what amount to near political vacuums suggests instead that it is more by default than by mass popular support that the Islamicists are succeeding.

Finally, it is becoming increasingly evident that Islamicists, having emerged as the major force within the opposition, are confronted not only by the state but also by secularists who are seeking to undermine Islamicists' influence. In the wake of the arrest of as many as 3,000 Islamicists in May–June 1987, the lawyers syndicate committee responsible for protecting the rights of members was conspicuous by its lack of vigor in moving to the defense of Islamicist attorneys. Despite protests and allegations of connivance with government by Islamicists, the syndicate continued to move only lethargically. When it was revealed that several prominent Islamicist physicians were among those rounded up, the doctors syndicate moved with less haste to protect them than Islamicists, who control a majority of positions on the board, felt was appropriate. Again they held secularists responsible.[139] In the 1987 parliamentary elections the Wafd and the NPUP both vehemently attacked Alliance candidates. The governmental strategy of dividing and ruling the opposition was clearly beginning to bear fruit.

THE STATE'S RESPONSE
TO THE ISLAMICIST CHALLENGE

As Sadat's vice president, Mubarak learned firsthand of the danger of providing symbolic and actual targets for Islamicists. Subsequently he has taken care to ensure that neither the presidency nor any practices or policies associated with it stimulate widespread negative reactions among them. He wisely refrained, for example, from making martyrs of the Sadat assassins by ensuring that most of those involved received relatively light sentences. Additionally, he has tolerated a wide variety of initiatives associated with symbolic Islamicization, without actually conceding much of substance. As part of the customs and tariffs reforms of 1986, excise duties on imported wine and spirits were allowed to rise to a prohibitive 1,700 percent. Nothing, however, was done to impede the distribution or consumption of locally produced alcoholic beverages. The ban on "pray-ins" in public squares on important Islamic holidays, which had led to numerous violent confrontations and clashes, was relaxed in 1987. A vigorous campaign by Islamicists to return women to the household, which it is claimed would both free up positions for young unemployed males and reinforce family life, met with a favorable response from some leading public-sector companies. In March 1987, several public-sector spinning and weaving companies announced they would no longer employ women. The timing of this decision, which was issued during the parliamentary election campaign, suggests it was a concession by Mubarak to Islamicists.[140] The indicment in September 1986 of almost fifty police and state security agents, including several high-ranking officers, for torturing Islamicist prisoners reduced the political tension associated with this very emotional issue. The Minister of Information, Safwat al-Sharif, took initiatives in 1985 to ban "immoral, indecent and vile" television advertisements and to censor from television serials anything "inconsistent with the *sharia*."[141] The regime has been sparing in its use of the charge that disturbances precipitated by Islamicists have been the work of "outside agitators." In the middle of the widespread religious disturbances of February-March 1987, for example, Minister of Interior Zaki Badr declared unequivocally that the activists involved were not being financed from abroad.[142] Members of campus-based *gama'at* who have been arrested for participating in violent demonstrations on campus have typically been released within a few weeks.[143] In April

1987, Mubarak himself urged the Islamic establishment to find a role for the *gama'at* in spreading Islam.[144]

The government has also refrained from undertaking policy initiatives that would provide a focal point for attack by Islamicists. Despite the debilitating economic and fiscal effects of inordinately low interest rates paid on deposits in secular public and private-sector banks and continual pressure by the IMF, USAID, and various other bilateral and multilateral aid agencies to increase those rates, the government has raised them only marginally and informed those agencies that its reticence is based on its fear of the Islamicist reaction.[145] Out of the desire both to avoid a confrontation with and to stimulate a pluralization of the Islamicist movement, the government has permitted the establishment of quasi-political libraries in mosques, and it has allowed Islamicists to organize seminars, to present their views on television, to visit Iran, and to publish books and magazines.[146] The Liberal Party has been permitted since 1983 to publish *al-Nur*, a weekly Islamicist newspaper. Continued prohibition of the publication of a newspaper by the Moslem Brotherhood suggests governmental intent is to perpetuate fragmentation of the Islamicist message by preventing it from being channeled through a single, dominant organ.

Another element of governmental strategy has been to employ the state-controlled Islamic establishment to counter oppositionist Islamicists. This tactic, however, has not met with much success, primarily because establishment *ulama* have undermined their credibility with many Islamicists by exchanging their independence for governmental patronage. It is precisely this point of weakness that the opposition, both Islamicist and secular, has exploited. Shaikh Gad al-Haq, Mubarak's longserving Shaikh al-Azhar, which is the premier post for Egypt's *ulama*, was in 1986 the subject of an opposition campaign against his profligacy and abuse of power.[147] Even Egypt's much beloved and ascetic star "television *imam*," Shaikh Mitwali al-Sharawi, lost some of his credibility when it was revealed as a result of a burglary that he had amassed a small fortune in jewelry.[148]

But the most damaging erosion of the credibility of established Islam occurred as a result of the government's inability for over a year to find a successor to the *Mufti*, Shaikh Abd al-Latif Hamza, who died in September 1985. The *Mufti* is nominally the highest Islamic legal authority in the land, responsible primarily for delivering official rulings on Islamic law, as well as performing a host of other religious and educational duties. Prior to 1961 the *Mufti*, like the Grand Shaikh of al-Azhar, was chosen by the leading *ulama* of al-Azhar, but since that time both have been chosen by the government. The Shaikh al-Azhar is subordinate to the Minister of Religious Affairs and the *Mufti* is under the Minister of Justice. Islamicists seized on the opportunity of the 1985 vacancy to demand that Nasser's 1961 reforms be rescinded and that the right of the religious establishment to select the *Mufti* and the Shaikh al-Azhar be restored. This the government refused to countenance, but the subordination of the religious hierarchy to the state and its bureaucratization had created a problematical anomaly. The position of *Mufti* has only quasi-legal standing in the civil service and as such has no associated pension entitlement and a salary that is less than that of ministerial undersecretaries, the post from which *Mufti*-s have been recruited since 1961. Thus the government, facing the resistance of Islamicists, had also to contend with the problem of finding a suitable candidate within the state-controlled religious establishment who would be willing to make a financial sacrifice to become *Mufti*. Moreover, secularization of al-Azhar and the associated decline in standards of the religious studies faculties have resulted in the preparation of fewer well-qualified individuals for the posts even of *imam*-s of mosques, to say nothing of that of *Mufti*.

After more than a year of unseemly delay, discussion, and criticism, the government finally appointed Muhamad Sayid Tantawi, whose various sojourns as educator in Libya, Iraq, and Saudi Arabia presumably resulted in sufficient financial independence for inadequate compensation not to pose an obstacle. The choice seems also to have been made with the reaction of Islamicists in mind. Tantawi was not from the ministry itself but is associated with al-Azhar. His Ph.D. thesis, "The Sons of Israel in the Quran and the Sunna," has, because of the contemporary political interest in that topic, been regularly reprinted since 1967. Tantawi, who hails from a village in Sohag Province in Upper Egypt, spent the years from 1967 to 1980 at the Asyut College of Religion, first as professor and then as dean, so is well acquainted with Islamicists in that hotbed of religious activity. But while Tantawi's appointment solved the immediate problem, the basic issue of state control over the religious establishment remains unresolved. The state will be subjected to renewed pressure to release its grasp on the posts of *Mufti*, Shaikh al-Azhar, and others. In the meantime the political and religious legitimacy attached to those positions and to the Islamic establishment generally will continue to erode.[149]

The government has also confronted difficulties further down in the Islamic establishment. Egypt has some 40,000 mosques, all of which are now "nationalized" (i.e., under state rather than private control), but less than 6,000 *imam*-s. The vacuum has since the early 1970s been increasingly filled by autonomous Islamicists, frequently of radical viewpoints and commonly with great appeal to their congregations.[150] The state would like to gain undisputed control once again over mosque pulpits, but al-Azhar has not been producing enough qualified graduates despite reforms in 1979 that reestablished a college specifically designed to produce *imam*-s. While the shortage may eventually disappear as a result of the excellent job prospects for those obtaining credentials in Islamic studies, there remains the possibility that the conversion of all *imam*-s to civil servants will not be enough to neutralize the appeal of

Islamicism to significant numbers of them. In the meantime the government has sought through other means to counteract propaganda and recruitment activities by Islamicists. In the spring of 1987 it announced the formation of a Supreme Council for *Dawa* (call) Affairs, the task of which is to spread the message of established Islam and regulate the activities of the Islamicist competition.[151]

If the government had no other tool than the Islamic establishment with which to contain Islamicists, it would be in trouble. While it is taking steps to upgrade the state's religious infrastructure, the efforts of Islamicists may well negate any improvements. The government, therefore, is simultaneously seeking to maneuver the conservative wing of the Islamicist movement into the position formerly occupied solely by the official religious hierarchy and from which a message supportive of establishment views can be widely propagated. It hopes that the Supreme Guide of the Brotherhood and his coterie of followers come to perform a political function similar to that of the Shaikh al-Azhar and the *ulama* generally, whereby they counteract radical appeals and, by virtue of their association with the state, legitimate it. Out of a position of weakness the government, in short, is having to try to ride this comparatively tame Islamicist tiger. It is willing to take this risk because the conservative elite of the Islamicist movement, of which the most important element is that within the Brotherhood, is not a system-challenging one; because the socioeconomic gap that separates elite from mass in the Islamicist movement is so great it will permanently inhibit the formation of a powerful, coherent political force; and because secularism in its ideological and organizational manifestations will continue to provide a heavy counterbalance.

Following the 1987 elections the government strategy of weakening the Islamicist movement became more evident. NDP deputies began publicly to probe their counterparts in the Brotherhood about their stances on such contentious economic issues as landlord-tenant relations, subsidies, the public versus the private sector, Islamic investment companies, and so on. The intent of the government was to demonstrate that the claim "Islam is the solution" is in reality a veil to hide the conservatism of the Brotherhood's elite and its lack of a systematic program. The government also began to relax its pressure on the Wafd Party, the premier embodiment of secularist political sentiment. Said Abd al-Khaliq, editor of "The Sparrow" column in *al-Wafd*, was not only acquitted on charges of accepting a bribe, but his nemesis, Abd al-Rahman al-Baidaini and Baidaini's accomplice, former Minister of Housing Abd al-Rahman Labib, were indicted. *al-Wafd* duly responded by attacking various elements in the Islamicist movement, including the Brotherhood.[152]

A final element in the strategy to contain Islamicism is to keep the specter of religious violence and disorder firmly before the public. The government's calculation is that the great majority of Egyptians, frightened by these events, will turn away from Islamicists and toward the state. The 1987 election results vindicated this assessment, for in those provinces where religious disturbances had been most severe, including Beni Suef, Asyut, and Kafr al-Shaikh, the NDP performed comparatively well.[153] Additionally, by associating violence with Islamicism, the government is forcing the movement's leadership to disassociate itself from radicals; in so doing it is opening up visible cracks in what prior to 1986–1987 had appeared to be a monolithic movement.

THE CHALLENGE PERSISTS

Mubarak's strategy then is considerably more complex than Sadat's, who first cultivated Islamicists and then attempted to clamp down on them. Mubarak has given ground on symbolic issues while holding firm on matters of substance. He has enabled the movement to enter the political arena but on terms that are unfavorable to it and are likely to exacerbate discord within the movement. He has sought, apparently with success, to gain political advantage from religiously based violence, and he can at any time bring into position the secularist counterbalance.

The fact that Mubarak has played the political game well and that the state's resources remain superior to those of the secular and Islamicist oppositions should not, however, obscure the fact that Islamicism remains ideologically and organizationally potent, that religious tension and violence persists, and that Mubarak's personal legitimacy is yet to be established. Suffering from declining capabilities as a result of the ebbing of resources away from the state and into private hands, the system of control is being asked to make finer discriminations between political friends and enemies than it did under either Nasser or Sadat. The Mubarak stategy requires the security apparatus to distinguish between good and bad Islamicists, with countless shades of gray between them, and to change those evaluations in line with shifting government policy. While there is no reason to believe that the state cannot manage that challenge in the short and medium terms, it will remain a critical one and as such will consume a major share of time and resources available to the political elite and the system of control. Moreover, meeting the challenge posed by the Islamicist and secular oppositions may well impair the state's management of the economy, to say nothing of the development of it. Political pressure resulting from protracted economic crisis can, therefore, be expected to persist. Pressure could in future be channeled through opposition organizations, but because of the state's vigilance and the president's ability to manipulate organized political actors, it is unlikely that a challenge from this quarter would be fatal. What may instead happen is that state and opposition alike become irrelevant to the concerns of those in the potentially explosive and largely anomic urban lower and lower-middle classes, and they simply take to the streets to seek redress. While the system of control can monitor organized threats, it has a far more difficult task in confronting the mob. The CSF could not be counted on to stand for long, while the riots in January 1977, in which obviously wealthy Egyptians immediately became the targets of the poor, indicate what sort of bloodletting could occur. In such circumstances all manner of semi- or well-organized radical groupings would join the fray, as they did in February 1986, and the political outcome would be unpredictable.

It is precisely this scenario that alarms Egypt's U.S. ally and conditions the aid program that has throughout the Mubarak era been running in excess of $2 billion a year. Whether that aid, the large U.S. community in Egypt associated with its delivery, and the U.S. connection generally have the effect of reducing or increasing the possibility of widespread anomic violence leading to profound political change is one of the issues to be analyzed in Chapter 7.

NOTES

1. Gilles Kepel, *Muslim Extremism in Egypt: The Prophet and the Pharaoh* (Berkeley and Los Angeles: University of California Press, 1986), epilogue.

2. The Moslem Brotherhood has adhered to this line since the emergence of the Islamic *gama'at* in the mid-1970s. See Israel Altman, "Islamic Movements in Egypt," *The Jerusalem Quarterly*, 10 (Winter 1979), pp. 87–105.

3. Robert Springborg, "Patterns of Association in the Egyptian Political Elite," in George Lenczowski, ed., *Political Elites in the Middle East* (Washington: American Enterprise Institute, 1975), pp. 63–108.

4. This distinction was drawn by Ali al-Din Hillal, "The Last Page," *al-Ahram al-Iqtisadi* (3 November 1986).

5. Baha al-Din Hassan, *The Elimination of Election Games* (Cairo: New World Press, 1984) (in Arabic), pp. 52–57.

6. *The Arab Strategic Report 1985* (Cairo: al-Ahram, 1986) (in Arabic) draws attention to this point, pp. 326–327.

7. Hassan, *The Elimination of Election Games*, p. 272.

8. *al-Musawwar* (9 March 1984) cited in *ibid.*, p. 53.

9. "Police Campaign Against Members of the Labor Party in Gahina," *al-Shaab* (22 July 1986).

10. *al-Ahram* (22 March 1987).

11. On the 1987 elections see Bertus Hendriks, "Egypt's New Political Map," *Merip Middle East Report*, 147 (July-August 1987), pp. 23–30.

12. For descriptions by prominent journalists associated with the SLP of their treatment by security forces when attempting to attend party rallies outside Cairo, see Fathi Radwan's column in *al-Shaab* (31 March 1987) and Muhamed Abd al-Quddus's column in the same paper on 24 March 1987.

13. *al-Akhbar* (12 April 1987).

14. These data were compiled from *al-Akhbar* (30 July 1986); *The Arab Strategic Report 1985*, pp. 326–327; Muhammad al-Tawil, "Conflict Between the Opposition and the Speaker," *Oktober* (29 June 1986); and "What the Opposition Says," *al-Ahram al-Iqtisadi* (24 June 1986).

15. The reason offered by the government for the long interruption to the parliamentary session was the October presidential referendum and the consequent

need to form a new government. Spokesmen for the secular and Islamic oppositions saw the recess as "a deliberate design by the government and the National Democratic Party to suspend the Assembly's function." Statement by Saif al-Islam al-Banna, Moslem Brother MP, cited in Mahmoud Nafadi, "There Is Too Much of a Runaround in Parliament, Opposition Says," *Middle East Times* (1–7 November 1987).

16. Imani Qandil, "The Peoples' Assembly . . . How it Supervises," *al-Ahram al-Iqtisadi* (17 June 1986).

17. The annual reports on circulation are to be found in *al-Akhbar* on 20 September 1986 and in *Akhbar al-Yom* on 21 September 1986.

18. *al-Wafd* (3 July 1986).

19. "Struggle on Columns of the Egyptian Press," *al-Magallah* (25–31 December 1985).

20. Bahira Mukhtar, "The Egyptian Man . . . and His Preferred Newspaper," *al-Ahram* (28 May 1987).

21. Hussain Abd al-Raziq, cited in *Middle East Times* (16–22 November 1986).

22. Even the respected economic and political weekly *al-Ahram al-Iqtisadi* suffers from lapses of professionalism. In an article by Gamal Zaida, "The Doors Are Open for Migration to America, Canada and Australia," for example, which appeared in the 22 September 1986 issue, the author claimed on the basis of interviews with consular officials representing those three countries that Egyptians could expect preferential treatment and that their chances of securing the necessary visas were excellent. When the officials concerned read this they were aghast, for in their interviews with the reporter they had all stressed that not only would Egyptians not be treated preferentially but that migration opportunities were exceedingly limited. One of the concerned consular officials raised the matter informally with the Ministry of Foreign Affairs, which informed him that he could rest assured that his and the other countries were not being singled out for this sort of treatment, for distorting the facts was a common practice among Egyptian journalists.

23. *The Arab Strategic Report 1985*, pp. 334–335.

24. I am indebted to a well-informed diplomatic source for this information.

25. "Accident . . . Or Assassination Attempt?" *al-Wafd* (25 September 1986).

26. The three defendants were acquitted of all charges in June 1987, and Baidani and former Minister of Housing Abd al-Rahman Labib, who *al-Wafd* alleged had taken bribes from Baidani, were placed under investigation. In July 1987 an order was issued for Baidani's personal property to be seized by the state. Labib was subsequently found innocent of all charges.

27. For a description of governmental harassment, see Muhammad Abd al-Quddus, "Children of the Country," *al-Shaab* (21 July 1986).

28. Mubarak made this allegation while speaking to a group of editors on 4 November 1986. Cited in *Middle East Times* (16–22 November 1986).

29. This incident received extensive coverage in the opposition press. See *al-Ahrar* (31 March 1986); *al-Shaab* (18 March 1986); and *al-Wafd* (19 March 1986). See also Imam Ahmed, "Egypt Media Scandal Raises Furor over Advertiser's Influence on Press Policy," *Middle East Times* (13–19 April 1986).

30. Sayed Marei, interview (23 March 1986).

31. Abd al-Wahab Masri, "So That President Mubarak Will Be a Witness to These Facts," *al-Ahrar* (11 March 1986).

32. Cited in *Middle East Times* (15–21 February 1987).

33. Introducing an article in which the dense network of relationships that tie together the television "mafia" are described, an *al-Shaab* reporter commented that "The president of broadcasting is a believer in the means of *shilla*-s and all the workers in broadcasting know the details." "The *Shilla* of Anis . . . In Broadcasting?" *al-Shaab* (5 August 1986).

34. Several such persons described their experiences in pre-program "briefings" to the author.

35. In one such case a promising young graduate in accounting from Cairo University who had obtained a good position in a joint-venture firm then joined the NPUP. The SSA undertook a campaign of intimidation against him that culminated in his losing his job. Having no alternative, he went to work as a laborer in a bakery. A close friend explained his plight to the author.

36. Sabri Abu al-Magd, "Words Not Lacking Frankness," *al-Musawwar* (27 June 1986).

37. *al-Akhbar* (30 September 1986).

38. *al-Akhbar* (3 November 1986).

39. Tony Walker, "Cairo Left," dispatch filed with *Financial Times, Sydney Morning Herald,* and *Melbourne Age* (28 July 1987).

40. *Ibid.*

41. Raymond A. Hinnebusch, Jr., *Egyptian Politics Under Sadat: The Post-Populist Development of an Authoritarian-Modernizing State* (Cambridge: Cambridge University Press, 1985), p. 195.

42. "The Amount of Competition Is a Guide to the Existence of Democracy," *al-Akhbar* (30 March 1987).

43. He further claimed, "You can multiply that figure by five members in each Egyptian family." *Middle East Times* (28 September–4 October 1986).

44. Mahmoud Nafadi, "Independents Rush to Compete in April Poll, but Chances Seem Slim," *Middle East Times* (29 March–4 April 1987).

45. See interview with Wahid Rifat in *al-Musawwar* (20 June 1986) and Karim Gabr and Ibrahim Khalil, "The Wafd Falls into the Pasha's Grip," *Ruz al-Yusuf* (7 July 1986). The author attended the extraordinary general assembly of the Wafd and estimates attendance at around 1,000. There are, however, extenuating circumstances, described below, that account in part for the low participation rate.

46. Abd al-Hamid Yunis, "We Have More Than Twenty Parties," *Oktober* (11 May 1986).

47. On the composition of the NPUP, see Hassan, *The Elimination of Election Games,* p. 60.

48. *Ibid.,* pp. 259–283.

49. See *The Arab Strategic Report 1985,* pp. 332–334.

50. "*al-Shaab:* Socialist or Islamic?" *al-Ahram al-Iqtisadi* (3 November 1986).

51. *al-Ahram* (12 April 1987).

52. See for example Bertus Hendriks, "Egypt's Election, Mubarak's Bind," *Merip Middle East Report,* 129 (January 1985). For an excellent account and analysis of the 1984 elections, see al-Sayid Yassin and Ali al-Din Hillal, *The 1984 Parliamentary Elections: Comment and Analysis* (Cairo: al Ahram, 1985) (in Arabic).

53. For statements by the principals involved in these events, see *al-Wafd* (15 November 1985) and *al-Mugtama* (10 November 1985), the latter of which appears in *Foreign Broadcast Information Service, Near East* (1 April 1986).

54. Particularly aggravating to Sirag al-Din was that the president of the lawyers syndicate, Ahmad al-Khawaga, an ambitious lawyer who had for several years cooperated with Sadat in controlling the syndicate, refused to support him. Khawaga was widely suspected of trying to use the syndicate as a springboard for his career within the Wafd. Moreover, Khawaga is a close relative of Speaker of Parliament Rifat al-Mahgub, the bête noire of Sirag al-Din. As if waving a red flag to a bull, Khawaga proclaimed in June 1986 that "al-Mahgub and I were brought up in the school of the Wafd and our teacher was his father." See the interview with him in *al-Musawwar* (27 June 1986); and Moushira E. El Giziri, "The Role of the Bar Association in Egyptian Politics," 1952–1981, unpublished M.A. thesis, American University in Cairo, June 1984.

55. Mustafa Bakri and Suliman Abd al-Azim, "Siragiyun and Nahhasiyun," *al-Musawwar* (20 June 1986).

56. Gabr and Khalil, "The Wafd Falls into the Grip of the Pasha," and observations by the author.

57. The government press provided extensive coverage of the assembly and negative reactions to it. See for example "How Sirag al-Din Directed Debate on the New By-Laws," *Akhar Saa* (2 July 1986).

58. *al-Musawwar* (20 June 1986).

59. Nagi was bitter because Gomaa, despite being younger, had succeeded in becoming Sirag al-Din's favored protege. Gomaa had consolidated his position by organizing seminars in competition with those offered by Yassin Sirag al-Din. See interviews with Nagi and Gomaa in *al-Musawwar* (27 June 1986), and see Bakri and al-Azim, "Siragiyun and Nahhasiyun."

60. Interviews with Ahmad Abu Ismail (18 June 1986) and Ahmad Abaza (24 March 1986). That Abu Ismail's view was closer to that of the Wafd's MP is suggested by the results of a poll of MPs conducted by *al-Ahram*. Twenty-seven Wafdists and 184 members of the NDP were asked, among other questions, what they thought should be done about subsidies. Of Wafdist MPs, 14.8 percent thought they should remain, 3.7 percent that they should be canceled, and 81.5 percent that they should be retained but directed toward the needy. NDP MPs responses were 19.6 percent, 8.7 percent, and 71.8 percent, respectively. See Mahmud Murad, "Scientific Research Conducted by *al-Ahram* in Order to Know the Views and Thoughts of 211 Deputies," *al-Ahram* (3 March 1987).

61. In the *al-Ahram* poll referred to above, 92.6 percent of Wafdist MPs wanted to retain the public sector and only 7.3 percent wanted it abolished. The comparative percentages for NDP MPs were 94 percent and 6 percent, respectively.

62. Hinnebusch, *Egyptian Politics Under Sadat*, pp. 213–214.

63. See Riad Hilal, "Interview with Dr. Wahid Rifat," *al-Ahram al-Iqtisadi* (28 October 1985). See also ibid., p. 214.

64. "The Shaikh of al-Azhar Imposes Silence About the Allocation of a Maadi Villa to Him," *al-Wafd* (3 July 1986); and "Dangerous Secrets in the Case of the Allocation of a Maadi Villa to the Shaikh of al-Azhar," *al-Wafd* (10 July 1986).

65. Hinnebusch, *Egyptian Politics Under Sadat*, pp. 209–210.

66. Murad, "Scientific Research Conducted by *al-Ahram*."

67. Abd al-Azim Ramadan, "The Opposition Parties: Between Reality and Desire," *Oktober* (19 October 1986).

68. Hinnebusch, *Egyptian Politics Under Sadat*, pp. 187–190.

69. Ramadan, "The Opposition Parties."

70. See Kamal al-Din Hussein, "National Front of All Parties and Tendencies . . . Is it Possible?" *Ruz al-Yusuf* (21 July 1986); and Riad Hilal, "Formation of a National Front," *al-Ahram al-Iqtisadi* (28 October 19850.

71. This caused the mercurial Shaikh Salah Abu Ismail, who had in the previous year been thrown out of the Wafd Party, to resign from the Liberal Party.

72. See the issues of 12 and 19 October 1986.

73. "1986: The Year of Mass Movements," *al-Ahali* (7 January 1987).

74. That the government does not take peasant apathy for granted is suggested by its reluctance to implement additional changes to the agrarian reform laws that would further disadvantage peasant tenants, smallholders, and the landless. Although the NDP agriculture committee firmly supports such measures and the government indicated in early 1986 that it would introduce such legislation, when the CSF riots occurred in February of that year the government backed down out of fear of stimulating further political violence.

75. "1986: The Year of Mass Movements," *al-Ahali* (7 January 1987).

76. *al-Ahram* (10 June 1987).

77. For their names, ages, and vocations, see *al-Ahram* (2 September 1986). The backgrounds of those in the Video Group are similar to those of the persons arrested and charged with belonging to the *gama'at* accused of attempting assassinations of Hassan Abu Basha, Makram Muhammad Ahmad, and Nabawi Ismail. Of the 31 suspects transferred to the Higher State Security Court for trial on 15 November 1987, all were male, their average age was 29.6 years, and none was a peasant. Thirteen were tradesmen, lower-level civil servants, or small merchants, and 15 had at least some professional credentials or training in accountancy, engineering, pharmacology, veterinary science, or education, although it is probable that many were not employed in those fields. There was 1 student and 2 unemployed who apparently lacked secondary or tertiary educational credentials of any sort. *al-Ahram* (16 November 1987).

78. Khalid Ikram, *Egypt: Economic Management in a Period of Transition* (Baltimore: Johns Hopkins University Press, 1980), p. 246.

79. *Ibid.*, pp. 246–247.

80. *Ibid.*, pp. 134–135, 247. See also Bent Hansen and Karim Nashashibi, *Foreign Trade Regimes and Economic Development: Egypt* (New York: Columbia University Press, 1975), p. 227.

81. In May 1985 parliament endorsed a recommendation of its religious affairs committee for the gradual application of the *sharia* through a two-step procedure: first, preparation of public attitudes for the change; and second, purification of existing laws of material incompatible with the *sharia*. Islamicists assailed parliamentary Speaker Rifat al-Mahgub for terminating debate on the issue after only 12 of the 40 deputies scheduled to speak had actually done so. See *The Middle East Reporter* (22 June 1985).

82. That Islamicists participated in this fashion in the CSF riots has been corroborated by several eyewitness accounts.

83. Adil Hamuda, "The Camp of *al-Jihad* Swells," *al-Hawadeth* (16 May 1986); and Hamied Ansari, "Sectarian Conflict and the Political Expediency of Religion," *The Middle East Journal*, 383 (Summer 1984), pp. 397–418.

84. For an account of this incident, see *al-Shaab* (7 October 1986).

85. At Cairo University the government temporarily closed "informal" mosques to prevent them from being utilized for political purposes by Islamicists. See *al-Ahrar* (11 November 1986). According to *Sawt al-Arab* (26 October 1986),

Minister of Interior Zaki Badr and Secretary General of the NDP Yusuf Wali closely coordinated their strategy during the student election campaign. This charge was subsequently denied by Badr. See *al-Akhbar* (1 November 1986).

86. On these incidents see Magda Abd al-Ghani, "What's Going on Outside Cairo," *al-Akhbar* (3 November 1986).

87. Estimates of those arrested varied widely. Minister of Interior Zaki Badr claimed not more than a few hundred were under arrest, while opposition sources claimed that as many as 5,000 had been rounded up. A generally accepted estimate is 3,000. See John Kifner, "Islamic Fundamentalism in a Troubled Egypt," *New York Times* (12 July 1987).

88. Ahmed Lutfy, "Egyptian Security Forces Close in on Suspects Accused of Terrorist Attempts," *Middle East Times* (23–29 August 1987).

89. "The Dialogue Continues About the Radical *Gama'at*," *Akhar Saa* (18 June 1986).

90. Wafa al-Shishini, "What Is Behind the Radical Societies?" *Akhar Saa* (4 June 1986).

91. Israel Altman, "Islamic Movements in Egypt," *The Jerusalem Quarterly*, 10 (Winter 1979), pp. 87–105.

92. See for example John Kifner, "In Egypt, Fundamentalists' Institutions Are Rivaling the State's," *International Herald Tribune* (30 September 1986). Kifner has also reported that "The Islamic sector put as much as $6 million into the Brotherhood's (1987) electoral campaign. . . ." "Islamic Fundamentalism in a Troubled Egypt."

93. "Egypt's *Ulama* Conduct Dialogue with the Extremists in Liman Tura," *al-Musawwar* (4 June 1982).

94. *Oktober* (19 April 1987).

95. *al-Musawwar* (17 April 1987).

96. "Children of the Country," *al-Shaab* (15 July 1986).

97. "Our Call Is for the Rejection of Violence," *al-Hawadeth* (19 September 1986).

98. "What Is the Truth About a Relation Between the Brothers and the *Gama'at* and the Conflict Between Them?" *Akhar Saa* (11 June 1986).

99. For an example of this view, see al-Dimirdash al-Aqali's comments in Usama Agaah, "Religious Radicalism . . . and What is the Stand of the Parties?" *Akhar Saa* (11 June 1986).

100. Fadwa al-Guindi, "Veiling *Infitah* with Muslim Ethic: Egypt's Contemporary Islamic Movement," *Social Problems*, 28 (1981), pp. 465–483.

101. Nemat Guenena, "The 'Jihad': An 'Islamic Alternative' in Egypt," unpublished M.A. thesis, American University in Cairo (September 1985).

102. This is the view of Ali al-Din Hillal, as presented in a seminar at the University of California, Berkeley, 22 September 1987. See also Hinnebusch, *Egyptian Politics Under Sadat*, p. 204.

103. This information was made available to the author by Muhammad Subiah, a journalist who was closely associated with *Misr al-Fatat* and subsequently director of Dar al-Taawun publishing house.

104. Adil Hamuda, "The Exit from the Cave," *Ruz al-Yusuf* (23 June 1986).

105. "These Societies!" *Akhbar al-Yom* (17 May 1986).

106. Kifner, "Islamic Fundamentalism in a Troubled Egypt."

107. See the interview with Mustafa Kamal Murad in *Akhar Saa* (11 June 1986).

108. On the various organized groups that compose the Islamicist movement, see Robert Bianchi, "Changing Patterns of Interest Representation in Modern Egypt," unpublished manuscript, American University in Cairo, n.d.; and Hinnebusch, *Egyptian Politics Under Sadat*, pp. 200–204.

109. On Osman's role, see Adil Hamuda, "The Brotherhood Renounces Violence," *Ruz al-Yusuf* (21 July 1986); and "Moslem Brotherhood Between the Conflict of Two Trends," *al-Hawadeth* (30 May 1986).

110. Kifner, "In Egypt, Fundamentalists Institutions are Rivaling the State's."

111. Hassan Fathi, "Mustafa Mahmoud Brings His Faith and Science to the Service of the Needy," *Middle East Times* (13–19 September 1987).

112. For a sympathetic review of the activities of these organizations, including interviews with several directors of them, see Abd al-Rasul al-Zarqani, "The Islamic Gama'at . . . How They Perform Their Role," *al-Nur* (4 June 1986).

113. Kifner, "In Egypt, Fundamentalists' Institutions Are Rivaling the State's."

114. *al-Ahrar* (30 June 1986).

115. *al-Akhbar* (11 September 1986).

116. A small front-page article in *al-Akhbar* on 8 November 1986, for example, announced the arrest of five radicals outside a mosque in Suez for distributing leaflets that attacked "the system of rule and the political leadership and provided misleading information about events in Asyut." The five included a physical education teacher and four of his students.

117. "The Islamic Societies in Egypt's Universities Are Victorious in the Student Union Elections," *al-Mugtama* (7 January 1986), cited in *Foreign Broadcast Information Service* (1 April 1986).

118. *Ibid.* Whether this is the consequence of Islamicism having greater appeal to higher-achieving and more well-off students, or to the "absolutist" nature of the subject matter in the physical sciences as compared to the relativism of the social sciences, is a subject for keen debate among Egypt's academics.

119. *al-Shaab* (24 March 1987).

120. Ali al-Din Hillal, seminar.

121. Karim Gabr, "Asyut University Under the Control of the *Gama'at*," *Ruz al-Yusuf* (28 April 1986).

122. Hassan Nafaa, "On the Margins of the Elections of Cairo University Faculty Club," *al-Ahali* (30 April 1986).

123. On these incidents see Ya'acov Lamdan, "Growing Conflict with Moslem Fundamentalists," *Jerusalem Post* (3 June 1986); Richard Clifford, "Students Demand Islamic Law," *Middle East and Mediterranean Outlook*, 36 (January 1987); Hamuda, "The Camp of *al-Jihad* Swells."

124. For a review of and comment on this incident, see Fahmi Huwaidi, "Not in Defense of the Veil," *al-Ahram* (13 May 1986). See also Ghada Ragab, "Medical School Dean Attacked in Furor over the Wearing of Veils in Class," *Middle East Times* (4–10 May 1986).

125. On these events see *al-Ahrar* (9 June 1986); and *al-Shaab* (2 June 1987). In 1987 the government press provided extensive coverage of the "pray-ins," replete with photos. See for example *al-Ahram* (29 May 1987).

126. This terminology was employed by Philip Gallab, "The Last Page," *Ruz al-Yusuf* (17 February 1986).

127. Mustafa Bakri, "Yusuf al-Badri—The Man Who Defeated the Minister of War Production in the Elections," *al-Musawwar* (17 April 1987).

128. The last of this series of six articles appeared on 28 July 1986 and was entitled "The Exit from the Cave."

129. Abd al-Moneim Said Aly and Manfred W. Wenner, "Islamic Reform Movements: The Muslim Brotherhood in Contemporary Egypt," *The Middle East Journal*, 36, 3 (Summer 1982), pp. 336–361.

130. Hamuda, "The Camp of *al-Jihad* Swells."

131. Salah Azama, "Was There a Coup in the Brotherhood?" *al-Musawwar* (6 June 1986).

132. This account of the succession struggle in the Brotherhood is based on diplomatic sources, discussions with informed observers, and press reports. Among the most informative of the latter are Abd al-Qadir Shuhaib, "Inside the Brotherhood: The Conflict Between the Rich and the Holy," *Ruz al-Yusuf* (16 June 1986); "The Problem of the Brotherhood After the Departure of al-Tilmisani," author identified as "a prominent Islamicist," *al-Musawwar* (30 May 1986); and in the same issue the interview with Abd al-Rahman al-Banna; Adil Hamuda, "The Moslem Brotherhood in the Middle of the Conflict of Two Trends—Radicalism and Flexibility," *al-Hawadeth* (30 May 1986); Yusuf Fikir and Mustafa Bakri, "Hamid Abu al-Nasr the Provisional Guide Speaks to *al-Musawwar*," *al-Musawwar* (6 June 1986); Mustafa Bakri, "Muhammad Kamal Abd al-Aziz: The Candidate for General Guide of the Moslem Brotherhood," *al-Musawwar* (16 May 1986); Lutfi Abd al-Latif, "*al-Ahrar* Alone Presents First Conversation with the Supreme Guide of the Moslem Brothers," *al-Ahrar* (2 June 1986); and Wahid Abdul Meguid, "Muslim Brotherhood Unites to Select New Leader," *Middle East Times* (22–28 June 1986).

133. Observation by the author.

134. Azama, "Was There a Coup in the Brotherhood?"

135. Fuad Ajami, *The Arab Predicament: Arab Political Thought and Action Since 1967* (New York: Cambridge University Press, 1982), pp. 108–122.

136. See for example the interview with Zaki Badr in *al-Musawwar* (27 April 1987), in which he states that there are no more than a few hundred members of radical *gama'at*.

137. On the connections within *al-Jihad* and its various factions, as well as its ties to *Takfir wal Hijra*, see Yusuf Fikri, "Provocative Confessions of the Accused of the Video Fires," *al-Musawwar* (5 September 1986); Sayid Abd al-Qadir, "Secret of the al-Samawi *Gama'at*," *Akhar Saa* (8 October 1986); and "Violent Religious *Gama'at* Think About Assassinating Mubarak!" *al-Hawadeth* (19 September 1986).

138. "The Islamic Societies in Egypt's Universities Are Victorious in the Student Union Elections," al-Mugtana (7 January 1986).

139. For an Islamicist's perceptions of these events, see Muhammad Abd al-Quddus, "Children of the Country," *al-Shaab* (2 and 9 June 1987).

140. Secularists objected vehemently to this decision. See for example Mustafa Amin, "Injustice to Women," *al-Akhbar* (23 March 1987).

141. *The Middle East Reporter* (22 June 1985).

142. *al-Ahram* (21 March 1987). On 11 May 1987, however, the government expelled the last Iranian diplomat remaining in the country on the charge that he had "acted in a way inconsistent with the requirements of diplomatic tradition," implying that he had assisted radical *gama'at*. That decision, however, may well have been taken out of foreign rather than domestic policy considerations. In August 1987 the attorney general, Ragaa al-Arabi, accused Iran of funding radical *gama'at. al-Ahram* (29 August 1987). That the announcement was made by this comparatively low-ranking official, rather than by a cabinet minister or by the

President, suggests that the government did not want to attempt to smear the Islamicist movement as a whole with the "outside agitation" charge.

143. Those arrested at Asyut University during riots at the outset of the academic year in mid-October 1986 were, for example, released in mid-November. *al-Ahram* (19 November 1986).

144. *al-Ahram* (17 April 1987).

145. Information provided to the author by officials of the IMF and USAID.

146. A list of the concessions made by government to Islamicists is provided by Abd al-Sitar al-Tawila, "Playing with Fire," *Ruz al-Yusuf* (25 August 1986).

147. "Shaikh al-Azhar Imposes Silence Around the Assigning of a Maadi Villa to Him," *al-Wafd* (3 July 1986); and "Serious Secrets in the Issue of Assigning a Maadi Villa to the Shaikh al-Azhar," *al-Wafd* (10 July 1986).

148. *al-Wafd* (31 March 1987). For an interview with Shaikh Sharawi, see Ahmed Lutfy, "Sheikh Sharawi—Loved by Millions," *Middle East Times* (1–8 June 1986).

149. On the problems associated with the selection of a new *Mufti*, see Zakariya Abu Haram, "Where Is the Monastic Egyptian *Mufti?*" *Akhar Saa* (12 May 1986); Ahmad Hussain and Sayid Abu Duma, "New *Mufti* of the Arab Republic of Egypt in a Special Conversation with *al-Ahram*," *al-Ahram* (1 November 1986); and Ahmed Lutfy, "Muslim Leaders Push Greater Autonomy in Running Islamic Affairs," *Middle East Times* (2–8 February 1986). *Mufti* Tantawi's first major decision was in support of the government and against Islamicists. He ruled in November 1987 that a law prohibiting female students from wearing the *niqab* (veil) "does not violate the *sharia*." Middle East Times (8–14 November 1987). Like the position of *Mufti*, the role of *al-Ashraf* Association, which is comprised of those ostensibly descended from the Prophet Muhammad, has deteriorated markedly in recent years. It has not had a leader since its last president died in 1953. In 1987, amidst accusations that the Associations was selling phony certificates attesting to descent from the Prophet, the grand shaikh of Sufi orders and various other religious notables called for its dissolution. See Hassan Amer, "Venerable Society Attracts Ridicule with Offer of 'Holy' Certificates," Middle East Times (11–17 October 1987).

150. Hassan Amer, "Islamic Extremists Filling Gap Left by Lack of Teachers," *Middle East Times* (7–13 September 1986).

151. *Middle East Times* (30 August–5 September 1987).

152. The three defendants in "The Sparrow" case were finally acquitted in early June 1987, just as the public prosecutor was announcing his charges against former Minister of Housing Abd al-Rahman Labib and Baidani.

153. Ali al-Din Hillal, seminar.

7

ECONOMIC ASSISTANCE AND THE LIMITS OF POLICY LEVERAGE

DEPENDENCY IN THE ABSENCE
OF MULTINATIONAL CORPORATIONS?

The political economy of Egypt since the mid-1970s has come to resemble in at least two key respects the Latin American pattern of dependent development. By following exclusionist policies the Sadat and Mubarak regimes have demobilized lower strata, a process that has continued to gain momentum. Additionally, the bureaucratic-authoritarian state has progressively become more closely linked to bourgeois interests, although the Egyptian state retains more autonomy from the class substructure than does the Latin American archetype. But the third trait of dependent development, which is penetration and eventual domination of the national political economy by multinational corporations (MNCs), is conspicuous by its absence from Egypt. Commenting in the early 1980s on the possibility that MNCs, through Egyptian affiliates, "could infiltrate the Egyptian elite and dominant class and wed them to the interests of the core," Waterbury raised the caveat that "it is not at all clear that the MNCs are interested in taking over Egypt, although the country may be there for the taking."[1]

By the mid to late 1980s no appreciable change has occurred in the cautious, hesitant approach by MNCs to Egypt. If there is any slight attitudinal shift among the captains of international industry, it could well be that Mubarak's Egypt is thought by them to be even less hospitable than Sadat's had been. Foreign private capital remains concentrated in the oil and banking sectors, but declining profitability in the latter had by 1987 led to a considerable shakeout of international banks. The agreement in that year by Bank of America to sell its 40 percent share in Misr America International Bank to the Islamic investment company al-Rayan symbolized the broader failure of international capital to displace local secular and Islamic banking and financial operations, a consequence of governmental protection and the deterioration of the Egyptian economy.[2] In 1984 direct private U.S. investment in Egyptian industry and agriculture did not exceed a very modest $61 million and it has not risen substantially since then.[3] The high-profile GM agreement, which was intended by the U.S. Embassy and some Egyptian decision makers to demonstrate to other MNCs the advantages of doing business in Egypt, backfired. Against the backdrop of a depreciating Egyptian pound and a toughening bargaining position by the Ministry of Industry and the public-sector firm NASCO that was to be involved in the joint venture, GM executives finally declared in August 1987 that they would make no further offers in order to salvage the project. While some U.S. based MNCs had in the meantime established branches in Egypt, such as Safeway, Pioneer Seeds, American Standard (a ceramics manufacturer), and the agribusiness division of Bechtel International, these operations were small and frequently their presence was due to special circumstances. Bechtel's agribusiness division and Safeway, for example, did not invest their own capital but worked on management contracts for local and foreign investors.[4] Bechtel's involvement was also intended as a flag-flying exercise, for that huge engineering company had successfully bid for the construction of one very large U.S.-financed power plant and was seeking further such contracts. Nor have all MNCs been operating profitably. Those producing mass consumption items, such as soft drinks, have complained bitterly and persistently about governmental interference and vacillation as the cause of financial losses.[5] Structural factors, including inadequate infrastructure and a modern consumer market that is estimated to constitute no more than 2 million of Egypt's 50 million citizens,[6] combined with government policy that under Mubarak has as a rule favored national as opposed to international capital, have discouraged significant new investment by MNCs.[7]

MNCs have yet to subordinate the Egyptian political economy to their will and integrate it into the world capitalist order on unfavorable terms. To Egyptian equivalents of Latin American *dependistas* this is not an indication of the inapplicability of the dependency model. According to them that inexorable process requires a preliminary phase, unlike the Latin American prototype, in which the path must be cleared for MNC penetration. For these firms to operate profitably infrastructure must be put in place, consumerism stimulated, and most of all, appropriate policies implemented and supportive elites entrenched in the commanding heights. *Dependistas* claim these tasks are, in Egypt's case, to be performed by foreign economic assistance and the governments and multilateral agencies that dispense it.[8] The new orthodoxy of development, which calls for export-led growth to be propelled by privatization, is the guiding dogma of USAID, the IMF, the World Bank, and many other Western bilateral aid agencies, precisely because they are to play the key role in levering open the Egyptian political economy. Their strategy is to encourage the growth of indebtedness and then to make further economic assistance conditional upon policy "reform," while simultaneously cultivating a constituency among the comprador bourgeoisie and, most importantly, within the state itself.[9] Because the United States has since

1979 provided approximately two-thirds of all economic assistance to Egypt and because it plays the leading role in the IMF and the World Bank, it is the principal force behind these efforts.[10]

INCREASING COMMITMENT TO POLICY LEVERAGE

While virtually all of those involved in channeling aid to Egypt through either bilateral or multilateral organizations vehemently disagree with most contentions of Egyptian *dependistas*, they do not contest the claim that assistance is utilized for policy leverage. Indeed, a missionary zeal has spread among the experts and officials involved in assistance programs in Egypt. They believe that by forcing Egypt to accept the tenets of the new orthodoxy they will save it from itself. By encouraging the growth of the private at the expense of the public sector, by forcing relaxation of controls over producers, especially those in agriculture, by inducing economic decision makers to devalue the currency, raise interest rates and rationalize consumer subsidies, they will help establish an economically viable, productive, and ultimately more independent Egypt. In their thinking MNCs can assist this process by providing capital, technology, expertise, and access to international markets.[11]

Because USAID is far and away the dominant force within the large community of foreign organizations involved in distributing economic assistance, its efforts to exert policy leverage not only have the greatest direct impact, but they also influence the approach of smaller donors. Since 1985 USAID has become increasingly single-minded and effective in tying project assistance to policy reform. That it took some ten years for this qualitative change to occur is due to several factors. Replacement of Carter appointees by loyal Reaganites began at the top layer of USAID and gradually moved down into the ranks. Personnel turnover was paralleled by a shift in the agency's agenda from satisfying the basic human needs of the poorest sectors in developing countries to an emphasis on the need to free up potentially productive private initiatives that previously had been bottled up by government. This change was accomplished almost simultaneously with the completion of the first generation of USAID's projects, which had been designed in part as information-gathering exercises to lay the bases for second-generation projects. During this preliminary phase frustration had accumulated in USAID as the Egyptian economy showed few signs of "taking off," despite the infusion of about one-fifth of total U.S. foreign assistance.[12] Media criticism in Egypt and the United States of USAID's role in this "failure" further exacerbated discontent. As these internal changes in USAID were beginning to dovetail into a consensus to more actively develop and utilize policy leverage, the Egyptian economy went into a nosedive. Deteriorating oil prices, combined with reduced tourist receipts and worker remittances in 1985–1986, as well as the need to make the first annual installment of almost $600 million on the military debt owed to the United States, rendered the Egyptian economy uniquely vulnerable to economic pressure. This conjunction of events confirmed for *dependistas* the soundness of their theory. Foreign aid and increasing indebtedness have gone hand in hand and in so doing created vulnerabilities that the United States immediately seized upon. For USAID officials the need for and opportunity to reform the decadent state capitalist legacy of the Nasser era were long overdue. That Egypt had not managed that task itself suggested that some assistance by a foreign but interested and concerned friend was necessary and justified.

The attack launched in 1985–1986 was across a broad front. The pledge of up to $200 million of USAID funds to support GM, an amount equivalent to some 40 percent of annual project assistance to Egypt during the Mubarak era, was part of a general reallocation of U.S. assistance in favor of the private sector. Although $32 million had been allocated to private industrial firms through the Development Industrial Bank in 1976, the bulk of those funds remained undisbursed five years later.[13] Between 1975 and 1982 private Egyptian businessmen, mainly importers, obtained slightly in excess of $100 million from USAID in credits toward the purchase of U.S. goods and services, or on average less than $15 million annually.[14] By comparison, USAID's 1986 allocations included $235 million in credits to be disbursed to private businessmen over a three-year period, or more than $77 million per year.[15] Other USAID programs also targeted the private sector for increased benefits. In agriculture $123 million was in 1986 authorized to continue and to expand the Small Farmer Production Project (SFPP), a scheme whereby credit is made available to private farmers. Previous funding of the SFPP had been at a level less than one-sixth this amount. According to USAID's 1986–1987 Action Plan, "The emphasis of USAID's industry program shifted markedly from public to private-sector in FY (Fiscal Year) 1985." The Private Sector Production Credit project doubled its expenditures in that year, and for fiscal year 1986 one quarter of all commodity imports financed by USAID were earmarked for the private-sector. For 1987 the private sector's share of commodity imports was to be further escalated to one-half. Public-sector industry, according to USAID's long-range plan, was to receive no further assistance whatsoever.[16]

In addition to redirecting economic assistance to the private sector, USAID from 1985 sought to tie allocations to the public sector to specific policy reforms. Authorizations for agriculture in 1986 were made on the condition that actual disbursements would be contingent upon Egypt achieving five specific policy objectives, including raising the cotton procurement price; reducing red meat prices; privatizing the marketing of corn, broadbeans, and some part of the rice crop; eliminating subsidies to fertilizer and farm credit and encouraging private competition in these areas; and legalizing and encouraging private-sector exports of oranges and other high value crops.[17] By 1986 all proposed USAID projects were evaluated principally from the perspective of how much policy leverage they would buy. Technical, social, and other criteria that had been deemed relevant and appropriate in the first ten years of USAID's experience in Cairo were all but ignored. Finally, USAID seized on the opportunity offered by Egypt's strained financial circumstances of 1985–1987 to coordinate its program with the lending activities of the IMF, the World Bank and to a lesser extent, other bilateral donors. USAID, IMF, and World Bank officials throughout 1986 and into 1987 worked together closely in drawing up a plan that would exert pressure on Egypt to adopt policies consistent with the new orthodoxy of development in exchange for debt rescheduling.[18]

RESPONSES TO POLICY LEVERAGE

By 1986–1987 it was evident that Egypt, which had for more than a decade managed to delay, dilute, or simply ignore most of the reforms recommended and then demanded by USAID and the IMF, was going to have to give ground. It had to have access to additional funds to avoid defaulting on loan repayments to the United States, which would automatically render Egypt ineligible for further U.S. military and civilian aid, to say nothing of the consequences for its access to further supplier credits and assistance from other sources. Further, the current account deficit threatened to balloon to as much as $4–5 billion, or more than twice export earnings, unless the government could devise a strategy to mobilize the savings of individual Egyptians, generally estimated to be in the $40–50 billion range.[19]

The first of what was to become a series of steps was the proclamation in March 1986 of Ministerial Decree 121, by which the private sector was given permission to import corn and a wide range of foodstuffs. Six months later several tourist hotels that were owned and operated by the Egyptian Hotel Organization, a particularly inept public sector company, were leased on longterm bases to European hoteliers, an innovation that was interpreted by some observers as a preliminary move in selling off the public sector.[20] During the preparation of the five-year plan to take effect from 1 July 1987, it was announced that the private sector had been allocated 38 percent of scheduled investments, an increase of more than 10 percent over the previous plan. Minister of Agriculture Yusuf Wali, who already had declared that privatization of the agricultural sector was "one of our major targets," announced during the 1987 election campaign that mandatory deliveries to the state of all crops except cotton, sugar cane, and half the rice crop were no longer to be required and that all legal charges previously laid against producers for nondelivery of lentils, beans, wheat and corn crops would also be dropped.[21]

The major breakthrough came in May 1987, when the government announced reforms associated with an 18-month standby agreement for a new IMF loan and access to other lines of credit, which would in turn pave the way for renegotiation of some $12 billion of Egypt's foreign debt of $40 billion. The pound was devalued from the bank incentive rate of $1=£E1.35 to $1=£E2.20, and it was declared that in future its value would be set daily by a committee of bankers. Devaluation was accompanied by measures intended to bring the Islamic investment companies and black market money changers under control and to direct foreign currency away from them and into government coffers. The 1987 budget froze support for consumer subsidies at the 1986 level of £E1.7 billion, which in constant pound terms was a decrease in one year of at least 20 percent and a much larger one since 1984–1985, when over £E2 billion had been budgeted for subsidies. Of greater significance for subsidies was the fact that the government pledged to the IMF to phase out by the end of the year concessionary exchange rates (chief of which is the "commercial" rate) for all food imports other than wheat and flour, purchases of which by the state would continue to be made in dollars made available at the rate of $1=£E.70. Since hidden subsidies, to which artificial exchange rates have been a major contributor, were estimated at £E7–8 billion in 1985 and 1986, or some four to five times the government's official budgetary allocations to subsidies, the deval-uation amounted to a drastic cutback of governmental support to con-sumers. The rate of inflation of prices paid for basic foodstuffs, which was at least 20 percent in 1986–1987, was estimated to at least double in 1987–1988.[22]

In the wake of the May reforms the government identified several small unprofitable public sector firms engaged in service activities as suitable for sale to private interests. It commissioned a study to devise a means to base pay and promotion in the administration and public sector on merit rather than seniority.[23] With regard to agriculture it declared that the government subsidy on corn would be terminated by the end of 1987; that the private sector would henceforth be permitted to import fertilizer; that the Principal Bank for Agricultural Development and Credit (PBDAC), the state's main credit and marketing arm, would reschedule debts to private producers to facilitate investment; that the government would no longer farm reclaimed land but would confine its activities to installing infrastructure in newly reclaimed areas prior to selling the land to private investors;[24] and that the Ministry of Agriculture had established in the summer of 1987 an Agricultural Investment Office in order to provide data free of charge to potential agribusiness investors and to guarantee a response in one week to any proposals they might make.[25] In August 1987 for the first time an incumbent cabinet minister, Fuad Sultan, called for selling the public sector to private interests.[26]

While these reforms appear to be substantive and could, if further strengthened, become as important as those implemented in the wake of the 1973 war that led to Sadat's *infitah*, the question remains as to whether they are the result only of Egypt's vulnerability and IMF arm twisting or if in fact a domestic political consensus in favor of the new orthodoxy of development has finally emerged. If the reforms were announced only as a consequence of temporary financial necessity and IMF pressure, they presumably will not be followed by further steps and may in fact be rolled back when Egypt's financial circumstances permit, which with the upturn in 1987 in earnings from the "big four" (oil, tourism, Suez Canal tolls, and worker remittances) may soon occur. On the other hand, there are indications that what Albert 0. Hirschman has referred to as a reform coalition and what *dependistas* see as Latin American-style dependent development may have finally taken hold.[27]

EMERGENCE OF A REFORM COALITION?

The military is a powerful political actor, and the prevailing ethos among at least those officers employed in its productive enterprises is supportive of developmentalism's new orthodoxy. Field Marshal Abu Ghazala has much more influence over selection of cabinet ministers than anyone other than Mubarak. Many of the key economic portfolios, including those of Economy, Finance, and International Cooperation, have since the demise of Mustafa al-Said in April 1985 been awarded to reformers, which may well reflect Abu Ghazala's preferences and influence. The Washington-based lobbyist employed by the Egyptian government to put its case to the U.S. congressional and executive branches has close ties to Abu Ghazala and devotes a substantial part of his efforts to the U.S.-Egyptian military connection. Officers employed in the military sector of the economy are generally contemptuous of the civilian administration and of the public sector and prefer to deal with MNCs or, failing that, local private sector firms.

U.S. military assistance has contributed both to the enhancement of the military's political role and to its increasingly conservative outlook. Over 200 officers a year are trained in the United States as part of the military assistance program. A larger number have short-term training on weapons systems purchased with U.S. aid from private manufacturers. Weapons procurement has served to establish close relations between Egyptian officers and various U.S. corporations, and additional such relations have resulted from the military's involvement in various economic activities. The agreement announced in the summer of 1987 to permit Egyptian military industries to manufacture the most advanced armored weapons system in the U.S. inventory, the M1 Abrams tank, paves the way for a broadly based collaboration between those industries and General Dynamics and manufacturers of the tank's components.[28] While the initial authorization of $168 million to facilitate commencement of the Abrams program was drawn from the $1.3-billion annual U.S. military assistance to Egypt, Abu Ghazala's and the military's appetite for sophisticated weaponry has more than consumed available aid despite the fact that all U.S. military assistance was converted to grants rather than loans from 1984.[29] Like the Israeli military that wanted financing for the Lavi jet fighter on top of the "normal" military budget, the Egyptian military can afford the Abrams and maintain the rest of its procurement program only if it can induce the civilian sector to forgo a large slab of butter. The military has given no indication that it is contemplating reducing its appetite for F16s, Mirage 2000s, and other expensive weapons systems, so the assumption has to be that the military will in the coming years obtain an increasing share of the state's budget.[30] The Egyptian military's rejoinder to its civilian critics is that joint venture industries it establishes to produce weapons will also manufacture goods for civilians, to say nothing of employing them. Supported as it has been by the largest U.S. military assistance program to a Third World country, the Egyptian military may also be opening the door to MNCs across a much broader front than just weapons production.

But it is not only the military that favors privatization, liberalization, and closer association with MNCs. While the productive bourgeoisie independent of the state, many of whom are associated with the Wafd Party, strongly favor a reduced role for government and, less unanimously, endorse a role for MNCs in Egypt, they are marginal political actors, removed as they are from the state apparatus. Those within it, however, have been courted by USAID for the purpose of winning them over to the new orthodoxy, a strategy that has enjoyed some success, although rather less than its equivalent in the military sector. The Peace Fellowship Program, one of the "peace prizes" awarded Egypt for signing the Camp David accords, sent 1,900 Egyptians to the United States for university training. Several thousand others have spent varying periods in educational and training courses in various U.S. universities, businesses, and so on. As a result the civilian administration has, in the opinion of Cairo USAID's chief economist, come to resemble a sandwich—with middle-level, middle-aged, East Bloc-trained, and sympathizing administrators surrounded at the bottom by younger recruits with U.S. training and at the top by older senior administrators educated in the West prior to Egypt's turn to the USSR during the 1960s. The strategically placed middle layer is able to block policy initiatives from the top and to frustrate the advancement of younger, more Westernized and, in the view of USAID officials, more competent administrators.[31]

Selective backing by USAID of potential allies in the administrative and political elites results in part from the problems perceived to be caused by the sandwich-like structure of the civil service. Promising individuals are identified, provided additional training if necessary, and then supported by being given appropriate roles in USAID projects. Yusuf Wali, for example, while working in the Ministry of Agriculture's international relations department under his close friend, the then-Minister Mustafa Dawud, came to the attention of the director of USAID's agricultural program. Wali was brought into several projects, which in turn provided him with patronage resources as well as general visibility. He in turn brought to USAID's attention other individuals, such as

Ahmad Goueli, Osman al-Khuli, Hassan Khadr, and others, who as a result were also involved in USAID projects. As clients of Wali's they have enabled him to broaden his political base, with Goueli becoming governor of Damietta, Khuli being appointed president of Minufiya University, and Khadr being awarded an undersecretary post in the Ministry of Agriculture from which he could mind the store while Wali has been off playing politics. Similarly, Atif Ubaid, a U.S.-trained management expert, was consistently involved in USAID projects prior to his inclusion in the cabinet as Minister for Cabinet Affairs and Administrative Services. In 1986, while still in the cabinet, Ubaid was selected by USAID to direct a very large training program, a patronage position that he could be expected suitably to exploit.

The U.S. government has also supported and even brought into being pressure groups of prominent businessmen. The Egyptian American Business Council was created in the wake of Sadat's *infitah* for the purpose of improving communications between Egyptian and U.S. businessmen and influencing the government to be supportive of business interests. The Commercial Section of the U.S. Embassy worked behind the scenes in the early 1980s in helping to create the American-Egyptian Chamber of Commerce, several leading members of which obtained lucrative USAID-financed contracts.[32] Scores of wealthy and prominent businessmen have received subsidized loans through various of USAID's private sector credit programs. These efforts, taken jointly, suggest a concerted campaign by the United States to create a base of political support within the military, the state, and the bourgeoisie for the United States and its current policy preferences.

SCENARIO ONE: BREAKTHROUGH

As a result of the reforms of 1986–1987 and associated political developments a plausible scenario is that Egypt, having now broken decisively with the Nasserist past, will go on to implement the basic tenets of the new orthodoxy of development. Infrastructural improvements have been made and consumerist attitudes and practices spread. Egypt has, in the minds of *dependistas*, been "Americanized," a process in which USAID has played a leading role. Construction in central Cairo of large parking garages, the installation of a freeway grid around that city, and plans to construct a freeway from Cairo to Aswan reflect to these critics an inappropriate infatuation with the automobile and a misguided enthusiasm for spreading U.S. car culture to relatively impoverished Egypt. Additionally, to *dependistas*, upgrading the road system was part of a USAID strategy to enable U.S. car manufacturers to operate profitably in Egypt. Similarly, USAID's emphasis on marketing, especially with regard to foodstuffs, is interpreted as an intentional design to diffuse consumerist habits and facilitate the growth, among other things, of U.S.-style supermarkets. Before Safeway can operate profitably Egyptians have to be instructed in the advantages of prepackaged, hygienic, properly stored food items and become accustomed to paying more for them. The establishment in 1986–1988 of several large, Western-style supermarkets is an indication that this strategy is succeeding. Phase one of Egypt's dependent development, in which foreign economic assistance paves the way for MNC penetration is, in this view, coming to an end and phase two just beginning.

Much of the necessary political spadework has, according to this interpretation, also been completed. Those of the lower strata who previously had been sensitized by Nasserist ideology and recruited into cooperatives, labor unions, syndicates, the ASU, and so on have now been desensitized and demobilized. Simultaneously the bourgeoisie has conquered the ideological high ground with its condemnations of the remnants of Arab Socialism and its promises of vastly improved economic performance under the banner of the productive *infitah*. The bourgeoisie has also constructed a network of pressure groups while colonizing much of the state apparatus, particularly the NDP and parliament.

But even to those who see major and continuous reforms as now virtually inevitable, there remains a nagging doubt about the political will behind the economic liberalization. It is generally recognized that a last major redoubt of opponents situated in the state and in the shadow it throws into the economy is yet to be overrun. This redoubt is comprised of those who have benefited from the state's control of the economy and who fear for their political and/or economic futures in a system in which the state's dominant role is undermined. To those who believe the new orthodoxy will ultimately prevail, the privatization of patronage, the process whereby the state farms out to the private sector through joint ventures the task of supplying patronage resources, will ultimately erode loyalties to the state apparatus and replace them with private sector connections, a process that most concede will require additional time.

A good political barometer of these underlying economic changes is, according to some observers, the degree of political party reorganization. It can be anticipated that as the privatization of patronage erodes the state apparatus, a new political party will emerge out of a coalition of liberals in the Wafd and the NDP. Wafdist economic nationalists who oppose MNCs will drift away to other parties. NDP apparatchiks who do not want to or cannot make the transition to the new era of the alliance between the bourgeoisie, the state, and MNCs will shift into alliance with Marxist or bourgeois economic nationalists. The result of these political realignments will be the emergence of a dominant political party that is committed to and an effective proponent of the new orthodoxy of development.

SCENARIO TWO: A TEMPORARY RETREAT

A contending view is that the paradox of an attempted liberalization by the organizational legacies of Nasser's bureaucratic-authoritarian state, including the NDP, cannot be resolved. The state will never voluntarily surrender its powers of control over the economy, for its political authority ultimately rests on that control. It will seek to exploit economic assistance and MNC participation in Egypt in order to bolster its position, rather than to transform the political economy. The state will persist in its efforts to fragment the bourgeoisie, while constantly holding before the public the prospect of social disharmony and political breakdown if the government were forced to abandon its central role as arbiter and guarantor of the social contract. The reforms of 1986–1987 are in this view fated to be epiphenomena for they lack the necessary support that only a coherent, organized political constituency could provide.

In this alternative scenario the reforms of 1986–1987 are analogous to the prevarications of Khedive Ismail in the face of those international bankers who sought to recover their loans to that profligate nineteenth-century ruler of Egypt.[33] Like this predecessor, Mubarak has had no choice but to adopt some of the recommendations of his creditors in order to maintain the state's solvency and to induce private Egyptian investors to part with some much-needed capital, but he has no intention of putting the house in order according to the dictates of his creditors. Mubarak's plight at this stage is equivalent to Khedive Ismail's before his expensive tastes led him so far into debt that his creditors decided it was safer to jettison him than to throw more good money after bad.[34] Mubarak still has considerable room to maneuver before reaching Ismail's ultimately ruinous state, a situation he has appreciated and exploited.

Mubarak courted the Soviets from the outset of his presidency and was rewarded at his moment of greatest need by them. In April 1987 they agreed to cancel interest owed on $3 billion of outstanding debt, to suspend repayment of principal for six years, and to allow Egypt to repay the balance over 25 years. Clearly the Soviets did not see it in their interest for Mubarak and Egypt to be brought to their knees before Western creditors. Similarly, the oil exporting Arab states of the Gulf, confronted with the Iranian threat and desperate in the wake of erratic U.S. policy as revealed by Irangate to shore up their position, looked to Egypt in 1987 to provide a counterbalance to Iran. To make the offer sufficiently attractive they combined restoration of diplomatic ties that had been severed in 1979 in the wake of Sadat's peace treaty with Israel with hefty sums of cash and promises of more to follow.[35] The growing threat of Islamic fundamentalism throughout the region has enhanced the image of Egypt as the only Arab state capable of containing it while simultaneously raising the specter that the fundamentalist whirlwind could sweep the Mubarak regime away if too much financial pressure were applied by the West. The original incentive to the United States for the vast aid commitment to Egypt, which was to remove it from the Arab-Israeli military confrontation and to place its weight behind the peace process, remains.

As a result of these factors Egypt's position is less desperate than that of other countries confronted with equivalent economic crises but lacking significant strategic resources to trade off against further infusions of cash. Terms offered by the IMF and the 18 member states of the Paris Club, or "Club of Friends" that had been formed in 1977 of Egypt's major creditors and that convenes in Paris, were accordingly generous by recent world standards.[36] Moreover, by the time the reforms were announced in May 1987, the worst of the economic crisis may already have passed. Earnings from the "big four" were back up and the likelihood of further significant transfers of funds from the Gulf was high.[37] As a result of these windfalls Egypt began to stiffen its resistance in the second round of IMF negotiations that commenced in September 1987, and in October IMF officials were expressing their concern that Egypt was not living up to its May commitments.[38] Simultaneously those agencies of OECD (Organization for Economic Cooperation and Development) countries that guarantee export credits began to withhold cover for contracts to Egypt in order to bolster their side in the various bilateral negotiations between Egypt and the Paris Club member states.[39] This, however, was more an indication of the unprecedented magnitude of concessions Egypt was demanding than a manifestation of commitment by the Paris Club to forcing Egypt to adhere to those reforms already declared.[40]

LIMITED IMPACT OF THE REFORMS OF 1986–1987: FISCAL AND MONETARY POLICIES

Egypt's improved economic and strategic positions in the second half of 1987 may cause some of the reforms agreed with the IMF to remain dead letters and others subsequently to be rolled back. Even were backsliding not to occur, however, the reforms as declared in 1986–1987 were not sufficient in and of themselves to be the battering ram that would once and for all break down resistance to implementation of the new orthodoxy. Key aspects of fiscal policy, including treatment of capital markets, which remain poorly developed and under close governmental control, were untouched despite concerted pressure by the United States.[41] Egypt devalued its currency and established a semifloating exchange rate not to create an open, relatively unregulated market for investment capital, but to pry foreign currency away from the black market and into the national treasury. In the process the private sector was actually penalized, for its access to foreign currency was greatly reduced. Within days of the reforms businessmen were complaining bitterly that they were being forced to suspend operations because the black market had been closed down and because the bulk of foreign currency flowing into government accounts was being claimed by the public sector.[42] The Ministers of Economy and Finance declared deposits in the formal banking system were exceeding expectations, while independent economists assessed the flow as a relatively meager trickle.[43] Branches of foreign banks that since the mid-1970s had been major sources of foreign investment were essentially prevented from doing further business because they were prohibited from exchanging Egyptian for foreign currencies.[44] Various anomalies in exchange rates remained and operated to the disadvantage of the private sector. Airline companies, for example, had to continue to sell tickets at the £E1.05 rate but could only remit profits at a special rate of £E1.52. Most importantly, the so-called commercial rate of exchange, at which the government sells foreign currency to cover imports of most basic commodities, was retained. Although the government promised to phase it out, previously such promises have never been kept.[45]

The government took no immediate steps to resolve these various problems. Indeed, most of its actions suggested that fiscal policy was not to be overhauled and would remain based on the principle of "beggar thy private sector neighbor." It undermined the attractiveness of private financial instruments by declaring in the fall of 1987 that it was studying the possibility of a new bond issue to attract worker remittances.[46] In the previous year it had issued $500 million worth of such bonds, which yielded 12 percent tax-free, and were guaranteed to be immune from confiscation or seizure. They were oversubscribed. Private firms engaged in productive ventures clearly had difficulties in attracting foreign currency investments in competition with these terms. The government also continued to require banks to place hefty shares of their deposits with the Central Bank without payment of interest. It further refused to comply with demands by the IMF to allow interest rates to rise to the level of inflation so that the various distortions resulting from negative real interest rates could be eradicated. The government finally agreed to an interest rate increase of only 2 percent, indicating that it was far less interested in attracting private investments through appropriate incentives than in continuing to keep the state's interest bill low, in part through its policy of semiconfiscation of bank deposits. As a result Egyptian capital markets have not benefited from the reforms and remain small and isolated. Egypt's bourse, the oldest stock market in the Middle East, was completely unaffected by the precipitous fall of share values on world markets in October 1987. Far from being a sign of economic health, this demonstrated the extent to which Egyptian fiscal policy remains tied to the legacy of the closed economy.

Reforms other than those of fiscal policy were also of a relatively limited nature. That the new five-year plan for 1987/88–1991/92 awarded almost 40 percent of investments to the private sector should be interpreted more as a statement of the government's desire to tap private savings than as an indication that it is abandoning the public sector. Moreover, since 54 percent of all private investment in the previous five-year plan had been in housing, an increase in investment by the private sector was not likely to have an across-the-board impact.[47] The privatization of hotel management, even if it extended well beyond the half dozen government-owned hotels leased out in 1986, would not constitute a radical reform. During the Nasser era some publicly owned hotels were managed on this basis. The hotel and tourist sector more generally are akin to the oil industry in that they are more enclaves than trend-setters for the national economy. Minister of Tourism and Civil Aviation Fuad Sultan's call in 1987 to sell off the public sector was immediately countered by Mubarak, who declared that the government had no such intention.[48]

LIMITED IMPACT
OF AGRICULTURE POLICY REFORMS

Reforms in agriculture, a sector that had been targeted for special attention by USAID and the IMF because it is dominated by private producers anxious to be free of governmental controls, were tempered by countervailing measures.[49] With regard to the key issue of commodity prices, the 1986/1987 reforms institutionalized the neoclassical market pricing mechanism only very unevenly. The mixed system that came to prevail in the wake of the reforms also created some unfortunate anomalies. In the poultry industry, for example, producers were caught between the gradual removal of the subsidy on corn, the chief ingredient in chicken feed, and the continued imposition of price controls on chickens and eggs.[50] The announcement on 11 September 1987 by Minister of Agriculture Wali that as of 1 January 1988 the corn subsidy would be lifted entirely was the last straw. Those chicken and egg producers still in business (80 percent of the former and 50 percent of the latter had since 1984 ceased production) were able to secure an agreement from Wali that loan repayments would immediately be suspended for three years and that price controls on their products would soon be lifted. But the new Minister of Supply, Gamal Abd al-Dahab, whose urban consumer constituency demands cheap food, refused to cooperate, just as his predecessor Nagi Shatla had done. Abd al-Dahab instead offered the Poultry Breeder's Association a compromise whereby the Ministry of Supply would purchase 10 percent of the output of chickens and eggs to sell in the Ministry's shops and would authorize a small increase in the controlled price. Abd al-Dahab would not agree, however, to let prices be determined by market forces.[51]

Conflict between the Ministers of Agriculture and Supply over the price of poultry products is one battle in a much larger war. The Minister of Agriculture has an institutional interest in securing optimal prices for producers. That some prices were increased in 1986/1987 and others decontrolled may well reflect Wali's increased influence rather more than a broader desire in the political elite to adopt market pricing mechanisms. If so, these price reforms could be rolled back if the Ministers of Supply and Industry, whose domains are the two principal institutional interest groups for consumers of agricultural commodities, regain their normally dominant position over the Minister of Agriculture. Another aspect of the price reforms that indicates they may be temporary palliatives is that declared increases of controlled prices were, in hard currency values, nominal or even negative in light of the May devaluation. That many price increases beneficial to producers were announced just prior to the April 1987 parliamentary elections caused the opposition to deride them as government promises that were bound ultimately to be broken.[52]

Other measures indicated that the government was attempting to thwart the efforts of USAID, IMF, and other agencies to force relaxation of the control of the agricultural sector. While the government promised to comply with the USAID demand to terminate corn subsidies by the beginning of 1988, which was in accordance with a package of proposals intended by USAID to substantially reduce production of red meat, other policy initiatives appeared designed to frustrate that intent. Virtually simultaneously with the announcement that the corn subsidy would be lifted, PBDAC declared that producers of red meat would continue to be eligible for medium-term development loans that had since the late 1970s played a key role in stimulating expansion of the red meat industry.[53] That Egypt was possibly not dealing with USAID in good faith was also suggested by the fact that it originally agreed to terminate the subsidy for corn on 1 July 1987, but then delayed that measure for a further six months.

Declarations in 1986/1987 granting the private sector the right to import a range of agricultural inputs, including chemicals and fertilizer, were also severely restricted in practice. The public sector retained privileged access to foreign currency. The Ministry of Agriculture continued to subject all imported chemicals to elaborate testing procedures, a requirement that constitutes a significant and probably intentional hurdle to private sector imports. PBDAC did not reduce its demand for commissions for the distribution of privately imported inputs, which are officially stated to be 3 percent of the retail price but in fact are as high as the market will bear. Those importers who chose not to pay the "commissions" suggested confront the probability that their merchandise will sit in PBDAC storage facilities as long as it takes for it to trickle out the "back door."[54] Retail prices are not set by importers themselves but by the Office of Marketing in the Ministry of Agriculture, which has demonstrated scant regard for such factors as overheads and capital costs. It frequently set prices at unprofitable levels. But the greatest deterrent to private sector profitability is the massive leakage into the black market of subsidized inputs provided by PBDAC, where they sell at prices below those for which they can be privately imported and profitably marketed.[55] It is one thing for the government to grant permission to the private sector to import and sell agricultural inputs, but altogether another one for it to create the institutional and policy environments in which the private sector can truly flourish.

Another bone the Ministry of Agriculture has thrown to USAID and the private sector is the privatization of virtually all reclaimed land, permission for ownership there to exceed maximums declared in the agrarian reform areas, and an extension of the period of utilization from ten to forty years granted to foreigners who reclaim land. This, too, is essentially a strategy designed principally to attract capital out of investors' pockets while not diluting state control. Indeed, it may well enhance it, for the public sector land reclamation companies under the Ministry of Land Reclamation "reclaim" the land (i.e., install some irrigation equipment and maybe plant some trees or vines) and then sell it for very substantial profits that accrue to the state. Since this reclamation is mainly of virgin desert, the new owners and ownership patterns are of no threat to established agricultural communities or rural politics and land tenure patterns in the Nile Valley. In fact, virtually identical calculations in the 1960s led the government to invite the Soviet Union to demonstrate the advantages of large-scale mechanized, collectivized agriculture in newly reclaimed areas.[56] The physical remains of those efforts have now been sold off to private interests or distributed to peasants, suggesting that given another turn of Egypt's wheel of political fortune today's private farms being carved out of the desert could in some new regime be collectivized. In the meantime land tenure in the Nile Valley has remained unaffected by these experiments in the sand with capitalism and socialism.

Although the Ministry of Agriculture supported those aspects of the USAID-recommended reform package that were consistent with its institutional interests, it also took initiatives that ran counter to the thrust of those reforms. Under sustained pressure from the opposition, which had used the widening food gap as a political club with which to beat Yusuf Wali, wearing as he has the twin hats of Minister of Agriculture and Secretary General of the NDP, the government announced in 1986 a new agricultural policy that was to attain "food security." It embodied a rejection of the policy that Wali had advocated in the wake of Sadat's assassination and convinced Mubarak to adopt. This policy had entailed a downgrading of cereal production in favor of high-value human and animal feed crops. By 1987 some four fifths of the bread consumed in Egypt was baked from imported flour, agricultural exports were stagnant, Egypt's overall food dependency had grown to alarming proportions, and the opposition's indictment of Wali's failure to achieve his stated goals had to be countered. He did so by declaring what amounted to a policy of self-sufficiency through import substitution, with particular emphasis on expanding acreage under cereal crops. This ran counter to the thrust of USAID's policy recommendations that Egypt concentrate on high-value food crops for which the country enjoys a natural advantage, which is certainly not the case with wheat.

The Ministry of Agriculture was also not disengaging from direct production and marketing activities as recommended by USAID. Despite an intense effort by USAID to force the Ministry to allow the private sector to play the leading role in mechanizing agriculture, by late 1987 it had to admit defeat. A principal stated goal of Wali's new agricultural policy was to blanket the country with government-operated agricultural machinery centers, which reminded USAID staffers of the Bolsheviks' machine tractor stations. As part of its new policy of "food security," the Ministry of Agriculture began in 1986 to install and operate large numbers of greenhouses. While some were to induce the private sector to adopt plasticulture (i.e., production under plastic cover), the Ministry continued to play a significant role not only in plasticulture research but also in production. USAID's push to privatize and improve marketing of foodstuffs was sidetracked by the Ministries of Agriculture and Supply, both of which wanted a share of the marketing action. In competition with the private sector the Ministry of Supply embarked on a program of upgrading its retail outlets so that at least in urban middle-class districts they would become virtually indistinguishable from private supermarkets. The Ministry of Agriculture responded to criticism of government-controlled fruit and vegetable markets by pledging not to turn markets over to the private sector, as USAID preferred, but to build new ones under the Ministry's control on the outskirts of major cities.

Still further indication that decision makers in the agriculture sector were reluctant to endorse an across-the-board liberalization was that they did not want to be publicly associated with the leverage being applied by USAID to achieve those reforms. As a result key provisions of various agreements between the U.S. government and the Ministry of Agriculture, as well as other ministries, were not publicly announced. Following the uproar in parliament in 1984 when the Wafd objected to alleged infringements of Egypt's sovereignty contained in the self-help provisions required of Egypt in order to be eligible for U.S. Public Law 480 surplus food commodities, the government had ceased to announce in that forum annual revisions of the self-help measures.[57] In 1986 neither the Ministry of Agriculture nor the Ministry of International Cooperation wanted publicly to be associated with five major reforms included in the extension of the Small Farmer Production Project. The impasse was resolved by placing these conditions in a side letter that was not made public.[58] These practices suggest that Egyptian politicians and senior administrators do not perceive liberalization, especially when it is under U.S. auspices, as a program on which they should stake their careers. Economic substructural changes that may facilitate the eventual emergence of Albert Hirschman's predicted reform coalition may be taking place, but by 1987 economic changes had not so affected the political superstructure that reformers had the power and self-confidence to move to the center stage of Egyptian politics. Part of the explanation of the continuing weakness of the reformist trend is due to the institutional instruments through which the new orthodoxy is being disseminated.

INSTRUMENTS OF LEVERAGE

The Egyptian Military

Through its economic activities the military has direct connections with MNCs that may facilitate linkages between them and local capital.

But whether the military economy will develop into a real bridgehead or remain principally an enclave remains in question. Few MNCs have so far crossed the divide from the military into the civilian economy. This may be because of product specialization or because of comparatively unfavorable profitability in the civilian sector. Before the coalition of state, indigenous bourgeoisie, and MNCs that may be taking shape within the military economy can be further generalized, it may be the case that more reforms will be required of the civilian economy.

In the meantime those threatened by the economic and political power of the military, including a large share of the public sector and the President himself, have an interest in isolating the military and containing any spillover from its enclave economy. As discussed in Chapter 4, Mubarak has plucked projects away from the military and awarded them to the civilian administration and public sector. Among many close observers of the long-running GM negotiations with NASCO, there remains the suspicion that the agreement was finally scuttled by Mubarak himself because GM's case had been championed by Abu Ghazala and because its spinoffs benefited the military. Had the GM deal materialized in a form that involved that MNC simultaneously in automobile and military vehicle component production, it would have provided strong indication that the military would in future serve as a bridgehead for MNC penetration. That it did not eventuate in any form is indicative that barriers continue to divide the civilian from the military economy.

Other interventions by Mubarak suggest he seeks to ensure the military's isolation from non-Egyptian influences to prevent foreign contacts undermining the institution's nationalist integrity and his authority. In October 1987 Mubarak transferred Chief of Staff Ibrahim al-Arabi to the directorship of the Arab Organization for Industrialization, which is the heart of Egypt's military-industrial complex. Arabi's presence in that vital post provided Mubarak a counterweight to Abu Ghazala and his client, Minister of War Production Gamal al-Sayid. Arabi's replacement as Chief of Staff, Saif al-Din Abu Shanaf, has long had close ties to Mubarak. To prevent the military becoming too closely associated with the United States, barriers have been erected to impede U.S. access to it. U.S. military advisers and contract personnel are issued passes only for limited periods and on specific installations. If they need to gain broader access, they must lodge formal requests through the high command. After-hours fraternization between Egyptian and U.S. officers is discouraged, as are U.S. journalists' contacts with the Egyptian military. The annual Bright Star joint military maneuvers, which commenced during the Sadat era, are no longer publicized in the Egyptian media. In 1983 negotiations between Egypt and the United States for financing the upgrading of the airbase at Ras Banas were broken off because Egypt refused to grant permission for an overt U.S. presence. Mubarak steadfastly refused to yield to pressure from the Reagan Administration and from elements in the officer corps to allow the

Egyptian military to become involved in the campaign to topple Qadhafi.[59] Diversification of arms procurement, including purchase of Mirage 2000 jet fighters from France, is intended to dilute U.S. influence over the Egyptian military. All of these steps suggest that Mubarak is extremely sensitive not only to the role of the military in Egypt's foreign policy but also to any factors that may erode its commitment to the state as currently constituted. It is highly probable, therefore, that he would view with trepidation the proliferation of military-MNC contacts and their spillover into the civilian economy. His strategy of control of the military rests primarily on his indulgence of it, but the quid pro quo he will probably demand is that it remain an enclave, both politically and economically.

The "Club of Friends"

USAID, the World Bank, and many of the member states of the Paris Club agree in principle that through the application of economic pressure Egypt should be induced to liberalize. By 1985–1986 coordination between them was extensive, but there remained sufficient divisions within and between these donors and creditors to tempt Egypt to seek as an alternative to a drastic belt-tightening to maneuver between them and play one off against the other. The IMF team negotiating the standby agreement in 1986–1987, for example, eventually split over the conditions to be offered. One senior member ultimately resigned in protest over their comparative leniency. As USAID was attempting in 1986–1987 to force privatization of the supply of agricultural inputs by tying project assistance to specific policy reforms, the World Bank approved concessionary financing for construction of a network of government-operated agricultural machinery stations and for the purchase of tractors, harvesters, and so on. The Ministry of Agriculture leapt at this opportunity to perpetuate its dominant role in the countryside, to enrich those bureaucrats who would be involved in the purchase of that machinery, and to ward off USAID's assaults on it. Debt rescheduling negotiations between Egypt and its creditors in the Paris Club, which were to be completed within six months of the May 1987 standby agreement, dragged on past that deadline.

Agreement could not easily be reached because Egypt sought to take advantage of its improved economic position, because of differences of opinion within the Paris Club, and because of the "Arab factor." Kuwait, the only Arab member of the Club of Friends, is the key Arab counterbalance to pressure from OECD states. Kuwait urged its co-members in the Paris Club to accede to Egypt's requests and demonstrated its commitment by participating in a $1-billion Gulf Cooperation Council Loan to Egypt, which was announced prior to the rounds of bilateral negotiations.[60] France, the first country successfully to complete negotiations to reschedule its large debt with Egypt, abandoned its original position that interest rates be calculated at market levels and instead agreed they be paid at LIBOR (London Inter Bank Offered Rate) plus 0.25percent. With that concession in its pocket and with Kuwait's backing, Egypt in the fall of 1987 set about the task of trying to induce other creditors to accept yet further reductions in interest rates, with a figure of 3.5percent, or about half the prevailing market rate, being mentioned.[61] Simultaneously Egypt stiffened its stance against the IMF in negotiations for the second phase of the standby agreement, which was to have been concluded in October 1987. Its new strategic importance in the Gulf and its role as bulwark against Islamic fundamentalism were "intangibles" that different elements in the IMF and the Club of Friends were willing to assign greater or lesser weight, which in turn conceded to Egypt additional room to maneuver. Since that entailed little if any cost or risk to Egypt, whereas undertaking wide-ranging economic reforms clearly would, it is hardly surprising that more energy was concentrated on extracting the best possible conditions from creditors than on creating the domestic economic environment that could over the long haul reduce the need for their benevolence.

United States Agency for International Development

USAID, the largest development assistance agency operating in Egypt, embodies in microcosm deficiencies that plague most organizations utilizing economic assistance for policy leverage. The principal limitations are a lack of organizational coherence, an inability for legal and political reasons to work with forces external to the state, and the fact that even USAID's funds are insufficient and too scattered to force Egyptian policy makers to submit to the will of its bureaucrats. Of the $1.3 billion in nonmilitary economic assistance that Egypt has been receiving annually from the United States since 1984, USAID has control over some $815 million, of which only $500–700 million has been in discretionary project financing, with the remainder provided in the form of cash transfers ($115 million in 1986 and 1987) or through the Commodity Import Program.[62] The $500–700 million is divided between projects in eight categories (infrastructure, industry, agriculture and irrigation, social services, decentralization, finance and investment, science and technology, and "other"). Its impact has been further diluted by the lag time between authorization and actual disbursement. By 1983 project aid had consumed only 50 percent of allocated funds and the pipeline of unexpended assistance was $2.5 billion.[63] Moreover, USAID cannot actually withhold congressionally authorized funds if Egypt does not agree to its terms; in that extent all it can do to reach agreement on a portfolio of projects that utilize 100 percent of the funds available is to delay disbursement of the balance until the end of the financial year. Between 10 and 35 percent of USAID funds are consumed by consultancy fees, the bulk of which are paid to U.S. consultants.[64] As much as 75 percent of all U.S. economic assistance is returned to the United States through the purchase of U.S. goods and services.[65] In 1986 USAID's annual project assistance was less than the $554-million annual interest bill on Egypt's military debt to the United States. So, while the U.S. provided Egypt between 1979 and 1987 some $20 billion in economic assistance (accounting for about 20 percent of all U.S. foreign assistance in that period and constituting between 5.7 percent and 9.7 percent of Egypt's GNP—depending on exchange rate and year), because these moneys are Egypt's "peace dividend" and replacement of Arab funds lost as a result of the peace treaty with Israel and because of other constraints, they cannot easily be manipulated to affect Egyptian domestic economic policy.[66]

The complex political-administrative environment within which it operates and its internal fragmentation further vitiate USAID's attempts to exert policy leverage. Senior staff in the Cairo USAID office perceive themselves as caught between an Egyptian government that wants to convert all economic assistance to cash transfers, thereby terminating USAID's presence, and important elements in the U.S. government who would like to do the same. The U.S. Embassy in Cairo is necessarily more concerned with the near rather than medium or long term future of Egypt and is, therefore, more sensitive to Egypt's viewpoint and more apprehensive about the large U.S. presence associated with USAID. U.S. diplomats in Egypt, many of whom are Arabists, generally have a low regard for their USAID counterparts, who are development rather than area specialists. USAID policy makers fear that the Embassy will not provide backing for their demands or that the State Department or the Egyptian government will, through their own channels to the White House or U.S. politicians, influence matters in a way unfavorable to USAID's cause. Visiting U.S. politicians are a constant worry to USAID, for it is feared they will curry favor with the Egyptian government by pledging to increase the cash component of the assistance program.[67]

USAID's anxiety about its backing by other branches of the U.S. government has the added effect of causing it to adopt a cautious approach in the allocation of project assistance. Fearful of the impact of negative newscoverage of its efforts, particularly in the United States, and very keen to have its projects favorably described, the public relations aspects of potential projects have become major considerations in the approval process. USAID has been associated with U.S.-built buses that rapidly and noisily disintegrated on Cairo's potholed streets; a cement factory that required a decade to construct; automated bakeries that did not bake bread; fish farms that produced no fish but did give rise to embezzlement charges against the U.S. project director and some of his Egyptian counterparts; a housing project that consumed more than $100 million without producing a single new dwelling unit; a sewage project in Alexandria that dumped effluent on the city's beaches; pumping stations along the length of the Nile that remained uncompleted years after the pumps had been delivered; and various other embarrassing debacles that received greater or lesser attention in the Egyptian and U.S. media.[68] As the number of such foul-ups has mounted over the

years and USAID's position become more embattled, so has it become
increasingly wary of projects that might attract negative comments in
the media. A proposal to provide financial assistance for the construction
of schools adjacent to mosques was rejected because Cairo's USAID
director feared some U.S. journalist might associate in print U.S. taxpayers'
moneys with Islamic fundamentalism.[69] Conversely, favorable comments
by a congressman who had visited farmer beneficiaries of the Small
Farmer Production Project and its generally positive treatment by the
U.S. press caused USAID to vastly upgrade that project and use it as
the vehicle through which large blocks of funds could be dumped into
the agricultural sector.[70]

The Egyptian government has exploited USAID's vulnerability to
negative public relations by tolerating and maybe even fostering exposes.
In the fall of 1982 *al-Ahram al-Iqtisadi* ran a series of articles critical of
USAID operations, including its "suborning" of Egyptian researchers
and accumulation of what was alleged to be vital security information.[71]
Although Lutfi Abd al-Azim, the then-editor of that weekly magazine,
was subsequently dismissed because of his leftist inclinations and replaced
by Issam Rifat, a comparatively conservative economist associated with
the American University in Cairo, continued leakages to the opposition
press of damaging information about USAID's activities suggest the
government did not call the hounds off the chase altogether. While some
of the allegations in the opposition press are so farfetched as to be
utterly preposterous to all but the most fanatical anti-Americans, many
are close to the target and achieve results. The ceaseless campaign
against USAID's financing of trilateral projects involving U.S., Israeli,
and Egyptian personnel and technology as part of the normalization
process prescribed in the Camp David accords has contributed to Cairo
USAID's increasing reluctance to collaborate with Israel.[72] The attack by
Islamicists on USAID's support for birth control, especially its involvement
with the al-Azhar University Hospital, has had similar results. Criticism
of the quality of construction of parking garages in Cairo and of the
proposal to construct a freeway from Cairo to Aswan contributed to
USAID's downgrading of its commitment to the motor vehicle related
transportation infrastructure.

USAID Caught in the Crossfire. External interventions into USAID's
decision-making processes at both the Washington and Cairo ends of
the bureaucratic chain impair the agency's ability to target its resources
to achieve maximum policy leverage. In Washington various individuals
and groups with an interest in Egypt, USAID, the development process
more generally, or just their own professional or pecuniary advancement
work through USAID, Congress, the State Department, and/or the White
House to achieve their ends. Egyptian policy makers and potential
beneficiaries of USAID projects follow these interventions avidly and
seek to turn them to their own purposes. The long-running battle over
USAID's agricultural program provides an example of how these inter-

ventions cause USAID to be consumed with its internal affairs, thereby reducing its policy leverage.

The initial phase of USAID's agricultural program was intended to facilitate information-gathering. That stage terminated more or less simultaneously with the transition from the Carter to the Reagan Administration. As Cairo USAID was beginning to turn its attention more systematically to how it might use its newly acquired information to allocate its resources in such a way as to encourage Egypt to create a policy environment more conducive to enhanced agricultural production, a lobby comprised of U.S. agricultural experts hoping to become involved in USAID projects entered the scene. Access was provided through Professor E. T. York, a prominent Florida-based educator who had a tie to the new President through their mutual friend Peter McPherson, Reagan's newly appointed USAID director. Within months of taking office, McPherson dispatched York as head of Reagan's Presidential Commission to investigate USAID's flagging agricultural program in Egypt and make recommendations. From the old school of thought about agricultural development, York firmly believed that effective extension is the key to rapid growth for it provides the needed linkage between research station and farmers' fields. Enhancing Egypt's research and extension capabilities would also involve significant numbers of U.S. experts.

This approach was anathema to many on the Cairo USAID staff, who were in fact more in tune with the Reagan Administration's commitment to privatization than was York himself. They had become disillusioned with extension activities in Egypt, which they saw as part of the Nasserite system of control over producers. They believed that sufficient biological and other agricultural technology appropriate for Egypt was already available; that a further infusion of "white-skinned" agricultural advisers was counterproductive; and that USAID's funds should be used in carrot-and-stick fashion to cajole the government into lifting its heavy hand off the agricultural sector. But these USAID employees lacked York's access to Washington-based decision makers, so the report of his Presidential Commission came to serve as blueprint for the agricultural program.

For the next three to four years a bureaucratic war raged between those who were for or against the York approach. The casualty rate among Cairo USAID agricultural staff became so high that from 1982 to 1985 tenure in the key positions of agricultural program director and chief agricultural economist averaged a little more than one year. But the dogged perseverance of those opposed to York finally paid off. The bulk of the USAID bureaucracy gradually swung behind the idea that agricultural extension as practiced in Egypt was inimical to liberalization and should not, therefore, serve as the focal point for U.S. assistance. While York made one last effort in the summer of 1985 to rally support at the Cairo end for his approach and continued to receive back-channel communications from his sole remaining loyalist in the Cairo USAID agricultural program as late as 1987, the signing of the new agricultural program by the Egyptian government in October 1986 marked the end of the York period.

For their part the Egyptian government and those Egyptians involved in the administration of agriculture sought to turn this domestic squabble in USAID to their own advantage. They backed York, for the extension department was indeed a key element in the agricultural control system that few in government wanted to dismantle. Nor did administrators or policy makers want the anti-York Americans, who were committed to tying USAID projects to policy reform, to prevail. Additionally, individuals and institutions within the Egyptian agricultural bureaucracy struggled among themselves to extract maximum benefit from the USAID largesse. The Agricultural Research Center, an institute that employs 25,000 staff and that is autonomous from the Ministry of Agriculture, had become the primary beneficiary of USAID projects. It, rather than the Ministry, was assigned responsibility for conducting USAID-financed research, for which it was provided lavishly equipped laboratories and other research facilities. The Agricultural Research Center also used the argument that close cooperation between research and extension would expedite the dissemination of new technologies to pry much of the authority over the extension service away from the Ministry. Not surprisingly the Director of the Center, Dr. Ibrahim Shahata, became closely associated with York. Minister of Agriculture Wali was furious that Shahata had snatched these plums out of his grasp and set about the task of levering Shahata out of his post. Wali also sought to regain exclusive control over the extension department, first by cultivating York and then, when it became evident to Wali that York's influence was waning, by approaching York's opponents in the USAID mission. Only when it became absolutely clear in 1986 that USAID was going to abandon its previous commitment to extension though did Wali change his tack and similarly disassociate himself from the extension program and seek funds for other activities that he and the Ministry, rather than Shahata and the Center, controlled.[73]

Out of this tangled web of policy making and patronage an agricultural program finally did emerge that was more or less supportive of the overall strategy of inducing Egypt to adopt the new orthodoxy of development. This cumbersome policy process, however, had resulted in wastage of funds, excessive personnel turnover, and delay. Moreover, USAID's internal bickering had enabled the Egyptian side actively to engage in the agency's internal policy-making processes. Across the entire front of USAID's activities similar penetration has been facilitated by two interrelated factors. The first director of Cairo USAID, L. Dean Brown, surrendered control of the project development fund to Egypt so that it could participate in the formulation of projects. With that decision USAID lost the financial resources required effectively to plan new projects, thereby further weakening its position vis à vis the Egyptian government.

Searching for Allies. USAID's potential leverage is further limited by legal restrictions contained in its formal agreement with the Egyptian government and by associated political constraints. USAID must, according to the terms of the agreement, work directly with the Egyptian government, within which individuals associated with and committed to the legacy of Arab Socialism remain. This results in the paradoxical situation in which USAID and its Egyptian allies are seeking to liberalize the political economy with Nasserist institutions and loyalists. Those whose power rests on control of the state and in turn on the state's control over the economy stand between USAID and the secular bourgeois opposition, whose interests are supportive of the new orthodoxy of development. Extensive contacts between USAID and the political opposition would, of course, be construed by the Egyptian government as unacceptable meddling in its domestic affairs. For the same reason, the U.S. Embassy is circumspect in its dealings with the opposition. Organizations that constitute the official U.S. presence therefore cannot play an active role as reform-monger, helping to cobble together a broadly based reform coalition of those elements, whether of the government or opposition, that want to liberalize the political economy. Indeed, it may be the case that economic assistance, much the largest share of which goes directly to the state, serves to perpetuate its dominant role.

Although the political superstructure is more or less out-of-bounds to USAID, the economic substructure is accessible. But is USAID's increasing allocation of funds to the private sector likely to bring about economic conditions that will result in political demands for liberalization? In the view of *dependistas*, such assistance will lead to the emergence of a powerful comprador bourgeoisie that will ultimately attain the political clout required to undo the last vestiges of Nasserism. In fact, however, USAID private sector assistance is presently too limited to have a substantial impact, economically or politically. The amount of assistance that reaches Egyptian businessmen is actually even less than the relatively limited funds allocated to the private sector, for U.S.-based companies active in Egypt also have access through partners in joint ventures to such assistance. While GM is the most noteworthy case, there are many smaller examples. The GM case also illustrates the reluctance of Egyptian entrepreneurs to commit capital to long-term investments in industry, even when such investments provide access to concessionary financing from USAID. A major element of the GM deal was to be associated component manufacturing by up to twenty joint-venture companies formed of Egyptian investors and foreign corporations. Incentives to Egyptian participants were to be offered by USAID in the form of concessionary loans made even more attractive because they were to provide access to dollars at the £E1.35 rate at a time when the prevailing black market rate was £E2. Nevertheless, over a year after the GM deal had been signed, there had been few demonstrations of interest by potential investors.[74]

Although a comprehensive profile of individual recipients of USAID private sector assistance programs is not available, it is evident that many of those beneficiaries are in fact entrenched in the state apparatus and are, therefore, highly unlikely to change their basic outlook as a result of a handout from USAID. The chairman of the *Shura* Council's Foreign Relations Committee is a case in point. From a large and powerful family that has been politically active throughout this century and that has been associated with the public, private, and Islamic sector, depending on their relative profitability at any one time, this NDP loyalist, whose personal wealth is in the millions, has had two sizable loans from USAID. He has utilized these to invest in irrigation equipment for large tracts of newly reclaimed land that he and his family own, one block of which he sold off after equipment financed by USAID was installed.

Because a large proportion of USAID private sector assistance has been utilized by those well connected within the state apparatus to turn quick profits, frequently in importation, the head economist of USAID Cairo and the majority of the six deputy directors, all of whom are advocates of liberalization, oppose the private sector loan program. They believe it provides essentially parasitical elements guaranteed and quick profits and minimal advantage for the national economy.[75] As far as the Egyptian recipients are concerned, it is doubtful if USAID is buying converts to capitalism. More likely they are thankful for their contacts that put them in touch with USAID. The USAID private sector loan programs, in sum, are in their present form unlikely to so alter the economic substructure that political support for the new orthodoxy of development will become irresistible. Indeed, USAID's programs may be having a negative impact by encouraging the perpetuation of parasitical economic activities and providing sufficient funds to obviate Egypt's need to seek relief from creditors.

POLITICS AS USUAL

The year 1966 was the high-water mark of Arab Socialism. As a result of an incident in the Delta village of Kamshish, which pitted radical cadres in the ASU against remnants of the old landlord class, the political elite had to decide whether to embark on an unprecedented mobilization of workers and peasants against "exploiting classes" or to fall back on the army and the state apparatus to contain these antagonistic social forces. In the event, self-preservation dictated that the weak authoritarian state had to chose the latter, for to throw its weight behind one social class or another would have resulted in the transformation of the state itself into a mobilizational or much more conservative one, probably displacing the incumbent elite in the process.[76]

The collapse of the GM-NASCO agreement in 1987 may have marked the outermost swing of the pendulum in the opposite direction. Had the agreement been implemented, it would have signaled that the coalition of state, bourgeoisie, and MNCs was finally emerging in tangible form and that Egypt was at least tentatively embarking on a path of dependent development. The agreement may have bridged the divide between the military and civilian sectors and paved the way for other MNCs to move between the two. It would have subordinated the public sector firm NASCO to GM, on which it would have become dependent for technology, organization and recruitment of labor, marketing, and access to capital.[77] It may have attracted into Egypt other MNCs involved in component manufacturing. Finally, it would have demonstrated that bilateral economic assistance from the Untied States could act as the necessary lubricant in linkages between MNCs and Egyptian firms. That the deal misfired suggests that the necessary reform coalition, consisting of elements drawn from the state and the bourgeoisie, was too weak to overcome opposition mounted from various quarters. Confronted with the choice of swinging to the right, the weak authoritarian state once again chose to follow a course of politics as usual, in so doing preserving its essential character.[78]

Failure of the GM-NASCO agreement to come to fruition is not the only indicator that the Mubarak regime has opted for the tried and tested over the unknown of wide-ranging economic and political reforms. Patterns of recruitment into the political elite indicate that the President is anxious to retain a balance between reformist and statist tendencies. Prime Minister Kamal Hassan Ali, a dedicated supporter of the new orthodoxy of development, was jettisoned from the cabinet before he could have a significant impact. His successors, Ali Lutfi and Atif Sidqi, while attuned to the need for fiscal austerity and significant reform of the public sector, subsidies, and so on, are nevertheless not ideologues. They are pragmatists who do not reject all aspects of Nasserism out of hand, in part because both have ties to its theory and supporters.[79] Prior to his appointment as Prime Minister, Ali Lutfi was best known for his campaign against tax evasion during his brief tenure as Minister of Finance under Sadat. Lutfi had personally recorded license plates of late-model Mercedes, traced their ownership, and inspected taxation records to see if the owners had filed returns and declared incomes sufficient to indulge their known tastes in automobiles. Both Lutfi and Sidqi were strongly backed by Usama al-Baz, the most influential adviser to Mubarak with Nasserist leanings. In addition to being director of the Central Organization for Accounting before being appointed Prime Minister, Sidqi was also a member of a consulting firm that included Rifat al-Mahgub, the speaker of parliament with strong Nasserist connections, and Mustafa al-Said, the controversial Minister of Economy who failed in an attempt to undermine the power of *munfatihun* in the early months of 1985.

Sidqi's recruitment was also due to the fact that he was a member of the French-speaking elite recruitment pool. The French connection was seized upon by Mubarak to create an obstacle between his Prime Minister and the United States, thereby reducing its influence over the government. Mubarak bolstered Sidqi's defenses by appointing to the cabinet formed on 12 November 1986 five other ministers whose advanced degrees were from France or, in the case of Minister of Education Ahmad Fathi Surur, had served in diplomatic posts in Geneva and Paris but never in English-speaking countries. Of the other five new entrants to that cabinet, only two had U.S. degrees. This was the largest contingent of Francophiles to enter the cabinet since the *ancien regime*. That three of its members constituted the core of the government economic team (Prime Minister and Ministers of Economy and Public Finance) was of added importance. In response to this tactic the U.S. Embassy and Cairo USAID began to comb their ranks for French-speaking expertise, the relative paucity of which enhanced the gambit's effectiveness. Maybe because of this Mubarak included yet another French-educated technocrat in the group of four new ministers recruited into the cabinet formed immediately after his reelection in October 1987.[80]

It is also noteworthy that the two leading proponents in the cabinet of closer economic relations with the United States and of radical reforms consistent with the new orthodoxy have seen their once rapidly rising career trajectories gradually flatten out. Atif Ubaid, who has been backed by USAID and the U.S. Embassy, rose meteorically in the early Mubarak period and was predicted by some to succeed Kamal Hassan Ali. However, he was passed over for Ali Lutfi and subsequently for Atif Sidqi. The U.S. connection, which had been an advantage in the early stages of his career, was clearly a liability in Ubaid's quest for the higher post. That was also the case with regard to Fuad Sultan's political career. Dedicated to privatization, he was kept away from the sensitive economic portfolio and given instead the much less visible and crucial Tourism and Civil Aviation ministries.

Recruitment into the NDP and from that party into parliament further suggests that Mubarak encourages the statist counterbalance to the reformist trend. From NDP Secretary General Yusuf Wali on down through the ranks of the party committee chairmen and provincial secretaries, the majority of incumbents are still apparatchiks, a large percentage of whom began their political careers in Nasser's ASU. While most are from the bourgeoisie and some have benefited directly from the privatization of patronage, it is their penetration of the state apparatus that has provided access to resources, a fact that they can hardly ignore. Most, however, are willing to adopt the style of reformers if that is necessary to obtain further patronage. It is that posturing that attracts such outside actors as USAID. Yusuf Wali, for example, has appeared to many USAID officials as a dedicated reformer because of his advocacy of raising agricultural prices. But these and other reformist positions he takes partly out of the imperatives of his agricultural portfolio. Additionally, there is the strong possibility that he and other members of the elite are posed by Mubarak as pro-U.S., just as Nasser had Zakariya Muhyi al-Din play a similar role and Ali Sabri a pro-Soviet one in order to boost Cairo's ties to the two superpowers. Wali and other politicians of course use their access to foreign-source patronage to their own advantage, but this is not by any means proof of their dedication to a reform program. Most no doubt appreciate that the fit between any theory of development propagated on an international scale with the economic and political realities of their particular environment is sufficiently poor to make it very risky indeed to tie one's career to an abstract conceptualization that in practice may not work.[81] It can be anticipated that most of Egypt's politicians will not commit themselves on a programmatic basis to a reform coalition, but will take their stances issue by issue according to prevailing circumstances. As a result the pace of change will remain moderate, and the possibility of an ultimate breakthrough is not great.

The assumption that brief training of officers and civilian administrators will have significant policy implications over the long haul may also be fallacious. The short duration of many such programs causes recipients to consider them as pleasant interludes from their careers. The Peace Fellowship Program, for example, imposed a one-year maximum period of U.S. residence, too short a period for attendance in degree programs. For most it became an extended holiday.[82] But even those officers and civilians who are more thoroughly acculturated to the United States as a result of a significant period of residence and involvement in U.S. institutions do not necessarily constitute a dynamic force for change within their own cultural and institutional environments. The U.S. colonel in charge of the Land Forces Military Assistance Program bemoans that most returnee officers quickly reassimilate to the prevailing milieu of the Egyptian officer corps, which he adjudges as authoritarian and stifling of initiative.[83] A frequent consultant to USAID's educational program who has worked with many young returnee Ph.D. students from the United States finds them in private to be outgoing, analytical, and creative. But when dealing with the same individuals in the presence of their administrative peers and superiors, they become deferential, uncritical and reserved.[84] The norms to which these young administrators have been exposed in U.S. educational institutions are incompatible with the Egyptian bureaucratic environment and, accordingly, are shed. The head economist of USAID Cairo compares Egypt unfavorably to Southeast Asian nations in the ability and willingness of those in the political and administrative elites to reach down into the system and pull up those young recruits with expertise acquired overseas who exhibit competence and dynamism. To him the comparative inflexibility of Egyptian administrative structures strongly militates against the contribution of foreign training to systemic reform.[85]

The Washington-Cairo relationship is insufficiently developed to provide a broad-based stimulus for the reform of the Egyptian political economy. The 150 or so permanent USAID staffers in Cairo, even when backed by more than $500 million annually in semidiscretionary "patronage," are no substitute for the density of business, political, and even ethnic community ties that link many Latin American states to the U.S. Members of U.S. strategic business and political elites who are closely associated with and who benefit substantially from U.S.-Egyptian relations are very few indeed. A comparison to U.S.-Iranian relations during the era of the Shah is instructive. While David Rockefeller, the veritable personification of the U.S. financial system, has made precisely one business trip to Egypt, and that during the Sadat period, he was in effect the Shah's banker and was closely associated with all aspects of U.S.-Iranian relations, as the decision to admit the Shah to the United States for medical treatment in 1979 revealed.[86] The Iranian lobby in the United States during the era of the Shah was quarterbacked by the effervescent and big-spending Ardeshir Zahedi, Iran's ambassador in Washington. His efforts and those of the lobby he headed dwarfed the subsequent Egyptian-U.S. connection. The Egyptian lobby, in fact, consists of little more than a small consulting firm and the low-key Egyptian diplomatic presence. There is simply no equivalent to the network of supporters in U.S. business and political life that fanned out from the Iranian Embassy and who provided automatic congressional majorities for Iranian requests for the purchase of such items as advanced armaments. U.S.-based MNCs are disinterested in Egypt, as declining attendance at annual Joint Business Council meetings attests.[87] While profits can be made in Egypt, for almost all U.S.-based non-oil MNCs those profits depend on USAID or military assistance financing. For a variety of reasons, U.S. corporations that obtain contracts payable by USAID and military assistance are remarkably few in number.[88] Even if Egypt truly desired to broaden the base of its relations with the United States to include the U.S. corporate world, the lack of attractiveness of the Egyptian market combined with the scarcity of natural resources and other factors that impede competitive export-oriented manufacturing would continue to militate against widescale MNC involvement.

Mubarak's primary concern is to achieve balance between the reformist and statist tendencies rather than to build a dominant coalition of one or the other. He repeatedly has distanced himself from calls to sell off the public sector. His preferred phrase in 1987 was that the public and private sectors should be "equal partners." He has no compelling reason to forsake the relative safety of a compromise between the statist and reformist trends for a wholehearted endorsement of the latter. He lacks the charisma and even the legitimacy required to play that sort of innovative leadership role. His reelection campaign in 1987 focused on his ability to unite Egyptians rather than on leading them in a new direction, although he did chide them to produce more. The turnout for the presidential referendum on 5 October was, as usual, low. Although Minister of Interior Zaki Badr announced that 88 percent of the 14 million eligible voters had voted and that 97 percent cast ballots for

Mubarak, Western diplomatic sources put the turnout rate at less than 25 percent.[89] Rallies intended to build up enthusiasm for his candidature were sparsely attended, stage-managed affairs.[90] The possibility that Mubarak might try to realign the party system and draw together elements from the NDP and the opposition who truly support wide-ranging reforms is unlikely not only because of his relative weakness but because of the persistence of bitter animosities and rivalries that divide those various forces. That Mubarak might try to accomplish such a reorganization by permitting truly free elections that would assume the character of classic "ruralizing" elections that have occurred in Turkey and elsewhere and succeeded in placing democracy on reasonably secure footings was made even more improbable by his postponement for one year of local council elections that were to be held in the fall of 1987.[91]

Mubarak, in sum, is a weak leader of a weak state. The consequences of this match for domestic and foreign policy are the same—namely, that prevarication, balance and counterbalance of contending forces, and subterfuge will prevail over declared and dramatic policy initiatives. Mubarak will continue to seek to maneuver between the contending domestic political forces while trying to impose greater financial austerity in order to reduce the budget deficit and overseas borrowings, just as he will seek to continue to maneuver between his foreign creditors. So far the relative fragmentation of both the domestic political opposition and of the Club of Friends, combined with the sudden increase in "rents" in 1987, has made this course of action tenable. Even if it were not, however, the new orthodoxy of development would not be the only remaining alternative.

NOTES

1. John Waterbury, *The Egypt of Nasser and Sadat: The Political Economy of Two Regimes* (Princeton: Princeton University Press, 1983), p. 434. On Latin American dependent development see *ibid.*, pp. 3–40; and Peter Evans, *Dependent Development: The Alliance of Multinational, State, and Local Capital in Brazil* (Princeton: Princeton University Press, 1979).

2. The government, however, refused to approve the sale on the grounds that al-Rayan was not a suitable partner for such a venture. In June 1987, Chase Manhattan sold its 49 percent stake in Chase National Bank of Egypt, while First Chicago was rumored to be trying to sell its 20 percent interest in Misr International Bank. See *Middle East Economic Digest (MEED)* (8 August 1987). See also *Economist Intelligence Unit Country Report: Egypt*, 3 (1987). Profits for the leading joint-venture banks fell by about one-third in 1986. See *MEED* (26 September 1987). The refusal by the government to allow branches of foreign banks operating in Egypt to deal in local currency placed them at such a competitive disadvantage that by 1986–1987 none were performing well.

3. "Economic Trends Report: Egypt," U.S. Embassy, 17 April 1984, cited in Marvin G. Weinbaum, *Egypt and the Politics of U.S. Aid* (Boulder: Westview Press, 1986), p. 65. Most joint ventures established under the provision of Law 43 of 1974 have been locally financed. See Simon Commander, *The State and*

Agricultural Development in Egypt Since 1973, (London: Ithaca Press, 1987), pp. 16–17.

4. Safeway has a management contract for three supermarkets owned by a Libyan expatriate in Cairo. Paradoxically, all fresh fruits and vegetables marketed in these stores are produced by an Israeli agribusiness company operating in Ismailiya.

5. Ismail Osman, nephew of Osman Ahmad Osman, is the principal local shareholder in the joint-venture firm that produces Schweppes products. For several years, he has been the most persistent and outspoken critic of the government's policy of taxing soft drinks and imposing price controls on them. In 1987 Osman was seeking to sell his share in the firm.

6. For that estimate, I am indebted to Robert Mitchell, Senior Project Officer, USAID, Cairo.

7. Within a year of becoming President, Mubarak had promulgated a new investment law that extended the privileges granted to foreign investors to Egyptian private investors. "National capitalists" have continued to receive relatively favorable treatment since that time. For a general discussion of the relationship between government, national capital, and foreign capital in Egypt, see Kate Gillespie, *The Tripartite Relationship: Government, Foreign Investors, and Local Investors During Egypt's Economic Opening* (New York: Praeger, 1984).

8. Such views are frequently expressed in *al-Ahali* and *al-Shaab* and occasionally within the government press. For a typical indictment of U.S. economic assistance and MNCs, see al-Sayid al-Kholi, "Development . . . and the Mirage of Trans-National Corporations," *al-Ahram al-Iqtisadi* (15 December 1986). I am indebted to al-Sayid al-Kholi for his explanation of the views of Egyptian *dependistas*.

9. The figures on Egypt's indebtedness lend support to this proposition. Egypt's debt to the United States alone in 1987 was about $9.5 billion, or about one-half of all U.S. military and civilian aid to Egypt since 1979, the year in which that aid was very substantially increased. The total interest payable on that debt will, when the loans are finally discharged, amount to $9.8 billion, or some $300 million more than the principal. *Economist Intelligence Unit Country Profile: Egypt (1987–88)*, p. 43.

10. Marvin G. Weinbaum, "Dependent Development and U.S. Economic Aid to Egypt," *International Journal of Middle East Studies*, 18 (1986), pp. 119–134.

11. This interpretation is based on discussions with officials of the IMF, the World Bank, USAID, and other bilateral assistance programs, on documents produced by those agencies, and on public statements by involved officials. U.S. Ambassador Frank Wisner's speech to the American-Egyptian Chamber of Commerce on 26 October 1987 is typical of the latter. Wisner stated: "While Egypt has the talent and the resources to accomplish so much, it needs a commitment from both business and government to mobilize its resources for export-led growth. In an open economy, Egypt's new generation of entrepreneurs and their American and foreign partners [sic] will serve the public interest by serving their own . . . Egypt, and especially the Egyptian private sector, with encouragement from the government, must strive to get onto the new industrial bandwagon early. To meet this challenge . . . other steps will be needed. These include: First, an intensified effort by the government to remove obstacles to trade and investment, and to create the climate and policies necessary to free the market and encourage the private sector; Second, a commitment by private investors—Egyptian, American and foreign [sic]—to act as partners in growth." *Middle East Times* (1–7 November 1987).

12. Egypt's export earnings in 1981 of £E2.29 billion were only exceeded again four years later—in 1985—when they reached £E2.63 billion. In both those years, exports amounted to only 37 percent of imports. In addition, oil's share of total exports climbed steadily in the 1980s, reaching 67 percent in 1985. Industrial products, of which about $300 million have been exported annually in the 1980s, slipped to 6 percent of total exports in 1985. Agricultural production has been growing at about 3 percent annually since the mid-1970's, a rate below that of rising demand for food. As a result, Egypt's food gap has continued to widen in the 1980s.

13. Heba A. Handoussa, "Conflicting Objectives in the Egyptian American Aid Relationship " in Earl L. Sullivan, ed., *Impact of Development Assistance on Egypt* (Cairo: Cairo Papers in Social Science of the American University in Cairo, 7, 3, 1984), pp. 84–94.

14. Weinbaum, *Egypt and the Politics of U.S. Aid*, p. 76.

15. Christopher S. Wren, "U.S. Is Re-orienting Civil Aid to Egypt," *New York Times* (31 August 1986).

16. *FY 1986–1987 Action Plan* (Cairo: USAID/Egypt, 5 March 1986).

17. I would like to thank William Janssen, Deputy Director for Agriculture, and Kenneth Wiegand, Senior Agricultural Economist, USAID Cairo, for information on the policy objectives contained in the SFPP.

18. In September 1987, for example, the World Bank held out the prospect of large sectoral loans for agriculture, industry, and energy, possibly amounting to $1 billion, but requiring of Egypt agreement "on certain measures that would revitalise the economy and lead to recovery over several years." Those measures included large increases in energy prices and various policies favorable to the private sector. See *MEED* (19 September 1987).

19. *Country Profile: Egypt 1987–88*, p. 42.

20. *Middle East Times* (14–20 September 1986). See also Aisha Ibrahim, "Public Sector Hotels Turned over to Foreign Operators," *Middle East Times* (8–14 February 1987).

21. For Wali's declaration see the interview with him in *Middle East Times* (16–22 March 1986).

22. Imam Ahmed, "Egypt's New Government Moves Confidently to Resolve Old Problems," *Middle East Times* (25–31 October 1987). In an effort to contain inflation, the Central Bank decreed that banks not increase their loan portfolios by more than 2.5 percent for the first half of 1987. That decree was subsequently extended to the end of 1987, although several banks were granted exemptions and their new loan ceilings rose to 5–6 percent. See *MEED* (5 September 1987).

23. Ahmed, "Egypt's New Government Moves Confidently."

24. This measure received Mubarak's strong personal endorsement and was emphasized by him during a lengthy cabinet meeting. See Makram Muhammad Ahmad, "How Mubarak Holds His Ministers Accountable," *al-Musawwar* (7 August 1987).

25. Hani El Banna, "Egypt Reformulates Agricultural Policy to Attract Investors," *Middle East Times* (6–12 September 1987).

26. Redha Helal, "Mubarak Reiterates: The Public Sector Is Not for Sale," *Middle East Times* (11–17 October 1987).

27. Albert O. Hirschman, *Journeys Toward Progress: Studies of Economic Policy Making in Latin America* (New York: The Twentieth Century Fund, 1963), pp. 251–275.

28. The decision to permit Egypt to produce the M1 Abrams tank provides a good example of how U.S. military assistance is facilitating the emergence of a powerful coalition comprised of the Egyptian military, private, joint venture, and quasi-public sector concerns, U.S. weapons manufacturers, and other MNCs. The General Dynamics M1-A1 tank, if the agreement eventually comes to fruition, will be produced in a factory for which the military in October 1987 let the contract for construction to Osman's Arab Contractors. This factory, which is also to be used to produce other armored vehicles, is being equipped with mechanical and electrical machinery from one or more of the following companies: Taiwan's Ret-Ser Engineering Agency; Italy's Ital group; and/or a German joint venture comprised of Siemens and Thyssen. *MEED* (27 June 1987 and 17 October 1987).

29. In 1987 Egypt's military debt to the West stood at $11 billion, or more than one-quarter of the country's total debts. *Country Report: Egypt*, p. 15.

30. Defense expenditures in the mid-1980's amounted to 9 percent of GNP, the same proportion that prevailed just after the 1973 October war. Defense spending exceeds that on health, housing, education, and social services combined by over 50 percent and is about one-half of the total of public sector investments. Commander, *The State and Agricultural Development in Egypt Since 1973*, p. 73. The resumption of delivery of Mirage 2000s in the wake of the IMF agreement suggests that belt-tightening required as a result of that agreement and subsequent bilateral negotiations is not going to be at the expense of the military.

31. Peter Gajevsky, Chief Economist, USAID Cairo, interview (20 January 1986). This view is widely held among USAID officials.

32. For information on the role of the U.S. Embassy in establishing the American-Egyptian Chamber of Commerce, I am indebted to Anne Wolfe, a founder of that organization and President, Professional Business Services, Egypt.

33. For a fascinating account of this period, see David Landes, *Bankers and Pashas: International Finance and Economic Imperialism in Egypt* (Cambridge: Harvard University Press, 1958).

34. Egypt's indebtedness over the long term can probably be managed without great difficulty. 80 percent of its public debt is owed to official creditors and the effective interest rate on past debt is under 4 percent. Debt servicing, which in 1987 reached 29 percent of export earnings, has been growing and is now high but not disastrously so. It is in the short term, until the end of the 1980s, that Egypt confronts severe difficulties in debt servicing. In June 1986, Egypt's short-term obligations were $4.7 billion and debt arrears $4.3 billion. In early 1987, Egypt was about 20 months behind in payments of supplier credits worth over $8 billion. *Country Profile: Egypt (1987–88)*, p. 45.

35. In May of 1987, the Gulf Cooperation Council approved a $1 billion loan to Egypt to assist it in repaying its military debt. *Arab News* (16 May 1987), cited in *The Middle East Journal*, 41, 4 (Autumn 1987), p. 600.

36. According to one Western journalist, "The IMF Agreement is probably the feeblest in recent memory. The easy terms, said by Cairo diplomats to be 'unprecedented' in their leniency, drove a senior IMF executive to resign in protest." Peter Kemp, "Egypt: A Very Soft Deal," *Midddle East International* 29 (May 1987).

37. The value of net oil exports in the first half of 1987 totaled almost as much as the surplus in crude oil trade in all of 1986. The figures are $684 million and $686 million, respectively. *MEED* (10 October 1987). Tourist visits were up by 60 percent in the first six months of 1987 compared to the same

period in 1986. *MEED* (5 September 1987). Suez Canal tolls continued their gradual rise and reached $1.1 billion for the 1986–1987 fiscal year. While worker remittances may not have increased significantly, as a result of the May reforms a higher percentage began to pass through the official banking system, thereby making more foreign currency available to the government.

38. Redha Helal, "Agreement of Debt Rescheduling Unlikely to Be Finalized in October," *Middle East Times* (25–31 October 1987).

39. *MEED* (5 September 1987).

40. Indeed, by November refinancing had been agreed with the French, Spanish, and Americans. Negotiations with other members of the Paris Club were more or less on track.

41. USAID has for several years been seeking to develop a project to assist Egypt's Capital Markets Authority in obtaining leverage to liberalize government control over capital markets and to adopt supportive fiscal policies. That liberalization and development of capital markets are central to U.S. concerns is suggested by the remarks of Ambassador Frank Wisner to the American-Egyptian Chamber of Commerce, in which he stated that the new reforms should include "the mobilization of capital through the development of new financial instruments—government securities, commercial paper, common stock, negotiable certificates of deposit and bankers' acceptances. Debt instruments, such as bonds and mortgages, can be improved by making their yield more attractive. The stock exchange needs to be activated by easing the rules by which shares are traded." Cited in *Middle East Times* (1–7 November 1987).

42. The former director of the Central Bank also complained that the private-sector was being squeezed. See *MEED* (15 June 1987). In the late summer, the government prohibited importers from tapping the foreign exchange pool to pay debts acquired prior to 11 May 1987. *MEED* (5 September 1987).

43. Fuad Hashim, head of the Arab Investment Bank, said that he doubted the government's figure of $14 million daily flowing into the banking system. Hashim also observed that most official foreign currency transactions resulted from tourism, not remittances. See his remarks cited in *MEED* (3 October 1987). In early October, the government claimed $1.6 billion had been transferred through banks since the reform. *Middle East Times* (11–17 October 1987).

44. Favorable treatment, however, was given to Arab banks, which were allowed to open "booths" in public sector banks in which they could conduct foreign exchange dealings. This brought howls of protest from local branches of Western banks. See *MEED* (22 August 1987 and 5 September 1987).

45. *MEED* (29 August 1987). I am indebted to Bent Hansen for information about Egypt's unwillingness to abolish the commercial rate in the 1960s despite pledges to the IMF.

46. *MEED* (1 August 1987).

47. *Country Profile: Egypt (1987–88)*, p. 30. The Egyptian Businessmen's Association, in fact, objected to the government's effort to plan private sector investment. It also publicly cast doubt on the figure of £E18 billion that the five-year plan allocated to private sector investment. It claimed that the private sector has yet to invest more than £E1 billion in any year and that the government's figure of £E9 billion for private sector investment in the previous five-year plan was an exaggeration. See Abdel Rahman Akl, "Businessmen Call on Government Not to Interfere in Private Sector," *Middle East Times* (14–20 June 1987).

48. To further impress upon the Egyptian public that the government had no intention of selling off the public sector, a direct rebuttal to Fuad Sultan's

urgings consumed Makram Muhammad Ahmad's attention in his influential weekly column—"To Whom Shall We Sell the Public Sector?" *al-Musawwar* (14 August 1987).

49. 92 percent of agricultural land is owned by "individuals and the private sector." Khalid Fuad Sharif, "Privatization and the Extension of Private Sector Activity," *al-Ahram al-Iqtisadi* (22 June 1987). In 1973, which was prior to the commencement of Sadat's *infitah*, the private sector accounted for almost 98 percent of gross agricultural output. Calculated from figures in Waterbury, *The Egypt of Nasser and Sadat*, p. 160.

50. The £E2.5 billion poultry industry, which began to expand rapidly in 1978 as a result of subsidized feed, easy credit, and relatively high prices for chickens and eggs, has since 1984, when the price of subsidized corn was raised from £E60 to £E120 per ton, been demanding price increases for its products. The government, having permitted the price of red meat rapidly to escalate, has feared the wrath of urban consumers should the same inflation affect the only other major source of animal protein.

51. Hani El Banna, "Poultry Farms Fall Victim to Abundance and Archaic Laws," *Middle East Times (13–19 September 1987)*; and Hani El Banna, "Ministry Says Ailing Poultry Industry Will Continue to Receive Assistance," *Middle East Times* (20–26 September 1987).

52. See, for example, Mustafa Shurdi's column in *al-Wafd* (11 March 1987).

53. While estimates vary, it is generally agreed that not less than three-quarters of all PBDAC's "development loans" have been utilized for red meat production. See, for example, Jean-Jacques Deschamps, *Analysis of the Credit and Institutional Aspects of the Agricultural Production Credit Project*, Cairo, USAID, February 1986, p. IV-2.

54. I am indebted to Nasr Marei, an importer of Ciba-Geigy agricultural chemicals, for information about informal aspects of the relationship between PBDAC and private importers.

55. On the various impediments confronting private importers, see Kenneth Wiegand, "Agricultural Production Credit PID Design File–Inputs: Marketing of Agricultural Chemicals,, Cairo, USAID, 4 February 1986.

56. On this period see Robert Springborg, "Patrimonialism and Policy Making in Egypt: Nasser and Sadat and the Tenure Policy for Reclaimed Lands," *Middle Eastern Studies*, 15, 1 (January 1979), pp. 49–69.

57. On the Wafd's criticism of the self-help measures, see *Middle East Times* (25 May–1 June 1985). The self-help measures included in the 1986 PL 480 agreement with Egypt were as follows: (1) to improve the structure of prices and farm production incentives by increasing produce prices for export crops for which Egypt has been determined to have a strong international comparative advantage; (2) to rationalize subsidies for maize, beef, dry milk, and other agricultural products for which Egypt has no international comparative advantage; (3) to rationalize prices for nitrogen and phosphate fertilizer; (4) to encourage an increased percentage share for the private-sector in the domestic marketing and distribution of fertilizer and other chemical inputs; and (5) to continue studies by the Government of Egypt of the budgetary, nutritional, and other effect of possible steps to reduce eligibility for subsidized commodities. "PL 480 Self-Help Measures Review" (Cairo: USAID, 15 January 1987).

58. This information, the accuracy of which was confirmed by U.S. Ambassador Frank Wisner in a discussion with the author on 29 October 1986, was provided by USAID officials.

59. Bob Woodward, *Veil: The Secret Wars of the CIA 1981–1987* (New York: Simon and Schuster, 1987) pp 411, 435–436, 442–444.

60. Saudi Arabia also announced earlier in the year a loan of $200 million. *Country Report: Eqypt,* p. 8.

61. *MEED* (17 October 1987).

62. Between 1975 and 1982 project aid averaged less than 43 percent of total aid, which was $8.5 billion in that period. The highest annual amount was $529 million in 1980. Dina Gallal, "American Assistance: Where Does It Go and What Is Its Role?" *al-Ahram al-Iqtisadi* (22 June 1987).

63. Weinbaum, *Egypt and the Politics of U.S. Aid,* p. 70.

64. The exact proportion of aid that has been consumed by consultancy fees is a highly contentious issue, with estimates varying widely. Michael Stone, a previous director of USAID Cairo, claimed that 1 percent of total U.S. aid was allocated to consultants. "The U.S. Agency for International Development in Egypt," in Sullivan, *Impact of Development Assistance on Egypt,* p. 34. Stone's successor, Frank Kimball, stated that consultancy fees on USAID projects had ranged from 7 percent to 100 percent of the costs of individual projects, with an average of about 10 percent. Imam Ahmed, "Consultants Under Fire for Misuse of Egyptian Aid Funds," *Middle East Times* (27 July–2 August 1986). The leftist opposition contends that approximately one-third of all U.S. aid has been consumed by consultancy fees. Ibid.

65. David Kinley, Arnold Levinson, and Frances Moore Lappe, "The Myth of Humanitarian Aid," *The Nation* (11–18 July 1981), p. 42, cited in Weinbaum, "Dependent Development and U.S. Economic Aid to Egypt," p. 126.

66. That the United States has provided Egypt $20 billion in economic assistance, constituting 20 percent of all U.S. foreign aid, was stated by U.S. Ambassador Frank Wisner in an interview in *al-Ahram* (19 May 1987). That this aid constituted 5.7 percent to 9.7 percent of Egypt's GNP was claimed by Dennis D. Miller, "Egypt and the U.S.: An Aid or Trade Relationship?" in Sullivan, *Impact of Development Assistance on Egypt,* p. 75.

67. The visit of Vice President George Bush in the summer of 1986, while negotiations between USAID and the Egyptian government were at a delicate stage, was particularly nerve-wracking for USAID officials. They feared that Bush had authority to announce a significant increase in the cash portion of aid as an incentive to Egypt to come to an agreement with Israel on the Taba border dispute. In the event, the Egyptian-Israeli negotiating teams did not reach agreement while Bush was in Cairo.

68. While recognizing most of these failures, American USAID and Embassy spokesmen have generally attributed them to causes beyond USAID's control. See for example Stone, "The U.S. Agency for International Development in Egypt,"; and interview with former U.S. Ambassador to Egypt Hermann Eilts, *Middle East Times* (19–25 April 1987).

69. I am indebted to Wade Robinson, consultant to USAID, for this information.

70. I am indebted to members of the agricultural program of USAID for this information.

71. See for example Abd al-Monaim Said, "In Order to Describe Egypt in Arabic, or the Issue of the Freedom of Academic Research," *al-Ahram al-Iqtisadi* (8 November 1982); Mustafa Imam, et al., "The Description of Egypt in America," *al-Ahram al-Iqtisadi* (4 and 11 October 1982); and Muhammad al-Sayid Salim, "Fact and Fiction in the Issue of Joint Research," *al-Ahram al-Iqtisadi* (29 November 1982).

72. Dina Gallal, "America and Egypt: The Aid and the Relation," *al-Ahram al-Iqtisadi* (20 July 1987).

73. I am indebted to members of the USAID agricultural program and to consultants to that program for information about the involvement of these various individuals and institutions in the policy-making process.

74. GM had intended to attract investments to finance at least 18 such companies. By July 1987, only 1 company had applied to the government to obtain permission to operate in Egypt. "GM's Egypt Venture Stalled over Choice of Models," *Middle East Times* (12–18 July 1987).

75. Based on conversations with those individuals in 1986.

76. For an account of the Kamshish incident, see Hamied Ansari, *Egypt: The Stalled Society* (Albany: State University of New York Press, 1986).

77. GM, which assembles small trucks in Egypt, recruited and trained its own labor force while establishing its plant outside Cairo. According to one of its senior executives interviewed by the author, GM was not pleased with the prospect of inheriting NASCO's labor force and personnel problems. Accordingly, it imposed various conditions about recruitment and organization of labor in its negotiations and was planning a radical overhaul of personnel policies once the joint venture commenced.

78. For an explanation of the breakdown of the GM-NASCO agreement that identifies as the chief causal factor the weak state's lack of resoluteness and the absence of the necessary political base in the country for a reform coalition, see Khalid Sharif, "The Politics of Liquidation and Privatization," *al-Ahram al-Iqtisadi* (8, 15, and 22 June 1987).

79. The Economist Intelligence Unit found it curious that at a time when the government was encouraging the private sector, Atif Sidqi, "believed to be more sympathetic to a centrally planned economy than his predecessor," was appointed Prime Minister. *Country Profile: Egypt (1987–88)*, p. 5.

80. The new Minister for International Cooperation, which is an important post within the cabinet's economic policy-making team, was Maurice Makram Allah, who holds a Ph.D. from the University of Paris. The three other new ministers have Egyptian degrees.

81. The NDP is far from united behind liberalization measures. A significant faction within the NDP elite, including a group of parliamentary deputies and the head of the doctors syndicate, opposed cutbacks in subsidies to basic foodstuffs imposed as a part of the IMF reforms. "National Party Deputies Are Opposed to Lifting Subsidies on Broadbeans and Lentils," *al-Ahram al-Iqtisadi* (19 June 1987).

82. I am indebted to Ronald Wolfe, an administrator of the Peace Fellowship Program, for this information.

83. Colonel William Oldes, interview, Cairo (26 May 1986).

84. That person is Wade Robinson, to whom I am indebted for this information.

85. Gajevsky, interview, Cairo, 20 January 1986.

86. On this event and U.S.-Iranian relations in this period more generally, see James A. Bill, *The Eagle and the Lion: The Tragedy of American Iranian Relations* (New Haven: Yale University Press, 1988).

87. The meeting held in Cairo in the fall of 1986 was the source of considerable friction between the Egyptian and U.S. sides. U.S. corporations, having less interest in Egypt than they had during the heyday of *infitah* under Sadat, did not intend to send senior executives to the annual meeting. Instead they wanted to be represented by their local agents. This the Egyptian government objected

to, demanding the U.S.-based executives attend. Only some U.S. corporations acceded to this demand.

88. "In the late 1970's almost half of the U.S.-financed procurement contracts were for purchases from just twenty two U.S. megacorporations." Weinbaum, "Dependent Development and U.S. Economic Aid to Egypt," based on information in Kinley, Levinson, and Lappe, "The Myth of Humanitarian Aid."

89. John Kifner, "Mubarak Urges Action as a New Term Begins," *New York Times* (13 October 1987).

90. John Kifner, "Dancing for Mubarak: And a Cow Gives Its All," *New York Times* (6 October 1987).

91. *Middle East Times* (4–10 October 1987).

8

CONCLUSION

Threats to the stability and integrity of the Mubarak regime come from various quarters. The *infitah* bourgeoisie that prospered under Sadat has retained considerable influence despite a sustained effort by Mubarak to erode its economic preeminence and curtail its political access. The military, having lost much of its power during the Sadat era, has since 1981 established an economic empire that siphons scarce resources away from the civilian sector and provides a base from which political influence can and is being expanded. The two main counterbalances to the military, which are internal security forces and civilian political activists encouraged by the process of liberalization, lack the resources and will to contain either a sudden or a gradual annexation of the political order by officers. Secular opposition political parties are incapable of making serious inroads at the expense of the regime's party, but they have cast a shadow over the regime's legitimacy by revealing innumerable misdeeds of those in government and of others who have capitalized on connections to the authorities. Islamicists have demonstrated a capacity to mobilize and organize popular followings and to challenge the prevailing semisecular political order through both peaceful and violent means. Beyond the organized political constituencies remain vast numbers of apathetic, cynical, potentially violent members of Egypt's sprawling marginalized lower and lower-middle classes who have demonstrated a willingness to loot and burn in protest and who could conceivably be recruited in large numbers into radical movements. The end of the oil boom has left Egypt vulnerable to creditors who seek a rationalization of the Egyptian economy in order to extract loan repayments from it. The high-profile U.S. presence both embarrasses the regime and constrains its policy choices. And finally, Egypt's regional policy is fraught with peril. Since coming to power Mubarak has confronted the task of reconciling relations with Israel with Egypt's Arab character, role, and obligations. In 1987 the Arab World turned to Egypt to serve as a shield against Iran, thereby confronting Mubarak with yet more difficult choices.

Faced with this array of challenges to his personal rule, to the regime, and maybe even to the nation itself, Mubarak has adopted a nonideological, pragmatic approach, apparently out of the calculation that muddling through is less risky than seeking directly and simultaneously to resolve the basic issues. Mubarakism, consequently, is neither rallying cry nor legitimating myth. Nor does it appear to be a carefully articulated set of ideas or even a coherent, readily defined operational code that could stimulate others to champion or imitate it. Those seeking root and branch solutions to Egypt's pressing economic problems have not convinced the President that their prescriptions should be followed. His caution and the limitations of the weak state over which he presides are likely to continue to ensure that while some aspects of the new orthodoxy of development will be at least partially implemented, others will remain dead letters. Egypt under Mubarak will not imitate Turkey in its wholehearted endorsement of the basic canons of the faith of the new orthodoxy, including wide-ranging privatization. The Mubarak regime has yet to establish the political foundations required for such thoroughgoing economic changes, nor are there strong indications that such a political base is coalescing as a result of the partial liberalization. The politics of divide and rule, coupled to an economic policy that retains elements of the social contract while imposing greater fiscal austerity, is the most likely outlook for the short- and medium-term futures.

But where, then, will that leave Egypt in the mid-1990s, to say nothing of the year 2000 and beyond? A major portion of debts rescheduled in 1987 will come due once again in 1992. Prospects for increases in earnings from the "big four" sufficient to meet those obligations and to provide needed surplus capital for investments must be adjudged as poor. In the meantime Egypt must accommodate an additional 1 million people every ten months. By the year 2000 the population will be approaching 70 million. Already one of the most densely settled areas of the world, Egypt's Nile Valley could become one of the globe's ecological disaster areas. Political strain brought on by further economic hardships, exacerbated by a deteriorating environment, presumably would be too much for the fragile, semiliberal regime to bear. The main contenders to overthrow the weak state would be either the military or, much less likely, those able to channel the energies of the mob. In either case the experiment with limited democracy, which began under Sadat, would come to an end. The military would impose a version of the Latin American authoritarian state, whereas those associated with the other alternative would strike off in an egalitarian, militant, anti-Western direction.

There is, however, a different, less apocalyptic, and still credible alternative scenario. It is based on the assessment that change that has already occurred in Egypt under Sadat and Mubarak is more profound than the first scenario admits and on the assumption that it will continue to gather momentum. Liberalization, according to this interpretation, has stimulated a real increase in political participation, which in turn will eventually legitimate the regime in a rational-legal manner. More Egyptians engage in political debate, exercise their right to join interest groups and parties, and participate in electing candidates to offices than ever before. As they do so, they are laying the foundations for the emergence of a much stronger state and one that will not have to rely only on rents generated from sources external to the productive sectors of the economy, as its weak predecessor has done. As liberalization facilitates the emergence of a consensus behind the need for a sharing of burdens and benefits, the state's ability to extract and distribute resources will grow. The state, in short, will exchange some of its autonomy in decision making for access to some of the abundant resources held by its citizens.

The potential for economic development unlocked as a result of this trade-off will, according to this view, be further enhanced by social and economic changes already under way. The oil boom not only generated private savings, it stimulated the acquisition of new skills and talents that will increasingly be mobilized for Egypt's development as migrants return home. As a result of their new, relative affluence and of the lessening of controls over virtually all aspects of their lives, Egyptians are enjoying a far wider range of experiences than they did under the austere Nasser regime. Internal travel and tourism, which was the prerogative of the comparatively wealthy and/or politically acceptable some twenty-five years ago, is now commonplace. School children from even lower-middle class families now expect summer holidays along one of the country's excellent beaches. Children of the urban lower classes, who a generation ago were to be seen on city streets clad only in pajamas, now wear much less humble outfits, and the population as a whole is both better dressed and eating a more varied diet than it did in the 1960s. Underlying these visible changes are real structural transformations. In two generations the percentage of the workforce engaged in agriculture has shrunk from about two-thirds to a little more than one-third. Mechanization and the education of rural youths, combined with economic diversification, are freeing ever-larger numbers of those of peasant origins from the drudgery of fieldwork. The economy as a whole is more sophisticated and complex than it was in the days of Arab Socialism.

In this optimistic scenario even the population explosion is more opportunity than threat. Egypt, after all, is not just the Nile Valley. At present less than 5 percent of Egypt's total land surface is inhabited. Since the early Nasser era there have been attempts to induce the population to settle new lands. As the High Dam was being constructed in the 1960s, vast reclamation projects were undertaken, with mixed results. Under Sadat the rate of reclamation slowed almost to a halt, but the state's commitment to encouraging and supporting the geographical dispersal of the population continued in the form of the construction of new cities in the desert. The current regime is seeking to integrate and add to those earlier efforts. It has allocated a major share of investments in the five-year plan for 1987/88–1991/92 for the reclamation of yet more land and construction of appropriate infrastructure.

While many efforts to decentralize have come to nothing and much money has certainly been wasted, new communities, planned and spontaneous, are in fact springing up in the interior, along the Mediterranean and Red Sea coasts, adjacent to the Suez Canal, and in Sinai. A blueprint for a new Egypt recently unveiled by Mustafa al-Gabali, a former, highly respected Minister of Agriculture and Land Reclamation and leading proponent of land reclamation, would have appeared as utterly fanciful even at the end of the Nasser era.[1] The blueprint outlines ten major areas where new, productive communities are already established or that have the potential to support such developments in the immediate future. That hundreds of thousands of Egyptians now live in these communities, that they are contributing to rather than siphoning off national wealth, and that Egyptians of various backgrounds now talk enthusiastically about leaving the Nile Valley to live elsewhere in the country are facts that suggest Gabali's blueprint is much closer to reality than could have been imagined when he was supervising land reclamation projects under Nasser.

Egypt's future, therefore, is not preordained by either Malthusian or ineluctable economic or political forces. To be sure, the country is confronting severe challenges and its fate currently is being guided by a political system that rests upon the decaying foundations of a weak state. Whether the process of decay will be paralleled by the emergence of a more pluralistic, responsive political order, capable of rallying the population behind policies and mobilizing the necessary resources to accomplish them, or whether that transformation will be blocked by inertia or by the seizure of power by a yet more exclusivist, authoritarian order will be determined by the choices of those currently playing leading or secondary political roles. How Egypt resolves the dilemmas of development associated with having a weak state will be critical not only for its future but for the rest of the Arab World, which for so long has taken its cues from Cairo.

NOTES

1. The ten areas Gabali identified are Wadi Natrun; the Northwest Mediterranean coast; Maryut and West Nubariya; the new cities of Ten Ramadan on the road to Ismailiya and Six October on the road to Fayum; Salhiya; the New Valley; Lake Nasser; North Sinai; and South Sinai. See Mustafa al-Gabali, "New Societies and Confronting the Problems of Youth," *al-Ahram* (16 November 1987).

INDEX